AQA Philosophy

Exclusively endorsed by AQA

A2

Series editor
Martin Butler

John Appleby
Mike Atherton
Chris Cluett
Alan Dobson
John Foster
Dave Rawlinson

Nelson Thornes

First published in 2009 by:
Nelson Thornes Ltd
Delta Place
27 Bath Road
CHELTENHAM
GL53 7TH
United Kingdom

09 10 11 12 13 / 10 9 8 7 6 5 4 3 2 1

A catalogue record for this book is available from the British Library

ISBN 978 0 7487 9904 6

Cover photograph/illustration: Getty/ Jochen Sand

Page make-up and additional artworks by Hart McLeod Ltd

Printed and bound in Spain by GraphyCems

The authors and publisher are grateful to the following for permission to reproduce the
following copyright material:
Unit 3: p44, Fotolia; Unit 4: p43, Alamy: INTERFOTO/Fine arts; p115, Wilbur,
www.cartoonstock.com.

Every effort has been made to contact the copyright holders and we apologise if any
have been overlooked. Should copyright have been unwittingly infringed in this book,
the owners should contact the publishers, who will make corrections at reprint.

Contents

AQA introduction

Nelson Thornes and AQA

Nelson Thornes has worked in partnership with AQA to ensure this book and the accompanying online resources offer you the best support for your GCSE course.

All resources have been approved by senior AQA examiners so you can feel assured that they closely match the specification for this subject and provide you with everything you need to prepare successfully for your exams.

These print and online resources together **unlock blended learning**; this means that the links between the activities in the book and the activities online blend together to maximise your understanding of a topic and help you achieve your potential.

These online resources are available on  which can be accessed via the internet at **www.kerboodle.com/live**, anytime, anywhere. If your school or college subscribes to this service you will be provided with your own personal login details. Once logged in, access your course and locate the required activity.

For more information and help visit
www.kerboodle.com

Icons in this book indicate where there is material online related to that topic. The following icons are used:

💡 Learning activity

These resources include a variety of interactive and non-interactive activities to support your learning.

✔ Progress tracking

These resources include a variety of tests that you can use to check your knowledge on particular topics (Test yourself) and a range of resources that enable you to analyse and understand examination questions (On your marks …).

ⓘ Research support

These resources include WebQuests, in which you are assigned a task and provided with a range of web links to use as source material for research.

When you see an icon, go to Nelson Thornes *learning space* at **www.nelsonthornes.com/aqagce**, enter your access details and select your course. The materials are arranged in the same order as the topics in the book, so you can easily find the resources you need.

How to use this book

This book covers Unit 3 of your course. Each of the five chapters matches the five key themes in the specification.

The five chapters that match the five philosophical problems covered in Unit 4 can be downloaded from our website **www.nelsonthornes.com/aqagce/philosophy**. You will need to enter the following password to be granted access: PHILU4

The final chapter is an exam skills chapter which talks you through how to use the information that you have learning effectively in the A2 examination.

The features in this book include:

Learning objectives

At the beginning of each topic you will find a list of learning objectives that contain targets linked to the requirements of the specification.

 ## Key terms

Terms that you will need to be able to define and understand.

 ## Key philosophers

A short biography of the important people who have contributed to the topic.

 ## Think about

Questions for you to consider, based on what you've just learned.

Synoptic links

Links to relevant content in another A2 chapter or in a chapter from the AS book.

 **Examiner's tip**

Hints from AQA examiners to help you with your study and to prepare for your exam.

Learning outcomes

At the end of each topic you will find a list of learning outcomes, linked to the learning objectives, which show what you should have learned having worked through the topic.

 ## Summary questions

Short questions that test your understanding of the subject and allow you to apply the skills you have developed.

 Examination-style questions

In the exam skills chapter there are questions in the style that you can expect in your A2 examination, along with annotated example answers.

AQA examination questions are reproduced by permission of the Assessment and Qualifications Alliance.

Web links in the book

Because Nelson Thornes is not responsible for third party content online, there may be some changes to this material that are beyond our control. In order for us to ensure that the links referred to in the book are as up-to-date as possible, each web site is accessible through this Nelson Thornes site: www.nelsonthornes.com/aqagce.

Please let us know at **webadmin@nelsonthornes.com** if you find a link that doesn't work and we will do our best to redirect the link, or to find an alternative site.

1   Philosophy of mind

Learning objectives

- to understand what dualism is

- to identify, and distinguish between, different dualist approaches to mind and consciousness

- to understand how dualism relates to the mind-body problem and to the problem of other minds

- to be able to assess the strengths and weaknesses of dualist positions.

Key philosophers

Rene Descartes (1596–1650): French philosopher, scientist and mathematician. Widely regarded as 'the father of modern philosophy', Descartes remains a hugely influential figure in the philosophy of mind.

Aristotle (384–322 BC): Ancient Greek philosopher. Many of Aristotle's writings have survived and he has been incredibly influential in both philosophy and the natural sciences – although this latter part of his work has mostly been discredited over the past three centuries.

Key terms

Ontology: the branch of metaphysics concerned with questions about what there is, with what sort of entities exist. In the philosophy of mind ontological questions concern whether there are minds and brains, just brains, or just minds.

Dualism

Dualist theories in the philosophy of mind encompass a range of views that emphasise radical differences between mind and body; differences which lead dualists to construct arguments about why the mind cannot be treated as part of the physical world. Dualism has a long history: for Plato, particularly in his Phaedo (Plato, 1997), the radical difference between mind and body centred on the intellect. Since **Descartes**, however, it has centred on consciousness.

Varieties of dualism

Substance dualism

Substance dualism is the view that mind and body are two **ontologically** distinct substances, each having radically different essential natures. Substances are characterised by their particular properties or attributes but, more than this, substances are also those things that possess these properties. So, mind is a substance that possesses mental properties (such as believing or doubting), and body is a substance that possesses physical properties (such as height or mass).

The most influential substance dualist is Descartes. So influential in fact that substance dualism is frequently referred to as Cartesian dualism. As indicated in the introduction to this chapter, however, it should not be thought that his *Meditations on First Philosophy* is a book on the philosophy of mind: there was no such discipline in the 17th century. Arguably, his main purpose in this book was to provide a foundation for a new mechanistic philosophy of nature in keeping with 17th-century advances in science. This project involved discarding the **Aristotelian** philosophy of nature, which had been dominant for two thousand years, together with the Aristotelian view of the soul, or life-force, as laid out in his *On the Soul* (Aristotle, 1984). Aristotle held that an individual soul exists as the organising principle of a particular parcel of matter as living creature, organising matter into a living thing (man, animal or plant) and providing a living thing with its essential characteristics and functions. The new philosophy of nature, however, required changes in the states of bodies to be governed by physical laws: the notion of an immaterial soul as the form of the body had to be rejected. Mind had to be separated from matter. This, of course, is precisely what Descartes attempted to achieve.

Following the systematic doubt of the First Meditation, Descartes found his first certainty in the Second Meditation:

> I am, I exist, is necessarily true whenever it is put forward by me or conceived in my mind.

Descartes (1996)

Synoptic link

AQA AS Philosophy Chapter 10, The debate over free will and determinism, pp316–17; AQA A2 Philosophy Chapter 9, Philosophical problems in Descartes. This can be found at **www.nelsonthornes.com/aqagce**

Key terms

Substance: the notion 'substance' has various uses: it may refer to that which persists while attributes change (as in Descartes' example of the wax) and/or to that which is logically capable of existing independently (as, for example, in Descartes' view that mind could exist independently of body).

Key philosophers

Benedict Spinoza (1632–77): Dutch rationalist philosopher best known for his strong determinism, perceived atheism, and attempt to overcome Cartesian mind-body dualism. Spinoza's most famous work is his posthumously published *Ethics*.

Think about

If the claim that we perceive things when asleep seems counter-intuitive to you, consider why you wake up when your alarm clock goes off.

Conversely, there are states in which all forms of consciousness apparently shut down. This is how general anaesthetics work. Would 'I' cease to exist when on the operating table?

Much of the following discussion in the Second Meditation is devoted to what he existed as (the existence of body has yet to be established). Restricting himself to what he can claim with certainty, Descartes wrote:

> But what then am I? A thing that thinks. What is that? A thing that doubts, understands, affirms, denies, is willing, is unwilling, and also imagines and has sensory perceptions.

Descartes (1996)

Later in the Second Meditation he employed the example of a piece of wax to show that a clear and distinct conception of matter – which was not, at this stage of Descartes' argument, a proof that matter exists – grasped through the intellect rather than through the senses, is that it is

> merely something extended, flexible and changeable.

Descartes (1996)

Thus, mind and matter are (clearly and distinctly) perceived as two substances with different attributes and different essences: mind is a thing that thinks (the only attributes possessed by mind are states of thought); body is an extended thing (the only attributes possessed by body are states of extension). Bodies, rather than minds, are the proper objects of scientific study and the new philosophy of nature.

Descartes' use of the notion of **a substance** prompted some of the initial reactions to his work. **Spinoza**, for example, argued that neither mind nor body qualified as substances; rather they are attributes of a single, universal substance: 'God or Nature' (Spinoza, 1985). Hume argued that the notion of mind as substance lacked empirical content.

One problem for Descartes was to explain what kind of entity an immaterial substance is and, through this, to explain the unity of the mind. His view was that consciousness was the substance. But if this is the case then the subject 'I' does not exist when unconscious. Descartes appears to acknowledge this:

> I am, I exist – that is certain. But for how long? For as long as I am thinking. For it could be that were I to totally cease from thinking, I should totally cease to exist.

Descartes (1996)

His position is given that we have 'sensory perceptions' while asleep, we are conscious even when we do not seem to be.

Regardless of the adequacy of this response, it is clearly the case that a conception of mind as a thinking thing, as consciousness, is central to Descartes' project and the influence of his conception of mind is impossible to exaggerate.

Property dualism

Property dualism is the view that while matter is the only type of substance in the world, it possesses two distinct types of property: the physical and the mental are coinstantiated in the same objects. So a single object (for example, me) instantiates both the physical property of being short-sighted, and the mental property of believing that wearing glasses will alleviate my short-sightedness.

Property dualism is, perhaps, best thought of as a compromise position between substance dualism and materialism. Unlike substance dualism, the property dualist claims that mental properties are non-physical properties of physical substances (bodies) rather than non-physical properties of non-physical substances (minds). In other words, the existence of the mind as an immaterial substance is denied. Unlike materialism, however, the property dualist does not hold that it is possible to provide a purely physical analysis of mind: consciousness is seen as a genuine non-physical property of physical substances and property dualists do not accept that conscious states can be reduced to physical states.

We shall return to this question later in the chapter once we have considered both dualist and materialist positions on the mind.

Arguments for dualism

Some of the following arguments originate in Descartes and are covered in more depth elsewhere in this course. Furthermore, arguments for dualism may also be employed as arguments against some materialist positions on the mind. We shall consider arguments for and against materialism more fully later in this chapter.

Doubt and indubitability

Descartes' argument from doubt is that while I cannot doubt that I am a thinking thing, I can doubt the existence of my body and since, by **Leibniz's Law**, what I cannot doubt cannot be the same as what I can doubt, it follows that mind cannot be identical to body. This argument is also stated in the earlier *Discourse on Method*:

> Seeing that I could pretend that I had no body and that there was no world nor any place where I was, but that I could not pretend, on that account, that I did not exist ... on the contrary, from the very fact that I thought about doubting the truth of other things, it followed very evidently and certainly that I existed ... From this I knew that I was a substance the whole essence or nature of which was merely to think, and which, in order to exist, needed no place and depended on no material things. Thus this 'I' ... is entirely distinct from the body.

Descartes (1988)

That this argument will not do the work that Descartes requires was pointed out at the time by his critic Arnauld.

Arnauld employs a parallel piece of reasoning, concerning the properties of a right-angled triangle to identify the flaw in Descartes' reasoning. While I may not be able to doubt certain essential features of the triangle, such as that it is three-sided, I may (if not tutored in geometry) doubt that the triangle possesses the Pythagorean property (that the square of the hypotenuse is equal to the sum of the squares on the other two sides). However, from the fact that I can doubt this, it does not follow that the triangle does not possess the Pythagorean property.

Moreover, if it did follow that what can be doubted is not identical with what cannot be doubted then Descartes' position that 'I' am essentially a thinking thing becomes vulnerable. This is because it is perfectly possible to argue both that I cannot doubt that I think and that I can doubt that there exists a creature whose essential nature is to think, in which case it should be concluded that 'I' am not a creature whose essential nature is to think.

AQA Examiner's tip

Questions requiring an assessment of dualism, or concerning whether any form of dualism is tenable, cannot be fully answered through reference to substance dualism alone.

Synoptic link

AQA AS Philosophy Chapter 9, Persons, pp277–80.

Think about

Can you see any problems with this account? How do you think the two types of properties relate to each other? Find out the difference between property dualism and predicate dualism.

Key terms

Leibniz's Law: this law states the identity of indiscernibles. Simply put, if two substances, X and Y, have exactly the same properties so that there is no possibility of distinguishing between them, if all the attributes of X are also attributes of Y, and vice versa, then X is Y. To put it another way, if X has a property that is not possessed by Y then X is not Y.

Key philosophers

G.W. Leibniz (1646–1716) : German rationalist philosopher and mathematician whose interests ranged across metaphysics, theology, mathematics and science.

Synoptic link

AQA A2 Philosophy Chapter 9, Philosophical problems in Descartes. This can be found at **www.nelsonthornes.com/aqagce**

In the synopsis to his *Meditations* Descartes notes that, in the Second Meditation, he did not intend to make any claim about what is objectively the case but merely to record his subjective impression concerning his essential nature:

> So the sense of the passage was that I was aware of nothing at all that I knew belonged to my essence except that I was a thinking thing.

Descartes (1996)

In other words, his claim at this stage of his argument is 'I only know that I am a thinking thing' and it remains to be seen whether, objectively, it is the case that he is only a thinking thing.

Descartes' proof of the 'real distinction' between mind and body is typically referred to as the argument from clear and distinct perception. He writes:

> The fact that I can clearly and distinctly understand one thing apart from another is enough to make me certain that the two things are distinct, since they are capable of being separated at least by God … Thus, simply by knowing that I exist and seeing at the same time that absolutely nothing else belongs to my nature or essence except that I am a thinking thing, I can infer correctly that my essence consists solely in the fact that I am a thinking thing … accordingly, it is certain I am really distinct from my body, and can exist without it.

Descartes (1996)

In short, instead of the 'I only know that I am a thinking thing', position in the Second Meditation, Descartes is now claiming that 'I know that I am only a thinking thing'. Many have argued that this move is invalid on the grounds that he does not justify this transition.

However, it is worth questioning whether Arnauld's objection really is a parallel argument. Descartes' argument is based upon the claim that one cannot doubt that one thinks, because to doubt is to think. Surely, though, it can be doubted that the figure in front of me is a right-angled triangle? Moreover, for Descartes, neither the triangle nor the Pythagorean property can be understood as substances: complete entities capable of existing on their own. Mind and body, however, can be thought of as substances and as such are capable of existing on their own.

Still, there is a more serious objection, noted at the time, by Hobbes, and developed in the 20th century. As Hobbes put it:

> It may be that the thing that thinks is the subject to which mind, reason or intellect belong, and this subject may be something corporeal.

Hobbes (in Descartes, 1996)

Descartes opens himself up to this objection because there is a problem with his argument concerning the mind's independence from the body, hingeing upon the following passage.

> I can make judgements only about things which are known to me. I know that I exist; the question is, what is this 'I' that I know? If the 'I' is understood strictly as we have been taking it, then it is quite certain that knowledge of it does not depend on things of whose existence I am as yet unaware.

Descartes (1996)

What he is saying here is that as he knows he is a thinking thing, but is not yet aware that he has a body, then this knowledge does not depend on him having a body. However, this conclusion does not follow from the premises.

An example should clarify what is at stake here: The theory of Natural Selection was developed by Charles Darwin prior to the discovery of the inheritance of characteristics via genetic transmission. Plainly Darwin's theory was not based upon knowledge of genetics. However, it would be wrong to say that it did not depend upon genetics, as we have since discovered that genetic transmission is an essential mechanism for Natural Selection. In the same way, Descartes is correct to say that his knowledge that he is a thinking thing is not based upon knowledge of bodies (for, at this stage, he has no such knowledge), but that does not mean that he can therefore rule out the possibility that his 'I' is dependent upon a body. He confuses an epistemological claim (how he can know about his mind) with an ontological one (that his mind exists separately from his body).

Indeed, it is difficult to see how a mind could continue to exist as a thinking thing without a body or brain; it may even be the case that thinking is a physical process. If this is so then substance dualism ought to be rejected, although this is not incompatible with property dualism.

Indivisibility

One of the main ways in which Descartes draws a distinction between body and mind is his claim that whereas body is divisible, mind is not. He argues that as they possess distinct attributes, they must be distinct substances. Body, by definition, has the attribute of extension, and what is extended in space is divisible; mind, in contrast, is non-extended and, by definition, indivisible.

The obvious objection here is to question whether the mind is, in fact, indivisible. We regularly speak of faculties of the mind, such as imagination, and understanding. Does this not mean that we are dividing the mind when we speak of such things? Descartes says not:

> As for the faculties of willing, of understanding, of sensory perception and so on, these cannot be termed parts of the mind, since it is one and the same mind that wills, and understands and has sensory perceptions.

Descartes (1996)

In other words, he thinks that behind all the faculties there is an indivisible 'I' directing them.

Unfortunately for Descartes, most modern thinkers disagree with this. The various schools of psychoanalysis divide up the mind in differing ways, but one thing they all agree on is that there is a conscious and an unconscious aspect to it. While psychoanalysis is a controversial doctrine, there is also plenty of empirical evidence from other quarters involving individuals with multiple personalities, for example. It is hard to find any contemporary thinkers who agree that the mind is indivisible. Consequently this particular argument for substance dualism fails.

Perhaps, as many have argued, Descartes was seduced by the grammar of 'I' – the use of the first person singular that represents each of us as a unitary individual – whereas, in fact, no valid conclusion about the indivisibility of consciousness can be drawn from the grammatical use.

Think about

How would you argue for the possibility of the continuing disembodied existence of the mind?

Synoptic link

AQA AS Philosophy Chapter 9, Persons, pp290–8. This can be found at **www.nelsonthornes.com/ aqagce**

The properties of mental states

Further arguments for dualism, which can also be seen as versions of Leibniz's Law, concern properties allegedly possessed by mental states but not by physical ones. These properties of mental states appear to pose problems for materialist theories of mind and consciousness and, consequently, they will be covered in more detail later. However, it will be helpful to note them before we proceed.

- Privacy and privileged access have been proposed as features of mental states not possessed by bodily states. For example, I can know directly and immediately that I desire to visit Seville this summer, through introspection. Others might infer that I possess this belief and this desire from my behaviour but they cannot possess the first-person authority about my mental states that I possess.

- *Qualia* is the Latin term used to refer to the qualitative aspects of conscious experience, the 'what it is like to be' in a certain conscious state. These properties are subjective: they can be thought of as our particular points of view or as what it is like to experience the world as us, and, it is argued, what is subjective (conscious experience) cannot be reduced to what is objective (physical existence). We might say that while we can know everything there is to know about the physicality of another person, we cannot know what it is like to be that person.

- Intentionality refers to the fact that some mental states are about something, whereas physical states never are. Mental states, such as desires, beliefs, and memories, are about or directed towards something else, whereas no physical state possesses this feature. For example, you might have a memory of your first love: you may desire to see him/her again; you might believe that their life since losing touch with you has been one long downward spiral. All of these states are about, or directed towards, your first love. However, it is difficult to see how a physiological process, such as a neuron firing in a neural network, can be about anything. While it might be denied that all mental states are intentional states it will hardly be denied that some are so; by Leibniz's Law, minds with intentional states are distinct from bodies without mental states.

Free will

Synoptic link

AQA AS Philosophy Chapter 10, The debate over free will and determinism, p300.

Finally, some have argued for dualism on the basis that we have free will and this too can be seen in terms of Leibniz's Law. Bodies are in space and subject to the laws of physics; minds are in time, but not in space, and are not governed by the laws of physics. If a strong sense of freedom requires that our actions are not fixed by physical laws, and if we are to be held morally responsible for our actions, then a non-physical mind not governed by the same physical laws controlling the body may be essential for free will.

The mind-body problem

One problem emerging from Cartesian dualism is how to explain the relationship between mind and body. As Hume put it:

> Is there any principle in all nature more mysterious than the union of soul with body; by which a supposed spiritual substance acquires such an influence over a material one, that the most refined thought is able to actuate the grossest matter?

Hume (1990)

We shall now examine some attempts to answer this question.

Interactionism

Interactionism, which is the view that Descartes subscribes to, is the position that mind (or mental events) and body (or physical events) causally interact and influence each other. Descartes writes:

> Nature also teaches me ... that I am not merely present in my body as a sailor is present in a ship, but that I am very closely joined and, as it were, intermingled with it, so that I and the body form a unit.

Descartes (1996)

It is clear from the ensuing discussion that he believed that mental events could cause bodily events and that, in turn, bodily events could cause mental events.

Moreover, in a later work, Descartes identified the pineal gland as the site at which the interaction between mental events and bodily events took place. This, however, is unsatisfactory: the issue is not where interaction occurs but how it occurs. The bafflement concerning how this is possible is expressed in **Ryle's** contrast between the 'inner' world of the mind and the 'outer' world of the body:

> Even when the 'inner' and 'outer' are construed as metaphors, the problem how a person's mind and body influence one another is notoriously charged with theoretical difficulties. What the mind wills, the legs, arms and the tongue execute; what affects the ear and the eye has something to do with what the mind perceives; grimaces and smiles betray the mind's moods and bodily castigations lead, it is hoped, to moral improvement. But the actual transactions between the episodes of the private history and the public history remain mysterious, since by definition they can belong to neither series. They could not be reported among the happenings described in a person's autobiography of his inner life, but nor could they be reported among those described in some one else's biography of that person's overt career. They can be inspected neither by introspection nor by laboratory experiment.

Ryle (1968)

How can minds act on bodies? What kind of mechanism could do the work necessary to bridge two autonomous and ontologically distinct realms? Furthermore, if my mind stands in the same relation to my body as it does to yours (that is, if it is a 'thing' apart) why, when I want to scratch my nose, am I able to move my arm but not yours?

The interactionist doesn't appear to be able to answer questions like these. To which one might reply, so what? Questions of the type, 'how is it possible that ... ?', raise an issue for discussion: they do not constitute a refutation of interactionism. They merely show that some pressing questions have yet to be answered.

Perhaps we might accept that interaction occurs as a **basic belief**. For example, some philosophers have argued that our experience includes experience of 'the unity of the embodied self' and that:

> This experience of the self as embodied ought either to be shown to be illusory or to be taken as a fundamental datum in any attempt to determine the relation of body to mind.

Stout (1931)

Synoptic link

See AQA A2 Philosophy Chapter 9, Philosophical problems in Descartes for a detailed examination of this argument. This can be found at **www.nelsonthornes.com/aqagce**

Key philosophers

Gilbert Ryle (1900–76): English philosopher who became Waynflete Professor of Metaphysical Philosophy at Oxford University. Ryle was an ordinary language philosopher best known for his attack on Cartesian dualism in *The Concept of Mind*.

Key terms

Basic belief: one that might be seen either as self-evident, or an ultimate justification not to be justified in terms of something more basic.

Synoptic link

AQA A2 Philosophy Chapter 6, Philosophical problems in Hume. This can be found at **www. nelsonthornes.com/aqagce**

Key philosophers

C.D. Broad (1887–1971): Was Knightsbridge Professor of Moral Philosophy at Cambridge: University. While his main philosophical interests were in the history of philosophy, moral philosophy, epistemology and the philosophy of science, he was also interested in the philosophical aspects of psychical research.

In other words, given that the interaction between mind and body is a fundamental aspect of our experience, the onus of proof should be on those who argue that it cannot occur rather than on those who argue that it does.

One reason for arguing that interaction cannot occur is that mental events and bodily events are too unalike for this to be possible. However, in a similar vein to Stout, **Broad** argued that:

> No one hesitates to hold that draughts and colds in the head are causally connected, although the two are extremely unlike each other.

Broad (1925)

His view, drawing on Hume's account of causation as constant conjunction and particularly the view that 'the same motives always produce the same actions' (Hume, 1990) is that the fact that mind and body have different properties is not a compelling reason for arguing that they cannot be causally related. Broad also says that:

> It is of course perfectly true that an organism and the mind which animates it do not form a physical whole, and that they do not form a mental whole … But it does not follow that a mind and its organism do not form a substantial whole of some kind.

Broad (1925)

If, on the other hand, the argument against interaction is that mental events, being non-physical, cannot physically act on bodily events, then the claim, while true, is trivial.

A stronger argument against interactionism may be that it appears to contradict a basic principle of physical science: the conservation of energy. If the interactionist is right, and mental events are regularly causing physical events such as neural activity, then the level of energy in the universe would seem at least to fluctuate if not increase as mental states are somehow converted into physical energy thus contravening the principle. However, in response to this one might appeal to another principle of physical science: the indeterminacy of quantum laws implies that any one of a number of possible physical outcomes is equally compatible with known physical laws. If this is so then mental events may influence bodily events by guiding neurological processes, or by distributing neural energy, without there being any fluctuation in the total level of energy.

Psycho-physical parallelism and occasionalism

The earliest attempts to overcome Descartes' problem denied interaction between mind and body. This was done partly to preserve basic principles of physical science, as mentioned above. In psycho-physical parallelism, rather than causally interact, mind and body are presented as being in harmony with each other. This harmony is due to God. Leibniz argued that:

> The idea itself or essence of the soul carries with it that all its appearances or perceptions must be born from its own nature, and precisely in such a way that they correspond of themselves to what happens in the whole universe, but more particularly and more perfectly to what happens in the body which is assigned to it.

Leibniz (1908)

In other words, mind and body run in parallel like two clocks which have been set to the same time. If you decide (mental event) to go and buy a copy of Leibniz's *Collected Works* (physical event) this is not because your (mental) decision led to (physical) movement. It is simply that when God set the world in motion he arranged that you would experience a particular mental event to coincide with those particular bodily movements.

A similar view was proposed by **Malebranche** who argued that:

> It is clear that, in the union of soul and body, there is no other bond than the efficacy of divine and immutable decrees, an efficacy never without its effects. God … wills without ceasing that the various disturbances of the brain shall always be followed by the various thoughts of the mind … it is this constant and efficient will of the Creator which causes the union of these two substances.

Malebranche (1997)

This is occasionalism. The major difference between the two is that whereas for Leibniz, God simply set the world up so that the harmony between mind and body was pre-established, the more extreme occasionalists posit God as the efficient cause of everything; constantly intervening in His creation in order to act as the link between the mental and the physical.

Both of the above positions are typically (and, perhaps, unfairly) presented as substance dualism without interaction, and as theistic relics of the past. Both incorporate God in their explanation of the relationship between mind and body. Many modern readers of their work would probably not be persuaded by an appeal to God. Most religious commentators have also been resistant to Malebranche's concept of an interventionist God.

Epiphenomenalism

According to epiphenomenalism, mental events are caused by physical events but do not themselves cause physical events: the interaction is one-way. Mental events are pictured as epiphenomenal by-products of physical processes. An epiphenomenalist may hold that these by-products are properties of a non-physical substance – substance dualism, or that they are properties of bodies – property dualism.

T.H. Huxley argued that:

> Our mental conditions are simply the symbols in consciousness of the changes which take place automatically in the organism.

Huxley (1874)

So physical processes (e.g. brain states) cause other physical processes (e.g. bodily movement) and mental processes (e.g. emotions, desires) but these mental processes are simply 'the symbol of that state of the brain which is the immediate cause of that act' (Huxley, 1874). Mental states, as mere epiphenomena or symbolic by-products, do not cause anything. Huxley's view is that, like other animals, we are 'conscious automata':

> The consciousness of brutes would appear to be related to the mechanism of their body simply as a collateral product of its working, and to be as completely without any power of modifying that working as the steam whistle which accompanies the working of a locomotive engine is without influence on its machinery … If a greyhound chases a hare … he is a machine impelled to the chase, and caused, at the same time, to have the desire to catch the game by the impression which the rays of light proceeding from the hare make upon his eye, and through them upon his brain.

Huxley (1874)

Key philosophers

Nicolas Malebranche (1638–1715): French rationalist philosopher and priest whose interests were in epistemology, metaphysics and theology.

T.H. Huxley (1825–95): English biologist and advocate for the theory of evolution. His interests included the origins and development of man and man's relationship to other animals.

Think about

If we are conscious automata, can we still possess free will?

The problem of other minds

Whereas the mind-body problem raises ontological questions about what kinds of substances or properties there are in the world, the problem of other minds raises **epistemological** questions concerning how we can know the minds of others.

The reason that this problem is typically seen as belonging to the legacy of Cartesian dualism is that it appears to result from attributing certain properties to minds; especially those of privacy and privileged access which we noted earlier. Such access provides us with certain knowledge of our own mental states, whereas we can never be certain about the thoughts and feelings of others or even whether others are minded at all.

The problem of other minds is typically stated as grounds for rejecting dualism. It does not simply concern the grounds we have for knowing what others are thinking or feeling but whether we have grounds for knowing that there are others who have thoughts and feelings. Ryle notes that a Cartesian dualist has no good reason to believe that there are minds other than his own so that:

> Absolute solitude is … the ineluctable destiny of the soul.

Ryle (1968)

Thus, the mind, as construed by Descartes, leads to **solipsism**.

If this position is unacceptable (and it surely is) then, it is argued, there must be something wrong with the way that Descartes construes the mind and that there must be a better way to think about mindedness. We will now consider some attempts to address the problem of other minds itself.

The argument from analogy

Analogous argument works on the basis that if two things are similar in some respects then they are probably similar in other respects. Some philosophers accept that while one can never be certain that another person is thinking or feeling something, it is possible to justifiably believe that they are thinking or feeling something through analogy. One version of this argument was proposed by **Mill.**

> I am conscious in myself of a series of facts connected by an uniform sequence, of which the beginning is modifications of my body, the middle is feelings, the end is outward demeanour. In the case of other human beings I have the evidence of my senses for the first and last links in the series, but not for the intermediate link. I find, however, that the sequence between the first and last is as regular and constant in those other cases as it is in mine. In my own case I know that the first link produces the last through the intermediate link, and could not produce it without. Experience, therefore, obliges me to conclude that there must be an intermediate link which must either be the same in others as in myself, or a different one. I must either believe them to be alive, or to be automatons … by supposing the link to be of the same nature … I bring other human beings, as phenomena, under the same generalization which I know by experience to be the true story of my own existence.

Mill (1889)

Table 1.1 is an illustration of one example of Mill's argument. Note the missing link that gets filled in by analogy: I infer that others feel the same way as I do as when they suffer the same fate, they act in the same manner as I did.

Table 1.1 *An argument from analogy*

Stage	In my own case	In the case of others
Modifications to the body	On a freezing cold day I slip and fall over on an icy pavement.	I later notice that others are struggling to keep their feet, some fall over in the same spot that I did.
Feelings	I have a range of feelings: irritation (that the pavement hasn't been salted) and slight pain or discomfiture.	
Outward demeanour	I get up awkwardly, utter an expletive or two, and brush down my coat. I walk away more slowly.	I notice these others getting to their feet awkwardly. I can hear some of them uttering expletives, see them brushing down their coats, walking more slowly.

This argument is very straightforward but problematic. To begin with, we might question the implication that human social behaviour is uniform. For example, not everyone utters expletives when they fall over on icy pavements: many people laugh, although they may still get to their feet awkwardly, brush themselves down and walk away carefully. If I am able to make inferences about the feelings of others who, unlike me, do not utter expletives and who may laugh at themselves (and I am able to make such inferences) it is not purely from a consideration of my own case. This leads to three major criticisms:

1 A strong **inductive** argument reaches a general conclusion on the basis of a bank of particular examples. This inductive argument is weak because it draws a general conclusion (that others are minded) from a singular instance (my own case). It requires us to regard ourselves as typical, but our problem is precisely that we have no grounds for regarding ourselves as typical. It is rather like drawing the conclusion that 'all teenage males are idle' on the basis of encountering one idle teenage male.

2 The argument is applied to 'others' who I perceive as sufficiently like me (i.e. other human beings), but what about others (e.g. animals, aliens or robots) who are not like me in terms of outward demeanour? Focusing only on an analogy with beings that are like me, may blind me to the possibility that beings that are not like me may also be minded. Conversely, I may wrongly attribute mental states to beings such as robots that are unlike me on the basis that they are able to mimic my behaviour. We shall return to this point later.

3 Starting from one's own case is to argue from the assumption that one has no criterion for determining whether another human being does or does not have thoughts or feelings like one's own. A criterion is some feature that would settle the issue of whether it is reasonable to apply a psychological predicate, for example 'is irritated', to another human being: a feature that enables us to judge whether another human being is irritated or, if preferred, a feature that supplies us with logical grounds for ascribing irritation to another human being. If, for example, Mill possessed a criterion for determining mindedness in others he could apply it rather than reach a probabilistic conclusion from a consideration of his own case. Clearly, the outward demeanour or behaviour of other human beings is the obvious criterion to employ in judging whether or not to ascribe a particular psychological predicate to others. (Note that while behaviour constitutes logically adequate grounds for ascribing mental states to others this does not entail that a particular ascription is true.) Now, if I accept that the behaviour, or outward demeanour, of others is a criterion of mindedness, I do not need to engage in analogous argument and do

Key terms

Induction: a form of reasoning in which the reasons given support but do not entail the conclusion. The conclusion is a generalisation from a consideration of individual instances.

not need to accord a special priority to my own case. If, however, I do not accept behaviour as a criterion of mindedness, so that feelings are completely divorced from any behavioural episodes that might signify their presence, then it is not clear how I could argue analogously that 'other humans have the same feelings as me'. I possess no criterion to establish this sameness, no grounds on which I might judge whether another human is, for example, irritated, nothing that would count for or against such a conclusion. Indeed, the idea that there could be irritation other than my own is, perhaps, unintelligible if I have no idea of what would establish this. Reasoning from one's own case does not lead us out of solipsism, it leads into it.

We might be on stronger grounds if we saw Mill's argument not as an argument from analogy but as an **inference to the best explanation.** An inference to the best explanation is abductive rather than inductive: it is a method of reasoning, employed in the sciences, in which the hypothesis selected is that, which if true, would best explain the relevant evidence. (Although Mill himself certainly saw his reasoning as inductive).

The phenomena I must explain if I am to understand the world around me include the outward demeanours of others. For example, in a football match I kick an opponent when he doesn't have the ball and the referee isn't looking. Later he kicks me back. The best inference to make is that he was annoyed that I kicked him, remembered that it was I who kicked him, waited for an opportune moment and intentionally kicked me back.

In other words, the best inference – the hypothesis that provides the most simple, coherent and adequate explanation of his outward demeanour – is that he is minded.

The private language argument

This argument is highly critical of the argument from analogy. Originally developed by **Wittgenstein**, it attacks the root of the problem of other minds: the Cartesian starting point of beginning from one's own case; claiming to know what (private, inner) sensations and emotions are from a first person perspective. Wittgenstein employs the notion of a necessarily private language to show that this starting point destroys itself. The point is not that starting from one's own case leads to solipsism; rather that solipsism is untenable.

Wittgenstein begins by postulating a language describing mental states and inner experiences which only the speaker can understand: a necessarily private language. He notes that in order for this language to be necessarily private the terms employed by the speaker cannot be linked to any natural expressions of sensation because, in that case, others might come to understand it. He then considers the following example:

> 'What would it be like if human beings shewed no outward signs of pain (did not groan, grimace, etc.)? Then it would be impossible to teach a child the use of the word "tooth-ache".' – Well, let's assume the child is a genius and itself invents a name for the sensation! – But then, of course, he couldn't make himself understood when he used the word. – So does he understand the name, without being able to explain its meaning to anyone? – But what does it mean to say that he has 'named his pain'? – How has he done this naming of pain?! And whatever he did, what was its purpose?

Wittgenstein (1968)

So, he not only questions what it means for someone to name a sensation to themselves but also why they would bother.

They might bother if they decided to keep a diary charting their experience of that sensation: when they experience the sensation they record that experience in their diary by associating it with a name. But having named their sensation on day 1, how would they know that on day 153, when they use the name again, their usage is consistent with their previous application of the term? Because they have concentrated their attention on the sensation and impressed upon themselves the connection between the sensation and the name?

However, they only have a private 'impression' that they are using the term correctly. Can this impression of correctness guarantee correctness? Wittgenstein thinks not:

> 'I impress it on myself' can only mean: this process brings it about that I remember the connexion right in the future. But in the present case I have no criterion of correctness. One would like to say: whatever is going to seem right to me is right. And that only means that here we can't talk about 'right'.

> *Wittgenstein (1968)*

If the (necessarily) private language user has no criterion for correctness, they cannot determine whether they are using a term consistently, and so cannot be said to be using a language. Signs purporting to stand for something accessible only through introspection would have to acquire meaning through a private and unverifiable process. Wittgenstein's argument shows that if this is so, if others are excluded from our use of such private signs, then the private language user herself cannot understand what she means by the signs as she has no way of making a meaningful distinction between correct and incorrect use.

Moreover, even in a public language the meaning of words describing sensations and emotions can have nothing to do with introspectively attending to a private object (my pain, my jealousy etc.). Wittgenstein attempts to demonstrate this with his 'beetle in the box' example, where the box can be seen as analogous to the mind and the beetle as analogous to a sensation:

> Suppose everyone had a box with something in it: we call it a 'beetle'. No one can look into anyone else's box, and everyone says he knows what a beetle is only by looking at his beetle. – Here it would be quite possible for everyone to have something different in his box. One might even imagine such a thing constantly changing. – But suppose the word 'beetle' had a use in these people's language? – If so it would not be used as the name of a thing. The thing in the box has no place in the language-game at all; not even as a something: for the box might even be empty … if we construe the grammar of the expression of sensation on the model of 'object and designation' the object drops out of consideration as irrelevant.

> *Wittgenstein (1968)*

That is, it is the public rules governing the grammatical use of the word that are important: not the private object that the word refers to.

For example, if we were to try and teach a child what 'being ticklish' is like we might tickle under her arms so that she squeals and jerks away. We might say to her 'that is what a tickling sensation is like'. Suppose she felt (privately) something we can't know about; suppose that the second time we did this she felt something different; suppose she felt nothing. Does any of this matter if we try to determine whether she understands by the meaning of 'ticklish'? No, we determine whether she understands the term through the way she uses it in public language – the meaning of the term is the way it is used in public language.

Wittgenstein's approach was to focus on grammar, on the ways that words are used in our language. His target, in this instance, was not to solve the problem of other minds by advancing a philosophical theory but to dissolve philosophical puzzlement about the issue by removing the misleading concept leading to the bafflement. The misleading concept, in this case, is the notion that sensation words, such as pain, are the names of private phenomena. What Wittgenstein shows is that the meaning of such words derives from grammatical rules governing their use within a public language. In this way he rejects scepticism about other minds because, as the sceptic is engaging in a public activity by posing the question of other minds in the first place, her position is self-defeating.

The concept of a person

Strawson also targets the root of the problem in Cartesian dualism, arguing that:

> The concept of a person is logically prior to that of an individual consciousness … it is not to be analysed … as a secondary kind of entity in relation to two primary kinds, viz. a particular consciousness and a particular human body.

Strawson (1959)

Like Wittgenstein, Strawson holds that a necessary condition of ascribing states of consciousness to oneself is that one should be able or prepared to ascribe states of consciousness to others. The ability to other-ascribe requires us to recognise other subjects of experience – other persons. A person is a subject to which both predicates ascribing states of consciousness ('P-predicates') and predicates ascribing physical characteristics ('M-predicates') are attached. Briefly:

1 A necessary condition of ascribing P-predicates at all is that they should be ascribed to the same entities as certain M-predicates are ascribed.

2 It would be impossible to ascribe P-predicates to oneself unless one could also ascribe P-predicates to others.

3 The condition of considering oneself as the subject of experiences is that one should also consider others as the subjects of experiences.

4 This, in turn, requires us to be able to individuate different subjects of experience.

5 The condition for recognising others as the subjects of experience is that they should be entities, like oneself, to which both M- and P-predicates apply.

6 So, P-predicates couldn't be ascribed at all unless they were ascribed to persons.

Strawson notes that:

> Clearly there is no sense in talking of identifiable individuals of a special type, a type, namely, such that they possess both M-predicates and P-predicates, unless there is in principle some way of telling, with

AQA Examiner's tip

Wittgenstein's use of the word 'grammar' is wider than the accepted meaning. Rather than simply encompassing the formal rules of syntax, he means the entire network of (formal and informal) rules by which we impart meaning to language. You need to show that you aware of this point if talking about 'grammar' in the exam.

■ Synoptic link

For the stages in his argument see AQA AS Philosophy Chapter 9, Persons, pp278–80.

■ Key philosophers

P.F. Strawson (1919–2006): English philosopher. Waynflete Professor of Metaphysical Philosophy at Oxford University. His main interest was to offer a descriptive metaphysics in relation to the concepts commonly employed in our shared conceptual scheme.

■ Think about

Does this approach also have implications for the mind-body problem?

regard to any individual of that type, and any P-predicate, whether that individual possesses that P-predicate.

Strawson (1959)

Regarding self-ascription, it is noted that we do not always need to observe our own behaviour in order to self-ascribe: some self-ascriptions are based on behaviour but others are not. However, regarding other-ascription, the logically adequate criteria for ascribing states of consciousness are behavioural. This difference – between sensations that are felt but not observed and behaviour which is observed but not felt – appears to create room for the sceptical question whether I can know, from another's behaviour, what they are feeling or whether they are feeling anything at all. Strawson, however, wishes to deny the sceptic the space for this question. Using the concept of depression, and following the argument outlined above, he claims that in order for there to be such a concept as, for example, my depression, the concept must cover what I feel but do not observe in myself and what I observe but do not feel in others.

It should not be thought that Strawson avoids scepticism by adopting behaviourism (which will be discussed more fully later in the chapter). He is not claiming that a person's behaviour logically entails the presence of a particular mental state – perhaps one might fake depression or disguise it – merely that we have to accept behaviour as a logically adequate criterion for the ascription of P-predicates to others. Like Wittgenstein, Strawson's target is the sceptical question at the root of the problem. Strawson argues that in order to pose the sceptical position – I know from my own case that I am minded but I cannot know whether there are any other minded creatures – the sceptic is both accepting the conceptual scheme in which P-predicates are located (e.g. by ascribing depression to themselves) and rejecting it (by refusing to ascribe depression to others). He notes that 'this logical gap … swallows not only his depression but our depression as well' (Strawson 1959). If the sceptic cannot, or is not prepared to, say whether another person is depressed, there would be no possibility of ascribing depression to oneself.

Like Wittgenstein, Strawson's argument is not an attempt to solve the problem of other minds:

> These remarks are not intended to suggest how the 'problem of other minds' could be solved, or our beliefs about others given a general philosophical 'justification' … such a 'solution' or 'justification' is impossible … the demand for it cannot be coherently stated.

Strawson (1959)

Rather, if we pay attention to the conceptual scheme that we have, the conceptual scheme in which P-predicates function, the problem should not emerge as a genuine problem in the first place. So the sceptical position is unintelligible.

This conclusion has been disputed. In *The Concept of a Person*, **Ayer** argues against both Wittgenstein and Strawson. He questions Wittgenstein's view that 'an inner process is in need of outward criteria' claiming that

> the relation between the statements which refer to these experiences and those which refer to their outward expressions remains obscure … We are not allowed to say that the experiences are identical with their outward expressions; and yet we are not allowed to say that they are logically distinct.

Ayer (1963)

Synoptic link

For conceptual schemes, see AQA AS Philosophy Chapter 1, Reason and experience, pp23–9.

Key philosophers

A.J. Ayer (1910–89): Professor of philosophy at both UCL between 1946 and 1959 and, thereafter, at Oxford University. Mainly known for his work in the tradition of empiricism, including his support of logical positivism.

Outward expressions do not necessarily entail experiences because such expressions may be deceptive. If reference to 'inner' experience is not simply reference to its outward expression, then it must include a reference to something else as well; but what this something else might be is not addressed by Wittgenstein.

Ayer's main criticism is directed at Strawson:

> It seems to me … that Mr Strawson's argument needs a stronger premise than the one he states. It must hold it to be a necessary condition of one's ascribing states of consciousness to oneself not merely that one should ascribe them, or be prepared to ascribe them, to others, but that one should be sure of doing so successfully. It must, in other words, exclude the possibility of one's being invariably mistaken.

Ayer (1963)

He argues that we can conceive of a situation in which we learn to ascribe conscious states to ourselves at the same time as we learn to ascribe them to others, on behavioural criteria, where all of our other-ascriptions are false. He illustrates this by asking us to imagine a child raised, in isolation from other human beings, by non-conscious automata or androids. These androids are programmed to perform a limited range of 'actions' and utterances. At the same time, the child is instructed in the use of language by a voice which addresses him through a loudspeaker. Due to these instructions the child learns to ascribe states of consciousness to himself at the same time as he ascribes these states to the androids, as the voice stresses similarities between his feelings and their outward expressions and the outward 'expressions' of the androids. So he gradually learns to self-ascribe and other-ascribe sensations, emotions, beliefs etc. The problem is that all of his other-ascriptions are false.

In view of this, Ayer rejects the claim that scepticism about other minds isn't intelligible. Referring to the child in his example, he argues:

> If he were an infant philosopher, he might begin to wonder whether his companions really did have experiences in the way that he did and infer that they did from their resemblance to himself. Or perhaps if he were struck by some stereotyped quality in their behaviour he would rightly conclude that they did not. Whichever conclusion he came to, his scepticism would not be senseless. How could it be if it were actually justified?

Ayer (1963)

Ayer's treatment of this issue is epistemological – he is concerned with the gap between what the child can be said to know about his own mental states and what he can be said to know about the mental states of others. Arguably, however, this misses the novelty of Wittgenstein's approach in particular. With regard to emotions and sensations, Wittgenstein did not treat the relationship between subject and predicate in an epistemological way. For Wittgenstein the statement 'I know that I am in pain' was pretty much accounted for by 'I am in pain'. *He also thought that, as a matter of fact, we often do know that another person is, for example, in pain:*

> *Just try in a real case to doubt someone else's fear or pain.*

Wittgenstein (1968)

Similarly, Strawson was also more interested in the richness of ordinary language and of natural beliefs. Beliefs which are stubbornly held, such as belief in other minds which, even if apparently rejected by philosophers

Think about

Is there a solution to the problem of other minds?

after sophisticated reflection, remain beliefs that we are naturally and inescapably disposed towards.

☑️ *After working through this topic, you should be able to:*

- explain the differences between substance and property dualism
- identify and illustrate some arguments for dualism
- explain how dualism relates to the mind-body problem and to the problem of other minds.

Reductive accounts of the mind

Learning objectives

- to understand the key features of some reductive accounts of the mind
- to be able to assess whether such accounts provide satisfactory explanations of the mind and mental states
- to be able to give an account of the 'hard' problem of consciousness and say how one might attempt to throw light upon this issue.

Materialism

'Materialism' is a term that has been attached to a variety of philosophical approaches to mind and consciousness since the mid 20th century. Sometimes it has been used interchangeably with the term 'physicalism' (some past A-level questions have used the term in this way, for example) although physicalism is also frequently restricted to describe a specific type of materialist approach. While it is possible to identify some broad areas of agreement among materialists, it is also true that many disputes in contemporary philosophy of mind are disputes between materialists of different persuasions. Sometimes the dispute even involves disagreement about whether a particular theory should or should not be called materialist.

The materialist approach to mind and consciousness

The first point to note is that all materialists share the view that dualism is wrong. Thus, while acknowledging the influence of Descartes' work, Ryle commented:

> I shall often speak of it, with deliberate abusiveness, as 'the dogma of the Ghost in the Machine'. I hope to prove that it is entirely false, and false not in detail but in principle.

Ryle (1968)

One does not have to be a materialist in order to believe that Descartes was mistaken and, indeed, it is arguable whether Ryle should be thought of as a materialist philosopher. However, materialists do not believe that there are any such things as 'ghostly' Cartesian souls or minds. Humans (and other minded creatures or machines, if there are any) are physico-chemical beings, composed entirely of matter, so our movements, personal traits, dispositions, and attitudes can be fully explained in physico-chemical terms. In short, everything that exists is in some sense physical. Typically, this belief is seen as a posteriori: a result of tested and confirmed empirical hypotheses.

All of us possess some personal evidence of the material dependence of mental phenomena: if I alter the bio-chemistry of my body by drinking eight pints of lager, my conscious states are also affected. Similarly, if an

Think about

Does it necessarily follow that materialists reject mentality completely?

elderly relative can't remember who I am due to the onset of Alzheimer's disease, this is because areas of their brain have stopped functioning. We might also link this point to how successful scientific explanations have been over competing explanations in improving our understanding of mental disabilities and illnesses.

We shall see that some materialists do reject it, but it is not a necessary consequence of materialism. Many materialists hold that mentality can be accounted for within a materialist approach. Thus, most materialists accept that mental events occur, and it is appropriate to offer mentalistic explanations of human behaviour and actions.

Arguably the most straightforward interpretation of this claim is to say that mental events or phenomena are identical to certain physical processes or phenomena. For example, the mental state of believing that the world is round is identical to some neural process in the brain. In other words, the 'is' in 'everything that exists is in some sense physical' is the 'is' of identity. Papineau illustrates the point as follows:

> Consider two contrasting analogies from purely physical science, the theory of electromagnetism, and the theory of heat ... The theory of the electromagnetic field is a theory of an extra physical entity, of something additional to other physical goings-on, such as the movement of charged particles. The charged particles are one thing, and the field they produce something further. But the theory of heat does not explain heat in a similar way. Heat is not something extra to the kinetic energy of moving particles. Rather, talk of the heat in a body is just another way of referring to the kinetic energy of the particles in it. There aren't two entities here, the moving particles and the heat. It's not as if a 'heat field' arises when the particles move. Heat is nothing but the movement of the particles, described in other terms. Now, which of these is the better model for the relation between conscious feelings and brain activity? That is, should we expect a successful 'theory of consciousness' to show us how certain brain activities generate certain extra entities, the conscious feelings, on the model of the electromagnetic field? Or should we rather expect such a theory to show us how conscious feelings are nothing but certain brain activities, described in other terms, on the model of heat ... We can call a theory of the former kind a dualist theory, and a theory of the latter kind a materialist theory.

Papineau (2003)

Heat simply 'is' the kinetic energy of moving particles and theoretical explanations offered in the field of science concerned with, for example, the transfer of heat from one body to another, namely thermodynamics, are reducible to theoretical explanations found in another field of science concerned with laws governing the transmission of motion between atoms or molecules, namely mechanics. According to this view, just as thermodynamics is reducible to mechanics so too theoretical approaches to consciousness, such as psychology, are reducible to neuroscience (the study of the nervous system). This approach to the philosophy of mind, drawing from allegedly successful **inter-theoretic reductions** in the philosophy of science, is typically referred to as reductive materialism.

So according to this view mental properties and mental events, such as believing that something is the case, are both real and fully explicable in physico-chemical terms because mental properties or events simply are physico-chemical properties or processes.

Key terms

Inter-theoretic reduction: the reduction of one theory to another Implies a change of ontological attitude towards reduced entities (so that, for example, mental states come to be seen as physical states), while simultaneously assuming the existence of both: both mental states and physical states really do exist just as heat and motion really do exist.

A word of caution before we proceed to consider those philosophical views that have attracted the label of being reductive: just as the term 'materialist' is employed loosely, so too is the term 'reductive'. Some reserve the term 'reductive materialism' for a particular position in the philosophy of mind, while others refer to a range of views as reductive. Thus, when considering different materialist views that have been proposed it is perfectly reasonable to question the extent to which they are materialist views and, if so, whether they are reductive views and, if so, what the nature of the reduction is.

Behaviourism

While it is true that, as with other positions in the philosophy of mind, the term 'behaviourism' has been applied to a variety of theoretical positions, it is possible to broadly identify some common ground between them. The motivation behind behaviourist arguments has frequently been epistemological: argumentation has been concerned to show how we can come to know the mental states of others and with how we are able to verify claims about those mental states. The behaviourist response to the problem of other minds has been to attack the Cartesian view of the mind and mentality as some radically private, 'inner' process: rather, minds are viewed as being largely if not wholly constituted by 'outer' behaviour.

So while Ryle, for example, regarded Descartes' position on the relationship between mind and body as so influential that it deserved to be called 'the official doctrine' he also referred to it as 'the dogma of the ghost in the machine'; 'a philosopher's myth', and as 'a category mistake'. The alleged category mistake made by substance dualism is that it:

> represents the facts of mental life as if they belonged to one logical type or category … when they actually belong to another.

Ryle (1968)

He illustrates the concept of a category mistake as follows:

> A foreigner visiting Oxford or Cambridge for the first time is shown a number of colleges, libraries, playing fields, museums, scientific departments and administrative offices. He then asks, 'But where is the University? I have seen where the members of the Colleges live, where the Registrar works, where the scientists experiment and the rest. But I have not yet seen the University in which reside and work the members of your University.' It has then to be explained to him that the University is not another collateral institution, some ulterior counterpart to the colleges, laboratories and offices which he has seen. The University is just the way in which all that he has already seen is organised … He was mistakenly allocating the University to the same category as that to which the other institutions belong.

Ryle (1968)

Analogously, Ryle thinks that it is an error to allocate the mental to the same category as observable activities such as behaviour.

Logical behaviourism

Most behaviourist philosophers have been reductivists, but not **eliminativists**. Behaviourism in philosophy should be understood as a linguistic thesis, concerned with the meaning of mental concepts. Logical

Think about

Try to come up with your own example of a category mistake.

Key terms

Eliminativism: the view that our everyday, folk, psychology of 'experiencing' this and 'believing' that is imprecise and deficient. It can and should be replaced with a better, more scientific, vocabulary.

behaviourism claims that statements describing mental states can be translated without loss of meaning into statements describing behaviour. We shall now consider two ways in which this might be done.

Hempel

Carl Hempel subscribed to the logical positivist view that a statement that claims to be factual has meaning only if it is possible to say how it might be verified. So, psychological statements are meaningful only if we know how to verify them and the conditions of verifying psychological statements are largely behavioural. For Hempel, the meaning of any psychological statement consisted solely in its successful abbreviation to descriptions of physical, or physiological, processes in the body.

> Thus, the assertion that Mr Jones suffers from intense inferiority feelings of such and such kinds can only be confirmed or falsified by observing Mr Jones' behaviour in various circumstances. To this behaviour belong all the bodily processes of Mr Jones, and, in particular, his gestures, the flushing and paling of his skin, his utterances, his blood pressure, the events that occur in his central nervous system, etc.
>
> *Hempel (2004)*

He advocates a strict analytical reduction of references to mental states, to references to behavioural states.

Ryle

Ryle is also sometimes regarded as advancing a logical behaviourist position. However, his position is very much 'softer' than Hempel's hard view that all statements about mental states are equivalent to statements about behaviour. Whereas Hempel, a materialist, was impressed by efforts to construct a scientific psychological behaviourism, Ryle's hostility to 'ghostly' Cartesian stuff was matched by his hostility to 'mechanistic' accounts of mentality:

> Man need not be degraded to a machine by being denied to be a ghost in a machine.
>
> *Ryle (1968)*

His references to behaviourism are at best lukewarm and he does not afford a privileged status to psychology as, specifically, the science of behaviour.

Ironically, perhaps, while Ryle's commitment to behaviourism was less than wholehearted, his approach in *The Concept of Mind* which, as he acknowledges, could 'undoubtedly, and harmlessly, be stigmatised as "behaviourist"', has undoubtedly been influential upon behaviourists. Ryle's motivation was to 'dissolve', rather than solve, the problem of other minds: effectively, to show that the problem was merely a pseudo-problem. As noted above, his approach draws upon aspects of 'agential' behaviour – our understanding of what we, and others, as agents are like through what we do and what our dispositions are – that we are already familiar with and can describe quite well.

> When a man is said to be a cigarette-smoker it is not being said that the man is smoking a cigarette now. To be a cigarette-smoker is to be in the habit of smoking cigarettes. The habit of cigarette-smoking could not exist unless there were such processes or episodes as smoking cigarettes. 'He is smoking a cigarette now' does not say the same sort

■ Synoptic link

AQA A2 Philosophy Chapter 10, Philosophical problems in Nietzsche, pp167–9. This can be found at **www.nelsonthornes.com/aqagce**

of thing as 'he is a cigarette-smoker' but unless statements like the first were sometimes true statements like the second could not be true.

Ryle (1968)

The term 'smoker' has both episodic uses and tendency-stating uses. The importance of this point is that when we ascribe a particular mental state or characteristic to somebody, we are neither describing a ghostly inner quality nor, necessarily, describing an episode of behaviour taking place now. Frequently we are describing a tendency or proneness to behave in a certain way.

Also, whereas some dispositional terms are highly specific (or determinate) insofar as there is only one sort of action predictable from the description of someone as, for example, 'a cigarette-smoker', other dispositional terms are more generic (or determinable).

> Dispositional words like 'know', 'believe', 'aspire', 'clever', and 'humorous' are determinable dispositional words. They signify abilities, tendencies or pronenesses to do, not things of one unique kind, but things of lots of different kinds.

Ryle (1968)

Thus, our knowledge of others does not consist in knowledge of 'ghostly', 'inner', episodes: it consists in our knowledge of their capacity or tendency to act in certain ways. Our descriptions of others as being, for example, clever or humorous, are not reports of observed behaviour or an observed incident but are connected to behaviour and incidents that might be observed. If this weren't so we wouldn't be able to understand talk about mental states. That is, if our descriptions of others are true they are the kind of statement that will be satisfied by some narrated incident – in the way that 'George is clever' might be satisfied by 'George got ten starred A grades in his GCSE exams'.

A further example of the way that Ryle attacks, what he calls, 'Descartes' Myth' is his treatment of 'heed concepts' such as noticing, concentrating, taking care, paying attention or minding what one is doing:

> When a person hums as he walks he is doing two things at once, either of which he might interrupt without interrupting the other. But when we speak of a person as minding what he is saying ... we are not saying that he is doing two things at once ... what is being described is one operation with a special character and not two operations executed In different 'places' with a peculiar cable between them.

Ryle (1968)

It would be a logical contradiction to claim that someone is absent-mindedly concentrating on what they are doing and logically odd to ask someone to pay attention without any indication of what it is that they are supposed to pay attention to. It will be remembered that Ryle's charge against Cartesian dualism was that it had led philosophers to make a 'category mistake' when assigning certain concepts to minds and we would be guilty of this error if we assign 'minding' to minds. So, we should not see 'minding' as involving some 'ghostly' monitoring process: rather, monitoring is itself a kind of behavioural performance just as being careful is a disposition to act in certain ways.

To conceptualise 'minding' as a 'ghostly' activity, taking place in non-physical minds, is according to Ryle, a philosophers' myth. Logically, or conceptually, mind is constituted by, or intimately connected to, outward behaviour. Philosophical problems concerning our apparent lack of knowledge of other minds and our bafflement concerning how to explain mind-body interaction arise from Cartesian. Their appearance as problems presupposes the legitimacy of the distinction between mind and body; their disappearance as problems results from denying the legitimacy of that distinction.

Objections to behaviourism

Behaviourism is false

This criticism results from two related points:

1 Behaviour is not a necessary condition of having experiences, beliefs or desires. If it was, then paralytics would not have beliefs, desires or experiences. However, it seems perfectly reasonable to say that a paralytic may believe that she is paralysed, may desire to be able to move and may feel despair at not being able to move. This might be countered through an appeal to dispositions so that, for example, her desire to move means something like 'she would (have the disposition to) move were she physically able to do so'. However, while this might be an appropriate counter-argument where non-behaviour is a result of physical injury, it is not appropriate where the reason for non-behaviour is psychological. **Hilary Putnam** imagines a race of super-Spartans who suppress all pain behaviour by willing themselves not to exhibit pain. In this case a dispositional analysis is not possible as it could not exorcise the mental – effectively it would amount to 'they would have the disposition to exhibit pain behaviour if they did not already have the disposition not to'.

2 Behaviour is not a sufficient condition of having experiences, beliefs or desires. One might imagine a race of super-pretenders capable of putting on convincing displays of the whole range of generic pain behaviours when not in pain.

So, the criticism is that behaviourism is false because it cannot draw distinctions between actually being in pain and pretending to be in pain and between not exhibiting pain-behaviour because pain isn't present and not exhibiting pain-behaviour although pain is present.

> Two animals with all motor nerves cut will have the same actual and potential behaviour (namely, none to speak of): but if one has cut pain fibres and the other has uncut pain fibres then one will feel pain and the other won't.
>
> *Putnam (1975)*

Moreover, we should remember that the behaviourist analysis applies to all conscious states and, as Putnam points out, if instead of pain we substitute a sensation the bodily expression of which is easier to suppress, then the point is even more firmly made.

Against this objection the behaviourist might argue that pretence, as the intention to deceive or entertain, is revealed in behaviour either through the context of the pretence (e.g. through role play) or because, no matter how good the actor, it is unlikely that they could successfully mimic or sustain all of the physiological symptoms of being in pain.

A further distinction ignored by behaviourists, and a further reason why it might be claimed that behaviourism is false, concerns the distinction between first person and third person ascriptions. It would seem that,

■ Key philosophers

Hilary Putnam (b. 1926): Emeritus Professor of Philosophy at Harvard University. His main interests have centred on mind, mathematics, language, logic and epistemology.

■ Think about

An example incorporating both pretence and non-behaviour might be that of homosexuals who 'pass'. Passing may involve suppressing any homosexual desires, which are present but also acting out heterosexual desires, which are not present.

■ Can we see 'passing' as behavioural or should we argue that the presence of homosexual desires which are never acted upon and the occurrence of heterosexual actions without the appropriate desires indicate that behaviourism is false?

■ Given that passing is surely an act of will does this rule out a dispositional analysis altogether?

■ Could we not phrase a dispositional analysis of the repressed desire along the lines of 'Bill would act upon this desire if homosexuality attracted less social stigma'?

However, it isn't clear that such an analysis exorcises the mental since it indicates Bill's concern or anxiety about social stigma. These difficulties indicate a further problem for behaviourism that we will return to.

according to behaviourism, the way that I learn about my beliefs is precisely the same as the way that I learn about yours: by observing behaviour. However, surely I do not need to observe my behaviour to know what I believe. This is not to say that such beliefs are not manifest in my behaviour or that I can never learn anything about my own conscious states through attending to my behaviour, but that there are other routes to self-knowledge I can employ. The old behaviourist joke is relevant here: after making love one behaviourist says to another 'it was fine for you, how was it for me?'

Behaviourism is vague

There is a difficulty in behaviourist accounts of specifying the particular behaviour, or behavioural disposition, which constitutes a particular mental state. For example, what piece of behaviour is the outward constitution of 'Henry believes that it will be frosty tonight'? Is it that Henry has turned the central heating up, is looking for a favourite pullover, or both of these things and more? Believing that it will be frosty tonight seems to be as generic, to use Ryle's term, as being clever.

Moreover, if statements like 'George is clever' are analytically reduced to 'George has a tendency to manifest lots of different kinds of behaviour associated with cleverness' then this is extremely vague. While, as noted above, we can provide reports of episodes when George has manifested cleverness, it must be remembered that, on the dispositional account, George's cleverness is not necessarily being actualised at a given moment. So there is a further difficulty of constructing a list of hypothetical statements explaining under exactly which conditions George's cleverness would be actualised. For example, it may be the case that 'George would have got ten starred A grades if …' but the problem is how long the list of conditional statements following the 'if' is: '… if he had not been depressed', '… if he did not suffer from hay fever', etc.

Thus, the task of explaining behaviour without reference to mental (non-behavioural) states does not look promising. It seems that it is not going to be possible to specify the conditions under which any given mental state will be realised in a particular episode of behaviour without referring to other mental states.

Behaviourism is non-explanatory

Even if we could specify the behaviour dispositions associated with beliefs, desires, experiences, attributes etc. it might still make more sense to introduce some internal state – either a physical state, such as a brain state, or a mental state – the presence of which explains a piece of behaviour, or a behavioural disposition, rather than claim that internal states are constituted by the behaviour dispositions themselves.

On a behaviourist analysis, Emma's desire to go to university and her belief that Nottingham University offers the best course for her is not the cause or reason why she applies to Nottingham University: rather, her application to study a particular course at Nottingham University is the main constituent of the desire and the belief. On a behaviourist analysis mental events are not causes of behaviour, or reasons for acting, because they do not exist independently of dispositions to behave in certain ways. But, surely, mental events do lead to behaviour.

There is an air of uninformative circularity about behaviourism. This is sometimes referred to as the intentional circle. For example, Emma may have the desire to be warm when she moves to Nottingham and, according to the behaviourist, this desire may be constituted by Emma packing several pullovers and coats. However, she will only do so if she believes that Nottingham will be cold. But this belief, according to the behaviourist, is itself constituted by packing several pullovers and coats and she will only do this if she possesses the desire to be warm.

Furthermore, there is a difference between action and movement and it is not clear that behaviourism pays sufficient attention to this difference. For example, 'I moved my leg' does not say the same sort of thing as 'my leg moved'. Clearly, if we are walking behind someone and observe them trip over a cat, we would not enquire 'why did you do that?' Whereas, if we observed them kick the cat we might well ask 'why did you do that?'

There are two issues here:

1 Movements like tripping over a cat are certainly accompanied by mental states such as feelings of irritation or embarrassment; actions like kicking cats are accompanied by mental states such as hatred of cats. Are they both, then, behavioural? Can a behaviourist distinguish adequately between behaviour and non-behaviour?

2 We are ordinarily inclined to see behaviour as motivated by an agent's attitudes, beliefs and desires rather than as merely mechanical. Thus, we might claim that behaviour isn't behaviour at all unless we presuppose an inner state which causes and explains it.

Behaviourism neglects certain features of mental states

Finally, behaviourism appears to neglect certain aspects of our conscious experience, both the subjective features, or qualia, of our experience, and the privacy of some aspects of our experience. Such experiences may be comprehensible only from the point of view of the conscious being that has them and any theory of mind that neglects this is, arguably, inadequate.

Despite Ryle's acknowledgement that biographical works would be incomplete as the subject of the biography would have some thoughts, dreams, etc. that would be unknown to the biographer as they have no behavioural manifestation, he nevertheless attempts a behavioural analysis of imaging, or 'visualising something with the mind's eye'.

Ryle suggests that there is:

> A person picturing his nursery is … not being a spectator of a resemblance of his nursery … he is resembling a spectator of his nursery.

Ryle (1968)

This does not seem right. If you are an A-level student reading this book, in what sense do you resemble a 6-year-old in a bedroom? Surely it is better to say that this is precisely the type of mental operation for which behaviourism seems false.

Eliminative materialism

While eliminative behaviourism has been largely abandoned, the project of eliminating our commonsense conception of the mind and mentality retains support in eliminative materialism. While contemporary eliminative materialism dates from the 1980s, support for eliminativism can be found in earlier, mid-20th century, materialist accounts of the mind and consciousness.

Eliminative materialism is not, on the whole, a reductive theory of mind. One feature of reductive theories is that they preserve the reality of what

Think about

Try to visualise what your bedroom looked like when you were 6 years old: is any behaviour attached to this?

is being reduced. However, the project of eliminative materialism is to eliminate, or reject, rather than preserve our conception of mentality; to replace references to mental states, and the theory in which references to mental states occur, with a better theory which does not refer to mental states at all. Eliminative materialism regards mental states as irreducible because, put simply, they hold that mental states don't exist. Eliminativists differ in their approach to which mental states do not exist and may hold a reductive position with regard to other mental states.

The most recent versions of eliminative materialism claim that **folk psychology** does not describe anything that actually exists; they predict that it will be completely replaced (hence, 'eliminated') when our scientific knowledge becomes sufficiently advanced:

> Eliminative Materialism is the thesis that our common-sense conception of psychological phenomena constitutes a radically false theory, a theory so fundamentally defective that both the principles and the ontology of that theory will eventually be displaced, rather than smoothly reduced, by completed neuroscience.

Churchland (1981)

Eliminativists, such as **Churchland**, target intentional states; others target subjective qualitative states, like the qualia of being in pain.

Eliminative materialism views folk psychology as a theory that we employ when using our everyday mental vocabulary to explain human action and interaction. According to eliminativists, folk psychology as a theory is comprised of both law-like generalisations and specific theoretical concepts. A law-like generalisation might be that if Charlotte has a desire to complete the London marathon and a belief that jogging four or five times a week, will help her to realise this desire, then, all things being equal, Charlotte will tend to jog four or five times a week. A specific theoretical concept, such as a belief, is typically assigned certain properties. So Charlotte's belief that jogging is a useful way of preparing to run a marathon possesses intentionality and is causally efficacious: the belief, coupled with her desire, leads her to jog. Eliminativists hold that this view of Charlotte's actions is profoundly mistaken and arguments for eliminativism are, essentially, arguments against the credibility of folk psychology.

The Churchlands argue that, from a scientific point of view, for something to merit the title of 'theory', it should offer both explanatory power and map out a fertile research programme which develops over time. They claim that folk psychology fails this test because:

- It lacks explanatory power in a number of important respects. For example, it either has nothing to say at all, or what it does say is flawed, about the nature of consciousness, certain mental disorders, or even why we dream. Neuroscience, on the other hand, does address these issues.
- It is stagnant. While it has been around for as long as folk have, it has not experienced much theoretical development over thousands of years whereas, in recent years, the neurosciences have been progressing.

They then offer the further criticisms that:

- It is extremely unlikely that the propositional features of beliefs – their syntactic structure and semantic properties – could be accommodated within a scientific account of mind. Where in the brain are we likely

Key terms

Folk psychology: our commonsense understanding of psychological events; the psychological concepts (such as belief and desire) we employ on a daily basis.

Key philosophers

Paul Churchland (b. 1942): American philosopher noted for his work in the philosophy of mind in general, and the philosophical implications of neuroscience in particular. He often works in collaboration with his wife, Patricia; another notable eliminative materialist.

to find any structure or process that resembles Charlotte's belief that 'jogging is a good way to prepare for a marathon'? Similarly, Charlotte's beliefs are about jogging and are directed at something outside of her and it is difficult to see how this feature of her beliefs can be causally responsible for how she acts.

- With regard to the qualitative features of mental states, the knowledge we already possess concerning neurological processes is too complex to map onto any vague folk psychological conception of the qualia to experience something, for example the what-it-is-like for Charlotte to feel grief on failing to complete the London marathon.

Consequently, folk psychology and the concepts it employs is doomed to the same fate that folklore has experienced: rejection and, ultimately, disappearance.

Objections to eliminative materialism

Eliminative materialism is counter-intuitive

What is persuasive about the Cartesian position is surely the view that even though we may attempt to question our knowledge, we know immediately and incorrigibly that we are minded. Thus, a thesis which claims that our commonsense understanding of the fact that we are minded, and of what our mindedness entails, is false seems counter-intuitive and obviously wrong. Mental states like belief and desire are so central to our grasp of social action and interaction that it would take very convincing argumentation to persuade us that our conception is mistaken. The issue is, then, whether eliminative theories are strongly persuasive. In this context we might then ask what kind of evidence would persuade us that, for example, we don't have subjective, qualitative, experiences and that qualia is a term that doesn't describe anything that is real?

Is eliminative materialism self-refuting?

Do we need to assume the existence of mental phenomena in order to advance the cause of eliminativism? If we do then eliminativism appears to be self-refuting. If, for example, eliminativism is intended to be a response to some alleged inadequacies of alternative theories then it appears to be self-refuting because it assumes the existence of some intentional property. Similarly, if eliminativism is true we cannot know that it is true because knowledge is typically defined as justified true belief and, according to at least some eliminativists, there are no such things as beliefs. Thus it would be self-refuting for an eliminativist to believe a thesis that states there are no such things as beliefs. Or, more precisely, it would appear to be self-refuting for an eliminativist to assert eliminativism because in order for eliminativism to be asserted as a thesis the eliminativist must believe the thesis to be true. It would seem equally odd for an eliminativist to assert that an alternative thesis is false given that, for this to occur, the eliminativist must believe the alternative thesis to be false.

Is folk psychology a theory?

It is not clear either that folk psychology is some kind of pre-scientific theoretical account of social action and interaction, nor that folk psychological explanations of action and interaction can simply be replaced with concepts drawn from neuroscience. **Searle** argues:

> The actual capacities that people have for coping with themselves and others are for the most part not in propositional form. They are

> ... background capacities ... matters of know-how, not theories. You distort these capacities if you think of them as theories.
>
> *Searle (1992)*

If, for example, Charlotte does not respond to a wolf-whistle as she walks past a building site it is probably not because she is entertaining a law-like theoretical proposition such as 'I have a desire to avoid a stranger invading my personal space and a belief that if I respond by looking up I might attract more unwanted attention so, all things being equal, I won't look up'. Rather, she has simply learned to cope with behaviour such as this. Part of the explanation of how she has learned to cope may involve the ability to put herself in the place of the wolf-whistler – 'what will he think if I look up?' It isn't obvious that the capacity to do this involves any kind of theoretical approach to the mind, folk psychological or otherwise.

Is folk psychology as hopeless as eliminativism suggests?

On the other hand, some have argued that folk psychology is a theory which successfully accounts how everyday communions with each other are conducted and, on the whole, such interactions are clear and well understood. It is not obvious that replacing these intentional terms with a terminology drawn from neuroscience would be as effective or that many of us would be able to employ such a terminology. Moreover, an inference we can draw from the long-lasting success of folk psychology in both accounting for and predicting behavioural responses to situations is that it offers a reasonably accurate account of many mental processes and certainly a more accurate account than eliminativists suggest.

Eliminative materialism may or may not turn out to be more scientifically respectable than eliminative behaviourism but it seems unlikely that folk psychology, the language employed by such simple folk as Dostoevsky, Camus and Joyce, will be replaced by neuroscience in the near future. Beyond this, we might claim that it is unlikely that it will be replaced at all.

Identity theory

Identity theory emerged in the mid to late 1950s and, like behaviourism, can be seen as a response to various problems stemming from Descartes' separation of mind and body. While most identity theorists acknowledge their indebtedness to logical behaviourism, there clearly is a range of mental phenomena, including experiencing, sensing and imaging, for which it does not seem possible to give a satisfactory behavioural analysis. So, if it is unsatisfactory to view mental states as non-physical states (as Descartes does) and unsatisfactory to define mental states in behavioural terms (as logical behaviourists do) it might be satisfactory to identify mental states with physical states. Identity theory is the materialist position that mental states are physical states; each mental state is identical to some physical state. The main division between different versions of identity theory concerns how to interpret the claim that every mental state is identical to some physical state.

Type identity and token identity

The main issue we face when attempting to determine whether mental events are the same as physical events concerns whether this question applies to kinds (or types) of mental events – whether pain, for example, can be regarded as a kind of sensation and whether, as a kind, it is identical to a kind of physical process – or to particular instances (or tokens) of mental events – whether this particular pain, experienced by this particular subject is identical to a particular physical process. An example should clarify:

How many words are used in the phrase 'forever and ever and ever and ever'?

There are two possible answers: three and seven. The answer 'three' regards the word 'ever', as a type of word. The answer 'seven' regards each time the word 'ever' is used as a token word.

Applied to mental phenomena, if ten people visit their dentist complaining that they have toothache and are in pain, then according to type identity theory all ten are experiencing the same type of mental event which is identical to a type of physical process (usually explicated in the philosophical literature as c-fibre excitation). That is, all instances of a particular type of mental state are also instances of a particular type of physical state. Type-type identity theory identifies types of mental states with types of physical states, so that, for example, pain as a type of mental event is numerically identical with c-fibres firing as a type of physical event.

According to token identity theory, however, each particular instance of pain is identical with an instance of a physical state of some type. That is, each instance of a particular type of mental state (such as pain) is also an instance of a physical state of some type (including c-fibre excitation but also other physical states such as, perhaps, physical states of beings that may not possess c-fibres). Token-token identity theory is the view that, for example my pain and your pain are tokens of the mental state of feeling pain and that the physical processes occurring in me and the physical processes occurring in you are tokens of a physical process associated with being in pain.

Type identity is a stronger claim than token identity; some objections to type identity theory will not apply to token identity claims; the division between reductive and non-reductive versions of materialism is also raised. Token identity is entailed by type identity because if mental types are identical with physical types then each individual instance of a mental kind will also instantiate a physical kind. However, token identity does not entail type identity because even if a particular instance of pain, as a mental kind, falls under a physical kind this contingent fact alone does not guarantee the identity of the mental kinds and physical kinds themselves.

The development of the identity theory of mind

Key philosophers

J.J.C. Smart (b. 1920): Scottish philosopher. Currently the Emeritus Professor of Philosophy at Monash University in Australia. His main interests have been in ethics and the philosophy of mind.

One of the early developers of identity theory was **J.J.C. Smart**. In his paper 'Sensations and Brain Processes' Smart was initially attracted by logical behaviourism, although he eventually rejected it in favour of type identity theory, and initially, focused largely on those conscious states which are resistant to behavioural analysis, such as sensations. He begins by considering:

> Suppose that I report that I have at this moment a roundish, blurry-edged after-image which is yellowish towards its edge and is orange towards its centre. What is it that I am reporting?

Smart (1964)

Smart wishes to resist the claim that this report is a report of something irreducibly psychical. He argues:

> There does seem to be, so far as science is concerned, nothing in the world but increasingly complex arrangements of physical constituents.

All except for one place: in consciousness … sensations, states of consciousness, do seem to be the one sort of thing left outside the physicalist picture and for various reasons I just cannot believe that this can be so. That everything should be explicable in terms of physics … except the occurrence of sensations seems to me to be frankly unbelievable. Such sensations would be **'nomological danglers'**.

Smart (1964)

Smart is aware that this is a statement of faith in science and the various reasons that he refers to include the simplicity and explanatory power of a scientific approach to consciousness. He also refers to **Occam's razor** as part of his reasoning: even if the identity theory and some form of property dualism are both equally consistent with an empirical fact, the former should be adopted in terms of its simplicity and its explanatory. So, with regard to what is being reported in the claim that Smart has a yellowish-orange after-image:

> The thesis does not claim that sensation statements can be translated into statements about brain processes, nor does it claim that the logic of a sensation statement is the same as that of a brain process statement. All it claims is that in so far as a sensation statement is a report of something, that something is in fact a brain process.

Smart (1964)

He is not claiming that talk about mental states means the same as talk about brain states; rather he is claiming that talk about mental states refers to the same thing as talk about brain states. Instead of a dualist two realms view, the identity theorist insists that there is only one realm and it is physical. Although we represent this realm in two conceptually diverse systems, science and folk psychology, and statements in one system have a different sense to statements in the other system, statements in both systems have the same referents.

The 'Australian materialism' of Smart was further developed, in the 1960s, by D.M. Armstrong. He did not accept that one could identify an internal mental process with external behaviour. Instead of identifying, or defining, mentality in terms of behaviour, Armstrong argued that it makes more sense to view mentality as the inner cause of external behaviour. So mental states are conceived as those states of an individual that are causally responsible for producing that individual's behaviour. In this account of the identity theory the definitive feature of mental terms and concepts is the causal role they play. Whereas Smart had initially confined his argument to those mental processes posing difficulties for the logical behaviourist analysis of mental states, Armstrong argued that all mental events were identical to physical processes in the brain. This view was eventually accepted by Smart.

Key features of the identity theory

The main points to stress when outlining the development of identity theory are:

1 It is, arguably, the most straightforward materialist theory of the mind. Its central claim can be simply stated as: mental states or events are identical with physical-chemical states of, or processes in, the brain. Given that it is an empirical rather than logical thesis, it can also be stated as: further scientific research will demonstrate the identity between all mental states or events and physical-chemical states of, or processes in, the brain. Put simply, to have a mind is to have a brain, minds are brains and mental events are brain processes.

Key terms

Nomological dangler: something which lies outside of a scientific law of nature.

Occam's razor: the view that the simplest explanation of any given phenomena is the best explanation. Entities should not be multiplied beyond necessity, so an explanation that refers to one entity and which does the same work as an alternative explanation that refers to two entities is to be preferred.

2 It is a reductive materialism that simplifies our ontology. Instead of the mental and the physical, there is only the physical.

3 It is an empirical theory. The claim is that scientific research will reveal the strict identity between mental states and brain states. So, the identity between mental states and physical states, while strict, is contingent. Determining which physical state (if only one state is involved) correlates with the mental state responsible for playing a causal role in our behaviour is something that can only be known a posteriori. The identity between mental states and physical states is not a conceptual truth: it is not being suggested that, through the analysis of concepts, philosophers will reveal the logically necessary, a priori, identity between mental states and brain states. This is in contrast to logical behaviourism, which does suggest that such a strict analytical reduction is possible.

Objections to the identity theory

Early objections

A number of objections to the theory, mostly connected with alleged violations of Leibniz's Law, appeared shortly after Smart's paper was published and prompted a response from Smart in a revised version of his paper. These included:

■ The epistemological claim that because we have direct knowledge of mental states while remaining completely ignorant about the physical states they are alleged to be identical to, mental states cannot be identical to physical states.

■ Mental states appear to have properties that physical states do not have. A yellowish-orange after-image, for example, has the properties of being yellowy-orange. A brain process, on the other hand, cannot be yellow or orange.

■ Brain states appear to have properties that mental states do not possess such as spatial location. If my sensation of an after-image is a brain process then it is located, roughly, two inches behind my eyes but it does not seem to be the case that the image itself is located two inches behind my eyes.

■ Sensations are private and first-person reports of sensations have a special kind of authority – arguably the person reporting the sensation cannot be wrong. Brain states are public. A neuroscientist with the appropriate equipment, such as a scanner, can observe states of my brain. While it makes sense to say that two or more people are observing a particular individual's brain processes it makes little sense to say that two or more people are having an individual's experiences.

Smart's reply to the first of these points is to accept that an illiterate peasant (his example) is able to talk about his sensations without knowing anything at all about brain processes, just as he can talk about lightning without knowing anything about electricity. However, this does not imply that sensations are not brain processes just as it does not imply that lightning is not an electrical discharge.

The second point is a stronger objection. We identify a sensation, such as an after-image, by its properties, such as being a yellow-orange patch of colour. Such properties appear to be distinct from, and something over and above, the properties identified in a purely physical framework. Moreover, it seems to be important that these properties are distinct because we can only identify a sensation with a brain process if we can first of all identify and describe the sensation in terms of some phenomenal property not possessed by brain processes. Thus, the identity theory seems to acknowledge a dualism of properties. Smart's reply is that we should describe sensations in 'topic-neutral' terms that favour neither dualism nor materialism. He says:

> When a person says, 'I see a yellowish-orange after-image', he is saying something like … 'There is something going on which is like what is going on when I have my eyes open, am awake, and there is an orange illuminated in good light in front of me, that is, when I really see an orange.

Smart (1964)

Smart's point is that we may be able to report that one thing is like another without stating in what respect they are alike. Because the respect in which two things are alike is not specified, the description is neither distinctively mental nor physical. Smart acknowledges that this reply may not be satisfactory and surely it is not: more or less everything is alike, or similar, similar to another thing in some respect; for example my computer is similar to the North Downs insofar as they are both in Surrey. Consequently if we do not specify the respect in which two things are similar, we cannot identify the distinguishing properties of sensations. Armstrong's identification of sensations, and other mental particulars, in terms of the causal roles they play – which is also neutral between mentality and physicality given that anything can bear a causal relation to something else – is a more sophisticated response although it is doubtful whether any attempt to remain neutral between mentality and physicality can work. Mental states, such as sensations, are distinctively mental: if a given state is a sensation then it will possess some characteristically mental properties.

Smart deals with the third point more successfully by making it clear that he is not arguing that an after-image is a brain process but that the experience of having an after-image is a brain process. So, while it is true that a brain state is not 'yellowy-orange' it is also true that the experience is not a yellowy-orange something. Smart claims that there is no reason that brain processes cannot include experiences of yellowy-orange after-images.

The fourth point, however, seems to be more problematic. Smart's response is to note that 'the language of introspective reports has a different logic from the language of mental processes' (Smart, 1964) and that, while we normally accept an individual's introspective report of his or her experiences, our acceptance of introspective reports is provisional on the further development, and improvement, of the identity theory. Until then we have no criteria for determining exactly what experience an individual is having. As Smart acknowledges, however, for the moment we typically do accept an individual's introspective reports and the problem arises of what we are to do if an introspective report conflicts with the report of a neuroscientist observing that individual's brain processes – if, that is, the individual claims to be in pain and the neuroscientist, not being able to find any brain activity relevant to pain, contradicts this. Due to the authority accorded to first-person reports do we assume that the neuroscientist is wrong – that, perhaps, she has missed something – or, due to the successes and status of science, do we assume that the individual is mistaken? Smart argues that an individual's introspective reports are not absolutely incorrigible but how can one make a mistake about whether they are in pain? Also, if we cannot always accept an individual's introspective report as accurate, there is the further problem of how we could set up a research programme to demonstrate psycho-physical correlations between the mental and the physical at all. This last point is also relevant to the following section.

Individual differences

The identity theory is an empirical thesis claiming that scientific research will, eventually, map the identities between types of mental states and types of neurological states. This project, however, does not seem particularly fruitful:

- Can we identify mental events of the same type? Can we say that my thought that 'Dustin Hoffman is a good actor' is the same thought as your thought that 'Dustin Hoffman is a good actor'? My thought may be linked to a range of his performances over time; your thought may be linked to your enjoyment of one film. Moreover, if I have this thought more than once, I may have initially thought 'Dustin Hoffman is a good actor' after watching one film, and only later will it come to be linked to a range of his performances. Is this the same type of thought in me? If we cannot say what a thought of the same type is then, clearly, there is little chance that a research programme mapping the identities of types of thoughts to types of brain processes could be successful.

- We know that when an area of the brain is damaged the brain compensates for this and another area of the brain takes over its function so it is unlikely that a given mental state can be identified with a given neurological state. Excessive consumption of alcohol may have decimated the neural network activated when I first had a positive thought about Dustin Hoffman but this should not be taken to imply that I can no longer have a positive thought about Dustin Hoffman.

At this point it should be noted that this is not a problem for token identity theory. Our thoughts, mine and yours, are tokens of thoughts about Dustin Hoffman. As such, they may be identical with brain processes and, possibly, with tokens of brain processes. That is, there will be a neural process of some kind going on every time you and I think about Dustin Hoffman but my neural process may be different from yours, and different in both of us at different times. However, if every thought and every brain process is in some sense unique, it is difficult to see what kind of empirical test we could employ to establish token identities.

Multiple realisation

Token-token identity theory may be more plausible than type-type identity theory insofar as it can deal with differences between and within individuals, and this might also lead us to question why we should restrict the identities between mental processes and physical states to human mental processes and physical states.

> The brain-state theorist is ... concerned to maintain that every psychological state is a brain state. Thus if we can find even one psychological predicate which can clearly be applied to both a mammal and an octopus (say 'hungry') ... whose physical-chemical 'correlate' is different ... the brain-state theory has collapsed ... Our mental states, e.g. thinking about next summer's vacation, cannot be identical with any physical or chemical states ... it is clear from what we already know about computers etc. that whatever the program of the brain may be, it must be physically possible, though not necessarily feasible, to produce something with that same program but quite a different physical and chemical constitution.

Putnam (1975)

Type identity theory claims that pain, for example, as a type of mental event is identical to c-fibres firing as a type of physical event. It follows, therefore, that creatures without c-fibres (some aliens perhaps) cannot feel pain. Somewhere in the universe it is possible that there is a life-form which does not possess the same physical-chemical constitution as human and non-human life-forms on earth but which does feel pain. If this life-form were to visit earth, be captured and tortured and demonstrated similar behavioural signs of distress and pain to those typically expressed by human and non-human animals it would be chauvinistic for us to assert that it cannot be in pain because it does not possess c-fibres.

This is widely regarded as one of the most damaging objections to type identity theory although, once again, token identity theories are fully consistent with the multiple realisability of mental states. Pain in the alien, for example, might be identical to d-fibres firing. Consequently, some theorists have abandoned type identity theory in favour of token identity theory while others have attempted to develop a more restricted version of the type identity theory. We will return to this point at the end of this section.

Irreducibility of consciousness

This objection to the identity theory stresses that conscious mental states involve the subjective point of view of the individual. There is something which it is like for an individual to be conscious or to be in a particular conscious state and this something, or quale, resists reduction.

This is illustrated in Frank Jackson's example, 'what Mary didn't know'.

> We suppose that we have a brilliant physical scientist, Mary, who is confined in a black and white room. There are no windows. She herself is, we may suppose, painted white all over and dressed in black. All her information about the world and its workings comes from black and white sources like books without coloured pictures and black and white television. However, the lectures she receives over the black and white television and the books she reads are amazing feats of exposition in physics, chemistry, biology and cognitive science, and she has extraordinary powers of comprehension and retention. In consequence, she is, despite the artificial restrictions in which she works, extraordinarily knowledgeable about the physical nature of our world, the neurophysiology of human beings and sentient creatures in general, and how their neurophysiology underpins their interactions with their surroundings including for instance the fact that on many occasions they produce words like 'red' and 'yellow' (if they speak English) when in front of blood and buttercups, respectively.
>
> Can she in principle deduce from all this physical information what it is like to see, say, red? It seems that she cannot. Despite her vast knowledge of the physical facts, there is something about our world and especially about persons' colour experiences she is ignorant of. This conclusion is reinforced by reflecting on what would happen should she be released from her room. Assuming that there is nothing wrong with her colour vision despite its lack of exercise during her imprisonment, she would learn what it is like to see red, and it is plausible that this would be learning something about the nature of our world, including especially the nature of colour experiences.

Jackson (2003)

The claim is that since consciousness is inextricably linked to the subjective experience and point of view of the individual, in this case

Mary, no objective or completely physical account of it is possible. Thus, via her new conscious experience, Mary learns something new – what it is like to see red – which is not physical knowledge.

Materialists have responded to this objection in various ways, generally by denying that Mary gains new knowledge. Some have argued that Mary acquires know-how, rather than knowledge of, through gaining new imaginative abilities, such as the ability to picture redness, and that she acquires a new means of mental representation; others claim that she is merely acquainted with what she already knew in a different way or that the only difference in her is that she has now seen colour. Many materialists continue to assert that the qualitative features of Mary's conscious experience depend, in an objective way, on her perceptual apparatus and, therefore, that whatever Mary's conscious states are like is also a physical matter.

The conceivability argument

A related objection to the above is one associated with David Chalmers. He identifies two types of problems associated with consciousness:

> The easy problems of consciousness are those that seem directly susceptible to the standard methods of cognitive science, whereby a phenomenon is explained in terms of computational or neural mechanisms. The hard problems are those that seem to resist those methods.

Chalmers (1995)

Chalmers does not deny that subjective experience is closely connected to physical processes in the brain (in humans) but poses the question of why physical processes in the brain should be accompanied by conscious experience at all (this is what he regards as the 'really hard problem of consciousness'). He employs the conceivability argument as an argument against materialism. The first premise of this argument is that it is conceivable that there is, somewhere in the universe, a zombie world in which there are beings that are physically identical to conscious human beings – they look like us, their neural states are just like ours, their behaviour is indistinguishable from our behaviour etc. – but these beings lack subjective conscious states. The second premise is that, as this is conceivable, such a world is metaphysically possible. Consequently, if there could be a world which is, physically, just like ours but in which there is no such thing as a subjective point of view or consciousness of what it is like to be a being in that world, consciousness must be non-physical.

Materialists have responded in various ways: for example, by denying that philosophical zombies are genuinely conceivable; or by claiming that even if they are conceivable they are not metaphysically possible. Much of the literature on this is difficult but, perhaps, you could form your own view after considering the following story.

Imagine that astronomers have discovered Twin Earth and that the technology of space exploration has improved to the extent that it has become possible for you to visit. Twin Earth is a planet indistinguishable from Earth: there is a twin of everything, including a twin you. However, unbeknownst to the people on Earth, every living creature on Twin Earth is a zombie.

You decide to visit your twin. Upon arrival, you inform the twin you of how delighted you are to meet them. Your twin responds by saying that they are equally (z) delighted to meet you (z delight is zombie delight – delight without the subjective feel of delight). After a while, you may proceed to discuss the difficulties of A-level philosophy with your zombie twin who is taking the twin examination. Indeed it turns out that your twin is (z) confused about the same issues that confuse you. All of this occurs without you noticing any major differences between you and your twin.

You enjoy your visit so much that you decide to stay, so you apply for a visa. There is a girl in your twin's philosophy class you find attractive (funnily enough she is exactly like a girl in your philosophy class that you also find attractive). This creates a problem because your twin finds her (z) attractive too. She finds you both (z) attractive. Your visa arrives, you are allowed to stay, and, despite (z) upsetting your twin, you get the girl.

Are the proposed identities between mental states and physical states contingent?

We noted above, according to the type identity theory, that the identities between mental states and physical states are contingent. This may be less straightforwardly materialist than it at first seems. Some have argued that it is compatible with property dualism. This is because we identify the states to be correlated in two different ways – for example, pain is identified as pain in virtue of the mental properties it possesses and as c-fibre. So, even if humans are purely physical, they remain beings that instantiate both mental and physical properties.

Similarly we noted in our discussion of eliminative materialism, that it is not obvious that folk psychology is a theory at all so it may not be a suitable candidate for reduction. As we shall presently see, this is one of the reasons behind the development of non-reductive, token, versions of the identity theory.

Some philosophers, notably Saul Kripke, have challenged the idea that the identity between mental states and physical states is contingent. To this end, he employs the notions of non-rigid and rigid designators:

- Some descriptions we employ refer to subjects contingently: for example, 'the first female prime minister of the UK' refers contingently to Margaret Thatcher as, had economic circumstances in the 1970s been otherwise or had an earlier male prime minister undergone a sex change, 'the first female prime minister of the UK' could have been someone else. So, 'the first female prime minister of the UK' is a non-rigid designator.
- Other descriptions we employ are rigid designators because they necessarily refer to something; there are no circumstances in which they could refer to something else. Kripke would claim that 'Margaret Thatcher' is such a rigid designator as it necessarily refers to a particular woman.

If the terms 'M' and 'P' refer to the same thing, and if both 'M' and 'P' are rigid designators, then the proposition 'M' is identical to 'P' is necessarily true. Kripke proceeds to argue that both the terms 'my pain' and 'my being in such and such a brain state' are rigid designators. To be in such and such a brain state, such as c-fibre excitation, is necessarily to be in such and such a brain state. To feel pain is necessarily to be in pain as one cannot be mistaken about this. This brain state is necessarily this brain state and this pain is necessarily this pain. So:

> The identity theorist who holds that pain is the brain state also has to hold that it necessarily is the brain state. He therefore cannot concede but has to deny that there would have been situations under which one would have had pain but not the corresponding brain state. Now ...

Think about
- Is any of this conceivable?
- Even if conceivable, is it possible?
- Is there any meaningful difference between your relations with the zombies on Twin Earth and those you had with the people back home?

this is very far from being denied. In fact it is conceded from the outset by the materialist as well as his opponent. He says, 'of course, it could have been the case that we had pains without the brain states, it is a contingent identity'. But that cannot be.

Kripke (1980)

Kripke's point that if pain were identical to a particular brain state it would be a necessary identity is employed to deny the identity between mental states and brain states. That is, he holds the view that pain is not necessarily identical to a particular brain state, because the link between pains and brain states seems to everyone, the identity theorist and opponents of the identity theory, to be contingent. Thus, if a pain is not necessarily identical to a particular brain state then pains and brain states cannot be identical at all. Notice that this objection applies to both type and token versions of the identity theory.

Responses to this might attempt to take issue with Kripke's assumption that pain is necessarily felt as pain, as there do seem to be situations where we may not be aware of a pain (if we become immersed in doing something, for example) so that while the assertion of pain may be a rigid designator, the perception of pain may be contingent. Furthermore, the assertion that one is in pain need not to be taken to determine that it is the same state every time this assertion is made and this may also open the door for a contingent relationship between pains and brain states.

Functionalism

Functionalism is the theory that the condition for being in any specific mental state should be given by the functional role of the state rather than by the intrinsic features of the state. In other words, what is important is what a mental state does. What makes a mental state a particular type of state is not its internal constitution but its function, or the role that it plays, within a given subject's cognitive system. Thus, the identity of a given mental state is described not in terms of its physical constitution but in terms of the causal relationships the state has with environmental stimuli – which (typically) produce it – with behavioural outputs – which are (typically) produced by it – and with other mental states.

Crucially, functionalism incorporates the view that mental states are multiply realisable: two or more physical systems with quite different physical constitutions can nevertheless be functionally isomorphic (i.e. they can do the same thing). For example, computational machines made from different materials can nevertheless perform the same functions. Just as a computer program can be realised in any number of physically different hardware configurations, a psychological 'program' can be realised in different organisms with different physical and chemical compositions.

Since the 1960s the development of functionalist theories of the mind has been subject to a wide range of influences and, as with other theories of the mind that we have considered, it is best to think of functionalism as a family of related theories. One broad difference is that some attempts to develop a functional characterisation of mental states have been influenced by information derived from research findings (and conjectures) – particularly research in neuroscience, cognitive psychology and artificial intelligence – while others have attempted to develop a functionalist theory of the mind through analysing the meanings of mental concepts.

AQA Examiner's tip

When describing functionalism it is crucial to refer to causal relationships between a mental state and other mental states as well as to environmental inputs and behavioural outputs. Accounts focusing solely on perceptual inputs and behavioural outputs are closer to descriptions of a relatively crude version of behaviourism.

Think about

Fred sees a bomb and runs off. Give two mental states which together would explain how this perpetual input produces the behavioural output.

Analytic functionalism

Analytic, or conceptual, functionalism is an attempt to develop an analysis of mental concepts in functionalist terms. The project here is to provide a topic-neutral, functional or causal role, analysis of mental concepts. This is in order to avoid the objection to the identity theory (previously discussed) that identifying mental states in one way and physical states in another way invites property dualism. Thus, analytic functionalism can be seen as an attempt to advance a position with materialist credentials. If one can provide a purely functional description of the concepts that we ordinarily take to be mental, e.g. pain or distress, then, whatever the internal states of a given subject, whether or not the subject is experiencing pain or distress is to be analysed in terms of a causal account of the relations between these internal states (which are regarded as overwhelmingly likely to be physical), external stimuli and outward behaviour.

Machine functionalism

Arguably, a more important strand in the development of functionalism has been the machine functionalism advocated by Hilary Putnam. The strategy here involves comparing mental states to machine states and particularly to the states of computing machines. Just as the same computer software can be run on different hardware, so the same type of psychological states, such as pain or distress, can be multiply realised in creatures with different physiological constitutions. To be in a particular mental state is to be in some physiological state that performs a causal role in producing behaviour in relation to external stimuli and other mental states.

Putnam acknowledged the influence of Turing's conjecture that it was theoretically possible for a computer to respond to questions in a way that would convince its interrogator that he was interacting with a human being. The Turing Test, as it has come to be known, was seen by Turing as a valid way to address the issue of whether a machine could think. Putnam developed this idea further by arguing that any creature or system that is minded can be regarded as a Turing machine, i.e. as a system operating according to some specifiable set of instructions or programme. Thus, Putnam's early functionalist model of the mind was that of a programme that, for each mental state and set of inputs, specifies the probability with which an individual 'system' will generate certain other mental states and produce some external output.

Synoptic link

For more on the Turing Test, see AQA AS Philosophy Chapter 9, Persons, pp282–5.

Psycho-functionalism

Psycho-functionalism has further developed a computational model of the mind in connection with developments in cognitive science and in artificial intelligence. Psycho-functionalism draws from cognitive psychology in holding both that behaviour is to be explained through reference to the internal physical states of a system and that humans, as well as other creatures or systems with psychological states, should be viewed as information processing systems. This approach to understanding behaviour focuses on how creatures or systems receive, process, store and use sensory information and sees behaviour as a result of the interconnected functional components. Similarly, research in computer science also links artificially intelligent behaviour to complex information processing and continues to provide a model for understanding human intelligence and cognitive abilities. Consequently, psycho-functionalism can be seen as the view that mental states and processes involve the entities and properties, and just these entities and properties, featuring in the best scientific explanations of human behaviour at any given time. Thus it differs from machine functionalism insofar as the best scientific explanation available at any given time may not be very much like early speculations about the similarity between the machine table representations of the functional roles of machine states and human physiological states. It also differs insofar as it concentrates on a scientific, rather than a folk, psychological account of mental states.

Teleological functionalism

The main feature of teleological functionalism, as the name suggests, is that it imposes a teleological requirement on the functional realisation of a mental state. That is, it requires the physical components involved in realising a functional description of a mental state to have organically developed for this particular purpose. A mental state plays the functional role that it does because its functional components have developed for this purpose and to the benefit of the organism. The impetus behind this move is the desire to avoid some of the excessively liberal interpretations of what kind of entity can be minded. These interpretations appear to result from considerations of the functional equivalence between machine and human psychological states (see below). We are not only to think of a thing's function in terms of what the thing is for, what its purpose is or what it is supposed to do, but also in terms of how it has evolved, or been developed, to perform this role. This approach is more biological than psychological and there is a tendency to restrict functionalist analysis to the roles played by the components, or **homunculi**, of human physiology.

The strengths of functionalism

We have already noted that functionalism can be seen as an improvement on other materialist theories while retaining their materialist credentials. For example, as noted, functionalism is less species-chauvinist than early versions of the type identity theory and allows for the plausible claim that creatures whose physiological or neurological constitution differs from ours can nonetheless experience the same types of mental episodes that we experience. Similarly, whereas some behaviourist claims are not only vague but may also be false – for example, the claim that Mary's belief that it is going to be sunny is to be unpacked in terms of Mary's disposition to, for example, search through the dressers in her room for a pair of sunglasses will only be true if Mary wishes to protect her eyes – functionalists can provide a more precise account of such a belief by adding a reference to the further mental state of desiring to protect one's eyes. This is because functional descriptions refer to the causal relations between perceptual stimuli (such as watching a weather report on television), the state of believing that it will be sunny and other mental states such as the state of wanting to protect one's eyes, and behaviour.

Moreover, most functionalist theories are closely linked to ongoing research programmes in relevant disciplines including:

- The research of computer scientists in determining what intelligent tasks computers will be able to perform.
- The research of cognitive scientists in determining how minds process, store and employ information.
- Research into biological **teleology** concerning why biological traits have evolved to play the causal roles that they do in a functioning system.

Key terms

Homunculus: the Latin term for little man. It is employed here to illustrate the functioning of a system in terms of the causal roles played by its component parts.

Teleology: from the Greek 'telos' meaning 'end'. Actions should be taken to achieve an end. Any doctrine which stresses necessary movement towards an ultimate goal may be teleological. For example, if you believe that humans have become more civilised as the ages have progressed and will continue to do so, you take a teleogical view of history.

AQA Examiner's tip

When developing an exposition of functionalism in essays it is not necessary to refer to every strand of functionalist theory.

Thus, the development of functionalism as a philosophical theory of mind is refreshed and reinforced by developments in other disciplines.

Objections to functionalism

The first point to make here is that, due perhaps to the vibrancy of the development of functionalist theories over the past 40 years, some quite well-known objections to functionalist theory have been offered by writers who are, or who have been, associated with the development of functionalist lines of thought themselves. Secondly, some objections, which may have originally been targeted at functionalist theory, have come to be seen as objections to materialism, or physicalism, generally. Thus, some of the objections to the identity theory that we have previously considered, such as the knowledge and conceivability arguments, may also be employed as objections to functionalism.

Liberalism

If type identity theory was too restrictive, or chauvinistic, the opposite claim has been made in relation to functionalist theories, particularly in relation to machine functionalism. That is, the worry is that certain functionalist theories are too liberal.

This worry may be raised in connection with the notion of functional isomorphism or equivalence. Table 1.2 provides an illustration.

Table 1.2 *Functional isomorphism between man and car*

Donald	A Renault Laguna
Donald is jogging by the side of the A331. Donald detects pain or discomfiture in his left calf muscle (sensory input). Donald is distressed (mental state). Donald grimaces, winces, begins to limp, etc. (behavioural output). Donald has a desire to rid himself of discomfort (intervening mental state). Donald slows down (behavioural output).	The Renault Laguna is speeding along the A331. The Renault Laguna detects low pressure or discomfiture in the passenger side rear wheel (sensory input). The Renault Laguna is distressed (mental state). The Renault Laguna flashes a light on the dashboard depicting that all is not well with the passenger side rear wheel (behavioural output). The Renault Laguna desires to rid itself of the discomfort (intervening psychological state). The Renault Laguna flashes a light on the dashboard indicating that it requires a service and that the driver should slow down (behavioural output).
Donald notices that there are people sitting outside in the garden of a pub on the other side of the road (sensory input). Donald wishes to avoid appearing pathetic (intervening psychological state). Donald adopts a serene facial expression and speeds up (behavioural output).	*And, depending on how much money we wish to spend on our cars* The Renault Laguna (which is fitted with a camera attached to a computer) notices a Mercedes parked on the other side of the road (sensory input). The Renault Laguna wishes to avoid appearing to be pathetic (intervening psychological state). The Renault Laguna (which is fitted with a device to reinflate tyres) activates this device and carries on speeding (behavioural output).

Both Donald and the Laguna seem to be running functionally equivalent distress programmes. Thus both the jogger and the car might be said to be psychologically distressed. However, it is counter-intuitive, and arguably too liberal, to hold that a car can be either distressed or proud.

Arguably, aspects of mentality that are missing in the car include the subjective, qualitative feel of distress and pride – in other words the qualia of distress and pride – and the lack of any view about the situation – in other words the intentionality of psychological states (we shall return to these points shortly).

Now, it might be objected that this illustration is not a genuine case of functional equivalence, as there is only a rough, crude, and very partial notion of equivalence here. However, because machine functionalists treat the functional realisation of a mental state (like distress) as being a matter of a simple correspondence between an individual creature's, or system's, perceptual stimuli, internal structural states (whatever they may be) and behaviour on one side and the defining input/state/output function of a programme on the other side, the problem arises that virtually anything might correlate, in some way, with some psychological process. Ned Block gives the economy of Bolivia as an example:

> Economic systems have inputs and outputs, e.g., influx and outflux of credits and debits. And economic systems also have a rich variety of internal states, e.g., having a rate of increase of GNP equal to double the Prime Rate. It does not seem impossible that a wealthy sheik could gain control of the economy of a small country, e.g., Bolivia, and manipulate its financial system to make it functionally equivalent to a person, e.g., himself. If this seems implausible, remember that the economic states, inputs, and outputs designated by the sheik to correspond to his mental state, inputs, and outputs need not be 'natural' economic magnitudes ... The mapping from psychological magnitudes to economic magnitudes could be as bizarre as the sheik requires.

Block (1980)

So, this account of the functional realisation of mental states is too liberal because it appears to lead to the ascription of psychological states to things and systems that do not have psychological states.

The problem of qualia

The qualia of experiential states, like sensations and emotions, are not captured by, and may be resistant to capture by, attempts at functional characterisations of mentality, characterisations of mental states in terms of their causal relationships to perceptual stimuli, other states and behaviour.

One argument employed against functionalism concerns 'inverted' qualia. For example, I may have an inverted colour spectrum so that what I see as red you see as violet; what I see as yellow you see as blue. However, I learned the names of colours in the same way that you did: when young and looking at a red rose (which I saw as violet) my mother said 'that rose is red'. Consequently, I call my violet-experiences red. Because of this, you and I are functionally equivalent with respect to our colour experiences: we have both learned to stop when a traffic light is red, you see it as red and I see it as violet but have learned to call this red; if we are both asked to go and buy some red baubles to use as Christmas decorations we will both look for and come back with red baubles, although I will see them as violet. The point is that while we are functionally indistinguishable the qualitative aspect of our subjective experience is different: so functional accounts of how 'seeing red' is realised do not distinguish between qualitatively distinct experiences.

A second objection concerns absent qualia: whether there could be creatures (such as the zombies we considered earlier), or systems functionally equivalent to normal humans whose mental states have no qualitative character at all. Ned Block illustrates the objection that machine functionalism is too liberal with some examples of systems which are functionally equivalent to you (for example) but, unlike you, have no subjective mental life. The best known of these is the 'China-Mind':

> Suppose we convert the government of China to functionalism, and we convince its officials to realize a human mind for an hour. We provide each of the billion people in China (I chose China because it has a billion

inhabitants) with a specially designed two way radio that connects them in the appropriate way to other persons and to (an) artificial body …

Block (1980)

Each citizen of China receives the equivalent of sensory input from the artificial body, via the transmission of radio signals, and is also connected to other citizens via his radio. Each represents a neuron and communicates with other neurons in a network, as neurons do. Collectively, the population of China constitutes a brain for the artificial body. Each responds to messages displayed on a series of satellites in the sky placed so that they can be seen from anywhere in China. Given the right input signal, a citizen will execute his or her particular task and communicate, via the radio, with other citizens. In this way the population of China mobilises the robot body so that the citizens of China have been arranged to resemble a particular mind.

Block argues that such a homunculi-headed system – or Blockhead as it has come to be called – would not have mental states with any qualitative character. So, again, states in the artificial body that are functionally equivalent to sensations or perceptions may lack their characteristic feels. He concludes by arguing that because machine functionalism holds that a given mental state, e.g. a particular qualitative state, is identical to a state playing a functional role within a system, then machine functionalism cannot be true. Functionalism errs in claiming that any system with the same functional organisation as you will have all the same mental states that you have: the qualitative properties of your mental states appear to be intrinsic properties rather than relational ones.

In response, some have disputed whether it is possible that creatures or systems with the same functional organisation as a human being but without the qualia of human experience could exist. Generally, their argument is that the above objection may appear plausible but only works against early and cruder versions of functional definitions. Psycho-functionalists, e.g., might deny that Blockhead is a counter-example to their version of functionalism because it is not an organic psychological system which cognitive scientists can study and about which cognitive science can offer a scientific psychological theory. Teleological functionalists would also argue that Blockhead is not a functional biological system because none of the homunculi in Blockhead have evolved to fulfil the purpose of mobilising Blockhead.

The problem of intentionality

We have already noted that intentionality is the term used to refer to the aboutness of mental states (believing that …, desiring that, etc.). It may seem that intentional states are easier to describe in functional terms but some objections have been raised here as well. Can an intentional mental state be described in purely functional terms?

Putnam uses a version of the Twin Earth scenario we considered above to cast doubt on this:

Every item on Twin Earth looks, tastes, smells and feels exactly the way things do on Earth. However, every item on Twin Earth has a different physical structure to its counterpart on Earth. So whereas the inhabitants of both planets drink water, the molecular structure of water on Twin Earth is XYZ rather than H_2O. While our Twin Earth counterparts may talk about water in the same way that we do, about how refreshing it is for example, their meaning differs from ours. Their beliefs about water are directed at XYZ and are, thereby, different from the beliefs that we have about water which are directed at H_2O. Representational contents are wide, affected by one's physical and cultural environment, whereas functional roles are narrow. Thus, a purely functional description of the role played by a mental state may fail to capture the representational content of that state.

Putnam's point is that two individuals may be functionally identical while their beliefs are about different things so that what they mean by believing something is different. Searle offers a well-known thought experiment which also undermines the idea that a functional role in a machine programme possesses intentionality. The point of his Chinese Room thought experiment is that a system running a functionally equivalent programme to a human may have no intentionality at all. Searle's target was Artificial Intelligence and particularly the strong AI views that developments in computer science point to how we can further our understanding of human intelligence and that any system or organism that genuinely realises such-and-such a program (e.g. believing that, desiring that, sensing that) is functionally equivalent to us and, like us, possesses mental states. However, his argument can clearly be employed against functionalism (and behaviourism) as well.

Chinese symbols are received (input) and sent out (output) through the door of the locked room. The man in the room is an English speaker and has no knowledge of Chinese symbols. By following the instruction book and posting the symbols through the door, it would seem, to outside observers, that the he understands Chinese.

Searle argues that the man in the room does not understand Chinese. He applies instructions and he understands these but he remains ignorant of the meaning of Chinese symbols. His conversational response does not possess intentionality, does not mean anything, and is not about anything. According to Searle this undermines the Turing Test and the ideas that minds approximate to computers and computer programs approximate to a computational model of the mind. Intrinsic intentionality is not present in any system which is merely running a program: manipulating symbols in accordance with rules produces mere 'as if' intentionality, as if belief, as if understanding. One way of representing this argument is to claim that computers lack semantics (they do not signify meaning) although they possess syntax (they can arrange symbols in accordance with rules). So, when you sign into a program on your computer and it greets you with 'Hello Tiffany' it is arranging symbols but it does not mean anything, it has no beliefs about you or about civility.

To say that there have been many critical responses to Searle's argument would be an understatement. The best known response is called the systems response. This suggests that the Chinese room example encourages us to focus on the wrong agent: the person in the room. The person in the room may not understand Chinese but the system taken as a whole (room, person, instructions, symbols etc.) does understand Chinese. Searle's response to this was to suppose that the person in the room internalised the system in their head, for example by memorising the rules. Searle maintains that the person still does not understand Chinese and is not a genuine Chinese speaker. This, perhaps, is not altogether convincing.

It is also worth noting that Searle can be accused of operating with certain dualist assumptions. His intrinsic intentionality is conscious intentionality and this is identified with a subjective point of view. While Searle insists that he is not employing any outmoded Cartesian assumptions – arguing instead that consciousness is a natural biological phenomenon (see below) – he also insists that the ontology of the mind is subjective in keeping with our commonsense folk psychological intuitions.

Does functionalism involve an explanatory gap?

This is an argument against materialism generally, but it may be useful to apply it here. It is linked to the hard problem of consciousness. Briefly, we might wish to argue that:

1 Materialist accounts explain, at most, structure and function.
2 An explanation of a creature's structure, or of the functional roles that parts of that structure play, is not sufficient to explain consciousness.
3 If something cannot be explained physically it is because it is not physical.
4 All forms of materialism are false.

This argument is controversial. Materialists would deny all stages of the argument and argue that materialist accounts of structures and functions do constitute an explanation of consciousness. However, as noted earlier, arguments against materialism are also arguments for dualism and you may feel that, following a consideration of points concerning qualia and intentionality, the dualist view that mental states are something over and above physical states is plausible.

Summary

It is clearly the case that functionalist arguments face significant problems but, as previously noted, many of these issues are disputed *within* functionalism and it is still possible to argue that functionalism is the dominant paradigm among those engaged in the philosophy of mind.

The development of psycho-functionalism and teleological functionalism means that functionalist theory is still supported by developments in relevant empirical sciences. Moreover, it is rightly claimed that these positions can avoid the charge of excessive liberalism that faced machine functionalism. Whether they are correct or not is another matter. Ironically, however, it is argued that these developments in functionalist thought have led it too far the other way and that functionalist theory is becoming chauvinistic. Psycho-functionalism is closely tied to cognitive psychology and neurology in looking for the best scientific psychological research on how human physiological components contribute to the functional realisation of mental states and teleological functionalism is heavily focused on human biology in looking for the purposes underpinning the evolution of functional traits. Effectively this is a return to the species chauvinism of the type identity theory which, of course, might lead us to deny mindedness to certain creatures or systems that do possess it.

It may be the case, therefore, that functionalist theories are either going to be too liberal or too chauvinistic, that no functionalist theory can avoid both.

☑ *After working through this topic, you should be able to:*

- give an account of the key features of reductive materialism
- distinguish between the various types of behaviourism, identity theory, and functionalism and assess their strengths and weaknesses
- assess the strengths and weaknesses of eliminative materialism.

Non-reductive materialism

- to be able to understand to what extent consciousness can be regarded as an emergent, or supervenient, property

- to be able to give an account, and assess the plausibility, of anomalous monism

- to be able to give an account, and assess the plausibility, of biological naturalism.

Key terms

Supervene: a supervenient property is one that is dependent upon its subvenient base without being reducible to that base, so that mental properties supervene upon physical properties without being reducible to them.

Fig. 1.2 *A wintry scene in Dartmoor*

Key philosophers

Donald Davidson (1917–2003): Professor of Philosophy at the University of California, Berkeley, between 1981 and 2003. His main interests were in epistemology, the philosophy of language and the philosophy of mind and action.

At the beginning of the last topic, we mentioned a second way of interpreting the claim that all mental events have a material basis. This is to say that mental events or phenomena depend or **supervene** upon physical processes or phenomena. So, to return to our earlier example, the mental state of believing that the world is round is supervenient upon, rather than identical to, some neural process in the brain. In this case the 'is' in 'everything that exists is in some sense physical' is the 'is' of constitution. That is, while the physical properties of a mental event determine its mental properties, so that all mental events are composed out of physical processes, a particular mental event is not strictly identical to a particular physical process and the mentalistic vocabulary, or psychology, we employ to describe a given mental event is not reducible to a particular physical description of that event. Consequently, this approach to the philosophy of mind is typically referred to as non-reductive materialism.

An example might be useful here: consider Fig. 1.2, the image of a wintry scene on Dartmoor. As 'everything that exists is in some sense physical' we might argue, from a reductive point of view, that the 'wintriness' present in this image is reducible to a particular configuration of pixels. The 'wintriness' really is a property of the image: this property is reducible to the arrangement of pixels and is nothing over and above the arrangement of pixels. Alternatively, we might say that the 'wintriness' of the image supervenes upon this arrangement of pixels, and indeed is nothing over and above the arrangement of pixels, but that the property 'wintriness' is not reducible to this arrangement of pixels. The property of 'wintriness' in some photographic images cannot simply be a particular arrangement of pixels because it is multiply realisable – in other words, different images and, consequently, different arrangements of pixels, can display 'wintriness'.

The term 'supervenience' has been used in different ways. Outside of philosophy, it is typically used to refer to something that occurs in addition to, or that emerges from, something else. In philosophy, it is used to mean that there cannot be a qualitative difference between two things if those things are exactly alike in all physical respects: so, if a given thing or event is perceived to possess value to an extent then any other thing or event which is exactly like it must also possess value to the same extent (the term was first employed in moral philosophy). The term was introduced to the philosophy of mind by **Donald Davidson** in 1970:

> Mental characteristics are in some sense dependent, or supervenient, on physical characteristics. Such supervenience might be taken to mean that there cannot be two events exactly alike in all physical respects but differing in some mental respects, or that an object cannot alter in some mental respects without altering in some physical respects.

(Davidson, 2001a)

To return, briefly, to the wintry scene, this means, first, that another photograph with exactly the same arrangement of pixels would be equally 'wintry' and, secondly, that we could not change the 'wintriness' of the image without making some change to the pixels that comprise the image. Applied to the philosophy of mind, no two events can differ in their mental properties without differing in their physical properties; a single event cannot change its mental properties without changing its physical properties. In slogan form: there cannot be an M-difference without a P-difference.

Anomalous monism

Anomalous monism is the version of token identity theory proposed by Donald Davidson. He adopts the view that, although token mental events and states are identical to token physical events and processes, mental types are not identical, or reducible, to physical types. He also insists that, whereas accounts of causal relations between events can be given in terms of neural, or physical-chemical, descriptions it is not possible to provide an account of mental causation in terms of folk psychological descriptions of events. Folk psychological descriptions are too indeterminate in terms of meaning and translation to occur in law-like statements connecting causes to effects.

In 'Actions, Reasons and Causes' Davidson argued for:

> the ancient – and common-sense – position that rationalization is a species of ordinary causal explanation.

Davidson (2001b)

That is, that mental events and bodily events influence each other: the reasons people give to explain their actions can be taken to be the causes of those actions. He calls a reason for action a rationalisation. Rationalisations include both beliefs and desires. For example, George, a teacher, is producing a PowerPoint presentation on anomalous monism because he believes that, because of the limited time and resources available to them, few of his students will read essays by Davidson in their original form, and because he desires that his students should know something about Davidson. This rationalisation of George's action can be taken to be the cause of George's action: the primary reason for his action (i.e. his token of a belief that … and his token of a desire that …) is the cause of his action.

However, rationalisation can function as a causal explanation only if it falls under some covering law (or generalisation) describing the relationship between reason and action. The problem is that such generalisations cannot be sharpened into the kind of law which would allow accurate predictions to be made. That is, it doesn't follow that every time George believes his students would benefit from a PowerPoint presentation, even where this is accompanied by a desire that they should advance their knowledge, he will produce one.

In George's case, for example, the above belief and desire may co-exist with a belief that if he sits at a computer ignoring his pet Alsatian much longer his dog will begin to chew the furniture. Consequently he does not complete the PowerPoint presentation. Davidson argues that a correct identification of a person's mental properties, George's for example, is always a holistic matter involving an interpretation of George's intentional processes and that this is too indeterminate to appear in a law-like account of George's actions.

So, whereas tokens of physical events (such as neural firings) belong to whatever physical type they belong to (a brain process), tokens of mental

Synoptic link

AQA A2 Philosophy Chapter 4, Supervenience in moral philosophy, p147.

Key terms

Anomalous: irregular, inconsistent, does not fall under a law-like (nomological) description.

Monism: single; there is only one kind of 'stuff' (in this case, matter).

events (such as believing this) belong to a mental type (a propositional attitude) only relative to certain background assumptions about the meaning and force of an individual's rationalisations. Because of this, there can be no strict laws connecting physical and mental events. But, it does not follow that even if laws connecting reasons and actions cannot be given in terms of rationalisations that they cannot be given at all. It only means that an explanatory law connecting mental events and physical events must avoid mental descriptions of events. So, each token of a mental event can be said to be the cause of a bodily event only if it figures in a law-like explanation, and it can only do this if it can be described in physical terms:

> If psychological events are causally related to physical events there must ... be laws that cover them ... the laws are not psychophysical so they must be purely physical laws. This means that psychological events are describable, taken one by one, in physical terms, that is, they are physical events.

Davidson (2001a)

Thus, we arrive at a version of the token identity theory. It is necessary to describe a token of a mental event in physical terms, to require an identity between mental tokens and physical tokens, in order to preserve the commonsense intuition that our mental states are causally responsible for the way we behave.

This is a non-reductive version of the identity theory. Mental events exist and have mental descriptions which are not reducible to physical descriptions. There is no equivalent to rationalisations, which include intentional properties, in the physicalist framework. Mental events are causally efficacious; rationalisations cause actions. However, the only way to account for this is if mental events also have physical descriptions. So that each token mental state is also a token physical state. Davidson did not develop a positive non-reductive account explaining the inter-relationship between mental properties and physical properties. He did briefly comment that:

> Although the position I describe denies there are any psychophysical laws, it is consistent with the view that mental characteristics are in some sense dependent, or supervenient, on physical characteristics. Such supervenience might be taken to mean that there cannot be two events alike in all physical respects but different in some mental respect, or that an object cannot alter in some mental respect without altering in some physical respect.

Davidson (2001a)

Neither dependence nor supervenience entails reducibility. It does not follow from the above that two events cannot be alike in all mental respects while different in some physical respects.

An objection to anomalous monism

Arguably, a materialism which wishes to treat mentality seriously requires more than an identity between token mental states and token physical states. It requires that mental states have a role in explaining actions as mental states and it is not clear that Davidson's position affords the mental the explanatory power that we want it to have. It would seem that, on Davidson's account, the physical-chemical properties of mental states do all of the explanatory or causal work and that the mental properties are epiphenomenal. That is, if mental events are causally efficacious only by virtue of their physical features then their mental features, qua mental, do not seem to do anything.

Davidson was not much impressed by this objection, arguing that causal relations hold between events rather than between descriptions of events. He says:

> Events instantiate a law only as described in one way rather than another, but we cannot say that an event caused another only as described.

Davidson (2001a)

Explanatory laws describe events in particular ways, ways that employ physical-chemical properties, and the same event described in folk psychological terms loses its explanatory force. Nevertheless, it is the same event so that mental events can be said to cause physical events.

Think about

Do you find this response convincing?

Biological naturalism

Finally, we turn to a position that requires that we should 'forget about Descartes, dualism, materialism and other famous disasters' (Searle, 2007) and begin again after reminding ourselves of what we know. According to John Searle, if we were to do so we would arrive at a position that he calls biological naturalism.

Searle reminds us of some traditional distinctions between mentality and physicality which form the basis of disputes between dualist and materialist conceptions of consciousness (Table 1.3).

Table 1.3 *Distinctions between the mental and physical*

Mental states	Physical states
1 Are subjective.	1 Are objective.
2 Have first-person ontology.	2 Have third-person ontology.
3 Are qualitative.	3 Are quantitative.
4 Are intentional.	4 Are non-intentional.
5 Have no spatial location.	5 Have a spatial location.
6 Are not extended in space.	6 Are extended in space.
7 Cannot be explained by physical processes.	7 Can be explained through physical processes.
8 Are incapable of causally effecting physical states.	8 Are part of a causally closed physical system.

According to Searle, both dualists and materialists say something which is true, and something which is false. His own position on conscious states is that they:

1 are ontologically subjective – they only exist as the experience of a given subject as part of a unified conscious field

2 are qualitative – there is a qualitative feel, a what-it-is-like, to be in a particular conscious state

3 are intentional insofar as they refer to, are about or are directed at objects, other subjects and states of affairs

4 have a spatial location

5 can be explained through microphysical processes – they are higher level brain processes and have a neural base, or are caused by, lower-level microphysical processes in the brain

6 are causally efficacious.

Think about

- Is this the best of both worlds?
- Can we have the best of both worlds?

Searle objects to materialist reductionism as:

> it is bound to fail because the ontologically subjective cannot be reduced to the ontologically objective.

Searle (1992)

He is also hostile to any form of dualism:

> I think one can accept the existence and irreducibility of consciousness as a biological phenomenon without accepting the ontology of traditional dualism, the idea that there are two metaphysically or ontologically different sorts of realms we live in, or two different sorts of properties in the world.

Searle (1992)

His main objection concerns the difficulty dualists experience in explaining the causal efficacy of mental states. Searle holds that under the property dualist approach mental states are either epiphenomena, with no causal powers of their own, or, should it turn out to be the case that the physical universe is not causally closed, then mental properties acting together with physical properties to cause a state of affairs produces causal over-determination (any explanation we give for our bodily movements will include too many causal stories).

Searle argues that conscious states are real parts of the real world and can neither be eliminated nor reduced. He claims:

> Mental events and processes are as much part of our biological natural history as digestion, mitosis, meiosis, or enzyme secretion.

Searle (1992)

Furthermore that:

> our conscious lives are shaped by our culture, but culture is itself an expression of our underlying biological capacities.

Searle (2002)

Hence, he argues for biological naturalism rather than for reductive materialism or property dualism. He claims that his position on consciousness is one that shares common features with other natural phenomena. For example, we can use an analogy with water. At the ordinary 'macro-level' of everyday experience we are aware that water is wet, odourless (if pure), refreshing if drunk, adopts the shape of the container it is in etc. These 'properties' are caused by the micro-level of water: millions of individual and invisible molecules made up of two hydrogen atoms and one oxygen atom. Similarly, conscious states (with qualia and intentionality) are caused by non-conscious micro-neurological states (without qualia and intentionality). Conscious states are not a different type of 'thing' to microphysical states but neither are they reducible to microphysical states.

Objections

Biological naturalism has attracted a number of criticisms to and responses from Searle. The most significant have been:

- Searle wants it both ways. The view that consciousness is a biological process is materialist and the view that consciousness is irreducibly subjective is dualist.

Think about

Isn't this a problem for materialism as well?

- The account seems contradictory. It is ontologically non-reductive but causally reductive. Is it reductionism or not? If it is, it is materialism. If it isn't, it is dualism.
- This is a form of property dualism. The physical universe is causally closed and Searle's irreducibly subjective mental items are, therefore, epiphenomena.
- If consciousness, with the properties that Searle attaches to it, is caused by brain processes then there are two distinct properties: the causes of mental states, microphysical brain processes, and the effects of microphysical brain processes, subjective, qualitative and intentional mental states. This is property dualism.

Searle's response has been to claim that such objections rest on mistaken conceptions of the mental and the physical as well as mistaken conceptions of reduction and causation. However, his positions are not entirely convincing. For example, with regard to why causal reduction does not lead to ontological reduction, he says:

> In the case of consciousness the causal reduction does not lead to an ontological reduction by redefinition, because the redefinition would take away the point of having the concept in the first place.

Searle (2007)

With regard to causation, he claims that:

> Many causal forces are continuous through time … causal relations are bottom up and simultaneous with the effect.

Searle (2007)

However, the first comment seems to express sympathy with, or faith in, a dualist ontology and the second point, despite his assertions to the contrary, seems to express a materialist ontology insofar as an effect that is simultaneous with its cause seems to be the same thing as the cause.

The objection that Searle has been most concerned to answer is that biological naturalism is, in fact, a form of property dualism and that, despite his desire to avoid the alleged mistakes of past philosophers, his position endorses, rather than departs from, dualist intuitions. He writes:

> I say consciousness is a feature of the brain. The property dualist says consciousness is a feature of the brain … The property dualist means that in addition to all the neurobiological features of the brain, there is an extra, distinct, non-physical feature of the brain; whereas I mean that consciousness is a state the brain can be in, in the way that liquidity and solidity are states that water can be in.

Searle (2002)

However, if this analogy does not lead us to materialism, as Searle maintains that it doesn't, it is difficult to see how his position departs from property dualism.

☑ *After working through this topic, you should be able to:*

- explain what non-reductive materialism involves
- assess the strengths and weaknesses of different non-reductive materialist theories of mind.

■ **Summary questions**

1 Do some materialist theories help to resolve the problem of other minds, or does this remain a problem?

2 Can consciousness be reduced to something physical?

3 Is it likely that we will be able to eliminate talk of mental states altogether?

4 If mental states are held to be supervene upon physical states are we necessarily led to epiphenomenalism?

5 Does naturalism succeed in advancing a position, which is neither materialist nor dualist?

■ Further reading

■ Chalmers, David, *The Conscious Mind*, Oxford University Press, 1996. Contains probably the best overview of and, arguably, one of the most interesting developments in, contemporary philosophy of mind. It is also written very clearly.

■ Heil, John, *Philosophy of Mind: A Guide and Anthology*, Oxford University Press, 2004. There are a great many philosophy of mind anthologies available. This one not only contains key papers by many of the thinkers featured here, it also provides accessible introductory essays to the various positions.

■ Maslin, Keith, *An Introduction to the Philosophy of Mind*, Polity, 2001. This is written by an experienced A-level teacher and is aimed primarily at A-level students. Includes chapters on the problems and positions covered by the AQA specification.

■ Ryle, Gilbert, *The Concept of Mind*, Penguin Books, 1968. This highly influential text is also clearly written and accessible.

■ References

Aristotle, *On the Soul*, trans. by J.A. Smith, in *The Complete Works of Aristotle: The Revised Oxford Translation*, ed. by Jonathan Barnes, vol. 1, Princeton University Press, 1984, pp641–92.

Ayer, A.J., *The Concept of a Person and other essays*, Macmillan & Co. Ltd., 1963.

Block, N., 'The Troubles with Functionalism', in *Readings in Philosophy of Psychology, Volume 1*, Harvard University Press, 1980.

Broad, C.D. *The Mind and its Place in Nature*, Kegan Paul, 1925.

Chalmers, David, 'Facing up to the Problem of Consciousness', *Journal of Consciousness Studies*, Vol. 2, 1995.

Churchland, P.M., 'Eliminative Materialism and the Propositional Attitudes', *Journal of Philosophy*, Vol. 3, No. 2, 1981, pp67–90.

Davidson, Donald, 'Mental Events', in *Essays on Actions and Events*, Oxford University Press, 2001a, pp207–27.

Davidson, Donald, 'Actions, Reasons and Causes', in *Essays on Actions and Events*, Oxford University Press, 2001b, pp3–19.

Descartes, René, 'Discourse on Method' in *Descartes, Selected Philosophical Writings*, Cambridge University Press, 1988.

Descartes, René, *Meditations on First Philosophy with Selections from the Objections and Replies*, ed. and trans. by John Cottingham, Cambridge University Press, 1996.

Hempel, Carl, 'The Logical Analysis of Psychology', trans. by Wilfrid Sellars, in John Heil, *Philosophy of Mind: A Guide and Anthology*, Oxford University Press, 2004, pp85–95.

Hume, David, *An Enquiry concerning Human Understanding*, ed. by Tom L. Beauchamp, Oxford University Press, 1990.

Huxley, T.H., 'On the Hypothesis that Animals are Automata, and its History' (1874), in *Collected Essays*, Macmillan, 1893.

Jackson, F., 'The Knowledge Argument', in *The Richmond Journal of Philosophy*, Issue 3, 2003.

Kripke, Saul, *Naming and Necessity*, Harvard University Press, 1980.

Leibniz, G.W., *Discourse on Metaphysics and the Monadology*, Open Court, 1908.

Malebranche, Nicolas, *Dialogues on Metaphysics and Religion*, Cambridge University Press, 1997.

Mill, John Stuart, *An Examination of Sir William Hamilton's Philosophy*, Longmans, Green & Co., 1889.

Papineau, David, 'Confusions about Consciousness', in *The Richmond Journal of Philosophy*, Issue 5, 2003.

Plato, *Phaedo*, trans. by G.M.A. Grube, in *Plato: Complete Works*, ed. by John M. Cooper, Hackett, 1997, pp49–100.

Putnam, Hilary, *Mind, Language and Reality*, Cambridge University Press, 1975.

Ryle, Gilbert, *The Concept of Mind*, Penguin, 1968.

Searle, John, *The Rediscovery of the Mind*, MIT Press, 1992.

Searle, John, 'Why I Am Not a Property Dualist', *Journal of Consciousness Studies*, Vol. 9, No. 12, 2002.

Searle, John, 'Biological Naturalism', in *The Blackwell Companion to Consciousness*, ed. by M. Velmans and S. Schneider, 2007.

Smart, J.J.C., 'Sensations and Brain Processes' in *Body and Mind*, ed. by G.N.A. Vesey, Allen and Unwin, 1964.

Spinoza, Benedict, *Ethics*, trans. by Edwin Curley, in *The Collected Works of Spinoza Volume I*, ed. by Edwin Curley, Princeton University Press, 1985, pp408–617.

Stout, G.F., *Mind and Matter*, 2 vols., Cambridge University Press, 1931.

Strawson, P.F., *Individuals*, Methuen & Co. Ltd, 1959.

Wittgenstein, Ludwig, *Philosophical Investigations*, trans. by G.E.M. Anscombe, Blackwell, 1968.

Wittgenstein, Ludwig, *Tractatus Logico-Philosophicus*, trans. by C.K. Ogden, Routledge, 1981.

2 Political philosophy

Human nature and political organisation

The state

Political philosophy is largely about the relationship between **the state** and the individual.

The state is recognised as the body that has the right to make laws and to support their use of power with punishment. It has the ability and the right to command and to use coercion and violence to enforce its laws. A state may be legitimate, but lack the power and ability to enforce the law and then is referred to as 'a failed state'. Such states are usually unable to combat insurgency and guerrilla warfare within their territory.

The extent to which a state commands or does not interfere with the private life of its citizens; the determination of what punishments are justified and how long citizens can be detained without trial; and the kind of protection it should offer against, for example, terrorism, economic hardship and international health concerns, is of course a matter of debate. Thus, as we shall see, conservatives, liberals, anarchists and Marxists all have competing **ideologies** about this relationship between the individual and the state.

The origins of the state

The justification of the state is a demand for an explanation of political obligation. Although I may believe that a law is morally justified or a legitimate religious duty, political obligation is about the sovereignty of the state and its right to enforce that law. So I may agree that paedophilia is morally unacceptable, but the enforcement of the law and the designated punishment by the authorities needs additional justification.

This justification of the authorities has often taken the form of a discussion about the origin of the state. Has it grown naturally? Is it founded on a contract? Or was it redesigned after a war or revolution? Yet the origin of a thing is rarely a conclusive explanation of its value, particularly as states evolve and adapt to new circumstances.

The following debate therefore should distinguish between how states arose or civilisation started, and the actual justification for the use of power. The social contract for example, loses none of its force, by its lack of historical accuracy, if it presents a cogent argument for why we should obey. Similarly, entertaining analogies, such as the comparison of the organic growth of a country to the natural operation of the human body or family should ultimately rest on whether they present a credible case for social control.

Human nature

MacIntyre in *After Virtue* states: 'a moral philosophy characteristically pre-supposes a sociology'. In political philosophy too, ideologies have been founded on what commentators take to be the universal and significant features of human nature, and they have appealed to essential characteristics of humanity to justify forms of political organisation.

Learning objectives

■ to understand why political philosophers have entered into a debate about human nature

■ to explain the conservative conception of human nature and the role of the state

■ to explore the classical liberal view of the state and its legitimacy

■ to assess why anarchists and Marxists see the state as an oppressor.

Key terms

The state: the body, or set of institutions, which governs a territorial area, and secures obedience from those who live within its boundaries. It is the entity that has sovereignty and jurisdiction over all matters within its boundaries.

Ideologies: in this sense simply means a set of ideas and values associated with different political standpoints.

Synoptic link

AQA AS Philosophy Chapter 5, Why should I be governed?, Disobedience and dissent, p155.

There are references in Hobbes, Locke and Rousseau to 'a state of nature' that is designed to strip human beings of all the attributes which are the result of living in a society in a particular time and place, in order to reveal the innate or inherited tendencies in all human beings, regardless of history and culture, which are fundamental and unchanging. The state of nature is meant to uncover how human beings would still behave if there were no laws or social structure.

Inevitably, philosophers have selected theories of human nature that suit their own ends. Thus Hobbes stresses the self-interest and satisfaction of power that drives individuals; while Locke emphasises the rationality which entails a sense of equality and autonomy. In other words, they are advocating the moral basis on which the interests of all human beings should have equal consideration.

In the AS Philosophy textbook, Chapter 5, 'Why should I be governed?', the state of nature is characterised as:

- A psychological thesis, which identifies the universal human dispositions, which stem from our biology and psychology.
- A moral thesis, which highlights those dispositions which any political authority must respect, and so provide its justification.

So, to paraphrase Wolff in *An Introduction to Political Philosophy*, political philosophy may begin with 'descriptive studies' about how things are, but becomes a **normative** account of what should be the case.

For example, particular attention should be paid to the use of the word 'natural'. Just because something is (supposedly) natural, does that make it right? Thus Marx argues that what appears natural is simply the order imposed by the dominant class. In the Victorian era it was portrayed as natural that there were different classes – 'the rich man in his castle' and 'the poor man at his gate'. But communism will 'subjugate' the means of production 'to the power of united individuals' to remove the class divide.

The primary function of the state

Nevertheless any account of human nature can be treated as worthy of consideration if pragmatically it proves a useful insight and valuable perspective. If we take Hobbes' well-known position that Man is by nature a selfish, egoistic creature, an individual who craves power and seeks his own wellbeing and is fearful of others, one might simply counter with Aristotle's dictum that 'man is by nature a social animal', that abhors solitary confinement, who forms herds and who flourishes through relationships. Both these are recognisable human traits, although they are simply two among many. Yet it can be argued they are important enough that any political doctrine should take account of them.

Hobbes in his description emphasises the horrors of life outside society:

> there is no place for industry, because the fruit of that is uncertain: and consequently no culture of the earth, no navigation ... no Arts, no letters ... but continual fear and the danger of violent death.

Hobbes (1982)

Interestingly, Aristotle concurs with some aspects of this: 'he who has no family and no State is either a beast or a God' (1962, Book I). Without order, people are sub-human and animalistic, or must have God-like qualities.

Think about

What should be the power of the state?

The following are examples of state control in different countries. Can you justify these laws and if not how would you argue for their repeal?

- a law that allows private citizens to own guns for self-defence
- a law that bans abortion
- a state that allows farmers to grow genetically modified crops
- a law that forbids religious dress in schools
- a state that keeps essential industries, e.g. electricity, water, rail, under public ownership
- a law that conscripts young people to spend a few years in the army or other defence forces
- a state that restricts the access of its citizens to the Internet
- a state that does not run a welfare programme, e.g. a National Health Service.

Key terms

Normative: relating to or deriving from a standard or norm.

AQA Examiner's tip

This provides you with two lines of attack on a political philosopher:

- Challenge the description – the facts that are first presented.
- Challenge the arguments that are constructed, to lead from the facts to values.

Synoptic link

AQA AS Philosophy Chapter 1, Reason and experience, p22 and Chapter 5, Why should I be governed?, pp123–54.

Think about

Under which heading would conservatives have problems with:

- a priori notion of natural rights
- large scale immigration
- a blueprint for a new democracy based on 'the common good'
- abolition of the Monarchy and House of Lords
- an economy, centrally planned and controlled by government.

Whether one fully accepts these views or not, surely Hobbes has identified a primary function of the state: to maintain security, safety and stability. Without this bedrock, any other civilised, social activity cannot happen. Whether the sovereign power should do more than this is a matter of contention, but law and order is a prerequisite for any other functions.

Noticeably, even Locke, a proponent of minimal government, concurs with the basic need for security. Having granted 'rational man' in a state of nature, extensive moral rights, he also accepts 'that mankind being such that they had rather injuriously prey upon the fruits of other men's labours … the necessity of preserving men in what honest industry has acquired … obliges men to enter into society with one another' (Locke, 1960).

So in this respect, Hobbes seems to have the upper hand; although he has also conceded that the naked exercise of power is never right unless it is legitimised, to deliver the benefits of personal safety.

The state as an organic entity: the conservative conception of the state

The key aspects of the conservative State are:

- A profound distrust of political rationalism and scepticism of theoretical political ideas, especially those that advocate radical change.
- A belief that the complex mysteries of government are best discovered through conserving traditional practice and gradual reform.
- A belief that Man is born into a society that has evolved over time from which he is given a place and an identity.
- They reject that there ever was a contract between autonomous individuals. We have ever and can only exist in society.
- The individual is a small part of the whole, and our ability to reason is limited.
- Ruling is an art, which most do not understand and only a few can acquire the knowledge and expertise.
- Law and order should be the primary concern of the state to guarantee the security of its citizens.

Conservatives argue that the individual is born into society and that there are obligations which are not the product of a contract, for example, parents must care for their children just as managers must care for their workers. The social practices and values invade our consciousness from the beginning, so our identity is constituted by our place in society and the institutions, which we are a part of. People are students, football supporters, club members and identify with a class or social group. We very early realise our dependence on others, whose welfare is as important as our own. Therefore, we develop a sense of loyalty and belonging, which transcends any contracts and 'artificial' obligations that we later make. So people are 'encumbered' with certain values, wishes and hopes etc., that result from their upbringing.

The individual discovers themselves as an individual, through contrast with other people and institutions, and this is fashioned by social rules and expectations. For example, individuality can be expressed through music but not through violence. Hence my political sense too arises out of these personal experiences of an ever-widening circle of family, school, workplace, country etc. The very notions of freedom, rights, consent, and private are a product of the social context in which we were brought up. In most organisations, an ethos is made clear through 'ground rules', policy documents and agendas, which allow managers to control behaviour and reach 'acceptable conclusions'. So our political concerns for freedom or justice grow out of our social environment.

The organic analogy

Conservatives characterise society and its institutions as organic, just as an organism grows and develops infused by the active power of life. It has evolved over centuries to increase its capacity to solve problems, accommodate new challenges and develop positive, harmonious internal relations that enable it to survive.

Aristotle compares society to a household and also the human body, to conclude that the 'whole' (the state) must have priority over the parts (the individual), since all parts can only function as part of a whole. Separate a hand or foot from a body and it is rendered useless, 'the whole must be prior to the parts. Separate hand or foot from the whole body and they will no longer be hand or foot … It is clear then that the state is both natural and prior to the individual. For an individual is not fully self-sufficient after separation' (Aristotle, 1962).

In a household there are natural superiors and inferiors. Just as every household will be ruled by its senior members, so as people associate in villages and city states, there will be a natural hierarchy. In order for all members to live a flourishing life, we must live in a wise and flourishing society where opportunities for companionship, education and the 'good things' of life are available. Thus we see also in Aristotle the key conservative themes: the natural inequality among people; the importance and priority of the community over the individual; and the need for common morality and order.

Furthermore, to understand what we are now, we must acknowledge the importance of the past and the practical wisdom accumulated over generations. Any disruption to the subtle working of the body could destroy its capability to function, so gradual evolutionary change is always preferable to revolution. **Oakeshott** contrasts the theoretical or 'technical knowledge' which forms the basis of any art with practical experience, in an analogy with cookery. The principles of cookery are contained within a cookery book, but successful cooking comes with practical trial and adaptation of the theory. Conservatives stress the importance of experience and developed expertise gained from our heritage, rather than rational ideals, which is why, they claim, that revolutions inevitably fail in their attempts to build new societies.

Evaluation of the conservative view

The first thing to note is that the origin of something can be quite independent of its desirability and acceptability. Aristotle advocated the natural superiority of men over women and slaves on account of their rationality. The wisdom of our elders has not always been apparent and whether a method is reliable, must be judged on whether it continues to deliver results in the here and now. In Mill's famous attack on 'custom', he argues that what was relevant in the past may not be appropriate for modern generations. Even if situations are similar, the accumulated wisdom will still have to be adapted to changing circumstances.

A similar doubt arises about the analogies of the state to the human family and body, which imply that what is natural, is desirable. While the interdependence of individuals is undeniable, other assumptions which

Think about

Can you analyse this in your own family? How might your family or school have shaped your views on freedom and justice?

Key philosophers

Michael Oakeshott (1909–90): From 1950 he taught political philosophy at the London School of Economics. He emphasised the crucial importance of moral and political tradition, and politics – the art of repair to keep the ship of state afloat.

are built into the word, such as hierarchy are questionable. Are there natural superiors? And while Aristotle is right to point out that a foot detached from a body is useless, equally a body without a foot is severely limited. The relative importance of individuals with regard to the whole is not as one-sided as he suggests.

One of the most important charges aimed at the conservative state is that it over-values harmony, order and social cohesion at the expense of truth, or at least competing conceptions of the truth. Propaganda and the perception of convenient 'myths', such as Plato's 'noble lie' that all people are born to the status of gold, silver or bronze appear inexcusable, except perhaps when the survival of the state is threatened, as in wartime. Whether it be a diet of capitalist consumerism or communist propaganda, it belittles and demeans the people.

There is a danger that conservatism in an extreme form could politicise all activity as significant in the achievement of a common good. So anything that threatens the stability of society becomes a political matter: art, sport, trade etc. For example, Plato banned artists from the Republic if they indulged in imitative art, and right wing regimes frequently control the media, on the grounds that it spreads seditious ideas.

And finally, much confusion surrounds this concept of 'the common good' or 'the whole'. There is a danger that what is perceived as the public interest might benefit the state, without actually benefiting the individuals within the society, or only a percentage of them. For example, a policy on free trade might enhance a country's reputation abroad and benefit a wealthy few, while leaving many jobs for ordinary people vulnerable to foreign competition. In terms of tenders and even wealth creation, this might benefit a state, but many citizens might not personally gain. Critics will argue that the only justification for talking of the common good is when at least the majority of individuals actually benefit. As we shall investigate later under Marxism, the dominant class represents their interests as the real interests of the state. Thus the bourgeoisie advocate freedom, which appears a very plausible good, but the class who actually benefits from more freedom is the wealthy middle class. The poor would probably do with less freedom and more equality and justice. Thus considerable care needs to be exercised before any policy can be genuinely proposed to be in the public interest.

The state as neutral umpire: the classical liberal view of the state

The key aspects of the classical liberal state are:

- The state has been founded by a social contract (Locke), and government has been chosen and put in trust by rational, autonomous individuals, who prior to any arrangements understand their own interests.
- Law is subject to moral scrutiny, so that absolute, universal rights (Locke) and necessary freedoms (Mill) override any legislation that a government may wish to introduce.
- Citizens as far as possible should lead their own lives with maximum negative freedom: freedom from coercion and restraint, unless that freedom collides with or harms another.
- Human beings are capable of developing a flourishing life when they are allowed to choose their own lifestyles, based on their deepest instincts and desires, so that their choices are meaningful and

Think about

Which policies would you regard as genuinely a common good?

- experimentation on animals to test new drugs
- the invasion of Afghanistan
- bringing the Olympics to London in 2012
- lowering taxes
- banning cheap holiday flights to save aircraft fuel.

appropriate, and they can learn from their mistakes. The self-chosen life is the most fulfilling.

- No authority has a monopoly of reason and wisdom. There are no definite answers to moral issues, so the state should accommodate value pluralism and acknowledge that different cultures are entitled to express their version of the good life.

- Society is made up of autonomous, independent individuals and institutions should reflect their wishes. This is an atomistic view of society emphasising the role of individuals rather than practices, traditions and institutions.

- The role of government is limited to umpire or referee disputes between individuals and protect rights and freedoms. Mill reduces the role of the state to defence, the maintenance of law and order and the protection of interests that ought to be considered as rights.

Granted that there probably never was a state of nature without some form of social control; and granted also that there are problems about how we actually give consent to a social contract, we can nevertheless consider the classical liberal model for a state.

First, many would argue that there are 'goods' perhaps rights which we owe to people simply as people, not because they are part of a social tradition. Part of our respect for humanity as a whole is that people should have the right to choose their lives. Locke in the 'Second Treatise' talks about 'keeping faith' with 'the whole of humanity', regardless of race or tribe. We might argue about the content, but surely there are rights which all human beings deserve purely as human beings, for example the right to life, and which no state can justly remove. These universal moral standards are therefore not a product of society but are a precondition of civilised society.

Secondly, we must not forget that happiness, suffering, pain and fulfilment are felt by individuals. Institutions do not feel pain and liberals therefore do not subordinate individuals to the practices of the state. At the end of *On Liberty* Mill reminds us:

> The worth of a State, in the long run, is the worth of the individuals composing it ... a State, which dwarfs its men ... even for beneficial purposes ... will find that with small men no great thing can really be accomplished.

Mill (1985)

The government should therefore always be the servant of individuals and should be flexible enough to adapt quickly to the changing needs of the citizens. Wherever possible people should be allowed to settle their own disputes and run their own lives. The authorities only need to step in to prevent harm to others: 'the sole end for which mankind are warranted in interfering with the liberty of action of any of their number is self-protection' (Mill, 1985).

Human nature

The classic liberal thesis puts a lot of faith in the autonomy of individuals. Granted that people are conditioned by society and to a large extent gain their identity from their place and time, given extensive freedom of choice and a progressive education that encourages diversity and fosters debate and questioning, we can develop independence, confidence and autonomy. People do learn from their mistakes and

Think about

Under which headings would classical liberals have problems with:

- an economy, centrally planned and controlled by government
- conscription into the armed services for the common good
- censorship of offensive articles in the press
- tough laws against immigration
- a paternalistic government that raised taxes to pay for more surveillance camera.

they should be given an extensive private life where they can conduct 'experiments in living'. Thus a very positive view of human nature emerges: that we are progressive, self-improvers, capable of learning from experience and cooperating (without force) to further our own interests. In *On Liberty*, Mill provides a cogent series of arguments for trust in the individual's own judgement:

- the experience of others may be too narrow or they may have misinterpreted it
- the circumstances of an individual's experience or his character may be very different from other people
- people who choose their own life plans develop sensitivity, judgement and mental abilities
- people know and care more about their own situation than anyone else.

Value pluralism

And surely, no-one has a monopoly of truth on moral and lifestyle choices. For those who have strong beliefs, surely the most effective way of strengthening faith is to allow them to be challenged, to allow others to find the error of their ways through their own choices, and not to be accused of arrogance by enforcing views on other people and creating 'the moral police'. The faith that survives challenge will be stronger, according to Mill, and progress can only happen if we allow people to experiment with life styles, provided society is protected from harm. As an example, in Chapter 5 in *On Liberty*, he tackles prostitution, fornication and gambling. He declares that society has no business to decide what is wrong, where only the individual is concerned. However, the state has a duty not to encourage promotion of these activities if they are considered bad. So although gambling and prostitution should not be advertised in public, people should be free to indulge, in private houses and to make private arrangements. 'They may be compelled to conduct their arrangements with a certain degree of secrecy and mystery' so only those who actively wish to gamble and be involved in prostitution will find out. Any more than this is an infringement of free trade and 'all restraint is an evil' (Mill, 1985).

Evaluation of the classical liberal state

However, the last case indicates a serious weakness in the liberal position. Liberals argue for certain fundamental values, e.g. freedom. Yet it is equally fair for others to argue that there are fundamental evils, which must be addressed by the state. Negative freedom has been labelled the freedom to starve. A society that turns its back on state intervention also minimises paternalistic support of health care, education and social security. Thus Welfare Liberalism, also referred to as New or Revisionist Liberalism, argues for democratic regulation of free market economics and a well-developed social justice programme to protect democratic freedoms for all citizens.

Conservatives also attack the liberal state for ignoring the very 'glue' that holds society together and promotes the social cohesion. Nobody can fail to notice the hypocrisy in condemning prostitution but allowing it to happen in private. Mill himself recognises the difficulty of separating off from public accountability, a private space for people to 'be themselves' and experiment. He quotes Donne 'that no man is an island', suggesting that everything we do affects others. His reply is that if I am not neglecting my clear public duties or directly harming others without their clear, undeceived consent, then I should be allowed to freely act. Countless papers have been written on the vagueness of what Mill calls 'harm', which I will not pursue. The issue of whether offence is harm is pertinent.

Conservatives believe that without a shared moral consensus propagated by family, church and state, social divisions can open up in a pluralist society which can destroy it. We have many examples in Eastern Europe and in Belgium where communities do not share wealth, culture, moral values or even language and are permanently at risk of civil strife.

These last issues emphasise the need for a state that is not only an umpire, and the danger of a government 'in trust' to the people. As purely a referee, in a liberal state, the authorities will still need to interpret the rules in order to dispense justice – yet is in turn beholden to the citizens and can be dismissed. The advantage is that government under these arrangements is less able to become tyrannical, but the demerit is that the referee is vulnerable to undue pressure from the players or the most powerful group of players. Thus a liberal umpire can become so responsive to the majority that minorities and objectivity in decision-making will suffer. Mill of course foresaw the 'tyranny of the majority' but his response was to try and limit its harmful effects through limiting government and its jurisdiction. But this does not solve the problem of hard pressed and accountable governments avoiding the difficult decisions.

What do we mean by neutrality?

The previous point claims that in practice it will be very difficult for a state with limited powers to remain neutral. But there has also been some confusion on what neutrality entails. Does the neutral state ensure that people of all political and moral persuasions flourish or at least have equal opportunities? This would require considerable intervention, for example laws on equal opportunities. Many would offer this interpretation of neutrality, that a government should not dictate how we live our lives and should ensure variety and diversity. The government is not a moral judge, so therefore intervenes to support minorities.

However, this conflicts with the classical liberal position of the neutral state that expects people to take responsibility for their decisions, and to suffer the consequences. People who choose unsuccessfully will suffer and learn from their mistakes. The classic liberal state aspires to minimum interference, so that Mill argues that even charity and 'philanthropic enterprises' is not a government duty, but a voluntary act conducted by private associations. In this sense, the neutral state does not get involved. People learn at their own cost. Those who support the former interpretation of the state as an enabler will argue that the classical liberal state:

- actually diminishes freedom, since many lifestyles need support
- is a tragic waste of potential human resources when people are left to fail
- is unjust in that only the wealthy will be able to indulge in diverse activities and so develop.

A liberal contract

Although Mill explicitly declares that society is not founded on a contract, he argues that duties are owed in return for benefits. The classical liberal Locke and modern liberal philosopher Rawls specifically

Synoptic link

AQA AS Philosophy Chapter 6, Tolerance, p174 and Chapter 5, Why should I be governed? p164. See also AQA A2 Philosophy Chapter 8, J.S. Mill's *On Liberty*.

■ Synoptic link

AQA AS Philosophy Chapter 5, Why should I be governed?, p118.

use the device to establish liberal values, and ground their version of the role of the state. Three difficulties with this social contract are presented below.

First, the notion of obligation and obedience to a contract presupposes moral values. Yet the contract is introduced to define the moral relationships between individuals and a state. This contract to succeed, however, assumes people in a state of nature have the moral understanding to create a binding contract. Built into the signing of a contract are assumptions such as:

■ all individuals in one respect are equally important

■ a contract is binding if people freely enter into it

■ like keeping our word, contracts ought to be upheld.

In essence, the concept of moral obligation is logically prior to the concept of a binding contract.

Secondly, the contract of itself will not necessarily deliver liberal values. It depends on the nature of the contract what benefits and what kind of society develops. Locke had to employ a theory of natural rights in order to create liberal freedoms, and deny the kind of conclusions that Hobbes comes to. Rawls also arrives at a notion of justice from the nature of the contract, which contains liberal values of freedom and equality. Now in the normal way of debate, people bargaining for the rules of a game would know their natural talents and advantages and would not regard the others as equals. To promote justice, Rawls insists that behind the veil of ignorance, people are ignorant of their natural assets and also how the future might work out. But in this respect, equality is not then a value derived from the contract, but is actually a built-in condition of taking part. Again it is a value that is presupposed rather than a value people would freely choose. Equality through ignorance is imposed on the participants to make them sympathetic to others and impartial.

A final difficulty with the contract is that consent can only take place in a particular situation, with certain conditions prevailing at the time. However, that does not mean that if the situation changes, in a completely new set of circumstances, I would continue to assent. In many contracts, such as marriage, it is generally recognised that re-negotiation is morally justified if a significant change of circumstances has occurred. Thus, once the social contract is underway, individuals might well wish to reconsider some of the liberal values built into the original agreement.

■ The state as oppressor: Marxist and anarchist views of the state

Anarchy

■ Synoptic link

AQA AS Philosophy Chapter 5, Why should I be governed?, p118.

Anarchists believe in freedom, equality, natural human sympathy and cooperation. The word 'anarchy' in this context is not a synonym for 'chaos', it simply means 'no ruling power'. Since these are the fundamental aspects of human nature emphasised by anarchists, the use of coercive power and aggression by the state is illegitimate, and is in fact responsible for the selfish, competitive, anti-social traits that are seen in societies around the world. Even if we accept Darwin's principle of evolution and 'survival of the fittest', cooperation and mutual support is the key to survival, rather than the 'war of all against all'.

Yet Hobbes might reply that it is our natural competitiveness, egoistic desires and enjoyment of power that led to the development of authoritarian states. Anarchists might concede this, but will still maintain that an aggressive authority with prohibitive laws will not foster the more positive aspects of human nature. **Proudhon**, one of the first anarchists, believed that coercive institutions could be replaced by voluntary, peaceful, social and economic agreements.

Kropotkin (1991) makes the case that laws interfere with the rational self-government which individuals are capable of. Instead of laws solving our problems, we are encouraged to depend on outside authorities to regulate our lives and provide answers. Thus we lose the ability to think for ourselves, use our own initiative, and manage and be responsible for our own affairs. We become reliant on the government to 'sort it out' and we lose 'all habit of thinking for ourselves', and resolving our disputes through rational and sympathetic discussion.

Furthermore, interference in whatever social arrangements individuals care to pursue is an unwarranted infringement of their freedom. People can be guided by their shared moral beliefs, state law is unnecessary. Surely what I choose to do, as long as it does not adversely affect others, should be no concern of the state.

Also, the state more often than not is an instrument of oppression employed to maintain the interests of a powerful section of society against the rest. Thus the majority of laws are in defence of private property. Laws of ownership and trespass, for example, protect the capitalist who has acquired (often through theft and unjust means such as Land enclosures in the 18th century, or invasion or conquest) land and capital for personal use, to exclude others from enjoying it. If land was returned to the common people and private possessions were restricted to only the produce and enjoyment of one's own labour, then it is argued that the whole arsenal of property law would become redundant.

It is not intended to give a full account of **Marxist** theory here, but to draw some parallels with the views just outlined. Quotations come from *The German Ideology* (1970).

Key features of the Marxist interpretation of the state:

- There is no fixed human nature; rather it is dependent on the economic conditions prevailing at the time. 'The essence of Men' is 'the sum of the productive forces' which determines the kind of relationship between people.

- The nature of the state and who is in control depends on who is in control of the means of production. 'Civil society develops with the bourgeoisie; the social organisations evolving directly out of production and commerce.'

- So the values and ideology of society are determined in a modern state by the wealthy middle class. 'The rule of a definite class of society, whose social power, deriving from its property has its practical idealistic expression in the form of the State'.

- So the law is not an expression of justice, but simply protects the interests of the dominant class. 'It has just as little independent history as religion.'

- People can only grow, develop and realise their potential through relationships with others. 'Men need and have always needed each other.'

- Freedom practically means the free association of individuals who can develop all sides of their character. 'Only in community has each individual the means of cultivating his gifts in all directions.'

Key philosophers

Pierre Proudhon (1809–65): French philosopher who coined the phrase, 'property is theft', and advocated local self-managing associations rather than state authority.

Karl Marx (1818–83): The author of The Communist Manifesto and Das Kapital.

■ In a capitalist state, work is soul-destroying and uncreative and life is stunted and alienated. 'Man's own deed becomes an alien power opposed to him', 'thwarting our expectations … out of control.'

■ Thus a revolution is needed to take control of the means of production in cooperation with all other workers to 'bring their existence into harmony with their essence' and 'the transformation of labour into self-activity'. Eventually with the development of a communist consciousness, the state will 'wither away'.

Thus for Marx, the social contract and liberal rights are a fiction propagated by the bourgeoisie to protect their status and property. Those who benefit from rights are those who are sufficiently well off to satisfy their desires. In practice, the poor cannot use their rights. However, if under communism, the people own their industries, they can achieve a harmony of interests and dissolution of conflict, which make a contract unnecessary.

Marx also attacks the liberal idea of the autonomous, independent, unencumbered individual. The proposition that such individuals could exist outside society is an absurdity. The very language we use and the expansion of consciousness derives from living and talking together. Individuals can only conceive of themselves as different, or free in the context of social interaction.

So our consciousness, our very nature, is shaped by our economic and social environment. People's beliefs and values predominantly derive from their class. Yet we also have a 'species essence'. Unlike other animals who simply react to their environment, human beings are conscious and creative and shape their environment to suit their needs – they labour. Since we are forever developing new needs, we have continuously adapted the world to suit our purposes. However, when workers are forced to carry out repetitive, tedious tasks, they are deprived of the opportunity to satisfy those needs and are alienated: losing control over their work, the development of their potential and the full value of their labour. The profit that the capitalist takes, increases his wealth and his power. He is able to influence the government through finance, lobbying, and ownership of the media etc. All this is a direct result of the division of labour.

Under this 'scientific' analysis of social dynamics, Marx does not seek to judge the moral status of the capitalist state, but to explain how it inevitably develops and the plight of the workers and its eventual demise through revolution. In this interpretation, communism is not a utopian idea, but an inevitable next stage, as the capitalist economic system develops crisis after crisis. This is sometimes referred to as 'scientific socialism'.

This is in contrast to 'utopian socialism' which argues for a communist state on moral grounds, appealing to fairness and justice. But since, according to Marx, moral aspirations have no power to change the social system, as all change is generated by the economic conditions, utopian socialism becomes irrelevant.

Nevertheless, at times, Marx seems to imply that he has a conception of justice, when he refers to capitalism as 'the muck of ages' and 'the violence of things'. Also 'exploitation' and 'alienation' are not morally neutral terms. When he describes how the worker does not receive the full value of his labour, this is a desert based notion of justice.

■ **Synoptic link**

See Marxism, pp70–1.

■ **Think about**

Look at his description of modern capitalism. Which words or phrases suggest that Marx is offering us values and not simply facts?

■ 'never in an earlier period have the productive forces taken on a form so indifferent to the intercourse of individuals'

■ 'and by universal competition, it forced all individuals to strain their energy to the utmost'

■ 'the contradiction between the individuality of each separate proletarian and labour, the condition of life forced upon him, becomes evident to him himself, for he is sacrificed from youth upwards'.

Evaluation of the anarchist and Marxist view of the state

It would be easy to cynically dismiss anarchism as far too radical and idealistic. But there are more substantial issues.

First, it appears to hold contradictory accounts of human nature: (1) that there are universal qualities (rational and sympathetic) but (2) that the self is shaped by society, constituted by the social environment. Now both theses may be possible, but how does one distinguish which is a universal and which is a social product? Similarly for Marx, the self is generated through labour and economic activity. Thus a worker in a capitalist society will be alienated, see other human beings as obstacles and believe in the false consciousness of rights etc. Now if human nature is malleable, moulded by our environment, it is difficult to see why people would become alienated. They would just accept their limited potential and since 'men depend upon their epoch and not upon human nature' they would simply absorb the role assigned to them. The emphasis on realising themselves, however, suggests there is a universal potential for complex and creative development. But if this is our species-essence, who is to say that it does not also include egoistic desires and the will to power?

Secondly, the anarchist society and the mature communist stage assume a moral cohesion, which is questionable. Could we live without laws and a state? Even assuming a high degree of cooperation and effective informal agreements, moral relationships imply some form of universalisation. It must be wrong for everyone, all the time to hoard or steal. It is difficult to see how life could happen without a predictable framework of behaviour. Marx argues that once the economic base is fair, social relations will harmonise. But does this not conflict with the very creativity of our species essence? Man will continually find new solutions to new needs and there will be disagreements and factions. If we are free 'to hunt in the morning, fish in the afternoon, rear cattle in the evening and criticise after dinner' (Marx, 1970), then some will defend the interests of hunters, while others pursue the interests of farmers and critics.

Furthermore, in the absence of laws, there is the real danger of tyranny. Where people associate in unregulated groups, then charismatic leaders always seem to emerge. It would be easy for powerful individuals to dominate, so that what might appear to be a voluntary agreement is actually swayed by those who have natural power. Anyone who has been to a meeting and witnessed the chaos as everyone struggles to be heard, understands that rules are necessary to ensure proper fair discussion.

And finally, in practice, communist societies have become associated with the deliberate shaping of people's attitudes and the manipulation of human nature (usually unsuccessfully). If people are regarded as malleable, rather than autonomous, independent agents, there is always the spectre of Big Brother and the horrors of George Orwell's *1984*.

When communist societies have restricted free speech, used propaganda and 're-education programmes', they have confirmed the liberal's worst fears.

> **Think about**
>
> Research the use of 'double think' in the novel *1984* by George Orwell.

After working through this topic, you should:

- understand the different theories of human nature that underpin political ideologies

- be able to compare conservative, liberal, and anarchic/Marxist conceptions of the role of the state

- be able to evaluate the different positions outlined in this chapter

- be aware of the descriptive and normative arguments employed in these positions.

Liberty

Learning objectives

- to understand what it means to be free

- to distinguish between negative and positive freedom

- to explore why liberty is valued and how it can be promoted and defended

- to explain how different political ideologies interpret the issues

- to evaluate the relationship between the law and liberty.

AQA Examiner's tip

In the exam, try not to use terms like freedom, equally or justice, without clarifying and defining what precisely you mean, for example what kind of liberty.

Synoptic link

AQA A2 Philosophy Chapter 8, J.S. Mill's *On Liberty*, pp74–114.

Synoptic link

AQA AS Philosophy Chapter 5, The state of nature, p121.

Rousseau is claimed to have said: 'freedom is for the animals – Man should seek liberty' (1968). He wished to distinguish between the rational liberty that citizens of a republic would seek and the wild, unthinking licence of the animal kingdom. In this chapter, freedom and liberty will be regarded as interchangeable terms.

What does it mean to be free?

Let your pet off its lead, or open the door of their cage and you can watch it delight in freedom. Doing as you please would seem to be an essential part of a flourishing life. Yet such freedom can quickly turn to undisciplined, lawless and self-defeating behaviour. Surely the trained and disciplined pet can enjoy more opportunities and gain a worthwhile freedom, as they extend their capacities. Education and self-control increase and enhance our freedom as we can achieve more. Similarly, when playing a musical instrument, the discipline of regular practice widens the scope of your repertoire. The opportunities to extend your musical expression are limited if you just play as you please.

One of the most comprehensive texts on freedom is Mill's *On Liberty* (1985). In the first few pages, he interprets history as a struggle for freedom. According to Mill, the most 'conspicuous' aspect of history is the struggle between liberty and authority as the people fight for rights and 'immunities' against tyrannous rulers. Then the second stage was to establish 'constitutional checks' so that the consent of the people was required for rulers to act. The third stage was the evolution of democracy when the rulers must represent the wishes of the people and could be removed from office. In this last stage, the rulers were identified with the people – in effect the people ruled themselves, as the laws simply enacted what the people wanted.

Already we can begin to see different aspects of what it means to be free: initially a life *free from* tyrannous laws and then eventually laws that express the real interests of the people and enable them to be *free to* realise their aspirations. This distinction in what really constitutes freedom has led to widely different ideologies and political systems such as liberal democracy and communism. To understand this we must examine a fundamental distinction between negative liberty ('freedom from') and positive liberty ('freedom to'). We shall find that the definitions in each case are complex and contested.

Concepts of liberty: negative freedom and positive freedom

Negative liberty

Hobbes defines liberty as the absence of obstacles, which impede the individual from exercising his power. Liberty is 'the absence of … impediments to action', where the obstacles or impediments are external to the individual. Anyone who is a prisoner or in chains is deprived of their freedom. Hobbes continues to argue that the law is also a barrier to an individual satisfying their desires, so liberty becomes famously 'the silence of the laws' (Hobbes, 1982).

Yet on Hobbes' interpretation, it would seem that no person is ever going to be free. There are obstacles to me doing things wherever I turn.

■ The weather often hinders me successfully growing vegetables.
■ The English Channel is an impediment to visiting France.

Yet we would not really cite these barriers as a lack of freedom.

A less broad definition is that we lack freedom if we are coerced by other human beings. The external obstacles are thus the actions of other human beings. So Mill claims that freedom is a lack of interference by others which prevents us from fulfilling one's aims:

> Pursuing our own good in our own way … and no-one attempts to deprive or impede our efforts to obtain it' or in short, 'freedom is doing what one desires'.

Mill (1985)

■ Synoptic link

Further debate on this can be found in AQA AS Philosophy Chapter 6, Tolerance, Tensions and applications, p184 and Chapter 5, Why should I be governed?, Dissent and freedom of speech, p165.

Live as you like

A common thread in accounts of negative liberty is what Aristotle rather disparagingly terms 'live as you like' (Aristotle, 1962) – carrying out your wishes, and exercising your power. Mill defines liberty in Chapter 5: 'Liberty consists in doing what one desires'. Thus being caught in a traffic jam is a frustrating absence of negative liberty in contrast with being a free rider on the open road.

Locke also defines this freedom:

> as a state of perfect freedom to order their actions and dispose of their possessions and persons as they think fit … without asking leave or depending on the will of any other man.

Locke (1960)

He justifies the imposition of minimal laws by government, only if it protects this freedom.

Yet this is also not without contention. I may be doing as I please; blissfully unaware that in fact I have no other possibilities. Could I then be considered free? Consider the scenario that you are free-wheeling downhill on your bicycle, happily ignorant of the fact that your brakes have failed. Some would argue that you are not free, because of a lack of opportunity to change course.

So freedom, according to Berlin is 'the absence of obstacles to possible choices and activities' (Berlin, 1967). I am only free when I can also change my mind if I desire and do otherwise. As Mill acknowledges, freedom also requires, 'a variety of situations' (Mill, 1985).

Evaluation of negative liberty

Now critics of negative liberty point out that the provision of alternative options, so that I can change my desire and still exercise it, may require assistance, guidance and intervention. The simple fact that there are no external obstacles does not ensure that alternatives are open to me which I can actually opt for. In our example, the runaway cyclist may look for an escape lane. But to make this option available, someone needs to create escape lanes and support people who want to use them. To be really free then, a lack of external obstacles is simply not sufficient. A more paternalistic account of freedom is necessary to solve the problems of poverty or lack of education, for example, which restrict access to satisfying more liberating desires.

A further problem is that 'acting as I desire' does not fully give sense to 'I could have acted otherwise'. Surely liberty demands that I can choose my desires as well as act on them, that I am free from internal constraints. Negative freedom does not take into account that to be able to choose freely, I should also be able to reconsider my desires, acquire new values and pursue different goals. This will be developed in the section on 'Positive freedom'.

An additional concern is that a lack of restraint from one party impacts on another. There is a danger that negative freedom actually destroys liberty and social cohesion and is self-defeating. For example, our freedom to drive wherever we wish in gas-guzzling 4×4s leads to traffic jams and pollution. Hobbes resolves this potential conflict with a Leviathan of a political ruler, which could severely limit individual freedom, although a dictator could allow citizens an extensive, unimpeded private life. Mill uses the harm principle to regulate conduct, which is a rather vague and clumsy instrument. Thus in Chapter 5, he defends the sale of opium to China on the grounds that interference with free trade is 'objectionable' because it is 'an infringement' on the liberty of the buyer! But is selling opium not harm!

Negative freedom can therefore be criticised in that it does not accommodate a moral sense. Can real freedom be divorced from morality? Berlin acknowledges that 'the freedom of the pike is death to the minnows' (Berlin, 1967). In an extreme state of negative freedom, we might live in constant fear of being dominated by others, unforeseen dangers and the threatening contingencies of life. In a laissez-faire economy, the wealthy can control the flow of ideas, access to good things, while the weak are left in poverty, unemployment and fear. Such 'alienation' is surely not compatible with freedom.

Positive freedom

In the realm of positive liberty, I do not just follow my desires, but I am able to reflect on and select appropriate desires. This gives full meaning to 'I could have done otherwise'. Plato's illustration of this is his analogy of The Beast. The animal (and its trainer) are not free because they simply pander to their lowest desires and habits, for example the lust for power. Freedom is to be able to make your own laws on what it is best to do, and then to exercise those choices. A free person is a decision-maker, who is sufficiently in control of him/herself to select opportunities which unlock potential and lead to flourishing – that is, being autonomous. Kant characterises this as being rational, able to choose the wiser, moral option. The emphasis is on being a free person rather than seeking uninhibited action.

Mill implies in *On Liberty* that left with an abundance of negative freedom, people will learn from experience, practise independent reasoning, and so will develop sufficient autonomy to choose more wisely, and make more discriminating judgement:

> he who chooses his plan for himself employs all his faculties ... reasoning, judgement, discrimination ... self control ... provided that he is left to carry his opinions into practise at his own cost.

Mill (1985)

Synoptic link

AQA A2 Philosophy Chapter 8, J. S. Mill's *On Liberty*, The harm principle, pp81–88.

So the development of positive freedom is parasitic on negative freedom.

Yet Mill's position is disputable. He describes an ideal that may happen; but it is equally likely that left to their own devices, people may just stagnate and remain trapped in superficial and destructive habits.

Those who advocate this 'higher liberty' usually stress the need for paternalistic guidance: that intervention and even coercion may be necessary to empower individuals to overcome their internal constraints (such as ignorance, weak will, lack of judgement) in order to achieve the self-control and vision integral to the real freedom of actual realisation of their potential. So the reluctant pupil coerced into attending school is 'forced to be free' (Rousseau, 1968) to learn skills that empower them.

Evaluation of positive freedom

However, it is these final steps in the case for positive freedom that are most contentious. The argument implies that acting wisely and rationally involves recognising that your real interest lies in not pursuing basic, selfish self-interest, but enlightened choices of self-discipline and self-control. This is frequently linked to accepting the common good of society as my good, or performing moral and social duties that help me unite with others in a 'higher' freedom. So one is encouraged to accept a set of values about what constitutes real freedom, for example self-control, self-challenge, group harmony and so on. Chillingly, one such value hung above the entrances to the Nazi concentration camps: 'Arbeit Macht Frei' – work makes you free. So instead of value pluralism, an ideal conception of 'the good life' is imposed – a monist political system which rests on the premise that leaders understand what makes us free. The individual is 'dwarfed' to use Mill's term – they 'misunderstand' 'are unenlightened', 'uninformed', 'misled' and so on, and need to be 're-educated' to understand the 'true purpose' in life. It is a slippery slope to the worst features of extreme communist and fascist states.

The final, questionable step is to convince the individual that this is what, he really would have chosen, if he were sufficiently wise and rational, so it is not in fact a tyranny that he is experiencing. He is merely being guided to realise his real interests as opposed to his ignorant, partial, shallow felt interest (Berlin, 1967).

Nevertheless, the concept of positive liberty can be disentangled from ideological **hegemony**, if guidance is genuine and open minded.

In Chapter 5 of *On Liberty* Mill gives the example of a person trying to cross an unsafe bridge. If the person is ignorant of the danger, then it is valid to stop them from crossing, without infringing their liberty; because Mill claims, his real desire is not to fall into the river. This is a clear instance of paternalism, as the action is taken to enable them to realise their deeper desires. However, if a person is in full possession of the facts about the bridge, then they must be allowed to make their own decision and stand the consequences. They can be remonstrated with, or persuaded by rational argument, but ultimately the decision remains theirs if they have 'full use of the reflective faculty'. Mill continues that unless they are 'a child, delirious or in some state of excitement or absorption', then they are capable of making a choice. So with this positive conception of human nature, he assumes an element of positive liberty – the ability to make an informed and rational choice.

Think about

Can you apply the model of positive freedom to examples such as:

- the problem of traffic jams
- learning to play a sport or musical instrument
- the 'nanny state'
- competition for world resources, such as oil
- over indulgence in sex, drugs and rock and roll.

Synoptic link

AQA AS Philosophy Chapter 3, Why should I be moral?, The healthy personality, p74.

Key terms

Hegemony: control of ideas.

Think about

Do you recognise a 'pure' or 'higher' self or are there just competing desires?

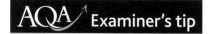
■ Think about

So the escaped prisoner is free from ... ... so free to ... ...

Poverty is freedom from ... ... in order to ... ...

The well-practised musician is free from ... ... to be able to ... ...

Negative liberty is a precondition of positive liberty

Paternalism, as the term suggests, presupposes that many adults are like children. But for Mill, the negative freedom of doing as one desires, with the responsibility of reaping the consequences, enables human beings to reflect on their desires and choose wisely. This is the province of positive freedom. Thus it can be argued that negative freedom is a prerequisite for developing positive freedom. This will be facilitated if people are not subject to strong social conditioning and the pressure to conform from 'the tyranny of the majority'. With this in mind, some commentators argue that positive liberty can be assimilated into a more sophisticated account of negative liberty. We cannot be free to choose, unless we are free from constraint.

Is the negative/positive distinction valid?

So the distinction between negative and positive freedom may not be clear cut and the popular description of negative liberty as 'freedom from' and positive liberty as 'freedom to' is also unhelpful since education is freedom from limited opportunities or freedom to gain knowledge and skills. Gaus summarises McCallum's view that all accounts of freedom refer to three elements:

1 an agent
2 an absence of restraint
3 an action.

So person X is free if they are free from a restraint to do something.

> All ascription of freedom concerns a claim that someone is free both from something and to do something.

Gaus (2000)

So the free motorist (in so many adverts) is free from other traffic so free to choose the appropriate route.

However, whether or not all instances of liberty can be accommodated by this schema disguises the fact that proponents of the two theories have different concerns. Berlin argues that negative freedom is concerned with restricting the law. It focuses on how much intervention in our private lives is acceptable, and law is an infringement of freedom. Those who advocate positive liberty will see laws as enabling and empowering and will be more concerned with how the laws are devised and who sets the agenda; the former is about absence of intervention, while the latter is about the kind of intervention. This will be further illustrated in the section on rights: negative rights, such as freedom from torture, and positive rights, such as freedom to a fair trial.

Liberty and political ideology

One must always beware of being too dogmatic or simplistic about political ideology, but broad trends can be identified.

Classical liberalism

Liberalism, as formulated by Locke and Mill, emphasises the importance of negative freedoms. For Locke, the natural state of human beings as God's creatures is one of rational and moral individuals acting as they choose without interference. So government is therefore based on consent, and its rationale is the protection of those freedoms. Laws are seen as obstacles, but a necessary, minimum restriction to preserve

Liberty. An unnecessary invasion of a person's natural disposition to dispose of their person and goods as they wish is tyranny. So the role of a government is that of a 'protection agency' **Nozick** or referee.

The referee ensures that free individuals do not collide in a way that harms anyone's freedom or is unjust. Governments can also advise and manage minimum bureaucracy, but Mill contests even this, arguing that it is better for private organisations to take on as many functions as possible, to avoid the risk of tyranny. He even claims that it is disadvantageous to attract 'high talent' into government, reminiscent of Plato's reluctant philosopher kings, to avoid a concentration of and desire for power in state hands: 'and the evil would be greater, the more efficiently and scientifically the administrative machinery was constructed'. The classical liberalism focus on political freedoms goes hand in hand with a laissez-faire attitude to the economy.

However, liberalism was revised at the end of the 19th century by philosophers such as Thomas Green. The classical emphasis on negative liberty meant that those who were vulnerable and needy could suffer and were not actually free because of limited resources. So the protection of liberty also required state intervention in the form of education and social welfare, and regulation of working conditions, notably health and safety. Nevertheless, the essential difference between liberalism and socialism is that the emphasis on positive liberty is to protect and enhance freedoms, rather than some other aim such as social justice.

Socialism

Socialism is much more concerned with equality and justice. The focus is on the lack of freedom inherent in economic systems, notably laissez-faire capitalism. 'The poor have no rights', for where there is a concentration of wealth and private property in a particular class, the resulting alienation and poverty limits opportunities. Marx's description of freedom under communism: 'I can hunt in the morning, etc … just as I have a mind' (Marx, 1970) requires control of production and economic power.

In addition, the belief that human nature is a product of economic and social circumstances means that institutions and practices can be structured to promote cooperation and freedom for all. The introduction of comprehensive education in the 20th century is a good example. Freedom is identified with the all-round development of the individual, the capacity to realise opportunities and to enjoy political freedoms, such as rights, which otherwise only benefit the prosperous. The positive liberty of socialism has the aim of equalising power so that all have control over economic and political agendas. Freedom as power can only be achieved in a just, well regulated democracy, where authority derives from all and applies to all, rule by the demos for the demos.

But central planning requires specialists, so there is increased authority for experts to manage the economic and social activity. This encourages the view that real freedom is submission to wise rules and regulations. Liberty is compatible with law.

Conservatism

Conservatism asserts that expertise is needed in order to rule, in accordance with Plato's description of the wisdom of the philosopher kings. Human nature is governed by irrational impulses and self-interest. So the attitude to liberty is complex.

On the one hand, there is a clear strain of positive liberty – the paternalistic provision of education and moral guidance through church,

Key philosophers

Robert Nozick (1938–2002): Professor at Princeton and Harvard. In *Anarchy, State and Utopia* he uses the conception of natural rights to set narrow limits on state legitimacy. For example, taxation without the consent of the taxpayer is forced labour.

Think about

What is the modern liberal position on the introduction of identity cards?

Think about

The law can be coercive and limiting or it can empower. Consider the rules on school uniform. On the one hand it restricts the expression of individuality, but on the other it fosters an inclusive attitude and negates any negative consequences of poverty.

Would liberty be possible if there were no laws? Sort these views into 'Yes' and 'No' and decide which opinions you could support.

In the exam, you may be asked to illustrate, explain or evaluate. Select some of these points to practise illustrating a point and/or evaluating it:

- a minimum number of laws are necessary to prevent disorder, e.g. laws that prevent harm to others
- laws restrict individual initiative and the ability of rational people to solve their own problems in their own way
- laws protect our natural rights, e.g. the right to free speech, and ensure our moral welfare
- laws create opportunities, e.g. access to free health care
- laws are imposed by the dominant class on the oppressed to protect their interests
- laws promote the common good and enact what all rational people would wish
- laws do not prevent crime. You will not stop theft and murder by laws on punishment
- laws are an expression of the tyranny of the majority enforcing conformity on the minority
- laws provide the religious and moral framework, so everyone knows what is expected of each other, and can plan their life accordingly
- laws intrude into our private lives and inhibit the original and creative development of individuals.

school and state. For example, Hobbes underlines that freedom depends on the enforcement of law and order, for security and safety. The decrease in crime allows everyone to take more advantage of opportunities.

Yet conservatives are critical of rationalism in politics. Social institutions should reflect the embodied wisdom of past generations, but the individual is limited. Burke declares, 'we are afraid … this stock of reason in each man is small' (Burke, 1975). So they reject the possibility of the rational construction of utopian ideals (despite Plato), and consequently there is also a desire for limiting government. The state should only concern itself with providing security and a legal framework to achieve social cohesion and a moral consensus. They reject 'the nanny state'. In this respect, there is an overlap between conservatism and liberalism.

So, for conservatives, a natural hierarchy of individuals will always exist and is acceptable. Any attempt to re-design social institutions to create equality will fail. Within the framework of a cohesive society, strengthened by support for the family, the church and traditional values, there is also a measure of negative freedom. Nevertheless, as we shall see in the section on rights, they reject the theory of natural, human rights. The freedoms that we enjoy have evolved over time because they are beneficial to individuals yet do not threaten the social order.

■ The relationship between law and liberty

There is an important debate about the origin and nature of law that impacts on the issue of law and liberty. First, stemming from traditional 'natural law' theory is the view that the law of the land should promote and enforce moral and religious standards. This is a 'substantive' concept of law, that the law is framed to produce concrete outcomes. The relationship between law and liberty therefore depends on the moral values that are held. Liberal values derive traditionally from a theory of natural rights (Locke) or utilitarian arguments (Mill). Either individuals are born with God-given rights to life, liberty and property or the most extensive realm of private life and negative liberty is conducive to individual and social progress and happiness. Conversely, some versions of Christianity and Shariah Law advocate strict regulation of sexual behaviour for example, and such states adopt a more interventionist approach to develop positive liberties. The debate is symbolised by the wearing of the burkah, which might to liberals appear a serious restraint of negative freedom, but which women also claim is liberating and life enhancing.

Marxism

For Marx, law in a capitalist society develops with the creation of wealth and private property. These laws will disappear when private ownership and class is abolished.

This is the first step, which will then enable workers to see labour as creative and fulfilling their needs. In these conditions arises 'the will to abolish competition and with it the State and the law'. Crime which embodies the isolated individual struggling against the dominant, capitalist conditions will cease to exist. As people are freed from subordination to the division of labour, to the dominant ideas and laws of the ruling class, there will be nothing to fight against. A socialist economy based on the principle of 'production for use' instead of the capitalist 'production for exchange', would eventually lose the need for money. Then, criminal law will become redundant. The social ills such as poverty, poor health and education, and unemployment, which foster crime, will have disappeared. So the key to freedom and the absence of law is planning. And communist states have attempted to build the centrally planned economy, with disastrous results! Why?

One inherent contradiction in the process is that economic planning requires experts. Doing away with the wastefulness and injustice of a free market, to replace it with a harmonious, cooperative and coordinated workshop requires specialist knowledge and leadership. But this contradicts the abolition of the division of labour and re-creates a managerial class – an elite.

Secondly, the free market, for all its problems is responsive to demands from individuals. To run a planned economy is difficult enough, but to respond to individual needs is nigh impossible. Inevitably the power in a planned economy stays at the top, which again contradicts the claim that under communism people will have the resources to meet a variety of new needs.

☑ *After working through this topic, you should:*

- be able to discuss various theories of what it means to be free
- understand the distinction between negative and positive freedom and evaluate these theories
- know how different ideologies interpret freedom
- be able to discuss the relationship between liberty and the law
- understand the issues with promoting and defending freedom.

Think about

How far should the law intrude into our private lives?

Synoptic link

The relevance of the Hart–Devlin debate is introduced in AQA AS Philosophy Chapter 5, Why should I be governed? in the section on 'Disobedience and dissent'.

Rights

Learning objectives

- to explore what we mean by human rights
- to assess how they can be justified
- to distinguish between natural and positive rights
- to explore a utilitarian justification for rights
- to discuss the relationship between rights, morality and the law.

The French revolution occurred in 1789. In 1790 Burke, an English conservative, published *Reflections on the Revolution in France*, attacking the reform of society based on an a priori conception of rights, natural rights (Burke, 1975).

In 1791, Paine published *The Declaration of the Rights of Man*, advocating human rights (Paine, 1987). A passionate debate ensued on an idea that had been argued for a century earlier by Locke and had been enshrined in the American constitution: the view that all human beings have rights, regardless of their nationality, creed, class, gender or age. These natural rights are pre-society and are in addition and prior to any legal rights that a society may grant.

It is the last set of rights that have been controversial, and the subject of philosophical debate.

Paine declares, 'natural law and right reason … are accessible to all rational persons'. So by appeal to the religious ethics of natural law, he

Synoptic link

AQA AS Philosophy Chapter 5, Why should I be governed?, The state of nature, p121.

concludes with our God-given reason, we can divine the purpose and law governing each living thing. This reveals that human beings are sovereign by nature, and possess freedom and integrity. These qualities must be respected by universal rights. This of course depends on the correct reading of God's will and the laws of nature.

Burke's more cautious conservatism favoured a gradual evolution of society with an 'insuperable reluctance to any established system of government, upon a theory'. He argued that generalisations about theoretical rights are meaningless. Liberty may be a good or a bad thing, dependent on the context: 'am I to congratulate a highwayman and a murderer, who has broke prison, upon the recovery of his natural rights'.

So natural rights cannot 'trump' and rank above good government. The shared traditions and wisdom of past generations about which freedoms are valuable should have precedence over abstract theories of liberty. We should be pragmatic, test any rights empirically and pay direct attention to the lessons of history. We can have too much freedom, too much faith in individuals and too idealistic plans for utopias. The rights that we grant each other, should only be the inherited rights (rights recognised by positive law) that our ancestors have incorporated into the legal system.

However, will these 'positive rights' be able to protect us against tyranny, exploitation and new moral challenges?

What are rights?

Before we evaluate these different approaches, we must be clear about what rights entail. It is generally agreed that rights confer advantageous positions on the possessor:

- They give a special justification for interfering with another's freedom, for example the right to prohibit trespassers on your land.
- They provide a justification to resist interference or coercion, e.g. the right to resist an arranged marriage.

So they offer control and autonomy over our lives and limit the power of others. Hohfeld identified four legal advantages of having rights:

1   liberties, which mean I do not have to refrain from an action
2   claims on others to perform duties
3   powers, which permit me to alter other people's liberties and duties
4   immunities which limit the power of others to interfere with my beliefs and actions.

Think about

Can you supply an example of a right to illustrate each of these aspects?

The distinction between natural and positive rights

To begin with, we will consider the justification for any rights at all and the difference between the two classical positions of Paine and Burke:

- Are there 'natural rights' over and above any legal/positive rights derived from natural law?
- Or are all rights 'positive rights' and simply 'a child of the law' and granted by the sovereign power?

To this is added a third position – the utilitarian argument which denies natural rights, but argues for moral rights that should guide legislation.

Examiner's tip

In the exam, be precise in any discussion on rights and distinguish between natural and human rights, and utilitarian and positive rights. Be prepared to defend and criticise each version.

Natural rights

A natural right is:

1 God-given and/or constitutive of what it is to be human

2 pre-social

3 universal and possessed by all human beings

4 absolute and trumps other (moral) considerations

5 inalienable – cannot be taken away.

So they are an entitlement independent of the law in any country, culture or epoch. At the end of the 18th century when landowners were given a legal right to keep slaves, this contravened natural rights.

Supporters of natural rights contend that they ground the law and can be used as a measure of whether a law is just. They provide a justification for challenging the law and, for Locke, this was a reason for rebellion against a tyrannous government. So that every law framed by Man is legitimate to the extent to which it is derived from the law of nature.

Locke interprets this in a classic exposition of natural rights, 'men living together, according to reason, without a common superior on earth, with authority to judge between them, is properly the state of nature':

■ a state of perfect freedom,

■ to dispose of their possessions and persons as they think fit,

■ a state also of equality … (without) subordination or subjection.

Locke (1960)

His supporting arguments are:

■ Because we are 'God's workmanship', no-one ought to harm another in his life, health, liberty or possessions. Even if we relinquish the religious reference, it may still be argued that human beings are valuable in themselves, 'a kingdom of ends' (Kant, 1972).

■ This implies a right to punish 'evil' as 'reason and conscience dictates'. As Man has been given Reason to discern moral values, this allows us to punish, not only our countrymen, but also foreigners ('aliens'), who behave irrationally and immorally.

■ Rational morality implies a form of universalisation, that all people are born equal and bound by moral law (even kings). We are all 'equal in the sight of God' and any 'unjust violence and slaughter' is a 'war against all mankind'.

■ Free and equal persons can expect a balance in the scales of justice, 'recovering from the offender so much as may make satisfaction for the harm'.

Thus we have natural rights to life, health, liberty, possessions, justice, equality and to punish, all founded on moral and religious premises.

Human rights

An alternative basis for rights is possible independent of religious beliefs, which we will call human rights. These stem from our essential nature and protect what is fundamental and integral to being human. Such qualities include foremost, autonomy (the freedom to choose) and may also refer to these other essential characteristics:

■ Synoptic link

AQA Philosophy AS Chapter 9, Persons, pp267–89.

- self-awareness and a sense of identity
- a sense of past and future interests
- self-control
- the need and ability to form relationships
- communication skills and a developed language
- rationality.

Thus rights can be awarded to beings that conceive of themselves as distinct entities and therefore have interests. Such beings understand the significance of life choices and have the ability to weigh up options. They also understand that co-relative duties are necessary and can compare their treatment with others. These needs and capacities underpin the necessity for moral relationships, which can be enshrined in rights. Thus law must contain at least a minimum of moral law. As the professor of jurisprudence Hart summarises, 'there are natural limits, imposed by basic features of the human condition, to what can count as law' (Hart, 1967).

Evaluation

The obvious advantage of natural or human rights is that they protect individuals all over the world from abuse and tyranny, from the misuse of child labour to the mistreatment of prisoners.

Also, while many rights are legal rights and apply within states, universal human rights can inform international relations and provide a framework for regulating behaviour between countries. This will be developed in the final section.

However, there are serious objections:

- that there are in fact such rights, and
- to the specific rights that have been identified.

First and most obvious is the reliance on a basis of natural law and religion. Apart from atheistic criticism, the interpretation of what is natural and rational is controversial. There must be a clear distinction between natural laws as scientific descriptions of how the universe functions, and attempts to read moral prescriptions into the order of events. A scientific, perhaps Darwinian, account will describe the natural world without the need to ascribe purpose, value and divine will. Even if we base human rights on an account of human nature, as we saw in the first section, there are two serious problems:

1 The version of human nature can be partial and selective, or there may be no human essence, or a nature that is malleable.
2 Even if we could agree on a human essence, there is a logical gap between Fact and Value. The fact that all human beings desire happiness, or that their unique faculty is Reason, does not entail that happiness is desirable or that we should act rationally.

Also, the following objections could be raised against Locke's points:

- As everything is God's workmanship, we can therefore never destroy anything, including dangerous bacteria. To treat human beings as unique or special is to assign a value to a species that is always questionable, and mocked by Sartre at the end of 'Existentialism and Humanism' – 'only a dog or a horse would be in a position to pronounce a general judgement upon man'.
- Reason is only the faculty of calculating: 'reasoning is reckoning' (Hobbes) or 'the slave of the passions' (Hume); it cannot discern

Think about

There are frequent new items about the infringement of human rights. Research the arguments surrounding a particular case that you can use as an illustration.

Synoptic link

AQA AS Philosophy Chapter 8, God and the world, What is the argument from design?, p223.

universal, moral absolutes. Locke's argument smacks of cultural imperialism.

- People are not born equal in any factual sense. This is a recommendation for an equal moral status, which is always open to question.
- Justice and a fair balance are highly contentious, as we shall see in the next section.

Furthermore, it is clear that rights are not possessed (like property) but are granted and conferred by others. Rights necessitate co-relative duties, recognition of claims and powers and reciprocal obligations. They must be a product of society rather than pre-social. Thus different rights have evolved in different cultures – even the right to life can be interpreted differently. In some countries, the right to life is subordinate to a virtuous life, and people are executed for adultery, treason and drug trafficking.

Marxist views

A Marxist criticism of rights is that they are simply a product of socio-economic conditions, so neither absolute nor universal but ideological. This perspective questions the rationality of some of the freedoms, for example the right to property. This is justified by Locke on the grounds that if one works the land, one deserves to own it and 'exclude the common right of other men'. But there is no logical connection between working the land and excluding others. It could easily be retained in communal ownership and loaned out to those who want to work it and look after it. And as Marx observes, with 'the concentration of private property', the working class 'never achieved an independent development'. Political rights are only ever in theory; in practice the poor can rarely exercise their rights due to lack of economic freedom. The cost, for example of going to court, means that many poor people cannot access the right to justice.

To be fair to Locke, he does include the condition that we should not take more than we need ('no wastage') and that there must be enough for everyone to have an equal opportunity to acquire land. But the first condition is very vague, I might argue the case that I need thousands of acres of wilderness; and the second is ignorant of the scarcity of world resources.

Marx would argue that rights leave real problems of division of labour, private property and classes intact. If all we do is redistribute income to the less well off – for example, the right to a minimum wage – we are not dealing with the conditions that cause the injustice.

Finally, rights overemphasise the importance of individuality at the expense of unity and solidarity. Rights encourage people to see each other as a threat, a separate and opposing force, rather than a comrade with whom they can cooperate.

Yet surely the freedom of the individual underlies all sense of obligation and is integral to most conceptions of the good life. Hart argues that if human beings enter into any moral relationships, then there is at least one natural right granted to all people, the equal right to be free. 'In the recognition of moral rights, there is implied the recognition that all men have a right to equal freedom'.

And surely the notion of human solidarity involves moral relationships, and endorses the right to equal freedom. So it is questionable whether Marx can escape the importance of rights.

■ Rights and utilitarianism

The idea of natural rights, however, was famously attacked by Bentham as 'nonsense on stilts' (Bentham, 1948). Rights cannot be based on metaphysical unknowns or a fictitious social contract, but are clearly granted by society and a product of debate and legislation. A natural right is 'a son that never had a father'. Nevertheless, Bentham argued that there were still moral rights, which were determined by the principle of utility, and the law ought to protect them.

Similarly, Mill dismisses the notion of 'an abstract right as a thing independent of utility' (Mill, 1985). Thus the utilitarian approach to rights is concerned with rights-based interests, which maximise wellbeing. Human beings have interests which need to be defended, such as protection from harm, which 'ought to be considered as rights', but are created by 'legal provision' or 'tacit understanding' and are justified by appeal to social utility. Whenever part of a person's conduct prejudicially affects the interests of others, then it may become a matter of constituting rights. To sum up:

■ My rights are those important interests, which if socially protected, maximise utility.

■ It is utility which rightfully constrains others from acting against my rights.

For example, my utilitarian right to freedom of speech is:

■ in the interests of the individual, as self-expression develops originality, appreciation of the truth etc., and

■ by recognising my rights, the development of individuals leads to social progress. Thus the institution of rights contributes to the greatest happiness of the greatest number.

So the utilitarian theory of rights is entirely consistent with Mill's rule utilitarianism. The provision of rights in a society enhances security of essential freedoms and so stops human beings worrying about their potential happiness.

The key issue for utilitarians is whether rights granted on the utility principle could be inalienable. Could people's rights be removed if it created greater social utility?

Rights and social utility

Social utility, the wellbeing of the majority, is the goal of utilitarianism. But suppose that respecting individual rights does not promote the good of the majority.

The difficulty for utilitarians defending rights in all these cases is that they must judge an action on the consequences of the action for the majority, and in a number of these instances greater utility and preference satisfaction is achieved by sacrificing individual rights for the greater good.

Evaluation of utilitarian rights

Even if utilitarians argue that a general rule that upholds generates more happiness, it is the principle of judging rights on their consequences that is at fault. Rights are **deontological** and are based on principles surrounding the value and respect accorded to each human being, regardless of whether that increases happiness or not. So all people have an equal right to be free, even if social utility is not obtained.

The two key problems are:

1 Rights based on utility are not inalienable.
2 Rights are deontologically valid and do not depend on consequences or utility.

The simple fact is that assessments of happiness, and the justice associated with rights, pull in different directions, creating a tension. Mill defends utilitarian rights on the grounds that they are essential to progressive human beings, who grow, develop and become valuable through experiencing essential freedoms, which he contrasts in Chapter 3 with the current state of people in China. But, supposing it could be demonstrated that these essential freedoms lead instead to conflict and uncertainty rather than the beneficial consequences of cooperation, common purpose and collective achievement. Thus, the approaches of rights theory and utilitarianism are quite different. The latter seeks to provide an end goal of behaviour, while the former is concerned with freedom, and sets limits to behaviour.

Positive rights

Positive rights are referred to here in the context of legal positivism. Hence it is argued that rights are simply created by laws and derive their force solely from the fact that these are an expression of the will of the sovereign power. Unlike utilitarianism, there is no independent moral justification in the form of utility. There are no natural rights or independent moral rights.

Sometimes it is the case that legal rights are immoral, or that opinion will be divided on whether a right is just. According to the Fugitive Slave Act 1850 (quoted in Gaus, 2000), owners still had the right to have escaped slaves returned to them. Victorian society also condoned a husband's right to commit his wife to a mental asylum, and until 1992 husbands still had a right to force their wives to have sex. Thus rights are only freedoms, powers and claims enshrined in law, and over time rights just like moral values and laws evolve.

One significance of this is that as rights are created by states, they cannot be used as a justification for disobedience and rebellion. In international politics, the European Court could not indict political leaders on the basis that they have contravened human rights, although a leader may still be regarded as cruel.

Rights, morality and law

So the exact relationship between these three political concepts is contested:

- either legal rights must conform to higher, natural law, or
- legal rights must respect human rights, which are determined by utility and/or moral rights, or
- there are only rights created by law, which may be considered just/unjust.

We have seen that it is difficult to establish any natural law or moral basis for incontrovertible rights, unless we accept that all men have a right to equal freedom. There is also no automatic connection between rights and utility.

AQA Examiner's tip

Use this exercise to construct useful examples of the conflict between rights and social utility that you can use in the exam.

Synoptic link

AQA A2 Philosophy, Chapter 4, Moral philosophy, Deontological Ethics, p169.

☑ *After working through this topic, you should:*

- understand how different philosophical theories justify the existence of rights
- be able to distinguish between natural and positive rights
- be able to evaluate the claims to universal human rights
- be aware of issues in relating rights to morality and to the law.

Justice

Learning objectives

- to understand the nature of social justice

- to understand what is meant by distributive justice

- to compare the competing principles of equality: desert and need

- to evaluate different conceptions of justice

- to explore the relationship between distributive justice, liberty and rights.

'It's not fair … it's always me and never him.'

'But you promised …'

'I have a dream … will not be judged buy the colour of their skin, but by the content of their character.'

'An eye for an eye, a tooth for a tooth.'

It seems we develop a sense of fairness and justice from an early age, and most would agree with Plato that the only life worth living is the just life. Yet philosophers struggle to define exactly what it entails. It surely encapsulates a sense of equality and treating people consistently; yet also allowing people freedom and rights; and recognising needs and deserts. Here are a few descriptions:

- Mill: 'to do as you would be done by, and to love your neighbour as yourself constitute the ideal perfection of utilitarian morality' (*Utilitarianism*, 1968).

- Kant: treat people as 'ends' and 'not means' (The groundwork of the *Metaphysics of Morals*, 1972).

- Hare: justice involves becoming an 'ideal sympathiser', putting ourselves in other people's shoes (*Moral Thinking*, 1981).

- Singer: 'equal consideration of interests is a minimal principle of equality … it does not dictate equal treatment' (*Practical Ethics*, 1993).

- Rawls: the principles of justice may be thought of as arising once the constraints of morality are imposed upon rational and mutually self-interested people (*A Theory of Justice*, 1999).

- Nozick: 'past actions of people … can create different entitlements or different deserts to things' (*Anarchy, State and Utopia*, 1974).

The crux of the debate about justice is: What is the nature of the principles that we should adopt? What is the content of a just law? What are the outcomes of a policy that can be accepted as fair? This is **substantive justice**, which tackles the ethical basis of a social system. It asks why and how we should treat people the same, distinguishing between needs and deserts; and relating opinions to our belief in human rights or fundamental moral values.

Key terms

Substantive justice: This refers to the content or substance of the decision and involves normative principles, such as equality of need, desert and rights.

Synoptic link

AQA A2 Philosophy, Problems in Plato, Knowledge and virtue. This can be found at **www.nelsonthornes.com/aqagce**

■ The relationship between distributive justice, liberty and rights

Distributive justice

So how should we allocate the good things in society – in income, welfare, services, status and honours?

The concept of distributive justice requires us to consider the ethics of how political and economic goods and benefits are distributed. The discussion largely centres on wealth and property, but can also include any desirable benefit. There are competing views on what principles the distribution should be based: such as desert, merit, human rights, needs and utility.

The classical liberal of Locke is that our natural rights include property rights and there should be no interference with what people deserve through their own labour. God gave the earth to the industrious.

The utilitarian position adopted by Mill is that the free market is the most efficient means of producing and distributing goods and that this freedom maximises happiness. Both these positions are compatible with a high degree of inequality in the accumulation of wealth, although utilitarianism faces the conflict that social utility might override rights to property, free trade and the benefits of negative liberty. Since both these theories have already been discussed, this section will attend to alternative theories.

Conservative ideology has tended to suggest a theory of natural justice, based on desert, as Plato outlined in *The Republic*. An alternative welfare liberal view is that an exclusive focus on desert will lead to unchecked and increasing levels of inequality and this restricts the liberty, opportunities and choices available to some individuals. A just society would be more egalitarian and would require some state intervention to regulate markets and redistribute property more evenly to secure fair opportunities for all. This is Rawls' theory of social justice, that social inequalities must be arranged to benefit the least advantaged.

In contrast, is Nozick's defence of classical liberalism, that any attempt to impose a 'patterned' notion of justice is inconsistent with individual rights and freedoms? A just society recognises the right and entitlement to legally acquire property and should not restrict or interfere with property dealings. Thus, in a just State, property could be distributed very unevenly and it would be unjust to interfere, through taxation, to change this.

Finally, there is the socialist perspective that the free market is wasteful and destructive and produces alienated individuals. A more equal distribution of goods according to need is required, which will maximise positive freedoms. Even this is insufficient for Marxists because it leaves an unjust, free market intact. Redistribution will not be necessary, if there is one class and identity of interests and control of the means of production.

Natural desert

Thinkers like Burke refer to the natural course of events or 'the workings of nature', so property ownership reflects the natural state of affairs, where in a free market, those who are more able take their opportunities. The accumulation of wealth should not be a subject of rights or based on needs, because it is matter of natural deserving. According to **Spencer**, 'each individual ought to receive the benefits and evils of his own nature and consequent conduct' (Spencer, 1982).

The argument goes something like this:

a I own my own body.

b I own my talents.

c Therefore I own the products of my talents.

Thus a star like David Beckham is entitled to enormous wealth as he works hard to make use of his rare and special talent. This view is compatible with a Darwinian model of the laws of nature which favour the survival of the fittest; and is exemplified by early pioneers who benefited from a gold rush. 'Equality of opportunity' existed for anyone to

Think about

Judge and jury: here are five examples of social injustice. Do you agree they are unjust? Can you explain why?

- Forms of sex discrimination, such as unequal pay for the same work.

- Enormous extremes of wealth and poverty, such as between Western nations and some African countries.

- A society that does not fund a welfare state, but expects citizens to ensure their own health care.

- Land reform that takes farms away from the white owners, through violence and intimidation.

- Positive discrimination for students from poor areas to give them a better chance of going to university, e.g. a quota system.

AQA Examiner's tip

In the exam be prepared to distinguish between these different principles and their relative merits, to provide a full discussion.

Key philosophers

Herbert Spencer (1820–1903): Originator of a general evolutionist philosophy.

stake a claim and get rich, so those who possessed the energy and skill to find gold deserved their gains.

However, many will point out that equality of opportunity is not necessarily equality of fair opportunity. While all children in theory have an equal opportunity to realise their potential through education, do they all arrive at the starting line together, with no particular advantage?

Because of the above, some will claim that we should intervene. It may even seem natural to help the less fortunate. Does an argument over what is 'natural' assist the debate? Should we not just assist the disadvantaged because it will benefit all of us to raise standards?

A possible reply is that intervention may be:

- too costly for those who have to pay for it
- ineffective because you cannot resist the workings of nature.

Redistribution of advantages will have little effect. Some people are better suited to survive, life is unequal and that is the harsh fact. Some geographical areas will always suffer droughts, poverty and famine.

Even if this grim scenario is accepted, however, it begs the question of what is fair. Just because a sequence of events is natural, that does not make it right.

Most of the arguments that follow suggest that human beings can take control of their situation, instead of resigning themselves to nature. They point to a weakness in the argument above about ownership of talents. The move from (b) to (c) is a 'non-sequitur'; it does not necessarily follow and so is invalid. In order to develop talents we usually need teachers, resources and facilities etc. Beckham will have received considerable support from the community to develop his talents and his career. He therefore owes a debt to society, which should be paid from the products of his work. This is the position of the welfare liberal, Rawls, that opportunities should be fair, and open to all.

Welfare liberalism

Rawls invites us to consider justice, impartially, behind a veil of ignorance. It is as though we are planning to play a game. We have no idea how our futures in the game may turn out, and we are agreeing the rules that we adopt. So we forget:

- specific information about out individual qualities
- our special interests, beliefs and values
- and are ignorant of our destiny.

Because of our ignorance, Rawls contends that we would wish to cancel out lucky advantages, such as natural talent and inheritance, so that any benefits that people earn are clearly deserved and not the result of accidental good fortune. This is equal, fair opportunity.

Secondly, not knowing whether we will thrive or fail, we will wish to provide the best possible support for the worst off in society. In case any of us sink to the bottom, we will desire 'the highest bottom' or maximise the minimum welfare provision (maxi min). We will therefore re-distribute wealth for two reasons:

- To ensure everyone starts with a fair opportunity, e.g. a good, universal education.
- To support the weak and vulnerable, e.g. a public healthcare system.

Rawls argues that people will accept this, not because it is natural or even utilitarian, but because it is just and is in our self interest.

He then sets out two principles, in order of priority:

First principle:

> Each person is to have an equal right to the most extensive system of equal basic liberties compatible with a similar system of liberty for all.

Second principle:

> Social and economic inequalities are to be arranged so that they are both
>
> ■ to the greatest benefit of the least advantaged …
>
> ■ attached to offices and positions open to all under conditions of fair equality of opportunity.

Rawls (1999)

Rawls clearly believes that we will wish to give priority to the most extensive rights and liberties to pursue our own lives and achieve our deserts. Yet the difference principle implies that where liberty leads to inequality, inequalities should only be allowed if they are to everyone's advantage. So, for example, a businessman can accumulate wealth that provides jobs for others or funds charities. So the freedom of the wealthy is permitted to the extent that it benefits the worst off.

Evaluation

Critics of Rawls point out that the top is tied to the bottom. The liberty principle is in fact subject to the difference principle. The fortunate will find their ability to exploit their initiatives and energy and to seek higher goals is tied to the redistribution of wealth to the poor and needy. As Mill would claim, this will hamper the development of the truly exceptional, the genius who requires very special soil in order to grow. Rawls would respond that geniuses can be free, as long as their achievements will eventually benefit all of us. But conservatives would criticise the danger to a strong family heritage, which requires generations of commitment and resources, to create some of our finest national treasures.

Secondly, it is highly questionable that behind the veil of ignorance, we would necessarily choose these principles. For example, those who confidently enjoy risk might prefer a system which gives more incentive to earn our deserts and only a minimum redistribution to provide a basic safety net of a welfare.

In other words, I may rationally prefer an unequal society, as long as there are some possibilities to reverse my fortunes or the minimum does not cause undue suffering. This does not have to be the extreme that inequality is only allowed if it benefits the least well off. Furthermore, a reasonable (utilitarian) position is that improving the average position in society will maximise happiness, because the number of poor may be a minority.

Furthermore, the problem of the veil of ignorance is that:

■ we might genuinely disagree over values, and not self-interest, about what model of society we favour

■ it is virtually impossible not to allow our values, beliefs and interests to affect our decisions

■ if we are ignorant even of our own conception of the good life, how can we even make a decision at all about what a just society would be like.

Think about

How would you respond to the argument that it is only through the resources of generations of private land ownership that some of our finest art collections or landscapes have been financed?

Finally, as has already been argued, the condition of ignorance prior to the contract is loaded in favour of equality. Far from equality being the choice of rational argument, it is a condition of taking part in the exercise. By removing all personal hopes and conceptions of what is good, people are required to believe that they are in a position of equality. It is a prerequisite, rather than a principle we would necessarily choose.

Yet the emphasis on the individual as part of a community will nevertheless receive a lot of support. Aristotle also presents an argument against extremes of wealth, so that the poor should not become too poor, or the rich too rich. He bases his argument on the benefit of everyone contributing to the whole. He argues that if the rich become too rich, they cease to care about the community because of their independence. For example, they can pay accountants to protect their income from taxes. The poor on the other hand are so preoccupied with their personal struggle for survival that they also can contribute little. For a society to be cohesive, and functioning to maximum potential, extremes must be avoided:

> Those who have superabundance … neither wish to hold office nor understand the work

and:

> Those who are greatly deficient … are full of envy [and] covet.

Aristotle (1962)

However, from another direction, one might enquire why inequalities of wealth are allowed at all. This will be discussed later.

Rights

Synoptic link

AQA AS Philosophy Chapter 5, Why should I be governed?, p136.

Locke's argument for desert, based on natural rights was examined in the last section. Here we will focus on Nozick's response to Rawls.

For Nozick (1974), equality is in conflict with liberty. Any policy to ensure an economic redistribution of goods will require constant intervention and interference with those who accumulate wealth. And the talented will always disrupt the drive towards egalitarianism.

He tells the story of Wilt Chamberlain, a popular, skilled basketball player. Wilt agrees to play if people pay an extra 25 cents. Now if millions of people pay the increased charge, Wilt has gained huge wealth:

■ with the voluntary agreement of his fans
■ without any unfair or illegal transactions.

No-one has been forced to contribute money, so consequently Wilt is entitled to keep the money. To redistribute his profit is to steal legal profit and to deny the wishes of the people, who gave their money to Wilt. Tax is like asking a person to spend part of their week, working for nothing. If you pay 20 per cent tax, nearly a fifth of your work is for the state.

Now if the right to property is an essential part of personal liberty, then redistribution of wealth contravenes that right. So the natural differences in human talent plus the rights to equal liberty and to hold possessions that are legally acquired means that inequality of wealth is justified and inevitable.

Nozick argues that if property is fairly acquired, or gained through free and legal transfer, it would be a violation of freedom to remove it. So a family should be free to give their wealth to their children. Wolff (1996) quotes Nozick to sum up his view: 'the socialist society would have to forbid capitalist acts between consenting adults' to achieve equality. Of course, Marx would not deny this or see it as a criticism.

Evaluation

Nozick's argument ultimately rests on the value of freedom, but the conception of freedom is negative freedom from coercion. However, it is also possible to have rights and duties that enhance positive freedom. Thus if Wilt is taxed appropriately, he will contribute to public services that will ultimately improve the amount and quality of his freedom. Public amenities which he has helped to fund will increase the opportunities where he can choose to spend his money.

Secondly, it is possible to query what 'fairly acquired' really means. A brief look at history shows that much wealth was acquired through robbery and imperialism. The notion of fairness and desert can only have substance in a shared set of communal values. In some parts of the world, one is entitled to land because it was an ancestral homeland, which is fair in a society that worships its ancestors. 'I deserve' can be interpreted in a number of different ways:

- I worked for it
- I was given it in sacred trust
- I really appreciate it
- I bought it
- I was brought up with it
- I have a moral right to it

and so on.

Desert or merit?

For those who emphasise the role '**desert**' plays in justice there is a potential clash with '**merit**'.

For example, someone may work hard and deserve success, but not reach sufficient competency to merit it. We all have met the irritating student who appears to do little work but merits a good pass grade on performance.

Some argue that justice should be about competency and merit and favour rigorous competition. This provides a problem for liberalism, in that competency entails agreed values, and will not encourage value pluralism. Indeed stringent criteria can impose narrow sets of values. We all know the difference between being told that 'you are doing well' in your studies, but not actually meeting the precise assessment objectives of the exam.

The more we define the competencies that people must achieve to merit the reward, the less freedom there is to consider broader notions of desert.

However, if everyone has had equality of fair opportunities, why should we not select on merit rather than desert? It will provide a clearer, more unequivocal notion of justice. In a more complex society, it appears necessary to precisely set out agreed success criteria. But if a society bases justice on merit, the following issues will arise:

- inequality will develop between the meritorious and the failures, some of whom would be considered deserving
- considerable power is given to those who decide the criteria, and success will be less open-ended

> **Think about**
>
> Would you prefer (a) a small decrease in your tax, or (b) to continue to pay for public utilities? If you choose (a), you will have a small increase in spending power. If you choose (b) everyone's small donation could be enough to fund a new theatre, swimming pool, hospital etc. Which would you choose? What could Nozick reply to this?

> **Think about**
>
> On what do we base desert?

> **Key terms**
>
> **Desert:** assesses effort and quality of work and therefore is backward looking.
>
> **Merit:** entails meeting criteria and therefore is forward looking.

there will be a demand for positive discrimination if any particular group consistently under-achieves.

Socialism and needs

When most people consider social justice or distributive justice, they mean redistribution of goods from the well-off to the needy. As Marx put it 'from each according to his ability, to each according to his need' (Marx, 1970).

It is important to distinguish this from desert. Under capitalism, it is argued that the worker may not be receiving his true deserts. If we agree that the owner purchases the labour of the worker and then by demanding longer hours, increasing efficiency or manipulating the market he makes a profit, then the worker is denied the true value of the product. Whether one accepts this or not, the argument is still about desert.

Although Marx employs a version of the previous argument, he also cites 'desert' as 'the narrow horizon of the bourgeois'. However, if everyone is to be valued as much as everyone else, then impartiality dictates that we must also satisfy basic needs. This is a simple matter of common humanity and the values of everyone's contribution to the community.

Furthermore, it will be remembered that equality of fair opportunity means that we are all on the start line before the race. To enable us all to start, natural disadvantages need to be compensated for. The aim is equal satisfaction of equal needs, so that every person can compete. A minimum level of resources is distributed to everyone so they can function. For example:

- a guaranteed minimum wage
- essential health care
- sufficient education
- social housing.

This is justified because it enables the needy to contribute to the good of the nation. The above ensures that everyone can be productive and begin to realise their potential.

However, tension will occur when 'being productive' may not necessarily be valued by some in the community. Supposing the well-supported citizen chooses to work abroad or have extended gap years. The socialist redistribution of wealth therefore generates a pressure to conform to values compatible with the common good. So social security payments are limited to socially useful and productive options, and the emphasis is on positive liberty empowering citizens to develop their 'higher' selves. Just laws coerce the citizen to be free.

Rawls draws up a list of 'primary goods', which are resources which everyone must have in order 'to pursue their aims in life' (Gaus, 2000). These include liberty, income, opportunities and the social basis of self-respect. Yet there is not a clear link between allocation of equal resources and needs being met. Some people and some countries have more extensive needs than others, and these may not be satisfied by an equal distribution of primary goods. Some countries in particularly harsh regions of the world will require more than an equal distribution of resources on a continued basis to counter drought, disease and climate change etc.

Synoptic link

See list of basic needs in AQA AS Philosophy Chapter 5, Why should I be governed?, p136.

Think about

Can you construct a case for continuing to support the least well off in society, if they are a continuous drain in resources?

Marxism

One strand of Marxism would dismiss this kind of justice as simply compensation. However, communism seeks to root out the causes of inequality. Justice according to need is still trying to reconcile the conflicting interests of individuals. But if the productive assets are owned by the community, no-one's needs should be neglected. If all we do is redistribute income from those who have, to the have nots then classes and alienation remain largely intact. But with common ownership comes identity of interest and others are regarded as supporting comrades in a shared vision.

However, this ideal has serious flaws, mentioned previously:

- Even if we have a shared vision, conflicts will still arise about how to achieve the vision. Moreover, Marx describes our species-essence as creative, and this is bound to stimulate differences of opinion.

- Conflict is unlikely to disappear while there is scarcity of resources, and Marx seems to assume that cooperative effort will create abundance. But as the history of communist regimes has shown, there is no necessary link between unity of effort and absence or shortage of materials.

- The public ownership of resources will, according to the theory, dissolve undeserved inequalities. But what about deserved inequalities? Supposing I use my free time to manage a vegetable garden. I then have an abundance of extra food, which I have worked for. I could swap my products for someone else's, and improve my standard of living. But note, I now have private property, which is not exploitative or an undeserved inequality.

It is difficult to see with the last example, how unity among workers can be maintained, without becoming, to use Mill's words, 'the rule of each by all the rest' and a 'tyranny of the majority'.

And finally, there will be considerable debate about what constitutes 'basic needs', and the distinction between a desire and a need. It is suggested that needs are universal and applicable to all human beings, but this can be challenged. A need in one society can be a luxury in another. Also this would necessitate having an agreed theory of human nature.

While it is self-evident that physical needs for food, shelter and health are universal, beyond that, whether we regard the essential human nature as egoist and self-interested, or rational and property owning, compassionate and not self-sufficient, or creative, self-developers will determine what counts as basic needs. The appeal to needs presupposes that we have a consensus on what it is to be a properly functioning human being.

> **AQA Examiner's tip**
>
> This point about human nature underlies much political ideology and could be employed as part of a conclusion to your essay.

☑ *After working through this topic, you should:*

- understand some of the principles integral to a system of social justice
- be able to explain what is meant by distributive justice
- be able to assess different theories and principles employed in different conceptions of distributive justice
- be able to explore the relationship between justice, liberty and rights.

Nation states

■ Introduction

Human beings have not always lived in nation states. These have evolved from tribal societies, nomadic groups and city states. Of the 160 or more nation states in the world, more than 20 were created after the Second World War, and some, like Israel, are still disputed. States do not necessarily coincide with nations, ethnic groups or even language users, as Belgium indicates.

A state is the centralised agency for the promulgation, application and enforcement of laws. It is a politically organised society. Nations as a collection of people with the same ethnic origin may not be politically organised; but with a nation state all people have the same government to promote cohesion and identity. The sign of a successful state is that laws are regarded as legitimate and generally obeyed by the citizens. A failed state will be unduly coercive, use extreme violence and degenerate into factions and civil war. Nation states retain borders and defend them and within these borders use the only form of legitimate violence – punishment.

The state and other states

There is one sense, at least, in which 'a state of nature' could be said to actually exist – the relations between nations. If we consider six aspects of the traditional notion of the state of nature, could they apply to states?

International morality

If one takes the view that the state is the ultimate moral authority, and laws simply embody the will of the sovereign power, then there is no higher moral authority to govern international relations. If rights are purely legal rights, then there is no higher authority and appeal to an international law would be seen to undermine the state. There would not be moral 'higher ground' from which to condemn barbaric practices in another society; and in these circumstances relationships between states would be a matter of power, might being right.

However, if one adopts a Lockean version of the social contract, then countries will subscribe to a higher moral authority in their dealings, as acknowledged in the UN Charter of Human Rights. Thus states, like citizens, would also be granted rights, such as the right to self-determination. However, another difficulty presents itself when not every state will accept the values enshrined in the code of rights. It is difficult to see how a liberal, pluralist ideal, with 'experiments in living' could operate at this level. Primacy must be given to international law rather than state law in the field of international affairs, and there may well be a tension between the two.

Further issues may also arise, when making the transition from applying moral rules to citizens, to the field of international relations. Some values, such as altruism, can be expected of individuals, but we could not expect a state to put the interests of foreign citizens before its own. Self-sacrifice could not be expected of countries.

Thirdly, we should enquire whether we can talk meaningfully about the good of a nation state. Surely this is only analysable in terms of the good of its citizens. Later we shall discuss whether a state can be a subject of rights. Yet some governments might perceive of a good which is the legitimate interest of the state, but not the current citizenship, for example a war, which entails the sacrifice of one generation for another. But in response, one could argue that is still a benefit for future individual citizens.

So, the most important aspect of the morality of nation states is that governments feel primarily obligated to their own people (internal duties) and secondly have external obligations to other countries. This promotes a self-interested attitude to international affairs. It would be a bold government that sacrificed or ignored the will of its own citizens in order to maintain foreign relations. The only solution is to make treaties which promote long-term mutual goals, so that the maintenance of a treaty can be weighed against the aspirations of the citizens. Whereas, for the individual morality may consist in overcoming self-interest, for the state it must be constitutive of self-interest.

The autonomy and independence of states rather supports, therefore, a social contract theory of international obligation.

Liberty

The classical liberal arguments for negative freedom from coercion and the encouragement of diversity, eccentricity and value pluralism look less plausible when applied to nation states. Is it possible to accommodate the resulting conflict on a grand scale, by for example allowing maverick states to develop nuclear weapons or eccentric states to condone child labour? The liberal response is to invoke natural rights or appeal to a shared conception of justice, such as the harm principle, to protect individual liberty. But the inconclusive nature of what constitutes harm is never more apparent than on an international stage. The free and open market, for example, develops into economic imperialism whereby whole cultures are annihilated, or transformed by aggressive, capitalist policies.

It would appear that liberals cannot have a neutral policy on the 'private lives' of states and the distinction between self-regarding and other-regarding actions looks precarious. The very food we eat, the clothes we wear and the fuel we burn have global consequences. The distinction between acts that 'directly' affect others and 'indirect' effects becomes increasingly blurred. Thus increased consumption of a commodity on one side of the globe produces a scarcity elsewhere; and this has ramifications for standards of living, financial policy and core, cultural values.

Yet liberals will be much more sympathetic to the free movement of people between cultures, since they foster respect for diverse values and a faith in the rationality of individuals. For conservatives, this poses much more of a problem. Conservatives stress that our identity derives from a framework of social relationships and institutional practices, and so progress and fulfilment are dependent on strong communal bonds and agreed values. Hence immigration can be viewed as a threat to these important social ties, and to our identity. An imaginative depiction of this problem is portrayed in *Practical Ethics* (Singer, 1993, Chapter 9), where after a nuclear war the residents of a nuclear shelter are debating how many of those still outside, at risk of radiation, should be let in.

Think about

Do people in your own country have a prior moral claim on you, rather than foreigners? Are you duty bound to help people of your own country before other peoples, if both are suffering equally?

Synoptic link

AQA AS Philosophy Chapter 5, Why should I be moral?, p86.

AQA Examiner's tip

Be prepared in Part (a) questions to explain and illustrate how conceptions of freedom, rights and justice pose problems when applied to nation states.

Think about

- The issue of extreme cultures is ever present. Should we allow the Taliban to treat women as they do; or communist states to forbid public religion; or tribes to practise cannibalism, polygamy etc.? How far should other states intervene to stop these practices?
- Look up this thought experiment, and decide for yourself what you would do, if you were in the shelter.

Think about

Here are some of the interests, which he mentions. Can you add to them? Do they help resolve the issue?

The interest

- of the refugee not to be persecuted or killed
- of the community not to lose jobs
- of people to live with others who share the same values
- of the community to have an effective, welfare programme
- of the world to avoid distressful situations
- of the abandoned country not to lose its citizens.

Think about

What problems might these rights cause, if granted to nation states?

- The right to self-determination.
- The right to self-defence.
- The right to protection of the law without discrimination.
- The right to a fair and public trial.
- The right to equal pay for equal work.
- The right of citizens to free movement within a country and abroad.

Synoptic link

AQA AS Philosophy Chapter 5, Why should I be moral?, p63.

The morally superior option, at first glance, would be the humane one of allowing people who are persecuted and in danger to enter into the community, but according to the scale, this could upset the vital balance and harmony in society that conservatives favour. Allowing in a large number of culturally diverse groups could disrupt social cohesiveness. But the alternative of rejection and repatriation ignores the common humanity that should exist between people everywhere, and elevates cultural homogeneity above multicultural dynamism. To solve this dilemma, some have made a dubious distinction between political refugees (fleeing from persecution), and economic refugees (fleeing from poverty and famine) and accepted in only the former. Is this a defensible policy?

This issue of the free movement of people faces problems both from a deontological, and a teleological approach. The former might take the form of an appeal to human rights, but as we shall see in the next section, rights can often conflict. Singer summarises 'an equal considerations of interests' that could be satisfied.

His conclusion is that countries should continue to take refugees, until the balance of interests has 'swung against a further increase'; and on 'present assessment', 'there is no objective evidence to show that doubling the refugee intake would cause (us) any harm whatsoever'.

Rights

The previous problems regarding freedom might be resolved by appeal to rights. Can states have rights?

If rights are purely legal, and not moral, then there is no basis for an international law that regulates the behaviour of states themselves. So treaties could be broken if it was expedient and world order rests on the inherent instability of enlightened self-interest. The scenario of the social contract as described by Hobbes would portray the situation accurately, except that there would be no Leviathan to ensure all parties adhered to the agreement.

International law therefore necessitates a shared basis for moral agreement, as enshrined in the UN Charter of Human Rights. These rights are universal and inalienable. From a positive view they protect vulnerable states from manipulation and conquest and defend minority cultures from interference. For all the countries who have signed up, they provide an objective moral framework to regulate and judge the behaviour of governments around the world. Thus the European Court of Justice can put on trial leaders accused of genocide or waging unjust wars etc. So international agreement on rights are an example of a real contract based on real consent, and illustrate Locke's model of autonomous, rational individuals entering into an agreement to mutual cooperation for the benefit of justice and order.

However, the problems identified with rights appear on a magnified scale in international relations:

- they promote individualism at the possible expense of cooperation, for example reckless consumption of resources
- rights often conflict and are not a coherent package, e.g. the right to self-defence and the right to freedom from fear
- human rights increase the likelihood of war because they provide a moral case to wage 'a just war'

- rights are largely political and do not protect against economic imperialism
- rights are ideological and reflect the existing power relations and so conflict with other religions and cultures.

Can a state have rights?

The assumption so far is that a state can be a subject of rights, in the same way as individuals. We do talk of 'crimes against the state' or of 'serving the community'. However, it is claimed that the state is merely a collective term for the individuals that compose it, or the people in government. So that when we talk of the rights of the nation state, we actually mean the rights of the infinitely complex jumble of individuals and groups that make up a nation. There is no clear rational interest that a state has, over and above its citizens, which could be the subject of rights.

Yet, on the other hand, if one uses the analogy of the state to a body, then the welfare of the whole body is more important than any of the parts, so one might argue that the body has rights over it security and welfare, which take priority over individuals. The state as a body can have rights, as the source of order, common welfare and harmonious civilised life.

Liberals will disagree. The metaphor of a body is a misleading analogy, they will argue. The state apparatus is nothing more or less than the will of groups of individuals. To award the state itself rights is to mask a despotism, which is the complete antithesis of the very rationale of human rights: to protect people from tyranny and to justly mediate in disputes between individuals.

Nevertheless, while it may be difficult or undesirable to apply rights to states, yet ultimately states are the protectors of rights for their citizens, and it is argued their role is crucial. Rights are not just enacted by declaring them in a UN charter. They have to be implemented by public policy and government action. If nation states are undermined, then the rights of citizens will be undermined too. It is within a nation that most people have a sense of belonging and conduct their business. So it is in the interests of human rights and for democracy to work, that nation states are supported by the rest of the international community.

Justice

Could nation states operate behind a veil of ignorance and choose the same principles of justice as individuals? While Rawls could expect individuals to discount personal talents and preferences, could the same be expected of nation states – that they ignore their cultural and geographical situation?

In this context, it might seem unrealistic to expect wealthy countries, rich in natural resources, to 'maximise the minimum', and for inequalities to be permitted only for the benefit of all nations. It makes the veil of ignorance seem increasingly impractical if people would be expected to ignore their nationality and cultural heritage when deciding on international law. What information would be left on which to base a decision? Remember also, that for a nation state that is self-sufficient, it would be feasible to stay outside the contract since nations, unlike individuals, could be independent and self-supporting.

> **Think about**
>
> Could the liberty principle and the difference principle proposed by Rawls be applied to nation states?

Yet the need for international justice is clear if we are to solve worldwide problems such as refugees, declining resources and so on. In fact, is the nation state part of the problem, when it seeks parochial and narrow self-interest? Two views will be presented, the first arguing for nation states, and the second against.

For the nation state

Conservative commentators usually defend the role of the nation state (Scruton, 2004).

In *The Need for Nations* (2004), Scruton argues that transcending nations states would lead to unaccountable bureaucracy and totalitarianism by distant supranational bodies. The more international law we have to conform to, the more difficult it is for law to reflect local traditions and to incorporate local checks and balances. Law must be bound up with a feeling of membership, and the larger the organisation (such as the European Community) the more difficult it is to feel part of the club. The law will then appear to represent 'them' and not 'us'.

Also, the law makers of international bodies will be far less accountable to ordinary people and so more difficult to remove. Scruton asks, 'Who will check the international lawmakers?', 'How could we repeal a law passed by the United Nations if it did not work for us?' The result will be an authority that is remote, undemocratic and far less responsive to the needs of the citizens.

So it is possible to defend the role of the nation state in determining justice for its people. Attempts to replace it will result in laws from outside the community being imposed from a source that is not necessarily impartial and infallible. We cannot rationally design a perfect world, so laws will just appear despotic. Here we have the traditional conservative scepticism of political theory. Instead, the way forward is with pacts and alliances between nations that are proven to work and stand the test of time.

Against the nation state

Many socialists would present an opposite point of view. Superpower politics rather lends credence to the Marxist theory of justice, that relationships between states are determined by the relative stage of the productive, economic means. Industrial production and commerce define the state and these interests are asserted in foreign policy, international relations and international law.

> The relations of different nations among themselves depend upon the extent to which each has developed its productive forces.'

Marx (1970)

Thus the bourgeoisie of each nation try to pursue their separate interests. This results in agreements between themselves and also exploitation of less developed nations, in the same way that the proletariat has been exploited. So, for example, cheap labour is used in other countries to maintain the economic interests of the most developed. Hence, it is an illusion that international law and justice are based on anything but the will of the international bourgeoisie.

However, as capitalism develops, those separate national interests will be overtaken by the development of 'big industry' and 'world history', when, 'all civilised nations and every individual member of them [is] dependent for the satisfaction of their wants on the whole world'. So

Think about

Would you prefer to be a 'citizen of the world' with free access across the globe, and ruled by the United Nations? You could abolish all state boundaries and allow people to live where they wished!

with the rise of global capitalism and international corporations, the individuality of nation states will disappear, and across the world, 'all natural relationships' will become 'money relationships', and life for the worker everywhere will become unbearable.

So justice will only be achieved when a collective, communist consciousness that transcends national boundaries creates a revolution, 'ridding itself of all the muck of ages'. Thus traditionally, communists have transcended the nation state and looked beyond to a time when 'workers of the world unite'. While the future is unclear, most commentators recognise some of the negative effects of rampant global consumption, as resources are depleted, and groups of workers feel powerless as their futures are decided thousands of miles away. Even national governments, have to negotiate now with 'big industry'.

While many may have sympathy with the criticisms of capitalism, the Marxist predictions may not convince. The following points are largely derived from *Contemporary Political Philosophy* (Kymlicka, 1990), where they are developed in much more detail:

- Marxists have traditionally opposed the free market. But then how are people going to be held responsible for their choices. If we waste our private lives in frivolous pleasure while another nation industriously uses their time in extra work, in the market this is registered as extra income. There must be some way to call nations to account for their choices.

- It is impossible to redistribute income to compensate fully for natural disadvantages. It is difficult on a personal level to fully equalise the circumstances of a severely handicapped person, but how could we compensate a country for infertile or Siberian conditions? Some peoples will never attain the fully realised ideal of the liberated worker.

- Marx has a 'perfectionist' theory of 'distinctive human excellence' – the human capacity for freely, creative, cooperative production. Now Marx argues that this will be achieved by abolition of the free market and division of labour. But how could such a planned economy work on such a huge, worldwide scale? The coordination would be impossible.

Marxists claim that revolution and war is inevitable and legitimate because of the goals of justice and freedom. So, the final aspect of justice is to consider whether it is possible to wage a just war.

Aquinas – the just war

Thomas Aquinas argues that a just war is permissible. The sovereign is God's representative on earth, which gives him moral authority to resist invasion and punish wrong doers. At all times, war can only be justified by doing good, but this can be both defensive (self-protection), and offensive (to establish and protect God's law). He sets out, however, three strict conditions:

1 The war must be waged by the legitimate sovereign and therefore moral authority (and not bandits), and only if redress cannot be gained by more peaceful methods.

2 There must be a sufficient cause, to right a wrong or prevent a wrong, such as to rescue the weak and needy from the wicked.

3 There must be a right intention, to promote good, with the object of securing a just peace. So there must not be gratuitous or excessive cruelty, but a proportionate response to rectify injustice.

Key philosophers

Saint Thomas Aquinas (c. 1225–74): Catholic priest and philosopher, generally held to be the greatest of the Scholastics; hence the sobriquet 'Angelic Doctor'. Enormously influential, he is generally credited with the introduction of Aristotelian philosophy into Christian theology.

The last point covers not only the morality of war, but how it should be conducted.

This theory may cause some uneasiness, as it could be used by any ideology. It is sufficiently vague to defend religious intolerance and ideological imperialism. Furthermore, as with any deontological decision, how does one resolve a clash of duties, say to uphold God's law and to respect and sustain God's creation.

On the other hand, it provides a clear criticism of empire building and the appropriation of resources and land, summed up in the grim joke, 'when the missionaries came, we had the land and they had the bibles. When the missionaries left, we had the bibles and they had the land'.

Rawls and the just war

In *A Theory of Justice*, it is suggested that the just principles derived from his 'original position' applies to nations as well as peoples, and also to war. So independent peoples have equal rights under the liberty principle, such as self-defence. The aim must be to secure a peace that is more just and preferable to the peace before the war.

So the conclusions are that natural interests defined behind the veil of ignorance are not best served by war and the only valid motive is to secure justice. It is not valid to go to war for world power or economic gain, but for rights, freedoms and basic equalities. Conduct in war should not degenerate into contempt for human life, since that contravenes the very basis of the contract, and conscientious objections should be permitted on the grounds that war is unjust.

Many of these principles would be regarded as acceptable, but two issues will be mentioned here, both focusing on the original contract and whether it will do the job that Rawls requires.

First, war can often be about deeply held beliefs that may not be accommodated by the liberal and tolerant ethos that Rawls believes would be impartially chosen. The 'most extensive liberties' would presumably include religious freedom and diversity, yet strongly principled cultures are occasionally mutually incompatible. Rawls argues that behind the veil, people will know that they have convictions, but do not know what those convictions are, therefore they will choose tolerance. By refusing to allow participants to know their religious beliefs, it could be suggested that Rawls has avoided the problem, not solved it.

Secondly, the weakness of the original position is that it is binding for all time. But as society develops, it may come to regret or wish to modify a decision made in ignorance. Rawls contends that the original principles are just and therefore cannot be altered, but their impartiality is born of ignorance. Once people develop lifestyles and allegiances, then impartiality is no longer valued. The liberal value of religious tolerance is itself just a value, which societies may wish to deny, for all sorts of reasons.

Marx

According to a scientific reading of Marx, the revolution is inevitable. He claims that, in history, whenever there is an increase in population, which determines a need for a new means of production to satisfy the increased demands of people, then war and conquest has been the result. Any political or moral justification has been manufactured to hide the real economic drive to expand because of 'the growth of wants'.

Synoptic link

AQA AS Philosophy Chapter 3, Why should I be governed?, p118.

Hence war has been a result of 'the struggle for trade', which fuelled the colonisation of newly discovered lands, which in time created animosity. These 'collisions in history' are but the precursor to the main class war (revolution) between the alienated proletariat and the demands of big industry.

This of course is not only a scientific thesis, it is a moral one. When Marx criticises philosophy because 'the philosophers have only interpreted the world, in various ways; the point is to change it' he betrays his aim of moral action to improve society.

As a scientific thesis, it can be challenged by alternative empirical data. A more compassionate capitalism has developed, and technical innovation has raised living standards for many workers, and those who remain exploited are in disparate countries, so that it may be difficult to generate a sense of unity and common cause. It is also possible that the dominant classes could just continue to manufacture consent successfully.

Heywood, in *Political Ideas and Concepts* (1994), also queries whether it is economic factors alone that cause revolutions. His assessment of various examples is that they are more likely to be caused, either when an unpopular power looks weak or releases its grip, or the expectations of a people, created by the government are not satisfied. In neither scenario, therefore, would revolutionary war be inevitable.

☑ *After working through this topic, you should:*

- understand various problems concerned with international justice
- be able to discuss how states should regard the liberty of other states and foreign citizens
- be able to explore whether a theory of rights is applicable to nations
- understand what some philosophers mean by a just war
- be able to contrast several different positions about war.

■ Think about

With regard to the moral position, previous arguments in this section should be referred to. Can you construct a moral case for not supporting revolutionary violence?

■ Synoptic link

AQA AS Philosophy Chapter 5, Why should I be governed?, p170.

 **Examiner's tip**

Try to present a balanced view, with points on both sides, on the question of just wars.

■ Summary questions

1. Assess the arguments of individuals who justify a refusal to obey the state.
2. Can it ever be right to restrict personal freedoms? Discuss.
3. Assess the view that liberalism attaches too much importance to individual liberty at the expense of other values.
4. Is the goal of distributive justice compatible with protecting individual liberties and rights?
5. Discuss the view that we possess inalienable rights.

■ Further reading

- ▨ Jung, C., *Wild Swans*, Anchor, 1992. A very revealing biography of life in Communist China under Chairman Mao.
- ▨ Orwell, G., *1984* and *Animal Farm*, Harcourt, 2003. Provide insightful views on political organisation and freedom.
- ▨ MacIntyre, A., *After Virtue*, University of Notre Dame Press, 1981. Presents the morality of war in Chapter 2 in an interesting way.
- ▨ Maslin, K., Woodfin, R., Johnson, S., Thompson, M. and Jackson, R., *Understanding Philosophy for A2*, Nelson Thornes, 2005. Has a chapter on Political Philosophy.
- ▨ Morton, A., *Philosophy in Practice*, Blackwell, 1996. Offers useful exercises and is a stimulating approach.
- ▨ Warburton, N., *Philosophy: The Basics*, Routledge, 1999. Contains a brief lucid account of many issues in the chapter 'Politics' as well as 'Philosophy: Basic Readings'.
- ▨ **www.nationstates.net** Inspired by Max Barry's novel *Jennifer Government*, 'Nation States is a free nation simulation game. Build a nation and run it according to your own warped political ideals'.
- ▨ There is a set of five BBC videos entitled 'The State we're in' which is presented by well-known comedians and takes a comic perspective on human rights in Britain today.

■ References

Aristotle, *The Politics*, Penguin, 1962.

Bentham, J., *An Introduction to Principles of Morals and Legislation*, edited by W. Harrison, Blackwell, 1948.

Berlin, Sir I., 'Two Concepts of Liberty', reproduced in A. Quinton (ed.), *Political Philosophy*, Oxford University Press, 1967.

Burke, E., *On Government, Politics and Society*, edited by B.W. Hill, Fontana, 1975.

Dworkin, R., *Taking Rights Seriously*, Duckworth, 1977.

Gaus, G.F., *Political Concepts and Themes*, Westview Press, 2000.

Hare, R., *Moral Thinking*, Oxford University Press, 1981.

Hart, H., 'Are There any Natural Rights?', reproduced in A. Quinton (ed.), *Political Philosophy*, Oxford University Press, 1967.

Heywood, A., *Political Ideas and Concepts*, Macmillan, 1994.

Hobbes, T., *Leviathan*, Penguin Classics, 1982.

Kant, I., 'Groundwork of the Metaphysic of Morals' in H.J. Paton, *The Moral Law*, Hutchinson, 1972.

Kropotkin, P., 'Law and Authority', reproduced in M. Palmer, *Moral Problems*, Lutterworth, 1991.

Kymlicka, W., *Contemporary Political Philosophy*, Oxford University Press, 1990.

Locke, J., *Two Treatises of Government*, Cambridge University Press, 1960.

MacIntyre, A., *After Virtue*, University of Notre Dame Press, 1981.

Marx, K., *The German Ideology*, Lawrence and Wishart, 1970.

Mill, J.S., *On Liberty*, Penguin Books, 1985.

Mill, J.S., *Utilitarianism, Liberty and Representative Government*, edited by A. Lindsay, Dent and Sons, 1968.

Nozick, R., *Anarchy, State and Utopia*, Basic Books, 1974.

Paine, T., *The Thomas Paine Reader*, edited by M. Foot, Penguin, 1987.

Pappas, N., *Plato and the Republic*, Routledge, 1995.

Pinchin, C., *Issues in Philosophy*, Palgrave Macmillan, 2004.

Plato, *The Republic*, Penguin, 1955.

Quinton, A. (ed.), *Political Philosophy*, Oxford University Press, 1967.

Rawls, J., *A Theory of Justice*, Oxford University Press, 1999.

Rousseau, J.J., *The Social Contract*, Penguin, 1968.

Scruton, R., *The Need for Nations*, Civitas, 2004.

Singer, P., *Practical Ethics*, Cambridge University Press, 1993.

Spencer, H., *The Principles of Ethics*, edited by T. Machan, Liberty Classics, 1982.

Wolf, J., *An Introduction to Political Philosophy*, Oxford University Press, 1996.

3   Epistemology and metaphysics

Key terms

Nihilism: nothing is true or worthwhile, therefore there is nothing to seriously care about.

AQA Examiner's tip

As we shall see, philosophical scepticism is a rigorous and carefully thought out position. In the exam it is important to distinguish it from the more everyday sceptical attitude.

The challenge of scepticism and a 'theory of knowledge'

Think of an assertion of knowledge as claiming a right. Having this right allows you to insist upon the truth of your assertion. Others can defer to your right or otherwise they can dispute it. The process of arbitrating between claims and counter-claims is the business of those in authority within a particular discipline or mode of enquiry. In a biology class, Angus asserts that photosynthesis is a method used by film-makers to superimpose one picture on top of another. Mary denies Angus's claim. Arbitrating, Mrs Mather asserts her authority as the biology teacher and upholds Mary's refusal to accept Angus's assertion: he must withdraw his assertion because his claim is false. Challenging one another in this way is not scepticism, even if Mary is sceptical about the legitimacy of Angus's claim. Neither is appealing to the authority of Mrs Mather part of the substance of a philosophical 'theory of knowledge'; even if such a theory might, at a distance, sanction her right to arbitrate on matters of knowledge. Scepticism and theories of knowledge are abstractions, hovering over the ground level disputes that occur between claimants. Scepticism calls into question whether we really have any rights at all: a 'theory of knowledge' tries to secure those rights absolutely, against the challenge of the **nihilist**.

Still, both sceptic and theorist see themselves as providing a comprehensive diagnosis of what is taking place on the ground: and this analysis will have implications. Such an analysis should transform our understanding of the process we are engaging in when we dispute knowledge. Perhaps the sceptic will realise that our knowledge 'rights' are merely wilful self-assertions. Or the theorist will fathom how to distinguish between the genuine and the sham; as they have identified what possessing genuine knowledge requires. And both scepticism and theory will insist they are motivated by a common feature in our everyday discourse about knowledge: the requirement that claimants should be able to justify their authority. Suppose I assert 'all emeralds are green' and it is true that all emeralds are green. Both sceptic and theorist agree that upon challenge, unless I can justify my claim by providing better reasons for believing 'all emeralds are green' than believing 'not all emeralds are green', then my claim lacks the proper assurance to qualify as knowledge. So the would-be knower is obliged to give reasons justifying their claim against the broad assault of scepticism.

Infinite regress?

Either the authority of a claim to know is derived from the legitimacy of another claim, or the authority of the assertion is unconditional: self-endorsing. Consider the first option. Mary claims that 'photosynthesis is the process in green plants and certain other organisms by which carbohydrates are synthesised from carbon dioxide and water using light as an energy source'. Angus is impressed and asks her how she knows this. Mary points to her text book. The authority of Mary's claim is derived from the legitimacy of another claim: a claim made in her biology text book; the authority of the claims made in the text book depends upon the authority of the scientific experiments and theory referred to by the text. Now suppose all claims were like this, so that determining the legitimacy of any claim always required appealing to some other claim for justification. If so, the authority of all claims would be conditional; having the form 'if … is legitimate then … is legitimate'. As such, whether an assertion of knowledge was legitimate would always 'depend'. Notice that merely being 'derived from …' is not sufficient to sanction genuine authority. Consider a would-be king: unless his ancestors were established as rightful rulers, his claim to the throne will remain uncertain, even if the line of descent is indisputable. At some point not just the derivation, but the credentials of the founder need to be established. A sceptic sees this, and so challenges the theorist to verify the founding authority upon which all other claims derive their legitimacy. So it appears that some judgements must be intrinsically authoritative if any judgements are to have absolute, rather than merely conditional, authority.

At this point the sceptic and theorist can both agree: if our claims to know are to have any authority then that authority must be derived from what is self-evident, or at least, beyond reproach: justification terminates or else 'I know' is merely usurpation. What would be the consequences if knowledge claims lacked proper authorisation? We want to be able to distinguish between judgements that merely reflect the prejudice, whim and partial understanding of some individual or community from those judgements that are open-minded, consistent with the facts and comprehensive enough to secure the agreement of any rational assessor. Judgements of the latter kind have objectivity about them, lacked by judgements of the former kind. Whereas the former kind of judgement appears to reflect the merely subjective point of view of the individual or community making the judgement, objective judgement is such that it captures the truth about mind-independent reality. Unless we have reason to believe we can capture reality as it is in itself, purging our claims of subjective elements, then it looks as if objectivity is impossible. If objectivity is impossible then prejudice, whim and partial understanding is all we have. Consider Nietzsche's observation:

> whichever interpretation prevails at a given time is a function of power and not truth.

Nietzsche (2000)

Derivation?

So only if the authority of the would-be king's claim is derived from an intrinsically authoritative source shall we be obliged to defer to his claim: and so no wonder a would-be king appeals to a 'divine right'. Descartes is equally ambitious: the authority of any claim to know is ultimately sanctioned by God. Derivation by blood ensures genuine royalty, so what is the equivalent with knowledge?

We derive conclusions by making **inferences**. Think of an inference as a guarantee. Some guarantees are unqualified: 'I promise to pay you £5'. If I make a genuine promise then I ought not, under any circumstances, fail to deliver. Likewise, a **deductively** valid argument is unqualified: it is impossible for the premises to be true and the conclusion false. No new information can degrade the validity of a deductive argument. That's what it is to be a valid deductive argument: logic studies the various forms such arguments can take. In contrast, other kinds of guarantees are qualified *all things being equal*; 'I'll do my best to

Think about

What does the expression 'intrinsically authoritative judgement' mean? Are any of your judgements 'intrinsically authoritative'?

Synoptic link

AQA A2 Philosophy Chapter 10, Philosophical problems in Nietzsche. This can be found at **www.nelsonthornes.com/aqagce**

Think about

How does Nietzsche's suspicion express doubts about the 'objectivity' of judgement?

Synoptic link

AQA AS Philosophy Chapter 1, Reason and experience, pp18–9.

Key terms

Inference: drawing a conclusion from supporting reasons or evidence.

Deduction: a form of reasoning that begins from general propositions. The opposite of induction, which begins from particular cases.

be there at 4pm'. A qualified guarantee can, by its very nature, be compromised; circumstance can defeat the obligation (cf. 'Sorry I was late, I had to finish writing this chapter'). Likewise, the introduction of new information compromises all non-deductive (i.e. inductive) arguments. So, inductive arguments are, by their very nature, the kinds of arguments where the premises cannot guarantee the conclusion without fail because, it might turn out, not all things are as equal as they seem. This becomes clear if we consider a familiar kind of inductive argument. Mrs Mather refers to Mary's previous performance as evidence justifying her estimation of Mary's final grade. She recalls that all the essays produced by Mary so far are 'A' grade essays: from this evidence Mrs Mather draws the conclusion that Mary will continue to produce 'A' grade answers when dealing with like questions in the exam and she estimates accordingly. The conclusion is, on the basis of this evidence, justified. But what if, unbeknownst to Mrs Mather, Mary employs a private tutor. If Mrs Mather had this information then she would assess the situation differently: in Mary's case, doing an exam question is not like doing an essay at home. So unlike deductive inferences, inductive inferences are vulnerable to the possibility of new information changing our appreciation of circumstances.

Why does this matter? The sceptic doubts whether we can legitimately claim to know. First, the sceptic can ask for the original credentials of this claimed authority: unless it is somewhere grounded in self-evident truth any claim to know must remain, at best, provisional. So there must be self-evident truths if there is genuine knowledge. Second, even if there are known self-evident truths, our inferences might fail to guarantee that their authority is preserved as it transfers throughout the lineage: our justifying inferences might not be truth guaranteeing: they might be inductive. The theorist will respond to the challenge of scepticism by insisting on (a) the self-endorsing warrant of some self-evident claims and (b) the provenance of those derivative claims inferred from the self-evident. Let's consider both (a) and (b).

(a) Self-evidence

For both sceptics and theorists alike, not only material things or public occurrences are 'evidence': the philosophical sense of 'evidence' also signifies what is evident or manifest to me as a conscious subject; and so the objects of my awareness also count as evidence. In this intimate sense, it is evident that, for instance, I am seeing these words on the page, that I hear a boiling kettle and that the air feels cold. What counts as 'evident' here, is having certain kinds of experiences. What do we mean by self-evident truth? A self-evident truth is known to be true independently of the truth of any other proposition or evidence; and the idea that it might not be true is, in one way or another, absurd. Think about the following example of a self-evident truth:

> 'I am presently experiencing seeing, feeling and hearing a computer keyboard'.

The truth of the proposition is conclusively verified, so not subject to any further confirmation, just by having the experience. For now, let's grant that this assertion is self-evident and ask: what can be derived from this kind of experiential 'evidence'?

(b) Under-determination of the inference by the evidence

Looking at the keys, sensing their resistance and hearing them click, I don't believe merely that I am experiencing a keyboard: I also believe that there is now, was before, and there will be for some time after, *this* keyboard, which I happen to be experiencing now as I type these words. My present experience is the self-evident foundation from which I make an inference to the independent existence of the keyboard. Hume puts it like this:

> we always suppose an external universe, which depends not on our perception, but would exist, though we and every creature were absent or annihilated ... This very table, which we see white, and which we feel hard ... preserves its existence uniform and entire, independent of the situation of intelligent beings, who perceive or contemplate it.

Hume (1975)

What kind of supposition is it? Assuming it is an inference, is it deductive or inductive? As we said, the mark of deductive validity is that it is impossible for the premises to be true and the conclusion false. If how things appear might not be how they are in reality, the inference from experience to what is independent of experience cannot be deductive and so must be inductive. Examples of illusions or hallucinations are instances where experience fails to lead to what there is; there is a misalignment between how things appear and reality. The inference that I make from the self-evident (e.g. 'the stick looks bent and so therefore it is') is undermined because of the introduction of new information which has led me to revise my appreciation of the circumstances ('the stick is submerged in water'). Because appearances do not yield necessary truths about reality, the inference from experience to what is independent of experience must be inductive. Once this is admitted, the sceptic can apply a powerful strategy:

1 Show that there are alternative, mutually incompatible, inferences that can be drawn from the very same self-evident premises, all of which are equally compatible with that evidence.

2 Show that there is no reason to prefer one particular conclusion over another.

The following application of this kind of argument in a familiar context should make this strategy clear and indicate its implications. Suppose you are accused of stealing money. The accuser reasons that whoever stole the money was in the room when it was stolen: you were in the room when it was stolen; therefore you stole the money. Certainly, the evidence is compatible with you stealing the money: you were in the room when the money was stolen and whoever stole the money was in the room when it was stolen. Hence the inference 'you stole the money' is compatible with the facts. What is your defence? If there were 23 people in the room besides you, then on the basis of the evidence regarding 'who was in the room' there is no reason to prefer the conclusion 'you stole the money' over 'Angus stole the money', 'Mary stole the money', 'Mrs Mather stole the money' and so on. The accuser's case is degraded by the admission of information about the number of people in the room. As such, you haven't got a case to answer – and neither does Angus, Mary or Mrs Mather. In a court, the judge would dismiss an accusation like this as a waste of everybody's time. Likewise, unless our inferences from the evidence of experience are any more determinate, we ought to dismiss any attempt to make a case as a waste of everybody's time. Let's apply the strategy.

Think about

What would it be like to believe that among everything you could imagine being the case no particular scenario is any more credible than another? Imagine trying to write a story about a person who 'believed' this: what would that person be like?

■ Synoptic link

AQA AS Philosophy Chapter 2, Knowledge of the external world, p30; AQA A2 Philosophy Chapter 9, Philosophical problems in Descartes. This can be found at www.nelsonthornes.com/aqagce

■ Key terms

Veridical: a veridical experience is a non-illusory experience which accurately captures reality.

■ The external universe

Unless there are conclusive signs that distinguish experience that is merely dreamt from experience that reliably makes contact with reality, how can I insist that having *this* experience, now, is sufficient evidence for concluding that I am in contact with reality? Descartes reflects:

> How often have I dreamt that I was in these familiar circumstances, that I was dressed, and occupied this place by the fire, when I was lying undressed in bed? At the present moment, however, I certainly look upon this paper with eyes wide awake; the head which I now move is not asleep; I extend this hand consciously and with express purpose, and I perceive it; the occurrences in sleep are not so distinct as all this. But I cannot forget that, at other times I have been deceived in sleep by similar illusions; and, attentively considering those cases, I perceive so clearly that there exist no certain marks by which the state of waking can ever be distinguished from sleep, that I feel greatly astonished; and in amazement I almost persuade myself that I am now dreaming.

Descartes (1968)

Like Descartes, we have all had an experience which appeared **veridical** as it occurred to us, which subsequently turned out to be a dream. Admitting this, our current experience is equally compatible with inferring either 'I am awake' or 'I am dreaming one of those very realistic dreams again': and there seems to be no reason to prefer one option rather than another; it would *seem* real either way.

As I dream, I do not simply misjudge particular aspects of my perceptual experience. Rather, when dreaming, the totality of my awareness is absorbed, unbeknownst to me, in falsehood. Suppose I dream that I was talking to you on the phone. In this case, whatever caused my experience of 'talking to you on the phone' it was not that I was talking to you on the phone – because I was not. Dreaming invites the possibility that what causes and sustains my attention might be different from what I think it is. The neurosurgeon Penfield recounts the case of a young woman suffering from epilepsy:

> ...who complained of seizures that were ushered in by hearing a song, a lullaby her mother had often sung to her... At operation, when the posterior portion of the superior convolution of the right temporal lobe was stimulated, she gave a little exclamation. Then after the electrode had been withdrawn she said 'I had a dream. I wasn't here'. After talking with her for a little while, the electrode was reapplied at the same point without her knowledge. She broke off suddenly and said 'I hear people coming in'. Then she added, 'I hear music now, a funny little piece'. The electrode was kept in place and she became more talkative, saying that the music she was hearing was something she had heard on the radio.

Penfield (1958)

Taking the perspective of the surgeon, we can see that the cause of the experience (stimulation by electrode of the posterior portion of the superior convolution of the right temporal lobe) is nothing like the effect it produces in her consciousness, the objects of her attention (hearing the music and the people coming in). Now consider this possibility: from the outside Penfield can see I am a brain in a vat; even if on the inside it *appears* to me totally otherwise:

> You do not know that you are not a brain suspended in a vat full of liquid in a laboratory and wired to a computer which is feeding you your

current experiences under the control of some ingenious technician/ scientist … For if you were such a brain, then, provided that the scientist is successful, nothing in your experience could possibly reveal that you were; for your experience is ex hypothesi identical with that of something which is not a brain in a vat. Since you have only your own experience to appeal to, and that experience is the same in either situation, nothing can reveal to you which situation is the actual one.

Dancy (1985)

So unless I have decisive reason for rejecting the sceptical possibility that I am a brain in a vat, I cannot *know* I am not a brain in a vat: at best I only *feel* certain I am not.

Still, we might insist that even in the brain in the vat scenario there is an 'external universe'. First, notice that I need not infer this 'external universe' is material. Descartes contemplates the possibility that the totality of my 'ideas' are products sustained by either divine or demonic immaterial intervention. But must there be something apart from my thought? What if my consciousness is merely a brute fact and all I experience is an aspect of me: like a spider weaving its web out of itself?

So I can infer from my current experience mutually incompatible conclusions, all equally compatible with the evidence: there is an external universe that is more or less as it appears; there is a material external universe unlike its appearance; there is an immaterial external universe unlike its appearance; there is no reality apart from my experience. On the basis of the evidence, how would you choose between them? If you cannot, then there is no worthwhile case to be made for accepting one option instead of another.

Universal structures: confirming generalisations

Experiential evidence is not just evidence for the existence or occurrence of particular things. Also, we generalise on the basis of our experience. For instance, after repeatedly seeing emeralds and noticing they are green, I not only believe that these particular emeralds are green; I conclude that 'all emeralds are green'. Although I do reason like this, should I? Hume points out that even if generalising from the particular has worked on some occasions (all those occasions I have applied the procedure until now) it does not follow that generalising will always work. Anyway, an argument justifying the method of generalising from the particular on the grounds that sometimes generalising inferences prove trustworthy, simply argues in a circle: the inference is a generalisation. So we have no way of legitimising our inductive inferences and cannot therefore insist that this is how we should go on: only, we can say this is what we do.

Suppose we permit inductive generalisations. All the available evidence underdetermines which generalisation ought to be extrapolated from the data: the data cannot promise a unique interpretation. Suppose Mrs Mather sends Angus out to confirm the hypothesis that 'all emeralds are green'. Angus returns with his confirming data: emeralds that are green. Mrs Mather then asks Mary to consider whether that same data confirms the hypothesis that 'all emeralds are grue'. The teacher explains to Mary that an emerald is 'grue' if she observes it prior to 2030 AD and it is green, or it is an emerald that she has not observed, and is blue. Mary then carefully observes the emeralds. Angus and Mary consider the same data: and it turns out all the data confirming the hypothesis that 'all emeralds are green' confirms the hypothesis that 'all emeralds are grue'. Every emerald that Angus identifies as green, Mary identifies as

> **Think about**
>
> What would someone mean if they asserted '"I am not a brain in a vat" expresses a subjective judgement'? What would be required to show that the judgement is objective?

> **Think about**
>
> If you don't know you are not a brain in a vat, then what else don't you know? Are all judgements ultimately 'subjective'?

grue. But emeralds being green and emeralds being grue are incompatible generalisations (because the former, unlike the latter, excludes the possibility of emeralds being blue). So we have a case of mutually inconsistent conclusions inferred from the same confirming evidence and no obvious way of deciding between rivals. How things appear does not validate, more or less, a unique interpretation of how things are.

Still, both Angus and Mary take it for granted that when Mrs Mather sends Angus out to confirm the hypothesis 'all emeralds are green' that Angus ought to find out about the colour of emeralds and not the colour of his tee-shirt: the color of Angus's tee-shirt is irrelevant. Consider a paradox identified by Hempel (1965). Notice that 'all emeralds are green' entails the prediction that whatever is not green is not an emerald. This implies that the observation of a yellow tee-shirt, a pink hat or a blue coat is relevant evidence confirming the generalisation 'all emeralds are green'. From a logical point of view, any generalisation that is compatible with the facts is confirmed by all the facts; because whatever is consistent with that generalisation is inductive support for it.

Hence, all the facts are evidence for whatever generalisation is consistent with those facts 'green' or 'grue': no wonder that the data cannot validate, more or less, a unique interpretation of how things are. This logical perspective appears to render the practice of gathering 'relevant supporting evidence' obscure: the fact that my car is blue is as much evidence for 'all ravens are black' as the fact that *this* raven is black. Suppose we persist with our everyday intuitions about relevant confirming evidence: if those intuitions are not sanctioned by logic, then what guides our judgement? Again, it seems that all we can say is this is what we do, without assurance that we should. But the sceptic's challenge demands a justification establishing the authority of our judgements, not a confirmation that such judgements are made.

Unless we have reason to believe that some claims and not others are genuinely authoritative then we will have no method for discriminating among competing claims. It could be that all claims to know ultimately 'depend' and we have no effective rational procedure for preferring one claim over another. It could be that all our claims lack 'objectivity': they merely express subjective responses to a reality the nature of which lies beyond our reach. Meynell sums up the predicament scepticism leaves us in as follows:

> We will either be left in a chaos of conflicting and arbitrary opinion, since on this account all opinions are equally well- or ill-founded; or we will have to resort to propaganda, coercion or whatever to secure agreement.

Meynell (1984)

How can scepticism be rebutted? Are there self-evident truths and can we derive from those truths, other truths that are uniquely preferable from among the alternatives? Do some judgements at least attain the status of 'objectivity' so that they may be, in Kant's phrase, 'presupposed to be valid for all men' (Kant, 2004). We shall compare three different thinkers trying to respond to the challenge of scepticism by tackling the self-evident, the nature of inference and the objectivity of judgement.

Think about

What makes evidence relevant?
What does 'relevant' mean?

Hume: mitigated scepticism

Hume restricts the self-evident to what we grasp by intellectual intuition or demonstration; and the ideas immediately occurring in consciousness, derived from preceding sense impressions. First, consider intuition and demonstration. We know by *intuition* that 'where there is no property there can be no injustice … [once we have defined] … the terms and explain injustice to be a violation of property' (Hume, 1975). We know by *demonstration* whenever we use our intuitive understanding to demonstrate something that 'cannot be known … without a train of reasoning and enquiry' (Hume, 1975).

For example, we demonstrate geometrical truths like the square of the hypotenuse is equal to the sum of the squares of the other two sides. Although these truths are self-evident, their function is limited. They regulate what is *necessary* (I cannot imagine things being otherwise) and what is *possible* (I can imagine things being otherwise). It turns out that this kind of self-evidence is just a case of definition (If that is how you define your terms then …) or some kind of logical-mathematical entailment (the axioms of geometry) which I 'intuit' by grasping the appropriate relations between ideas. Such self-evidence is consequently restricted to the realm of ideas and their necessary and possible relations: therefore, intuitions regarding *relations of ideas* cannot disclose truths about a reality independent of ideas. Only experience can be any sort of guide to reality: the impressions we receive through the senses. These particular sense impressions are directly known in conscious experience. Here Hume's scepticism presents experience as a guide to an independently existing reality: and then argues that for all we know, experience leads us astray. Intuition cannot determine what is; only what might be, and what might be is, for all we know, anything that is possible. As we have seen, Hume is sceptical about induction because nothing known intuitively, by reason, implies that anything is more or less probable: because anything possible follows logically from any particular idea or impression. So it appears that apart from what is known to be occurring or to have occurred in consciousness, I know nothing. Hume's scepticism is devastating.

But according to Hume, we should not fear that scepticism will 'ever undermine the reasonings of common life, and carry its doubts so far as to destroy all action, as well as speculation'. He contrasts the impasse of scepticism with the practical business of leading lives, interacting with the world and engaging in commerce with others: everyday experience. In this familiar context, scepticism cannot get a grip. The fantastic scenarios dreamt up by scepticism are not impossible; they only serve to remind us that our beliefs are engaged with experience, not philosophical abstractions. And so, the apparition of sceptical doubt dissolves:

> These principles may flourish and triumph in the schools; where it is, indeed, difficult, if not impossible, to refute them. But as soon as they leave the shade, and by the presence of the real objects, which actuate our passions and sentiments, are put in opposition to the more powerful principles of our nature, they vanish like smoke, and leave the most determined sceptic in the same condition as other mortals.

Hume (1975)

So scepticism is mitigated, or qualified, by our response to the actuality of experience. Although scepticism is unable to undermine our everyday assurance and conviction, Hume believes that it can be employed as a

Synoptic link

AQA AS Philosophy Chapter 2, Knowledge of the external world, pp19–21; AQA A2 Philosophy Chapter 6, Philosophical problems in Hume. This can be found at **www.nelsonthornes.com/aqagce**

AQA Examiner's tip

While the unit devoted to Hume does not focus particularly on his scepticism, demonstrating an awareness of the issues in this module should help you gain synoptic marks in the exam.

counterweight to the abstractions of metaphysics and the pretensions of reason: our instinctive disbelief when contemplating scepticism indicates the folly of contemplating a reality unlike familiar experience; or scepticism is a caution against calling into doubt our common sense maxims. Rather, we should confine our enquiries to the familiar sphere of common life and accept, more or less, its verdicts. This has implications for the practice and limitations of philosophy:

> philosophical decisions are nothing but the reflections of common life, methodized and corrected. But they will never be tempted to go beyond common life, so long as they consider the imperfection of those faculties which they employ, their narrow reach, and their inaccurate operations. While we cannot give a satisfactory reason, why we believe, after a thousand experiments, that a stone will fall, or fire burn; can we ever satisfy ourselves concerning any determination, which we may form, with regard to the origin of worlds, and the situation of nature, from, and to eternity?

Hume (1975)

The sceptic's possibilities are too remote: scepticism has no impact on belief. Hume's response is insightful: the unbelievable devastation of scepticism ought to make us suspicious of the reasoning generating it. However, rather than revise that reasoning, Hume draws the conclusion that reason plays no part in our factual inferences from self-evident occurrences in consciousness. Rather what regulates our belief and makes scepticism so unbelievable is a purely natural mechanism. Hume's **naturalistic** account of belief has the following features. First, it is reductive in the sense that it understands belief as nothing but a natural process. The sceptic cannot really deny

> the existence of body, tho' he cannot pretend by any arguments of philosophy to maintain its veracity. Nature has not left this to his choice, and has doubtless esteem'd it an affair of too great importance to be trusted to our uncertain reasonings and speculations.

Hume (1975)

And like the rest of us the sceptic is equally prone to the belief that apparent patterns disclose general principles or laws. As we carry out our business we rely on this disposition:

> When I throw a piece of dry wood into a fire, my mind is immediately carried to conceive, that it augments, not extinguishes the flame. This transition of thought from the cause to the effect proceeds not from reason. It derives its origin altogether from custom and experience.

Hume (1975)

The second feature of Hume's naturalism recommends that the best method for studying belief is to adopt the approach of the natural sciences. He hopes his own theorising will resemble the other sciences in all important respects, as he aims to uncover 'the secret springs and principles by which the human mind is actuated in its operation' (Hume, 2000). As far as Hume is concerned, human nature is subject to the same 'laws and forces by which the revolutions of the planets are governed and directed' (Hume, 2000).

So he uncovers the mechanisms which lead me to believe the wood will burn. What generates our inductive inferences and generalisations turns out to be merely the goal directed functioning of our natural sensitivity

Key terms

Naturalism: a philosophical position claiming that the world can be fully understood in scientific terms without recourse to metaphysics or theology.

toward patterns we see, hear, touch, taste, smell or introspect. By psychological association, repetition and a disposition to form habits, 'expectations' that like patterns will more or less repeat in the future are subsequently mechanically generated; just as it is with other animals:

> animals as well as men learn many things from experience, and infer, that the same events will always follow from the same causes … it is impossible that this inference of the animal can be founded in any process of argument or reasoning … Animals, therefore, are not guided in these inferences by reasoning: Neither are children: Neither are the generality of mankind, in their ordinary actions and conclusions: Neither are philosophers themselves, who, in all the active parts of life, are in the main, the same with the vulgar, and are governed by the same maxims.
>
> *Hume (1975)*

Humans form beliefs using the same devices as other animals: human belief is a natural, as opposed to a rational, phenomenon. According to Hume, a belief is a distinctive feeling accompanying an idea. Consider Angus thinking about the colour of emeralds. Angus is aware he 'believes' all emeralds are green because this idea is the liveliest among merely 'imagining' blue emeralds or only 'conjecturing' emeralds are grue or just 'guessing' emeralds are *this* colour. As we consciously weigh up our thoughts, belief stands out as:

> A LIVELY IDEA RELATED TO OR ASSOCIATED WITH A PRESENT IMPRESSION.
>
> *Hume (2000)*

So the belief that the sun will rise tomorrow is wrought immovable by the frequency of previous experience: Angus believes all emeralds are green because the emeralds he has so far seen have been green. This is how it strikes him.

Assessment of mitigated scepticism

We shall now consider whether Hume's response to the challenge of scepticism is adequate. In particular, we shall focus on whether the resources Hume affords us to meet that challenge are either immune to the sceptic's doubts or too restricted to provide a satisfactory account of human rationality, so conceding too much to the sceptic regarding the objectivity of judgement.

Circularity

Consider the criticism that you cannot explain what is wrong with scepticism by referring to the inevitable disbelief that emerges from our human nature: because doing so assumes what the sceptic doubts; the truth of naturalism. **Husserl** thinks that that such a response to the challenge of scepticism must beg the question:

> To expect from natural science itself the solution … is to be involved in a vicious circle.
>
> *Husserl (1965)*

The sceptic is asking for credentials legitimising the claims we make; and that includes the credentials of naturalism. So a response to scepticism cannot invoke the authority of the natural sciences in order to authorise its own claims. Many 19th-century successors thought that Hume's

> ### Think about
>
> Do beliefs form automatically? Do they vary in conviction depending on the intensity or frequency of the originating experiences that form them? If belief is a function of a natural mechanism does that make belief 'subjective' or 'objective'?

> ### Key philosophers
>
> **Edmund Husserl (1859–1938):** Austrian philosopher who did important work in the philosophy of logic and mathematics, but is best known as the founder of modern phenomenology. Husserl's influence upon philosophy is particularly notable.

attempt to reconcile a radical scepticism with a fondness for naturalistic explanations was a **reductio ad absurdum** of his kind of empiricism.

A favourable interpretation of Hume's appeal to naturalism sees him as recognising that we can never rule out the possibility of scepticism without presupposing that some standards are authoritative. We suppose that the standards employed by the natural sciences and used in common sense reasoning are authoritative. In this way, Hume's naturalistic explanation of our belief is presented to the sceptic with irony:

> See this, if you will, as the beginning of the **postmodern** recognition that theory always proceeds from an 'embedded' location, that there is no transcendent spot from which we can inspect our own theorizing.

Anthony (2008)

Belief and responsibility

Consider the criticism that even if we grant a naturalistic explanation for disbelief in scepticism, the force of scepticism is unaffected. Hume's naturalistic account of belief is non-volitional: we just believe as we do. If our beliefs are determined by natural processes and that is all there is to it then the sceptic will be happy to conclude we have no reasons, and could have no effective reasons, for believing anything we believe. Hume appears to imply that because we cannot help but believe that there is an external universe behaving in a uniform way, then it is a mistake to ask whether we ought to believe this. As such, talk about what ought to be believed looks a sham. If I cannot help breathing oxygen it is not clear what sense an imperative 'you ought to breathe oxygen' could have.

Certainly, the beliefs we have regarding our immediate perceptions are characteristically received rather than volunteered. Nevertheless, there are reasons for thinking belief formation can be subject to the will. I could refuse to consider evidence as relevant, I could attend to certain features over others, I could prefer to evaluate the evidence according to one set of criteria or another, I could suspend my judgement awaiting further evidence, I could choose when to stop or renew the investigation, or I could deceive myself. As such, it appears as if psychologically, belief formation can be subject to the will.

Consider the issue from a logical or conceptual perspective. We discriminate between responsible and irresponsible belief. According to Kant, Hume's fundamental misunderstanding is his failure to recognise that our beliefs are essentially normative; in as much as they derive their content and status from being regulated by rational principles. For instance, to count as a believer I not only feel an expectation when confronted by fire that it will burn: instead, I recognise that the source of heat is 'fire' and understand that whatever is 'fire' will accord with principles of universal causality such that 'fire burns'. Being a believer involves acknowledging that reason demands I believe 'fire will burn' and this involves grasping binding universal concepts: in this case, the concept of 'fire'. A person who does not acknowledge the guiding principles of reason, expressed through the application of binding universal concepts, is not a 'believer' but merely a mechanism. According to Kant, our capacity to be guided by binding universal concepts and accord with rational principles is a mark of 'objective' thought in contrast to subjective response. Such objective thought is accountable; other rational agents can require I make it clear why I reason as I do. In fact, that is just what the sceptic demands. For Kant, objective judgement expresses the freedom of being a rational agent responsible for their belief. The idea that following rules is expressive of freedom might sound paradoxical. However, is the student who recognises 2 + 2 must equal 4 more or less free than a 'random calculator' which might produce any number of possible 'solutions'?

Here's one way of focusing on this issue: think about Hume's advice that 'a wise man proportions his belief to the evidence' (Hume, 1975). This seems like a rational maxim discriminating between what is and what is not responsible belief. On what basis can Hume offer this advice? Chisholm is clear that Hume's scepticism:

> leaves us completely in the dark so far as concerns what **reason** he may have for adopting this particular criterion rather than some other.

Chisholm (1982)

Hume insists that this is what the wise do, whereas Kant insists that this is how you should judge if you are to qualify as wise, because that is what being 'wise' requires of rational free agents.

Rationality and human practice

Consider the overarching criticism that Hume's conception of rationality is too narrow. The operation of reason is limited to the regulation of relations between ideas. As such, reason permits sceptical possibilities (they are imaginable) and reason has no grounds for ruling against their actuality. Hume's scepticism is inseparable from his restrictions on what counts as legitimate reasoning. Should we accept Hume's restrictions? Consider the following suggestions as applications of legitimate reasoning:

- reasoning in conformity with the laws of deductive logic
- calculating mathematically
- understanding conceptual and linguistic relations
- extrapolating and testing generalisations
- assessing probabilities
- deferring to authoritative judgement
- adjusting means to ends
- choosing our goals
- accepting and acting on the commands of law
- conforming to the traditions of the community
- trusting our friends' advice.

Only the first three exemplify anything like Hume's relations of ideas. If there were other ways of being rational, unavailable on Hume's analysis, there might be other possible strategies for defeating the challenge of scepticism. It is worth thinking about the proper context for analysing notions like 'inference', 'reason', 'belief' and 'knowledge'. Hume's naturalism assumes that these notions are natural phenomena and can be appropriately understood by the natural sciences. However, according to **Brandom**, a distinction needs to be made between discursive creatures like us:

> subject to distinctively conceptual norms, from their non-concept-using ancestors and cousins. Conceptual norms are brought into play by social linguistic practices of giving and asking for reasons, of assessing the propriety of claims and inferences. Products of social interactions (in a strict sense that distinguishes them merely from features of populations) are not studied by the **natural** sciences – though they are not for that reason to be treated as spooky or

Think about

How does Hume's account of belief impact on the value of doing philosophy?

Key philosophers

Robert Brandom (b. 1950): American philosopher who mainly works in the fields of philosophy of language and philosophy of mind. Often regarded as a modern pragmatist, Brandom's theory of inferential role semantics is heavily indebted to Wittgenstein.

supernatural. In conferring conceptual content on performances, states, and expressions suitably caught up in them, those practices institute a realm of **culture** that rests on, but goes beyond, the background of reliable differential responsive dispositions and their exercise characteristic of merely natural creatures. Once concept use is on the scene, a distinction opens up between things that have **natures** and things that have **histories**. Physical things such as electrons and aromatic compounds would be paradigmatic of the first class, while cultural formations such as English Romantic poetry and uses of the terms 'nature' and 'natural' would be paradigmatic of the second.

Brandom (2003)

Although Hume is keen to stress the relation between belief and action, he presents thinking as the product of instinct, custom and habit:

which teaches a man to avoid the fire; as much as that, which teaches a bird, with such exactness, the art of incubation, and the whole economy and order of its nursery.

Hume (1975)

Still, although we might describe the bird's behaviour as intelligent, the intelligence of the bird is not much like the sort of ordinary intelligence we display on a day-to-day basis. **Ryle** brings out this distinction:

What is involved in our descriptions of people knowing how to make and appreciate jokes, to talk grammatically, to play chess, to fish or to argue? Part of what is meant is that, when they perform these operations, they tend to perform them well, i.e. correctly or efficiently or successfully. Their performances come up to certain standards, or satisfy certain criteria. But this is not enough. The well-regulated clock keeps good time and the well-drilled circus seal performs its tricks flawlessly, yet we do not call them 'intelligent'. We reserve this title for the persons responsible for their performances. To be intelligent is not merely to satisfy criteria but to apply them; to regulate one's actions and not merely to be well-regulated. A person's performance is described as careful or skilful, if in his operations he is ready to detect and correct lapses, to repeat and improve upon success, to profit from the examples of others and so forth. He applies criteria in performing critically, that is, in trying to get things right.

Ryle (2000)

Key philosophers

Gilbert Ryle (1900–76): English ordinary language philosopher; best known for his attack on Cartesian dualism in *The Concept of Mind*.

Think about

Do dogs have beliefs? What kinds of beliefs might they have? Are they like your beliefs more or less?

Key philosophers

J.L. Austin (1911–60): English philosopher of language best known for his speech act theory as laid out in *How to Do Things with Words*.

The social dimension of thought

Brandom and Ryle emphasise the social or cultural context in which we make inferences, form and express beliefs, justify and assess our conclusions and assert knowledge claims. Hume, however, assumes that the workings of human understanding unfold in the mind of the individual, regarding human understanding as essentially normative and cultural, and recommends we unpack epistemological concepts in the same way other essentially normative and cultural concepts are analysed. For instance, **Austin** draws a parallel between epistemological and moral and legal ways of talking. To assert 'I know' is, according to Austin, to assert one's credentials, obliging me to provide legitimate reasons, warranting others to trust me and claim things are as I say. Austin develops a comparison between knowing and promising:

When I have said only that I am sure, and prove to have been mistaken, I am not liable to be rounded on by others in the same way as when I have said 'I know'. I am sure **for my part**, you can take it or leave it: accept it if you think I'm an acute and careful person, that's your responsibility. But I don't know 'for my part', and when I say 'I know' I don't mean you can take it or leave it (though of course you **can** take it or leave it). In the same way, when I say I fully intend to, I do so for my part, and according as you think highly or poorly of my resolution and chances, you will elect to act on it or not to act on it: but if I say I promise, you are **entitled** to act on it, whether or not you choose to do so. If I have said I know or I promise, you insult me in a special way by refusing to accept it. We all feel the very great difference between saying even 'I'm absolutely sure' and saying 'I know': it is like the difference between saying even 'I firmly and irrevocably intend' and 'I promise'.

Austin (1961)

Think about

Is 'knowing' something you do in your head?

Objectivity

An implication of Hume's scepticism regarding the 'external universe' is that we cannot think objectively about the world. If objective judgement is targeted to a reality beyond our reach then we cannot think objectively; at least, we cannot tell we are making objective judgements. What if we think about 'objectivity' differently? Instead, what if we think of 'objective' thought as being able to judge according to rational principles which bind all thinkers whenever they consider those 'objects of thought' a particular kind of judgement is directed towards. Such judgement would need to be warranted, cohere with other related judgements, accord with accepted practice and be communicable to others. In this way, an objective judgement just is a judgement that is accountable to the principles of rationality.

According to Brandom, this sort of perspective suggests a way of theorising knowledge:

The natural world does not come with commitments and entitlements in it; they are products of human activity. In particular, they are creatures of the **attitudes** of taking, treating, or responding to someone in practice as committed or entitled (for instance, to various further performances). Mastering this sort of norm-instituting social practice is a kind of practical know-how.

Brandom (1998)

The sceptic will doubt whether our 'rational practices' are as rational as we believe. That implies that the sceptic has some way of making sense of the idea that how I think about reality might not be the way reality is. If we could close the gap between appearance and reality then that strategy will not be open to the sceptic.

■ Ayer: phenomenalism

Hume argues that inferential relations between distinct matters of fact are always only contingent. Hume also takes it for granted that the relation between experience and reality ought to be understood as a relation between distinct matters of fact: I am presently experiencing a keyboard; and then there is the independent fact which needs establishing that there is a keyboard I am experiencing. As Hume puts it, no experience ever entails a 'double existence'. Because the

Synoptic link

AQA A2 Philosophy Chapter 6, Philosophical problems in Hume; AQA A2 Philosophy Chapter 10, Philosophical problems in Nietzsche, pp167–169. These references can be found at **www.nelsonthornes.com/aqagce**

Key philosophers

George Berkeley (1685–1753):
Irish empiricist philosopher and priest. Bishop of Cloyne from 1734. Berkeley was an empiricist best known for his idealism.

Synoptic link

AQA AS Philosophy Chapter 2, Knowledge of the external world, pp55–7.

relation between experience and perceiver-independent reality is merely contingent anything possible could, logically, be the case. But what if we understood the relation between experience and reality differently? According to Ayer, **Berkeley's** great insight is recognising how the relation between experience and material objects ought to be conceived another way:

> What he denied was the adequacy of Locke's analysis of the notion of a material thing. He maintained that to say of various 'ideas of sensation' that they belonged to a single material thing was not, as Locke thought, to say that they were related to a single unobservable underlying 'somewhat', but rather that they stood in certain relations to one another... what Berkeley discovered was that material things must be definable in terms of sense content.

Ayer (2001)

If material things must be definable in terms of sense content how does that defeat scepticism? Asserting 'there is a table here' does not imply a double existence: there being both the experience of the table and the material table besides. Rather, 'there is a table here' only implies that if anyone were in my situation then they would have a series of sensations, or become aware of sense-content which the sign 'table' picks out. As such, my experience of a table is not evidence that there might be some further thing, the material table, lurking unobserved behind the experience. Instead, my experience of the table is what 'table' refers to: so experience must be sufficient justification for claiming 'there is a table here'.

Why must material things be definable in terms of sense content? Suppose we think of a material thing like a table as the unobservable independent 'somewhat' that might or might not be the origin of my present experience. If so, asserting 'there is a table here' asserts the existence of an unobservable entity. This contravenes Ayer's verification principle:

> We say that a sentence is factually significant to any given person, if, and only if, he knows how to verify the proposition which it purports to express – that is, if he knows what observations would lead him, under certain conditions, to accept the proposition as being true, or reject it as being false.

Ayer (2001)

Examiner's tip

It is important to remember that when Ayer talks about 'nonsense' he is not simply being abusive: he literally means that the propositions in question convey no meaning.

Because the sceptic insists that we are never in a position to decide whether an experience verifies the truth of the proposition 'there is a table here', the proposition 'there is a table here' is unverifiable. The verification principle appeals to the plausible intuition that propositions describing how things are ought to be settled, one way or another, by some evidence. The kind of scepticism that denies we are ever in a position to know reality beyond experience appears meaningless:

> anyone who condemns the sensible world as a world of mere appearance, as opposed to reality, is saying something which, according to our criterion of significance, is literally non-sensical.

Ayer (2001)

So we must be able to know reality if we can talk about 'reality' at all. We might wonder whether the verification principle gives a convincing account of what we mean when we talk about material objects. As Guignon puts it:

It seems clear that our ordinary claims to know things about the external world carry more weight than is contained in propositions about the data present to consciousness or propositions about the constituting activity of consciousness. Theories of language that attempt to buttress such views of meaning usually seem cooked up for this special purpose.

Guignon (1983)

Guignon insists that normally, when I say 'there is a table here' I do not mean that if anyone were in my situation then they would have a series of sensations, or become aware of sense-content which the sign 'table' picks out. But Ayer admits this. Nevertheless, 'table' refers to one and the same as the sense-content listed. Regardless of anything else it might be associated with, 'table' must be cashed out in terms of sensory elements I am acquainted with or would be acquainted with were I to experience a table. What are these sensory elements I might be acquainted with? Consider briefly what Russell says:

> Thus in the presence of my table I am acquainted with the sense-data that make up the appearance of my table – its colour, shape, hardness, smoothness, etc; all these are things of which I am immediately conscious when I am seeing and touching my table … I know the colour perfectly and completely when I see it, and no further knowledge of it itself is even theoretically possible.

Russell (2001)

According to Ayer's phenomenalism, asserting that some material object exists is not proposing the existence of an entity of an **ontologically** different kind from that with which we are directly acquainted in sensation. Rather, to say a material object exists is to assert a truth about actual or possible experiences. Resemblance and continuity are the features by which we individuate appropriately related clusters of sense-content so that we can pick them out with statements which refer to discrete particular material things. Propositions asserting the existence of material objects are referentially equivalent to propositions asserting that subjects would have certain sequences of sensations were they to have certain others: they come to the same. As Ayer puts it, physical objects are logical constructions out of sense content:

> What gives one the right to believe in the existence of a certain material thing is simply the fact that one has certain sensations: for, whether one realizes it or not, to say that the thing exists is equivalent to saying that such and such sensations are obtainable.

Ayer (2001)

If reference to material objects is just reference to sense content then what does the distinction between veridical experience and non-veridical experience comprise? I am currently experiencing 'there is a table, here' and I have to judge whether there really is a table or whether there just appears to be a table: perhaps I am hallucinating. According to Ayer, particular misperceptions are corrected by reference to experience in general: that is what the distinction between veridical and non-veridical experience amounts to. The following analogy might help: I can know that in a particular episode Homer Simpson is acting out of character; because the character of Homer Simpson in this episode does not

Synoptic link

AQA AS Philosophy Chapter 2, Knowledge of the external world, pp37–9.

Think about

How is sense-data supposed to be self-evident?

Key terms

Ontology: the branch of metaphysics concerned with questions about what there is; with what sort of entities exist.

resemble or is not continuous with the character Homer Simpson in the other episodes; this is not established by checking the cartoon character against a cartoon-independent 'real' Homer Simpson. Likewise, this table is like no other table I have experienced: I can put my hands through it as it walks across the room. As such, I am hallucinating.

Phenomenalism advances a reductive solution to the possibility of scepticism; as reality is exhausted by what is in principle knowable. But Ayer will point out that on his account it makes sense to talk about material objects enduring independently of experience, just as long as there is the potential that such yet-to-be-had experiences might become the subject-matter of propositions that can in principle be verified. Our inductive inferences are merely predictions from experienced patterns to patterns we have not experienced. Still, in principle, our inferences deal in the kinds of things we might experience, because they are about sense-content. How does Ayer defend the propriety of such inductive inferences? He thinks the problem of induction ought to be viewed as:

> a fictitious problem, since all genuine problems are at least theoretically capable of being solved ... We are entitled to have faith in our procedure just so long as it does the work which it is designed to do – that is, enables us to predict future experience, and so to control our environment. Of course, the fact that a certain form of procedure has always been successful in practice affords no logical guarantee that it will continue to be so. But then it is a mistake to demand a guarantee where it is logically impossible to obtain one. This does not mean that it is irrational to expect future experience to conform to the past. For when we come to define 'rationality' we shall find that for us 'being rational' entails being guided in a particular fashion by past experience.
>
> *Ayer (2001)*

Asking if the inductive method is rational is rather like asking if the entries in the dictionary are spelled right: the dictionary defines right spelling and being a good speller just means spelling according to the dictionary. Using dictionaries is a useful way of standardising spelling and aiding communication. Notice that Ayer's conception of what is rational is broader than Hume's scepticism permits.

> We trust the methods of contemporary science because they have been successful in practice. If in the future we were to adopt different methods, then beliefs which are now rational might become irrational from the standpoint of these new methods. But the fact that this is possible has no bearing on the fact that these beliefs are rational now.
>
> *Ayer (2001)*

Ayer admits there is no transcending standpoint from which the rationality of induction will be assured, but he thinks that making inductive inferences proportional to the available evidence is both permissible and advisable from where he is now. Consider permissibility: the sceptic demands a guarantee, but that demand is impossible because as a matter of logic, no generalisation can be guaranteed by a limited amount of data. Therefore, the sceptic's demand is nonsense and so has no force. Consider advisability: we can see induction works whereas flipping a coin has proved less reliable; a person who is guided by coin flipping rather than past experience is, from our standpoint, irrational.

Assessment of phenomenalism

Does phenomenalism provide a convincing response to the challenge of scepticism? The verification principle appeared to rule out the possibility that 'reality is unknowable' by clarifying the limits of what we can understand and know. As such, Ayer's response takes the form of what Kant called a *transcendental argument*. Kant explains that such an argument 'is occupied not so much with objects as with our mode of cognition of objects, so far as this is possible *a priori*' (Kant, 2004).

A transcendental argument does not appeal to metaphysical facts that go beyond experience: the transcendent. Ayer denies such appeal makes sense. What is transcending about a transcendental argument like Ayer's is that it makes explicit the necessary conditions for the possibility of intelligibility in general.

The verification principle

But does the verification principle succeed in doing this? Ayer admits that the status of the verification principle is open to doubt and he recommends it as a 'methodological principle'. Why should we adopt it? One argument in its favour is that it would allow us to meet the challenge of scepticism. What are the costs? If we take the principle at face value and limit our knowledge claims to the observable then we not only rule out scepticism, but also among other things, the possibility of historical knowledge. Scientists and historians assert claims about events which occurred either long before there were any observers witnessing those events (e.g. the Big Bang) or before any of us were around to witness those events (e.g. the fall of the Roman Empire). According to the verification principle, if these claims are meaningful then they have to be verifiable by actual or possible experience. As time travel is not an option, the only observations that could verify a historical claim are present or future experiences. Unless we take the implausible view that, on analysis, accounts of the Big Bang or the fall of the Roman Empire are really just about present or future experience (e.g. data about background radiation or interpretations of documents and artefacts we presently possess) the retrospective claims of the scientist and historian are meaningless. So the verification principle restricts our conception of reality within very narrow limits.

Realism and objectivity

As we said, Ayer's response to scepticism insists that reality is exhausted by what is in principle knowable: the 'idea' of a verification transcendent truth is not an idea at all. Consider Nagel's opposite stance: understanding the project of objective enquiry conflicts with any attempt to reduce reality to the limits of what we can comprehend:

> In pursuing objectivity we alter our relation to the world, increasing the correctness of certain of our representations of it by compensating for the peculiarities of our point of view. But the world is in a strong sense independent of our possible representations, and may well extend beyond them. This has implications both for what objectivity achieves when it is successful and for the possible limits of what it can achieve. Its aim and sole rationale is to increase our grasp of reality, but this makes no sense unless the idea of reality is not merely the idea of what can be grasped by those methods.

Nagel (1989)

If commitment to an ideal of objectivity means admitting that the truth outstrips what we are able to grasp, then scepticism is unavoidable. Scepticism and realism are two sides of the same coin.

> The search for objective knowledge, because of its commitment to a realist picture, is inescapably subject to skepticism and cannot refute it but must proceed under its shadow. Skepticism … has no solution, but to recognize that is to come as near as we can to living in the light of truth.

Nagel (1989)

Nagel's realism is a long way from Ayer's stress on working within experience.

Solipsism

■ Synoptic link

AQA AS Philosophy Chapter 2, Knowledge of the external world, pp57–9.

Another important objection is that phenomenalism only overcomes scepticism at the cost of advancing solipsism. Does my sign 'table' refer to the same as your sign 'table'? No. If 'table' refers to sense content and I cannot have your sense content as you cannot have mine, then you and I can never signify the same by 'table'. But this is just solipsism, as reality becomes identical to whatever I and only I understand reality to be. Even if solipsism is a possibility then it is hardly victory over scepticism. But in what sense does the solipsist 'know' anything? What would it be like for the solipsist to get it wrong? As Wittgenstein puts it:

> One would like to say: whatever is going to seem right to me is right. And that only means that here we can't talk about 'right'.

Wittgenstein (1998)

There is something odd about the way phenomenalism describes my epistemic situation. Is it true that I am immediately sensing visual arrays, textures, resonances, flavours and aromas occurring in consciousness out of which I construct a world of material objects? A more accurate description of my awareness would refer to the material objects I think I am experiencing and describe the qualities these material objects possess. In contrast to Ayer's private constructor, consider Dilthey's account of our shared experience of our 'life-world':

> Every square planted with trees, every room in which the seats are arranged, is intelligible to us from our infancy because human planning, arranging and valuing – common to all of us – have assigned a place to every square and every object in the room. The child grows up within the order and customs of the family which it shares with other members and its mother's orders are accepted in this context. Before it learns to talk it is already wholly immersed in that common medium.

Guignon (1983)

The space of reasons

Why assume that our knowledge of material objects must be built from resembling and continuous occurrences of sense-content? According to Sellars this prejudice is the result of confusing two distinct issues:

> The idea that there are certain inner episodes – e.g. sensations of red or of C# which can occur to human beings (and brutes) without any prior process of learning or concept formation.

Sellars (1997)

This is then taken to imply that such occurrences must be

> the necessary conditions of empirical knowledge ... providing the
> evidence for all other empirical propositions.

Sellars (1997)

This confuses the sensory context in which thoughts can refer with
the stage-setting in which thoughts make sense. How could a mere
occurrence be the basis of a claim to know anything?

If experiences play a role in authorising knowledge claims, then it is
because they can be articulated within what Sellars calls 'the logical space
of reasons':

> The essential point is that in characterising an episode or a state as that
> of **knowing**, we are not giving an empirical description of that episode
> or state; we are placing it in the logical space of reasons, of justifying
> and being able to justify what one say".

Sellars (1997)

This dimension is easily missed when focusing on individual
contemplators (the would-be knower) in relation to an object (the would-
be known); especially if this relation is conceived as unfolding for the
most part in the privacy of one's mind, or at least, inside the head.
Williams sees the situation as follows:

> As Kant made clear to us, the philosophical question is not one of simple
> fact (Where do our beliefs come from?) but one of right (What entitles
> us to hold them?). Historically, however, most philosophical discussions
> of knowledge have focused on identifying the source of knowledge ...
> Such talk encourages us to think that asking 'Does knowledge come
> from the senses?' is like asking 'Do diamonds come from South Africa?',
> whereas these questions are quite different in character.

Williams (2001)

Key philosophers

Michael Williams (b. 1947):
American philosopher whose
interests are focused on the
philosophy of language and
epistemology. Williams is
best known for his attacks
on scepticism (see Williams:
inferential contextualism).

Williams: inferential contextualism

A would-be knower makes a claim and the sceptic challenges the knower
to provide their credentials: can they justify what they claim to know?
Unless the would-be knower is able to provide these credentials then
the would-be knower has no right to assert their claim. This exchange
between would-be knower and sceptic looks familiar. Angus makes
a claim about the nature of photosynthesis and Mary challenges the
authority of that claim. However, the exchange that takes place between
Angus and Mary is nothing like the exchange between the would-be
knower and the sceptic. Ultimately, the sceptic demands a general
assurance for any claim whatsoever. In response, the theorist offers
general credentials: for instance, knowledge claims are credible to the
extent that they are derived from or substantiated by sense-experience.

Sense experience looks like a plausible candidate for self-evidence as long
as we restrict it to just that: experience. I can know that I am presently
experiencing a keyboard; nobody else is in a position to undermine first
person testimony regarding my subjective awareness. So the theorist
can appeal to a self-endorsing claim immune from sceptical doubt. The
sceptic is happy to admit this because that just focuses and dramatises
the problem: how can you justify your inferences from mere private and

partial occurrent 'experience' to public and uniform stable reality? The inferential equipment available to you is incapable of underwriting the credibility of your claims: for all you know, things might be different because any conclusion is radically underdetermined by the data. Mary can rightfully appeal to Mrs Mather for support. What can the theorist appeal to? If they appeal to the goodness of God or the authority of science then they are merely **begging the question**. Unlike the exchange in the biology class, the dispute between the sceptic and the theorist appears irresolvable. Confronted by the sceptic's challenge, the onus is on the would-be knower to justify their knowledge claims; but how? It appears that scepticism is ultimately successful and all assurance and conviction regarding the existence and nature of the external universe can only amount to a feeling or natural disposition, or a prejudice in favour of a particular way of seeing the world:

> The sceptic takes himself to have discovered, under the conditions of philosophical reflection, that knowledge of the world is impossible. But in fact, the most he has discovered is that knowledge of the world is impossible under the conditions of philosophical reflection.

Williams (1991)

Following Wittgenstein, Williams diagnoses both scepticism and the theory that tries to rebuff its challenge as forming around a misunderstanding of the grammar of 'know': on both sides there is a failure to appreciate the contexts in which 'know' is used and conferred. In particular, Williams wants to show that scepticism and theory are both allies in the same misguided debate: both assume there is a single story to be told about what 'know' means and the conditions in which it is attainable. He recommends what he calls a *deflationary* account of 'knowledge':

> A deflationary account of 'know' may show how the word is embedded in a teachable and useful linguistic practice, without supposing that 'being known to be true' denotes a property that groups propositions into a theoretically significant kind. We can have an account of the use and utility of 'know' without supposing that there is such a thing as human knowledge.

Williams (1991)

What Williams wants to reject is what he calls *epistemological realism*: the view that there really is something called knowledge that a theorist can study and a sceptic can undermine. Just as a scientist understands that boiling kettles, warming paving stones and expanding gas are instances of a single cohesive phenomenon, so

> The epistemological realist thinks of knowledge in very much the way the scientific realist thinks of heat: beneath the surface diversity there is structural unity. Not everything we call knowledge need be knowledge properly so called. But there is a way of bringing out the genuine cases into a coherent theoretical kind. By so doing – we make such things as 'knowledge of the external world' the objects of a distinctive form of theoretical investigation.

Williams (1991)

Recall Nagel's remarks about the 'pursuit of objectivity', our 'grasp of reality' and the problem of a world that transcends our 'representations'. This is high theory and, according to Williams, a red-herring. Wittgenstein has similar suspicions:

> Philosophical problems arise when language goes on holiday

Wittgenstein (1998)

He goes on to claim that the task of his philosophy 'is to bring words back from their metaphysical to their everyday use'.

In this sense, Wittgenstein and Hume both stress the place of ideas as we go about our business, but unlike Hume, Wittgenstein is not interested in anything like a theory of knowledge or a general account of the content and modes of human understanding as such, and he criticises the philosophers' 'craving for generality'. According to Wittgenstein:

> philosophers constantly see the method of science before their eyes, and are irresistibly tempted to ask and answer questions in the way science does. This tendency is the real source of metaphysics, and leads the philosopher into complete darkness.

Wittgenstein (1974)

Instead, Wittgenstein recommends that philosophers adopt a different mode of understanding: we should seek to achieve a clear view of the way words are used in context; what he calls the grammar of our concepts. As for Nagel's concerns about 'the objectivity of our representations', Wittgenstein's verdict is not favourable:

> In philosophy, all that is not gas, is grammar.

Wittgenstein (1998)

So in order to appreciate William's response to the details of scepticism and its alter-ego the 'theory of knowledge', we need to understand context and the grammar of 'know'. To begin, we have taken it for granted that when the sceptic challenges the would-be knower, the would-be knower is obliged to accept the challenge. This presupposes that 'knowing' is something you must secure a right to; by providing an adequate justification for the claims you make. The sceptic shows that, for instance, I cannot justify my claim that I am not dreaming right now, so therefore I cannot be a knower. Let's turn things around. Wright points out that:

> the impossibility of earning a warrant that one is not now dreaming does not imply that no such warrant is ever possessed.

Wright (1991)

According to Brandom, the context in which claims are made and assessed has a default and challenge structure of entitlement:

> Often when a commitment is attributed ... an entitlement is attributed as well, by default. The prima facie status of the commitment ... is not permanent or unshakeable; entitlement to an assertional commitment can be challenged. When it is appropriately challenged (when the challenger is entitled to the challenge), the effect is to void the ... authority of the corresponding assertions ... unless the asserter can vindicate the commitment by demonstrating entitlement to it.

Brandom (1998)

Think about

Is Nagel's notion of 'a view from nowhere' just gas?

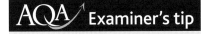

Examiner's tip

Wittgenstein's use of the word 'grammar' is wider than the accepted meaning. Rather than simply encompassing the formal rules of syntax, he means the entire network of (formal and informal) rules by which we impart meaning to language. You need to show that you aware of this point if talking about 'grammar' in the exam.

Constraints on objective inquiry

So challenging takes place in a context according to an etiquette. That context and etiquette assumes by default that my claims are justified; unless you are entitled to challenge my claim with an appropriate question. For instance, if Mrs Mather makes a claim about photosynthesis that Angus then challenges, Mrs Mather is not obliged to justify her claim: she can ask Angus to justify his doubts. Unless he can come up with some reason for questioning her authority ('I read in the Encyclopaedia of Biology that photosynthesis is…') then Mrs Mather can justifiably treat Angus's challenge as inappropriate and ignore Angus. As it stands ('Oh, I just thought I'd challenge you'), Angus is not entitled to an answer. What Williams tries to show is that this default and challenge structure constrains and undermines the intelligibility and rationality of the sceptic's doubts: such doubts are not appropriate challenges. Williams brings out five aspects of the 'stage-setting' that constrain the rational practice of assertion and denial. Throughout, the influence of Wittgenstein is clear.

Intelligibility constraint

Being entitled to challenge presupposes that your doubt is meaningful. But I can only make sense of your affirmations and denials if I assume you are right about most things in the same way that I am right about most things, that you assess the situation as I assess the situation and that you would doubt as I do and so on. But if you doubt everything or doubt without any recognisable motivation then I am not sure what it is you mean. Wittgenstein puts it like this:

> In order to make a mistake, a man must already judge in conformity with mankind … Suppose a man could not remember whether he had always had five fingers or two hands? Should we understand him? Could we be sure of understanding him? … If someone said to me that he doubted whether he had a body I should take him to be a half-wit. But I shouldn't know what it would mean to try to convince him that he had one. And if I had said something, and that had removed his doubt, I should not know why or how.

Wittgenstein (2001)

The intelligibility constraint is a general constraint on rationality: but there is an 'open texture' between sensible doubts and nonsense. The following constraints are set up variously, relative to particular context.

Methodological constraint

Being entitled to challenge presupposes that your doubt is in keeping with a particular line of inquiry. Suppose I go to hear a historian explain that documents recently discovered in eastern Turkey shed light on the development of early Christianity. In this context I can legitimately ask about the authenticity of the documents: but I am not entitled to ask the historian if she denies *this* world was produced five minutes ago by a deceiving demon. Notice that there is a close connection between intelligibility and methodological constraints. As we pursue certain lines of inquiry, some challenges shade into the unintelligible.

Dialectical constraint

Being entitled to challenge varies according to what Williams calls the dialectical environment. Consider Copernicus's challenge to the dominant geocentric view of the universe in 1543. Copernicus claimed that the sun, and not the earth, is at the centre of the universe. When he made the claim, all sorts of rational obstacles made Copernicus's heliocentric alternative appear, at best, a useful fiction: what was the earth suspended on; why couldn't we feel it move; what was so significant about the sun that God would put that at the centre of creation? However, as the model of the mechanical universe became so Copernicus's challenge now seemed perfectly reasonable. Wittgenstein puts it like this:

> I did not get my picture of the world by satisfying myself of its correctness; nor do I have it because I am satisfied of its correctness. No: it is the inherited background against which I distinguish between true and false … The propositions describing this world-picture might be part of a kind of mythology. And their role is like that of rules of a game … The mythology may change back into a state of flux, the river-bed of thoughts may shift. But I distinguish between the movement of the waters on the river-bed and the shift of the bed itself; though there is no sharp division of the one from the other.

> *Wittgenstein (2001)*

Economic constraint

Whether or not a challenge has any worth depends on the costs and benefits of making that challenge. If we gain a lot by being right and lose little by being wrong then challenges are less significant: if we lose a lot by being wrong and gain little by being right then doubts are more significant. Suppose I am doing a quiz. I can be asked as many as twenty questions over three minutes. If I know the answer to any particular question then I win £1,000 but if I get it wrong I lose 10p. If I mull over the answer to the first question, mentally eliminating every possible error, then I am not being rigorous; I am foolish. Imagine the same quiz with different stakes. If I know the answer I will be given 10p, if I get it wrong then I will be fined £1,000. Now, any possible doubt becomes extremely significant and I ought to take my time before I assert anything.

Situational constraint

The validity of a challenge varies according to the situation and our appreciation of that situation. Imagine the following: as Angus drives through the countryside he looks at the barns and comments on their authenticity. Mary challenges Angus: 'How do you know they are real barns?' Angus, justifiably, finds Mary's question difficult to make sense of. But unlike Mary, Angus has not realised that they have just driven into 'Barn Façade County'. If so, Mary's appreciation of their situation makes her question intelligible. Suppose Mary has no reason to think they are driving through 'Barn Façade County'. Unless Mary has some reason to think they are in Barn Façade County, then what sort of answer should she expect from Angus? If Mary has no reason to think they are in Barn Façade County, but it has occurred to her that it is logically possible they might be, what could Mary mean by asking 'how do you know they are real barns?' Perhaps she wants a philosophical discussion.

Think about

If Mary wants a philosophical discussion, is she really asking about the barns and Angus's knowledge of them?

The challenge of scepticism looks as if it is posing a question, but in fact it is creating a context for a theory of knowledge. How does scepticism achieve this? What is the *situation* we find ourselves in? Apart from the immediate objects of our awareness our situation is unknown to us. What about the *economics*? The costs of not knowing our situation is that reason is blind and we are unable to: discriminate appearance and reality; select the likely and relevant from the unlikely and unimportant. The sceptic's question is made *intelligible* by the theorist: I need to have an account of how consciousness connects with reality; I need to have an all-purpose guarantee making the way experience features in generalisations respectable. *Methodologically*, both sceptic and theorist agree on the line of enquiry: to discover the limits of human knowledge. And the *dialectical* environment is the history of the theory of knowledge. Outside of the theory of knowledge it is not clear scepticism poses a challenge. As Hume points out, scepticism cannot get a grip once we get on with our business. And it is not clear anything much is at stake: nobody thinks it serious enough to act on it. Whether or not consciousness connects with reality or whether there is an all-purpose guarantee making the way experience features in generalisations respectable, are not intelligible questions unless you have been especially initiated. What do the untrained make of the challenge 'how do you know you are not dreaming?' and what needs to be gone through to get them to understand the issue properly?

If this is the right analysis then scepticism and the theory of knowledge are engaged in a peculiar context of their own. It is not surprising that many of the great theorists also developed the most powerful sceptical arguments: consider Descartes, Hume and Russell. Even Berkeley and Kant were responding directly to the challenge of scepticism. Assuming that our conventions are those of default and challenge, in relation to non-philosophical contexts the consequence of the challenge posed by scepticism, even its intelligibility, is questionable. Wittgenstein says:

> When we do philosophy we are like savages, primitive people, who hear the expressions of civilised men, put a false interpretation on them, and then draw the queerest conclusions from it.

Wittgenstein (1998)

Think about

How might Wittgenstein's remark characterise the activity of the sceptic and theorist?

Assessment of inferential contextualism

Critics will respond by pointing out that Williams has only shown what Hume recognised: scepticism is peculiar. However, Hume also recognised what Williams fails to appreciate: the challenge of scepticism provides a more 'demanding context'. But Williams' point is that there is no obligation to see it this way. According to Williams, scepticism is not innocent, but rather its challenge comes with a theoretical baggage we are not obliged to take seriously. Let's briefly consider what this baggage is supposed to be and why we are not obliged to take it seriously.

Generalisations

Think about

Imagine a quiz in which you are asked 'what colour are emeralds?' A person who answers 'green' gets the point. A person who answers 'for all I know, any colour you care to imagine' does not get the point. Is it clear the latter just has more demanding epistemological standards?

Ayer's analysis of the problem of induction insists that the only context in which we assess the validity of inductive inferences is the context in which inductive inferences are made: the demand that inductive inferences conform to non-inductive styles of reasoning is nonsense. Still, Ayer looks for a general defence of induction and appeals to the utility of science as a reason for accepting the rationality of inductive thinking. Williams argues that inductive inferences need to be understood in context. In context, inductive inferences (which are, after all, just non-deductive reasons for accepting ...) can be more or less intelligible, responsible, relevant, and trustworthy.

Offering his own solution to the 'grue' hypothesis – what he calls the new riddle of induction – Goodman recognises how our reasoning is contextualised. He points out that 'All emeralds are green' is embedded or 'entrenched' in the way we understand and deal with emeralds:

interacting with emeralds and the wider environment, theory and practice have achieved a reflective equilibrium, over time. This reflective equilibrium is entrenched in the history of our observations and practices regarding emeralds, the concepts we apply to emeralds and regulate our judgements concerning them and the theories we construct that make 'being emerald' intelligible to us. Goodman is not baldly asserting that we 'know' all emeralds are green rather than 'grue' on the basis of our experience. Instead, he is challenging the sceptic to explain how the possibility that 'all emeralds are grue' could be regarded as equally rational compared to 'all emeralds are green'; where we understand being rational as encompassing more than the rules of deductive logic and including the history of our dealings with emeralds and the facts associated with them.

And Goodman's insight into embedded rationality sheds light on Hempel's paradox of confirmation. The paradox that 'anything that is consistent with a hypothesis confirms that hypothesis' need not be taken as posing a sceptical challenge. Rather we can turn the challenge on its head and see it as a *reductio ad absurdum* of the view that 'confirmation by evidence' is a merely logical, or 'syntactical', relation between data and hypothesis. Only if we understand 'confirmation' as involving entrenched meanings that make different kinds of evidence more or less relevant can we make sense of the scientists' practice of evidence gathering, theory formulation and prediction. Hempel came to the conclusion that his paradox showed

> the search for purely syntactical criteria of qualitative or quantitative confirmation presupposes that the hypotheses in question are formulated in terms that permit projection; and such terms cannot be singled out by syntactical means alone.

Hempel (1965)

The external world

Williams believes the sceptic trades on an unjustified account of the self-evident status of first person observational reports of 'appearances': the notion that even though reality might not be as it appears at least it must appear as it appears. But instead of thinking of these reports of 'mere appearances' as self-evidently authoritative, he follows Austin and Sellars in interpreting operators such as 'looks' and 'seems' as ways of distinguishing between those claims I assert unhesitatingly as a 'knower' who has rights to draw further inferences, authorising you to do likewise and so on, from claims in which I qualify my right to assert and your obligation to trust. Williams brings this out by considering three sentences in context:

- There is oil on the road.
- That liquid on the road looks like oil.
- It looks as if there is oil on the road.

He makes the following comments:

> In making the first claim, I commit myself to the correctness of everything I assert. In making the second, I introduce an element of 'qualitative looking': I commit myself to there being liquid on the road, but withhold commitment to its being oil. In the third example, the looking is 'existential': I am not committing to there being anything on the road (perhaps the road is just unusually shiny, so the appearance of oiliness is a trick of the light). The difference between qualitative

Synoptic link

AQA AS Philosophy Chapter 2, Knowledge of the external world, p30.

and existential looking is simply a matter of the scope of the 'looks' operator, the scope of determining which aspects of my claim I do and do not commit myself to.

Williams (2001)

The challenge of the sceptic contrasts appearance and reality: as if appearances were a domain of objects our conscious awareness contemplates with absolute assurance; contrasted with a world of material objects that are hidden from direct view and, for all we know, quite other than the objects of direct perception. Williams thinks there is no reason to take the sceptic's contrast seriously as it misconstrues the grammar of looks talk.

Relativism and objectivity

Synoptic link

AQA A2 Philosophy Chapter 10, Philosophical problems in Nietzsche. This can be found at **www.nelsonthornes.com/aqagce**

Key philosophers

Richard Rorty (1931–2007): American pragmatist philosopher with a wide range of interests. As controversial as he is influential, Rorty is perhaps best known for his rejection of analytic philosophy in favour of his own idiosyncratically nuanced version of continental philosophy.

Williams and Wittgenstein look as if they are saying that the notion of a 'theory of knowledge' arises out of confusion and that philosophy does not need it. Does this kind of response to scepticism leave knowledge suspended without foundations? If so, does this mean that what we 'know' is merely relative to particular contexts and that there cannot be any objective knowledge at all? Does it mean that philosophy itself is a sham: since Descartes at least, philosophy has seen itself as specifying the necessary conditions for knowing anything at all. If there are no such conditions then philosophy has no role. **Rorty** advances a kind of contextualism about knowledge and he seems to imply that what is real is merely a social construct, created by us:

there is nothing … except what we have put there ourselves, no criterion that we have not created in the course of creating a practice, no standard of rationality, that is not an appeal to such a criterion, no rigorous argumentation that is not obedience to our own conventions.

Rorty (1982)

And Rorty argues that:

Everything … is socially constructed, for no vocabulary … cuts reality at the joints. Reality has no joints. It just has descriptions.

Rorty (1998)

If reality is a social construct then there are no restrictions on what can count as reality. Various kinds of 'discourse' can create their own contexts; what is and is not rational is nothing more than what one group of 'thinkers' happen to be doing at a particular time and place, and that is all there is to it. If different groups engage in a different discourse then whether or not one 'language-game' has any bearing on another 'language-game' is a matter of the practitioners choosing to allow themselves to be moved by what each other says. As Rorty sees it, philosophy should re-invent itself as a kind of cultural commentator contributing to the 'conversation' in relatively edifying ways. Of course, other rationalities need not choose to listen and the philosophers' conversation is then just irrelevant. The philosopher has to admit that the notion of 'truth' can be replaced with whatever life-affirming criteria those engaged in the discourse find appealing or useful:

We think that there are many ways to talk about what is going on, and that none of them gets closer to the ways things are in themselves than any other … We suggest that the appearance reality distinction be dropped in favour of a distinction between less useful and more useful ways of talking … our purposes would be served best by ceasing to see truth as a deep matter, as a topic of philosophical interest, or 'true' as a term which repays 'analysis'.

Rorty (1989)

It seems that without a theory of knowledge fending off the challenge of scepticism, there can be no objective framework within which knowledge claims ought to be assessed, no way of deciding between good and bad theories. If we defeat the challenge of scepticism by abandoning a theory of knowledge then ultimately the sceptic is successful: there is no such thing as objective truth, better or worse reasons, or knowledge as opposed to mere opinion.

However, none of the sceptical implications follow from a proper understanding of Williams' contextualism, which merely points out that what we mean by objective truth and the marks by which we distinguish better or worse judgement is inseparable from an account of rational practice, or *praxis*. Scepticism and the theory of knowledge are abstracted from such praxis and, as such, have a dubious bearing on what 'knowing' involves. If the 'theory of knowledge' is a dead end it is not because scepticism and relativism have succeeded. Rather, eschewing a theory of knowledge is a corollary of coming to see that we are not obliged to take scepticism seriously. As Wittgenstein puts it:

> Where does our investigation get its importance from, since it seems only to destroy everything interesting, that is, all that is great and important (As it were all the buildings, leaving behind only bits of stone and rubble.) What we are destroying is nothing but houses of cards and we are clearing up the ground of language on which they stand …
>
> It leaves everything as it is.

Wittgenstein (1998)

> **Think about**
>
> Is Rorty saying the same thing as Nietzsche appeared to imply: 'true' obscures the fact that 'objective consensus' is just an expression of a dominant will to power?

☑ *After working through this topic, you should:*

- know why a 'theory' appears needed in order to rebuff the assault of the sceptic
- be able to assess the adequacy of mitigated scepticism
- understand the nature of belief, in relation to reason and practice and the notion of responsibility in relation to belief
- understand the link between inductive reasoning and rational practice
- understand the threat of empiricism collapsing into solipsism
- know the constraints on objective inquiry.

Metaphysics: universals and particulars

■ to grasp the way Plato understood the relation between universals and particulars and why he thought it was a significant issue

■ to grasp that Aristotle understood the relation between universals and particulars and why he thought it was a significant issue

■ to grasp why Hume believed that all general ideas are nothing but particulars.

AQA Examiner's tip

There is more material spread throughout the A-level on the issue of universals and particulars which you should be able to draw on in the exam.

■ Synoptic link

AQA A2 Philosophy Chapter 7, Philosophical problems in Plato, pp38–52.

The following account of universals in relation to particulars will contrast briefly three different responses to the issue. As we shall see, the issue reflects problems we have already been discussing. Because what 'the issue' amounts to is part of the issue, we shall concentrate on comparison rather than criticism. Begin by considering the claim 'All emeralds are green'. Both Plato and Aristotle agree that it is a fact about being an emerald that we understand and know when we grasp the truth that all emeralds are green. As such, Plato and Aristotle have been described as *realists* about universals.

■ Platonism

It is a fact that the ideal emerald is ideally green: this is the *Form* of being emerald. 'Ideal' does not imply that the Form is in anyway dependent on our ideas. Rather, a Form is ideal because it is a perfection of a kind of being (being emerald) which partakes in the perfection of Being itself: 'the Good' (the perfect Form of being emerald partakes in that which is 'Good'). To the extent that we understand 'what is', our ideas or words refer to and articulate ideals: not their inferior reflections. These ideals are not products of thought. Rather, they comprise the objective structure of reality which our thought aspires to grasp as it tries to make intelligible the world of particular events and things. As such, the Form of a particular being is a mind-independent universal that guides objective judgement. Matter which forms physical particulars, to the extent that it forms physical particulars that are emeralds, emulates the Form of being emerald. If you like, being per se has aspirations to achieve the fullness of its particular Form just as a plant grows into being the kind of plant it is. In this sense, the Form of being emerald is a universal realisation, towards which particular material emeralds progress. As such, a full understanding of the being of particulars must depend on a full understanding of the universal Form of particular kinds of being. So our grasp of the truth about what is emerald is acquired by increasingly insightful stages of conceptualising the ideal being (Form) of being emerald. Ultimately, true understanding must reflect a grasp of that which 'fully is' – the Form of the Good. Plato suggests various modes of thinking about reality, progressing from merely reflecting that a physical particular is, seeing similarities between particulars, drawing analogies, and offering generalisations and hypotheses. Whether or not these ways of thinking disclose the real contours of reality is only seen properly in the light of a proper understanding of the kind of being in question. Ultimately any genuine understanding and knowledge of emerald are derived from becoming directly intellectually acquainted with the Form of being emerald. Plato thinks truth comes in approximations as we understand further deeper degrees of reality. Grasping the Form of being emerald allows me to know that 'all emeralds are green'.

So, particulars partake in the being of the universal form which they exemplify. Ontologically, this universal Form is an ideal to which particulars aspire and particulars only achieve their fullest reality as they approximate towards this ideal: particulars, as they merely reflect their ideal form have the existential status analogous to 'shadows' and 'dreams'. Epistemologically and semantically, our ideas about reality ought to refer to mind-independent ideal Forms. To the extent that they do, we can share and enjoy sharply focused objective understanding. To the extent that our understanding fails to see beyond the multiplicity and change of the mere particular, our understanding is confused and subjective: merely reflecting how reality appears to us.

Aristotle had a great deal of sympathy with the notion that grasping real universals discloses the objective structure of reality. Aristotle's chief problem with Plato's account was that Platonism leaves the relationship between universals and the particulars that partake in these universals mysterious. Aristotle thought that it is a lot more fruitful to regard the universal as somehow inherent in the material particulars that exemplify form.

Aristotelianism

Universal essences determine the kind of being a particular being is. Our understanding seeks to grasp the universal essences instanced in particulars so that our categories, from which syllogistic deductions follow, are genuinely illuminating. As Aristotle puts it, genuine knowledge and understanding consists in recognising 'the why of it'.

What it is to be an emerald determines whether all emeralds are green. Particulars exemplify **essences** and accidents. It is of the essence of fire that it is hot, but merely accidental that one is currently occurring in my fireplace. If a property is 'of the essence' of being that particular thing then that particular thing must be that way: whatever is fire, must be hot. Likewise if all emeralds are green, it is because all emeralds share a common essence that makes them that way.

Aristotle, like Plato, thinks understanding universal Forms or essences at ever greater levels of abstraction allows us to make illuminating explanatory inferences from one categorical feature to another and from one category to a sub-category. These explanatory inferences aspire to generality and assuredness: secured by definitions and deductive orderings presented in the form of a syllogism. Unlike Plato, our understanding is not validated by appeal to a transcending reality. Rather our universal understanding is legitimated by a process of observation of the universal in the particular, the formulation of hypothetical universal deductions which are then tested for illumination by returning to the observed and seeing what light our universal explanation sheds on the particulars we observe.

Aristotle's account of universals also faces difficulties. In particular, Aristotle says that particulars share universal essences. However, what is it that they share apart from being relevantly similar in this or that way? If we are just talking about similarities between particulars, why suppose there is something else – the universal – apart from similarity between particulars? Empiricists like Hume wanted to insist that judgements about 'the general' were really judgements about particulars projected universally.

Think about

Why might Plato have thought that our grasp of the universal was not just a matter of having sense experience?

Think about

Is Aristotle's suggestion that 'kinds of things are as they are because they share an essence' just a philosophical elaboration of our common sense understanding of reality?

Synoptic link

AQA A2 Philosophy Chapter 6, Philosophical problems in Hume. This can be found at **www.nelsonthornes.com/aqagce**

Empiricism

It cannot be shown to be deductively valid from true premises that I can know all emeralds are green. Hume restricts what counts as legitimate reasoning. Flew puts it well: whatever is not deductive is defective. As such, 'the truth about emeralds', whatever that might be, cannot be that which determines that I judge 'all emeralds are green'. Instead, my judgements are determined by natural associations. My judgements do not range over 'all' of a certain type as my judgement is restricted to my limited experience; neither does my judgement penetrate the form or essence of things. Rather, my general judgements are just judgements about particulars I experience which, because of facts about human psychology, project imaginatively general features onto reality. Hume's analysis of the idea of universal causality is his classic exposition of this theory of general ideas. So, my judgement is restricted by the particular which stands for other particulars: particulars represent universal ideas. So even though it is true that I can entertain a 'universal' idea, the universal is, upon analysis, really only a particular idea ultimately derived from an experiential encounter with a particular. Ideas are always copies of particular impressions: applying a universal idea (e.g. 'green') to my ideas of 'emerald' does not involve any insight into the necessary universal properties of being emerald. Rather, applying a 'universal' idea involves entertaining a particular and associating by resemblance:

> all general ideas are nothing but particular ones, annexed to a certain term, which gives them a more extensive signification, and makes them recall upon occasion other individuals, which are similar to them.

Hume (1975)

'Green' is a universal just because when I think of a particular ideational 'object' that is green it triggers, mechanically, the thought of other 'ideational' objects that resemble '*this* particular green object' in some relevant respect:

> Thus when the term Horse is pronounced, we immediately figure to ourselves the idea of a black or a white animal, of a particular size or figure: but as that term is also applied to animals of other colours, figures and sizes, these ideas, though not actually present to the imagination, are easily recalled.

Hume (1975)

Think about

Can Hume explain how it is that particular ideas stand for and determine the universal judgements thinkers ought to make?

Nothing about my idea of the form or essence of being emerald entails anything about what *is* the case in reality: whatever *is* might not be, as I know by using my imagination and conjuring up other possibilities. Ontologically, epistemologically and semantically, universals are functions of the way particular ideas can stand for general ideas. However, our 'universal' ideas, for all we know, have no correspondence with reality, or the being of particular material things.

✔ *After working through this topic, you should:*

- be able to outline the reasons why Hume rejected Plato and Aristotle's accounts of universals and why he insisted we are only acquainted with particulars.

The analysis of knowledge

Learning objectives

- to understand claims to 'know' in relation to truth

- to understand the relation between belief and justification

- to understand the notion of 'reliabilism'.

What does an assertion require in order to qualify as an assertion of knowledge? Here we are not asking if our understanding of the world is as extensive or as assured as we tend to think, or doubting the possibility of objectivity and so on. Rather, we want to make explicit the criteria that an assertion needs to satisfy in order to achieve the status 'knowledge'. Asking this sort of question is a bit like asking 'What makes a footballer world class?' Suppose we all agree there are world class footballers. There are footballers we all agree are not world class. Also there are examples of footballers whose status we find difficult to determine. By asking the question and considering the examples we make explicit the criteria that guide our judgement. It is unlikely that any answer to this kind of question will be definitive for all possible cases, and as such we ought not to expect a comprehensive consensus. Is the question worth asking? Asking 'what makes a footballer world class?' not only makes the assessment of players more accountable and systematic, but also draws out assumptions and prejudices regarding the nature of the game itself. In this case, nobody would be tempted into thinking we are investigating a natural kind, like a scientist might investigate the atomic structure of various metals. Rather, we are exploring the conditions in which we decide to confer knowledge or deny it. No doubt what emerges from this analysis will have some bearing on the kinds of questions the sceptic asks, but an analysis of the requirements that need to be satisfied in order for a claim to be entitled 'knowledge' has to proceed by assuming that 'knowledge' is, at least sometimes, exemplified: otherwise, what is the analysis analysing? Before looking at what is called 'the standard analysis' it is worth pointing out that it is only 'standard' in the sense that it highlights a consensus that asserting what is false, judging erroneously, merely guessing or being indifferent towards our claims are not characteristics associated with knowledge claims. You do not find explicit formulations of and agreement about the standard analysis throughout the history of philosophy and Plato, who is often cited as formulating it, also offers an alternative account. So, it is a useful focus for discussion but can obscure the interesting things philosophers actually say, if it is taken to imply a standard all philosophers explicitly endorse or it is taken as a common story they are all keen to substantiate: it is not.

AQA Examiner's tip

It is important to bear in mind and demonstrate your understanding of this point if asked to write about the standard analysis in the exam.

The standard analysis

According to Ayer:

> the necessary and sufficient conditions for knowing that something is the case are first that what one is said to know is true, secondly that one be sure of it, and thirdly that one should have the right to be sure.

Ayer (1956)

So this analysis sets three conditions for knowing that: the **truth** condition, the **belief** condition and the **justification** condition.

S knows that P if and only if
i P
ii S believes that P
iii S has adequate justification or entitlement that P

Suppose Mrs Mather has lost her pen: "where's my pen?" Angus says 'I know', going into the technicians' room to bring it back. Entertaining the question, Angus thinks he remembers where the pen is. He goes into the technicians' room in the belief that the pen will be there. As a matter of fact, it is true that the pen is where he remembered it would be. His status as a knower is confirmed as he anticipated: he knew he had good reason. Mrs Mather recognises he knows what she did not: the whereabouts of the pen.

i The truth condition

Whichever way you understand 'truth', being true is a necessary condition that any assertion must satisfy if it is known. Because it is a conceptual necessity, denial results in incoherence. It is nonsense to say that 'S knows P, but P is false'. What about claims regarding fictional characters? For instance, watching television I reassure my little girl 'I know Dr Who will save the universe from oblivion' and he does. These assertions appear to be legitimate claims to knowledge, yet as nobody is Dr Who, my assertion hasn't anything to be true of. Evans proposes that with 'fictional realities', we 'connive' and treat the fictitious world as fact. In a conniving way you can know that 'Dr Who will save the universe from oblivion'

Philosophers have sometimes insisted that because knowledge requires truth, knowledge must be the product of an infallible mental process: one that leads to certainty. Socrates appears to be thinking like this when he distinguishes between the fallibility of the faculty of belief and the infallibility of the faculty of knowledge. But Ryle suggests this way of putting the issue commits a category mistake. Category mistakes occur when things or facts of one kind are presented as if they belonged to another. According to Ryle:

> the logical type or category to which a concept belongs is the set of ways in which it is logically legitimate to operate with it.

Ryle (2000)

According to Ryle, 'knowing that …' does not belong to the category of mental acts or processes: instead 'knowing that' belongs in the category of achievements with words like 'discover', 'solve', 'win'. Why might this be significant?

> The fact that doctors cannot cure unsuccessfully does not mean that they are infallible doctors; it only means that there is a contradiction in saying that a treatment which has succeeded has not succeeded.

Ryle (2000)

So the fact that assertions of knowledge cannot be false does not mean that such assertions are infallible; it only means that there is a contradiction in saying that an assertion of truth is false. Knowing is no more a unique infallible act or process for acquiring truth than 'curing' is an unique infallible act or process that acquires health for the remedied.

ii The belief condition

Belief looks like a necessary condition for knowledge. As Grayling puts it:

> It seems right to expect that if S knows that P, then … S must not merely wonder whether or hope that P is the case, but must have a positive epistemic attitude to it: S must believe that it is true.

Grayling (2002)

Synoptic link

AQA A2 Philosophy Chapter 1, Philosophy of mind, p19.

There might be instances in which it makes sense to say that a person believes something, even though the knower claims that they do not believe what they are supposed to know. For instance, we can imagine circumstances, say a verbal exam, in which a subject is so stressed that they insist that they cannot recall answers to the questions they are asked; nevertheless they proceed with the exam and all their answers are correct. If we know that they have prepared for the exam and that their answers are true then we will say they know the answers; even if they claim they do not believe anything they have just said is correct. What should we make of this kind of case? It shows that you do not always have to consciously affirm your claims for those claims to count as knowledge. Does it show that belief is not necessary for knowledge? Wouldn't we want to insist that the subject did believe? In fact, what the example shows is that belief is not necessarily a conscious occurrence.

Belief is often described as the subjective condition for knowledge. Whereas truth requires that our claims are in line with the way things are objectively, treating claims as expressions of belief allows us to admit that they are false according to the facts, but nevertheless regard these claims as providing insight into the way the facts strike an individual. We can agree that beliefs are subjective in this sense, but disagree about whether that implies belief is something like an internal episode or structure causing me to behave as I do. As we have seen, Hume understands belief as a lively feeling attaching to an idea, recognisable via introspection. This 'liveliness' is what makes beliefs stand out from the other thoughts I might be simultaneously entertaining. Hume's account has some positive elements. It recognises that a belief is not definable by its subject-matter. Hume argues that what distinguishes belief is not the content of the idea but the attitude one takes towards the object we are contemplating. Consider first, the distinction between belief and desire: both belief and desire are distinct states, but nevertheless belief and desire could both have the same content as in 'I believe we'll have a white Christmas' and 'I desire we'll have a white Christmas'. Hume is right to stress that in believing I am not merely entertaining a thought, so affirming the proposition 'p'. I have an attitude of commitment towards that proposition; beliefs are often described as *propositional attitudes*.

But let us consider briefly some reasons why this account of belief will not do. First, Hume's focus on 'liveliness' is vague and can appear ridiculous: consider Kneale's remark that:

> when we realize 2 + 2 = 4, we do not sweat with any feeling of supreme intensity.

Kneale (1952)

Hume's definition applies to beliefs we are currently contemplating. But beliefs are often dormant: most of the things you and I believe are not things you and I are thinking now. Rather, beliefs are dispositions. If this is right, then it might allow us to understand how the subject being examined could still be a believer despite their denial. A dispositional account analyses 'belief' as a proneness or tendency to act in a regular kind of way in certain circumstances. Pierce puts it well:

> belief does not make us act at once, but puts us into such a condition that we shall behave in a certain way, when the occasion arises.

Pierce (1958)

Synoptic link

AQA A2 Philosophy Chapter 6, Philosophical problems in Hume, pp17–20. This can be found at **www.nelsonthornes.com/aqagce**

According to Ryle, whether or not there is some internal structure (e.g. a subconscious process or physiological state of my brain) producing this disposition has no bearing at all on whether or not a subject ought to be described as exhibiting a disposition. My car is prone to wobble as it approaches 60mph, as is your car. What the cause of this wobble is and whether or not the cause is the same for both cars is a question for mechanics; irrespective of their explanation of what is occurring inside the car, it is true that both cars are prone to wobble as they approach 60mph. Even if the mechanic was unable to identify anything in either car which caused the cars to wobble, it would still be true that they both wobble as they approach 60mph. If you want, dispositions to believe can still be regarded as propositional attitudes. Saying that 'Angus believes all emeralds are green' allows hearers to infer that if Angus were asked 'Are all emeralds green?' he would, all things being equal, then reply 'Yes'. We are predicting that Angus will assume a certain attitude, all things being equal, to a proposition. However, this can be misleading if it suggests that beliefs are what Ryle calls one-pattern intellectual processes. Rather, that we believe something in particular and what exactly that belief involves shows in the inferences we make, the situations we imagine, what we do and do not say and how we act:

> However often and stoutly a skater avers to us or to himself, that the ice will bear, he shows that he has his qualms, if he keeps to the edge of the pond, calls his children away from the middle, keeps his eye on the life-belts or continually speculates what would happen, if the ice broke.

Ryle (2000)

Key philosophers

Daniel Dennett (b. 1942): American philosopher whose key interests are philosophy of science and philosophy of mind. Particularly well known for his work on the philosophical implications of evolutionary theory and his atheism.

Think about

Why might someone describe Dennett as an instrumentalist about belief?

Dennett suggests that when we try to make sense of behaviour we can take various 'stances' towards it. For instance, if I want to know the trajectory a diver will follow I can adopt the *physical stance*: this involves making sense of the 'dive' by referring to the kinds of explanations we find in physics regarding the behaviour of falling bodies. Alternatively, we could explain behaviour by taking the *design stance*. Here we make sense of behaviour in terms of proper functioning; the jogger's pulse will increase as he/she climbs the hill, all things being equal. Third, we can take the *intentional stance*, which involves attributing beliefs and desires to a subject and then predicting how the subject will behave *rationally* given those beliefs and desires. So Dennett sees 'belief' as an interpretative device that allows us to 'make sense' in ways that are useful to us. Are beliefs real? Dennett compares this to asking 'is the equator real?' We need to know what is at stake in asking the question. The navigator needs to know where the equator is, but a physicist cannot perform experiments on it. Unless we have some foolproof metaphysical insight into what can and cannot *be*, then Dennett doubts we need a once for all answer. Likewise, whether or not an animal or a child or a sophisticated machine can be understood as a believer depends on why we are asking: there is no metaphysical fact of the matter. Dennett's account of belief is often described as being instrumentalist.

Davidson agrees with Dennett to the extent that the attribution of 'belief' is a way of interpreting behaviour. Also, he agrees with Ryle that beliefs are not occurrences we introspectively recognise; neither are beliefs reducible to underlying causal structures. More Ryle than Dennett, Davidson thinks that 'belief' can only be attributed in the context of language and rational action, as we find ourselves speaking and performing. In order to bring this out, Davidson imagines encountering a creature for the first time and trying to make sense of the complex sounds it makes, by merely observing its behaviour in response to the environment. According to Davidson we find ourselves in the following situation:

> beliefs and meanings conspire to account for utterances … we cannot infer the belief without knowing the meaning, and have no chance of inferring the meaning without the belief.

Davidson (1984)

So if we are going to make sense of the creature in question we have to assume that it is rational, like us. And this involves seeing that creature as understanding its situation in much the same way we conceptualise that environment, having similar beliefs to our own about what is occurring and making similar inferences 'what would happen if …'. As Davidson puts it, we need to suppose that most of what the creature believes is true. And we must suppose the creature has desires and is able to rationally choose between those desires and adjust means to ends and so on as we do. Davidson calls this the *principle of charity*:

> If we cannot find a way to interpret the utterances and other behaviour of a creature as revealing a set of beliefs largely consistent and true by our own standards, we have no reason to count that creature as rational, as having beliefs, or as saying anything.

Davidson (1984)

Hence, according to Davidson 'belief' is inseparable from engaging with your environment rationally, and that rationality must be like the sort of judicious assessment any of us would make in the same circumstances. Information about the state of the creature's innards sheds no light on the content of the belief, even if there are common causal processes linking subject and environment which provide the stable background necessary for our being able to make sense of each other.

Whereas Davidson emphasises the shared causal framework relating subjects to their environment as providing the stage-setting for rationality, Phillips Griffiths makes the same point about the interrelation between truth and belief, but stresses the role of convention in regulating what counts as rational:

> one can speak of people as believing only so far as they can be conceived as thinking things true, and as accepting criteria which enable them to distinguish the false from the true. But one could speak of people as accepting these criteria of truth only in so far as in general they are willing to assert (that is, do assert unless there are some special reasons for doing so) what these criteria demand, on occasion when assertion is in place. And this means that there could not be said to be such a thing as belief, unless there were publicly intelligible standards of evidence and an actual tendency to use them: something like common sense, so to speak.

Phillips Griffiths (1962)

The discussion shows how we can agree that belief is a subjective condition for knowledge, without assuming that the subjectivity implies 'belief' must be understood as some internal occurrence or structure. Rather, the subjectivity associated with belief can consist in nothing but the recognition that with respect to the truth of this claim or that claim (but not with respect to the truth of *all* claims) the creature is in error; nevertheless that error can be interpreted as rational given for instance, the particular assumptions, situation, limited information and so on that the would-be knower has when making their judgement.

Think about

Given his analysis of belief, why might Davidson doubt that there could be a way of understanding reality radically different from the way we understand it?

iii The justification condition

According to the standard analysis, a claim does not qualify as knowledge unless it is justified. Consider the following case. I claim 'you are a thief' and my belief is based on my extensive reading of the old-fashioned theory of phrenology: the shape of your head arouses my suspicion. At one time this might have been a respectable belief but nowadays criminologists think that phrenology is a bad theory providing bad reasons for believing. Anyway, I have read about the theory, and being rather naïve, I find myself believing it completely. Also, it turns out you are a thief. I take it that your prison conviction confirms that I knew all along 'you are a thief'. But I did not know all along that you were a thief: phrenology has been shown to be thoroughly disreputable; it was only an accident that I got it right this time. Insisting that knowledge depends on good reasons is a way of maintaining a focus on truth: better reasons tend to produce more truth. However, as our discussion of scepticism showed, most of our reasoning concerning the truth is fallible (which does not mean it *is* false, only that it *might be*). This leads to an influential counter-example, casting doubt on the standard analysis of knowledge.

Gettier

Gettier imagines a situation in which I have good reason for believing as I do and what I believe is in fact true: nevertheless, my justified true belief is not an instance of knowledge. He assumes that:

> in that sense of 'justified' in which S's being justified in believing P is a necessary condition of S's knowing that P, it is possible for a person to be justified in believing a proposition that is in fact false.

Gettier (1963)

In principle, most of our inferences are defeasible: meaning that, from a logical point of view, they are capable of being undermined by further information. So Gettier's assumption is legitimate. He imagines the following case: Smith and Jones are going for the same job. Smith believes that 'the man who will get the job has ten coins in his pocket'. Why? Because he has been told by the boss that Jones will get the job and Smith also knows that Jones has ten coins in his pocket: for some peculiar reason he has counted up the coins in Jones' pocket. So knowing all this, Smith reasons that 'the man who will get the job has ten coins in his pocket'. Smith's inference is justifiable: he has good reason to believe that 'the man who will get the job has ten coins in his pocket'. In fact, Smith gets the job. Unbeknownst to Smith, Smith also has ten coins in his pocket. So Smith justifiably believes that 'the man who will get the job has ten coins in his pocket' and it is true that 'the man who gets the job has ten coins in his pocket', but Smith did not know he would get the job. Therefore, justified true belief is not sufficient for knowledge.

What should we make of Gettier's example? Certainly Smith believes something that is true: 'the man who will get the job has ten coins in his pocket' and he has some kind of justification for it. Gettier's example has been regarded as significant because it illustrates that the standard analysis

> does not state a sufficient condition for someone's knowing a given proposition.

Gettier (1963)

What Gettier shows is that the facts which make a proposition true might have nothing to do with our justified belief for believing it to be true. As such, the link between the facts and our beliefs appears accidental. As Plato puts it, we seem to be like a blind man on the right road. What we need is some alternative understanding of what it means to keep on track.

Responses to Gettier

Let's consider an externalist response to Gettier's critique of the standard analysis. In order to make sense of these *externalist* responses we need to distinguish between *externalism* and *internalism*. Recall the infinite regress problem, where we were required to show the derivation of beliefs from the self-evident. The sceptic appears to have assumed that authority must depend on my ability, in principle at least, to justify my beliefs by tracing the inferential relations that hold one belief to another. Ultimately this inferential structure will trace back to the self-evident, or else the sceptic casts doubt on the authority of any claim we make. This assumption is called internalism: my authority as a knower depends on my having access to supporting reasons for my belief. The default and challenge structure of knowledge called that assumption into question. Instead, in context my entitlements are assumed and only need to be established in the light of an appropriate challenge. Post-Gettier, philosophers have argued that we can claim to have knowledge even if there is no inferential structure leading back to unassailable foundations. The internalist model of knowledge that insists otherwise – the standard analysis – is faulty and so has little or no force. A more radical suggestion than the default and challenge structure argues that I can be said to 'know', even if I have no idea what the belief-forming process is that guarantees that I know. This position is called externalism. Instead, what we need is some other kind of marker that entitles us to claim we 'know': another kind of indicator that ensures our beliefs co-vary with the facts. What do we mean by this? Nozick gives an analysis of the conditions required for knowledge which bypasses internal justification:

> S knows that P if and only if
> i   P
> ii   S believes that P
> iii   If P were not true, S would not believe P
> iv   If P were true, S would believe it

What matters on this analysis, in place of justification, is that beliefs track the truth: made explicit by conditions **vi** and **vii**. So much for the formal analysis: what is supposed to do the job? Consider the suggestion that (vi) and (vii) can be catered for by a brute *causal* relation. The guiding idea is that there must be a belief-forming causal process that is independent of justification, but is nevertheless reliable, objectively. An objectively reliable process could be the behaviour of mercury in a thermometer, or the colour of litmus paper indicating acidity. A reliable process need not be anything conscious and it need not involve anything like making an inference. Instead 'nature' fixes the relation between input and output as there is some causal regularity that determines that whenever this then that. Goldman recommends his theory thus:

> With this in mind, consider how tempting it is to say of an electric-eye door that it "knows" you are coming (at least that something is coming), or 'sees' you coming. The attractiveness of this metaphor is easily explained on my theory: the door has a reliable mechanism for discriminating between something being before it and not being there.

Goldman (1976)

And reliabilism appears to link with an evolutionary perspective. Say my perceptual system behaves in causally systematic ways, describing it as 'reliable' says something more than that: because it behaves in causally systematic ways then it can function as a reliable device for regulating what I see, hear, taste, touch and smell. Reliability implies a function. Perhaps our perceptual system is 'reliable' in the sense that it functions well enough to allow us to survive long enough to reproduce copies of ourselves. Is this kind of causal *reliabilism* convincing? Such an approach can accommodate the idea that animals and babies, and even machines, have true beliefs and hence knowledge: even though they have no reasons they are aware of supporting their belief, they have reliable mechanisms instead. In this way, reliabilism picks up on the sorts of intuitions informing Hume's naturalism in which the beliefs of animals, children, the vulgar and the philosopher are all the products of the same kind of 'cognitive' process. Like the reliabilist, Hume thinks our 'understanding' does not reflect the kind of inferential architecture the sceptic assumes. Nevertheless, as we pointed out, naturalism takes for granted what the sceptic doubts. And the theorist is not going to find reliabilism satisfactory. Consider Stroud's complaint:

> suppose there are truths about the world and the human condition which link human perceptual states and cognitive mechanisms with further states of knowledge and reasonable belief, and which imply that human beings acquire their beliefs about the physical world through the operation of belief-forming mechanisms which are on the whole reliable in the sense of giving them mostly true beliefs … If there are truths of this kind … that fact alone obviously will do us no good as theorists who want to understand human knowledge in this philosophical way. At the very least we must believe some such truths; their merely being true would not be enough to give us any illumination or satisfaction. But our merely happening to believe them would not be enough either. We seek understanding of certain aspects of the human condition, so we seek more than just a set of beliefs about it; we want to know or have good reasons for thinking that what we believe about it is true.

Stroud (1984)

Unless we have a conception of truth and some reason to think our beliefs are true then talk about reliable processes leading to true beliefs will not get started. If so, it looks as if, at some point, justification is inescapable. The suspicion that reliabilism begs more questions than it answers is also apparent in Goldman's claim that the electric eye 'sees' anything; and not because electric eyes are not sophisticated enough causal mechanisms. Recalling the arguments referred to earlier about the 'logical space of reasons' the eye is certainly a reliable mechanism but nothing follows from that about its cognitive capacity if 'cognitive capacity' can only be spelled out in terms of conceptual ability and the stage setting that ability requires. Mrs Mather wants to increase Angus's and Mary's knowledge. She does not just set up appropriate causal conditions and hope her students have reliable processes for coming to believe truths. Mrs Mather also teaches her students to appreciate reasons and develop their own justifiable judgement. As they learn how to think about biology their knowledge of the subject is increased. This point is significant because it highlights 'true beliefs' have content and that content is inseparable from the rational network of things we say and do. Recall Ryle's skater whose beliefs about the ice were shown in various ways. Likewise, the content of Angus's true beliefs about biology can only be cashed out against a rational backdrop in terms of what he asserts and denies, the connections he makes, the consequences he anticipates and so on. None of this looks like the sort of thing animals, babies or machines do. If beliefs are ways of characterising complex dispositions interpretable as expressing rationality then animals, babies and machines do not have beliefs: although treating babies as if they do is a necessary condition for them acquiring them. Consider Collingwood:

> The child's discovery of itself as a person is also its discovery of itself as a member of a world of persons … The discovery of myself as a person is the discovery that I can speak, and am thus a persona or speaker; in speaking I am both speaker and hearer; and since the discovery of myself as a person is also the discovery of other persons around me, it is the discovery of speakers and hearers other than myself.
>
> *Collingwood (1958)*

Does that mean that reliabilism and externalism ought to be rejected? You could argue that in a modified non-reductive form they are particularly insightful. Reliabilism explains why we are prepared to default to what you believe you saw, touched, tasted, smelled, heard. It underpins the principle of credulity. As Swinburne puts it:

> it is a principle of rationality that (in the absence of special considerations) if it seems (epistemically) to a subject that x is present, then probably x is present; what one seems to perceive is probably so. How things seem to be is good grounds for a belief about how things are.
>
> *Swinburne (1979)*

And Plantinga asserts this default position as the expression of a basic epistemic right. A belief is basic for a person if that person

> doesn't accept it on the evidential basis of other propositions and, furthermore, he is justified in holding it in a basic way: he is within his epistemic rights, is not irresponsible, is violating no epistemic or other duties in holding that belief in that way.
>
> *Plantinga (2000)*

Externalism allows that the reliability of your testimony is not simply determined by reasons available to you: at least to some extent I can assess the reliability of your testimony independently of reasons you have for thinking your beliefs are true. I can rely on your beliefs and you can rely on my beliefs because we are both rational reliable persons. As Brandom puts it:

> Reliabilism points to the fundamental social and interpersonal articulation of the practices of reason giving and reason assessing within which questions of who has knowledge arise.
>
> *Brandom (2003)*

☑ *Having worked through this topic, you should have thought about:*

- the standard analysis of knowledge
- problems facing the standard analysis
- accounts of what it is to have a belief in relation to being a rational agent
- externalism and reliabilism and how they should be understood.

Summary questions

1. Explain what is meant by 'self-evident' and draw out why the self-evident is significant in the debate between the sceptic and theorist.

2. Explain the verification principle and its role in undermining the possibility of scepticism.

3. Explain how a close look at the grammar of 'know' is supposed to dissolve the challenge of scepticism.

4. Compare Williams and Ayer on the relation between appearance and reality. Which account is the most effective?

5. Explain the difference between internalism and externalism regarding justification.

■ Further reading

▪ The *Stanford Encyclopedia of Philosophy* (**http://plato.stanford. edu/**) – Contains several relevant articles. Also helpful for placing the concerns of this chapter into a wider context via its easy to use search facility.

▪ Ayer, A.J., *Language Truth and Logic*, Penguin, 2001 – Spells out Ayer's position, as outlined above, in a more detailed, but still quite readable manner.

▪ Rorty, R., *Philosophy and the Mirror of Nature* – One of Rorty's great strengths is his ability to write clearly and interestingly about difficult ideas. While setting out his own position, this book also provides useful accounts of several other thinkers considered above. Part Two is of particular relevance.

▪ Sosa, E., J. Kim, J. Fantl and M. McGrath (eds.), *Epistemology: An Anthology*, Blackwell, 2008 – For advanced students. Contains papers by several of the thinkers mentioned above, plus some others relevant to our concerns.

■ References

Anthony, L., 'Quine as Feminist', in E. Sosa, J. Kim, J. Fantl and M. McGrath (eds.), *Epistemology: An Anthology*, Blackwell, 2008.

Austin, J.L., *Philosophical Papers*, Clarendon Press, 1961.

Austin, J.L., *How to Do Things with Words: The William James Lectures Delivered at Harvard University in 1955*, ed. by J.O. Urmson, Clarendon, 1962.

Ayer, A.J., *The Problem of Knowledge*, Penguin, 1956.

Ayer, A.J., *Language Truth and Logic*, Penguin, 2001.

Brandom, R., *Making Explicit*, Harvard University Press, 1998.

Brandom, R., *Articulating Reasons*, Harvard University Press, 2003.

Chisholm, R., *The Foundations of Knowing*, University of Minnesota Press, 1982.

Collingwood, R., *The Principles of Art*, Oxford University Press, 1958.

Dancy, J., *An Introduction to Contemporary Epistemology*, Blackwell, 1985.

Davidson, D., *Inquiries into Truth and Interpretation*, Clarendon Press, 1984.

Descartes, R., *Discourse on Method and the Meditations*, trans. by F.E. Sutcliffe, Penguin, 1968.

Gettier, E., 'Is Justified True Belief Knowledge?', *Analysis*, 23, 1963.

Goldman, A.I., 'Discrimination and Perceptual Knowledge', *Journal of Philosophy*, 73, 1976.

Grayling, A.C., 'Epistemology', in *The Blackwell Companion to Philosophy*, Blackwell, 2002.

Guignon, C., *Heidegger and the Problem of Knowledge*, Hackett, 1983.

Hempel, C., *Aspects of Scientific Explanation & Other Essays in the Philosophy of Science*, Free Press, 1965.

Hume, D., *An Enquiry Concerning Human Understanding*, Oxford University Press, 1975.

Hume, D., *A Treatise of Human Nature*, ed. by David Fate Norton & Mary J. Norton, Oxford University Press, 2000.

Husserl, E., *Phenomenology and the Crisis of Philosophy*, Harper & Row, 1965.

Kant, I., *Critique of Pure Reason Kant*, Dover, 2004.

Kneale, *Probability and Induction*, Clarendon Press, 1952.

Meynell, H., 'Scepticism Reconsidered' *Philosophy*, 59, 1984.

Nagel, T., *The View from Nowhere*, Oxford University Press, 1989.

Nietzsche, F., *The Anti-Christ*, Prometheus Books, 2000.

Penfield, W., *The Excitable Cortex in Conscious Man*, Liverpool University Press, 1958.

Phillips Griffiths, A., 'On Belief', *Proceedings of the Aristotelian Society* 63, 1962–3.

Pierce, C.S., *Values in a Universe of Chance: Selected Writings of Charles S. Pierce*, Stanford University Press, 1958.

Plantinga, A., *Warranted Christian Beliefs*, Oxford University Press, 2000.

Rorty, R., *Consequences of Pragmatism: Essays, 1972–1980*, University of Minnesota Press, 1982.

Rorty, R., *Contingency, Irony, and Solidarity*, Cambridge University Press, 1989.

Rorty, R., *Truth and Progress*, Cambridge University Press, 1998.

Russell, B., *The Problems of Philosophy*, Oxford University Press, 2001.

Ryle, G., *The Concept of Mind*, Penguin, 2000.

Sellars, W., *Empiricism and the Philosophy of Mind*, Harvard University Press, 1997.

Stroud, B., *The Significance of Philosophical Scepticism*, Oxford University Press, 1984.

Swinburne, R., *The Existence of God*, Oxford University Press, 1979.

Williams, M., *Unnatural Doubts: Epistemological Realism and the Basis of Scepticism*, Blackwell, 1991.

Williams, M., *Problems of Knowledge*, Oxford University Press, 2001.

Wittgenstein, L., *Blue and Brown Books*, Blackwell, 1974.

Wittgenstein, L., *Notebooks 1914–1916*, Blackwell, 1981.

Wittgenstein, L., *Philosophical Investigations*, Blackwell, 1998.

Wittgenstein, L., *On Certainty*, HarperCollins, 2001.

Wright, C., 'Scepticism and Dreaming: Imploding the Demon', *Mind*, 397, 1991, pp87–115.

Moral truth

Introduction

Surely it must be wrong to kill an innocent person; surely individuals have undisputed rights over what happens to their own body; surely paedophilia is an evil? Those who exclaim in such fashion are demanding the acceptance of moral truths.

Philosophers have approached the subject of moral truth from a variety of starting points. Plato asked the question 'how ought we to live?' and searched for universal principles that would characterise the good life; Kant enquired into the nature of absolute duty; and utilitarians like Bentham sought for an objective principle to serve as a goal or end by which to judge actions. What they have in common is that absolute moral values are knowable and teachable. They explain that there are moral experts with special cognitive abilities who can advise on matters of right and wrong, whether they be acquainted with transcendent truths (Plato), or understand rational moral law (Kant) or have a wide experience of human nature and happiness (Bentham, Mill).

In the opposite camp are philosophers who deny that there are objective truths. They might claim that values are simply an expression of personal taste, 'a sign language of the emotions' (Nietzsche) or created by the choices and projects of the subject (Sartre); and moral statements are prescriptions and recommendations which people choose to make (Hare). Thus our moral outlook is contingent on a variety of historical and cultural factors, and there can be no claim to a privileged knowledge:

> ... since truth is a property of sentences, since sentences are dependent for their existence on vocabularies, and since vocabularies are made by human beings, so are truths ...

Rorty (1989)

and that includes moral truth. Moral values are not 'out there' waiting to be discovered (moral realism) but created by groups of language users and relative to that group. Moral language is not a mechanism, which is gradually taking on the true shape of the moral universe. So we should replace the question 'How do you know certain facts?' with 'Why do you talk that way?' In the absence of empirically verifiable or demonstrable certain moral truths, how can there be moral experts, or any judgement on moral progress? There are no criteria for maintaining that one society is morally superior to another.

So, can ethical claims be true or false? We can certainly make claims about what people believe – for example, Christians believe that God is Love – and these kind of propositions about beliefs can be checked out, by reading Christian texts. But with normative judgements about what actually *is* right or wrong, it is less clear where we can find a confirmation of our belief. With an act of killing, I can witness the events, observe who is responsible, note the suffering of the victim etc., but what actually indicates that killing is wrong? Where is the moral fact? Where is the 'wrongness'?

Learning objectives

- to understand and evaluate the case for God-independent transcendent moral truth

- to assess whether moral knowledge can be based on natural facts

- to examine the open question argument and the naturalistic fallacy

- to understand the analogy with secondary properties

- to explore the extent to which moral truths can motivate action.

Think about

Could you contest any of those values? Consider the case for euthanasia, anti-abortion and cultural views on children.

Synoptic link

AQA AS Philosophy Chapter 3, Why should I be moral?, pp73–97.

Think about

Research some of the unusual cultural practices of other societies and historical periods, for example, Hamilton (2003, p18). Can you make any case for moral superiority?

Now the first group of philosophers we mentioned are cognitivists. They argue that there are moral facts and the issue is how we connect to this external realm of value. Plato argues that through rational intuition and dialectic we can discern 'first principles' from which rightness, justice, beauty and so on can be deduced, which liken moral insight to mathematical insight. In contrast, empiricists develop ethics as a science. Armed with facts about human nature such as observations about 'wants that all men have' or the conditions of human flourishing, we can check our normative proposition against the natural qualities of someone's behaviour. Since human beings desire happiness, we can measure the utility of the action to produce happiness, and ethics is comparable to a social science.

However, our second group of philosophers are non-cognitivists who believe that there is nothing to be known and no realm of transcendent or natural facts. This thesis is accepted by emotivists, prescriptivists and existentialists, who deny that moral properties are a genuine feature of people and actions, which we can discover and describe. This camp may make use of the perceived distinction between facts and values and that no fact conclusively entails a value. Thus the fact that someone was kind does not necessarily entail that such kindness was a good thing. Can kindness be bad?

However, if we cannot derive a moral value from a fact, then how can moral claims be justified? If a moral principle, for example killing, is wrong, and it is derived from another moral principle, for example the value of life, then there must be an ultimate moral principle to ground all moral principles or we are left with a problem of infinite regress. Thus the search is on for an ultimate, self-evident moral truth, as the foundation of all values; and this was the search that Plato inspired.

Plato and the Form of the Good

In *The Republic* (1955), Plato argues that if we wish to lead a life worth living, and construct an ideal society, we must know and understand what goodness consists of. To achieve such knowledge and escape from uncertainty, moral disputes and relativism, we must enquire into what is necessarily and indubitably good: the essential nature of goodness that is the universal and significant feature of all good acts. If we understand this first principle, the Form of the Good, then we can assess whether particular moral acts conform to this truth. The enterprise is similar to mathematics, in that we can determine some self-evident axioms, we can then rationally deduce further truths, safe in the knowledge that they are coherent with our first axioms. So just as to recognise a circle depends on prior knowledge of what a perfect circle is, so to recognise a just act requires an insight into the nature of justice. Thus Plato unpacks what this first principle of goodness might be, that can explain all relative, competing transient, imperfect notions of what is right. This Form of the Good:

- is self-evidently *what people desire* – the good life is what all people seek and incorporates the aim of life and so motivates action
- is the *purpose* therefore of all action and the destination of the ship of state
- is the foundation of all *excellence* – an *ideal reality* and the paradigm of right behaviour with which we can become acquainted
- is an unchanging, constant *truth* which we can understand.

Think about

The fact–value distinction was introduced in AQA AS Philosophy Chapter 3, Why should I be moral? p86 and Chapter 5, Why should I be governed?, p155. Collect samples of how this fallacy is committed.

Synoptic link

AQA A2 Philosophy Chapter 3, Epistemology and metaphysics, p96.

Synoptic link

AQA A2 Philosophy Chapter 7, Philosophical problems in Plato. This can be found at **www.nelsonthornes.com/aqagce**

As with all the Forms, Plato assumed that what was true was also real. Since the Form of the Good does not exist in the physical world, it must exist in a transcendent realm. So to describe it, he has to use an analogy – and he compares the form of the Good to the Sun.

Table **4.1** *The Form of the Good compared to the Sun*

The Sun:	The Form of Good:
1 is the source of life – the essential ingredient of life	1 is the source of value – the embodiment of perfection
2 enables the living world to flourish	2 enables us to see what is right and just
3 and all plants and creatures seek the light (purpose).	3 and all human beings desire to contemplate and understand.

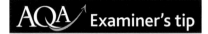

Examiner's tip

For ethics, the significance of the Good is that it is the source of absolute moral values. This should be the focus of your essay.

Synoptic link

AQA AS Philosophy Chapter 3, Why should I be moral?, p73.

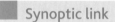

Synoptic link

AQA A2 Philosophy Chapter 2, Political philosophy, p78.

Practically, knowledge of the principle of goodness will enable us to function as a healthy, harmonious, wise happy individual, fully realising our potential, and contributing fully to a just society that makes it possible to have this good life.

This is a virtuous life, achieving excellence and maximising fulfilment for all. The principle of justice that allows this ideal state to develop is 'the having and doing of one's own', that is, giving whatever you can and receiving in accordance with your deserving. So the healthy individual achieves their soul's desire, controlling spirit and desire with reason which develops their potential, and are rewarded with their due.

This ultimate and absolute principle has been discovered by reason, in the same way that in maths we reason that a straight line is the shortest distance between two points, or the laws of thought such as the law of non-contradiction (nothing can be both *A* and not *A*). With regard to Plato's simile of the Divided Line, the Form of the Good is *A*, a product of intelligence that understands ultimate excellence and perfection.

Evaluation of the claim to rational, moral knowledge

Unfortunately this delightful vision of moral and psychic harmony has not convinced everyone.

First, there is some doubt about the nature of the Good, which seems to be visionary and mystical, rather than rational. Plato singularly fails to give a full account of this Form and resorts to allegories such as the Sun, which use language in suggestive and affective ways, rather than rational. The analogy rests on the logical move from the Sun being the source of life (fact) to the Sun being Good (value). Deriving values from facts is a controversial matter that is discussed later. Plato could claim that the hidden premise 'life is good' is a perfectly reasonable one, in which case the analogy successfully moves from facts to values.

Otherwise, Plato seems only to provide us with synonyms and the meanings of words. 'Excellence', 'perfection' and 'ideal' simply unpack how we use these words as broadly similar in meaning but they provide no substance as to what 'the Good' consists of. The definition of 'good' that 'it is what all men desire' does not significantly add to its meaning. We have to rely on the principle of justice to give content.

This principle is, however, not rational in the way that mathematics provides logically necessary truths. The harmony achieved by rewarding people according to their desert is not a necessary truth, but a value that is highly contentious. Why not distribute the rewards in society according to equal rights or need, and show respect for the unique value of all human beings? Why rank people according to desert? Harmony could similarly be achieved by valuing all contributions equally. Even if we accept the principle of desert, the criteria for what counts as desert is still entirely open to interpretation. Should the contribution of a philosopher ruler rank much higher than an artisan? Reason will not produce a definitive answer that is self-evident. Even the identification of goodness with harmony is questionable. Mill argues that disharmony in society is a means of social progress through conflict of opinion, and in music and the arts it can be a source of pleasure.

Neither is there a necessary link between performing a function and goodness. To perform a role in a society has no connection with *moral* goodness. How well we do something – be it teaching or motherhood or ruling – can be distinguished from being virtuous. Some of our most successful leaders, for example Churchill, would not be described as a paragon of virtue. There is a crucial confusion here between the words 'function' and 'purpose'. The former refers to the role that someone or something has in an organisation. A cog in a machine has a function. But the word 'purpose' also has overtones of value that this is what we *ought* to achieve or aim at. To be assigned a function in society is not necessarily the same thing as to be given a purpose. Function can be described purely as a series of operations, while purpose implies an ideal goal, what one ought to be doing. And can purposes in life be decided purely by rational thought? The problem with Plato's navigator in the simile of the ship is that the destination of a ship and the ultimate purpose of life are not comparable. Moral conviction is not like navigation.

This confusion lies at the heart of the Forms. Plato conflates 'the typical' with 'the ideal'. So the essence or Form of a horse defines what a typical horse is like, without the additional value of being an ideal. In fact there are probably many variations of opinion on what an ideal horse is like. So there is a crucial distinction between a typical man and a good man. Having the qualities denoted by the word 'man' can be separated from saying those qualities are good – the evaluative add-on. So we can define the essence of something without making any (moral) value judgements, and confusing it with an ideal.

Indeed, the fact that the word 'good' is applied to all good things does not indicate that they possess an identical quality. Good *may* be related to function, as for example a good striker scores many goals, but 'good fashion sense' can mean 'up to date' or 'appropriately dressed' or 'a good eye for colour and design' etc. The criteria for the perfect horse varies in a way that the perfect circle does not. So 'goodness' is not a separate quality that all good things possess, but a relationship between the speaker and the thing called good – a good striker or horse is *recommended*. 'That's a good horse' means it is commended or appreciated, but the qualities the horse has (speed, endurance, beauty etc.) are just the opinion of the speaker. It does not share a common, ideal quality with all other good horses (see 'Prescriptivism' later in the chapter).

Finally, Plato assumes that if we understand the Good, then we would *be* good and not live badly. So nobody willingly errs, and therefore a wise man must necessarily be virtuous and possess the character previously described.

Think about

Consider the honours system in this country. Is it fair that some people receive knighthoods and honours? If so, would you distribute them differently from the current system?

Weakness of the will

Yet we are all familiar with the experience of knowing what is good for us, but not being able to carry it out. For Plato, this possibility of being weak-willed is only if the understanding is incomplete, and therefore reason is not in control of desire. Being weak willed is accounted for by ignorance. For example, a chocoholic does not really understand the damage he is doing to his person. If he did, he would stop over-consumption immediately. Poor or immoral behaviour is a failure of education, and with clear knowledge, self-control would automatically happen.

The issue is whether reason and knowledge provide motivation. Some would say that reason by itself moves nothing, only when it is allied to desire does it motivate action. Hume (1969) encapsulated this in his famous dictum, 'Reason is and ought to be the slave of the passions'.

Plato (1955) in his account of the soul separates reason from desire, so that it is difficult to support his view that if we reason something, we shall be moved to act. In his simile of the chariot, 'it is the horses that do the pulling' (Hare, 1963), reason can only direct the horses. Yet elsewhere he claims reason 'has its own special pleasures', and that knowing the truth 'is the pleasantest life' and the rational philosopher's life is 29 times more happy than an unjust man (Plato, 1955, bk 587/8).

It is important to clarify that Plato is not offering enlightened self-interest. It is not a matter of calculation that it is my self-interest to do good. Plato is arguing that to know the good is to be so attracted; one therefore acts, and that my self-interest coincides with the virtue. The motivating factor is the rational knowledge of the Form of the Good. So we have to assess whether it would be possible, to know the Good and yet not wish to pursue it. Put another way, does a proposition that is necessarily true carry with it a prescriptive force – a categorical imperative? So, if it is intrinsically good, it must be obeyed.

Psychologically, this would not appear to be the case. We can possess knowledge yet ignore it or not exercise it, as in Aristotle's 'incontinent man'. It is possible to know the truth yet be moved by appetite. Not only do we need knowledge, we must learn how to apply it and this requires habituation and practice.

Plato also seems to have confused the necessity of accepting a rational proposition with the necessity of adopting a moral truth. But the necessity in a rational deduction lies in the cogency of the reasoning. The only prescriptive force is to accept the logic that relations of certain ideas cannot be contradicted. But if we sever the link between mathematical, logical reasoning and moral reasoning, then no necessity to act remains. To adopt a proposition because of its internal logic cannot be equated with moral imperatives.

The problem of weak wills could be alleviated if we discount reason as a motivating faculty. If we accept that all action is motivated by desire, then we could still distinguish between more rational and irrational desire. The former would be capable of being linked to long-term goals and social approval etc. So an enlightened egoist would allow a desire for long-term well-being to prevail over a more immediate short-term pleasure. However, this would dismantle Plato's project to link moral action to transcendental, moral absolutes and to refute the sophists and relativism.

Naturalism

An alternative to the use of reason to intuit moral truth, is to assert that there are natural facts, and that good can be identified as an empirical property, for example 'X makes everyone happy'. So moral absolutes can be derived from a study of human nature, for example 'it is a fact that suffering evokes human sympathy'. Moral properties are thus natural properties of people, actions and motives and to be good, an action must possess that unique quality of goodness. This is a form of **moral realism** and moral cognitivism: that there are moral facts and properties that are independent of people's attitudes about what is right, and that moral judgements can be true or false.

For example, psychological egoism states that people cannot help but act in their own self-interest and 'good' is whatever people perceive to be in their own interest.

Non-egoistic naturalism might agree that, 'nature has placed mankind under the governance of two sovereign masters, pain and pleasure' (Bentham, 1982), but claim that therefore every person needs to maximise the happiness for all – utilitarianism. But those two steps are not necessarily compatible. Why not?

Classical utilitarianism therefore needs to argue, either that maximising happiness for all is an 'enlightened act of self-interest', or that through natural sympathy for others we can become benevolent and disinterested and wish the happiness of the majority, rather than just our own. The natural facts are the human disposition to rational, enlightened, prudent calculation of self-interest or our capacity for sympathy. Both would account for our motivation to ethical behaviour.

The utilitarian theory is also particularly applicable to the formulation of laws, since a principle of social utility clearly indicates that we satisfy as many preferences as possible and achieve the greatest balance of happiness over unhappiness. This was Bentham's chief concern, to produce legislation that was justified, because it was based on the absolute and universal truths of human nature. So the law which embodies what is good, right and just is grounded in fact.

Virtue theorists, such as Foot, also claim it is possible to ground ethical judgements in facts about human flourishing. We can 'fix' the word good in the same way that we can determine the meaning of 'dangerous'. So, we can suppose that to call something dangerous contains a 'warning function', to prevent people from going near something. But we cannot warn people about absolutely everything, for to be meaningful there must be a possibility of real evil or harm. Likewise 'good' only makes sense if it is connected to real tangible benefits. We could not claim 'clapping three times before breakfast' was good unless a demonstrable advantage accrued. So 'good' can be fixed to those acts which advance human welfare and fulfilment – that is, natural observable facts. This point will be pursued later under 'thick' and 'thin' concepts.

Ethical naturalism was famously attacked by **G.E. Moore** in *Principia Ethica* (1968). He argued that the word 'good' is indefinable. In his 'open question' argument, he claimed that to define 'good' would be to reduce it to a tautology and yet naturalistic moral propositions are not tautologies. This led him to coin the term 'naturalistic fallacy' – that it is a logical error to reduce moral statements to psychological propositions and facts about human nature.

Key terms

Moral realism: this means that there is an ethical reality. Just as there is an atomic structure to the world, so there is one moral structure to events in the world, that local variations reflect.

Synoptic link

A discussion of this theory can be found in AQA AS Philosophy Chapter 3, Why should I be moral?, p61.

Synoptic link

AQA AS Philosophy Chapter 3, Why should I be moral?, p73.

Think about

What are the natural facts that must be attached to words such as kind or cruel?

Key philosophers

G.E. Moore (1873–1958): Cambridge professor of philosophy who proposed a theory of intuitionism, that good is a unique and indefinable property that we can recognise but not analyse.

Think about

Do the following lead to open questions?

- Survival of the fittest is good.
- We ought to be rational.
- Suffering is wrong.
- Preserving life is right.
- More evolved species are higher and better.
- Health is our (sole) good.

The open question argument

This argument points out that any definition should present synonyms, and therefore would result in a closed question. For example, a bachelor is defined as an unmarried man, so it is a pointless (closed) question to ask whether a certain bachelor is unmarried. It is a necessary condition of being a bachelor that you are unmarried. The statement is a tautology, and so the question is closed. The same cannot be said of the proposition, 'all bachelors are ugly'. This leads to an open question, since the answer could be 'yes' or 'no', as ugly is not contained within the meaning of bachelor. Moore argues that this is also the case with 'good'. Supposing, for example, that we define 'good' as 'pleasure' (hedonism) or as 'the survival of the fittest'. Now this would result in the open question: 'is pleasure good' for it is meaningful to answer Yes or No. It is perfectly reasonable to say that some are good and some are not. Whereas tautologies cannot be denied without contradiction, it is not a contradiction to say 'pleasure is not good'. So 'good' cannot be identified with pleasure, good cannot be defined as pleasure.

If one agrees that the above are open questions, then it is a fallacy to try to define good/bad in terms of natural properties. Moore approvingly quotes Mill (1948), who asks, 'how is it possible to prove that health is good?' and Mill's conclusion, 'that questions of ultimate ends do not admit of proof in the ordinary acceptation of the term'. Yet Mill himself stands accused of the naturalistic fallacy.

The fact–value gap

This argument points to the logical fallacy of deriving values from facts. Mill is a utilitarian and uses as his proof that happiness is *desirable*, the fact that happiness *is desired* by all people. Yet desirable means 'ought to be desired' or 'what it is good to desire' and the fact that people want happiness does not entail that they ought to want it or that possessing happiness is a good thing (value). There are bad desires as well as good ones, and the desire for happiness could be a bad desire. Moore terms the use of facts to determine values 'the naturalistic fallacy':

> Desirable does indeed mean 'what it is good to desire' but when this is understood, it is no longer plausible to say that our only test of THAT, is what is actually desired.

Moore (1968)

This logical flaw in many ethical arguments had earlier been indicated by Hume:

> In every system of morality which I have hitherto met with … the author proceeds for some time in the ordinary way of reasoning and establishes the being of a God or makes observations concerning human affairs; when of a sudden I am surprised to find that, instead of … is and is not, I meet with … ought, or ought not.

Hume (1969, Book III, Part I)

Yet the 'new relation' of 'ought' (value) does not automatically, necessarily and logically follow from an 'is' (fact). So Hume argues that there is no possibility through reason of deriving moral propositions from factual statements. Factual utterances describe the world, and their claims can be checked out to be true or false. Ought claims are emotive – expressions of approval, or disapprobation. They may evince attitudes, but they are not characteristics of events themselves. Values are not in the world but are projected onto it, and likened to secondary properties. This will be discussed later.

So we might agree on the facts, for example that:

- healthy food contains Vitamin C
- an orange contains Vitamin C, so
- an orange is healthy food

but the logic of the argument contains no value judgement about whether we *ought* to consume oranges. It is a matter of choice whether I value a healthy lifestyle or not. Thus Hume's distinction between 'is' and 'ought' entails an absolute separation of facts and values:

> Take any action allow'd to be vicious: wilful murder for instance. Examine it in all lights and see if you can find that matter of fact, or real existance, which you call vice. In which-ever way you take it, you find only certain passions, motives, volitions and thoughts. There is no other matter of fact in the case.

Hume (1969, Bk III.ii. 1)

So whereas a dispute about facts can in theory be solved by an empirical test, seem to be a quite different kind of discourse involving attitudes and recommendations, not facts about the matter. We can ascertain the facts about a killing, but where we disagree on its moral implications, no appeal to more facts can decide the issue.

According to Hare's theory of prescriptivism, discussed later, the word 'good' does not denote a moral truth, but instead guides actions. Thus once again we have a clear separation of factual terms and value words (Table 4.2).

Table 4.2 *Factual terms and value words*

Factual propositions:	Value propositions:
are statements	are commands
using **des**criptive terms	using prescriptive language
or indicative language	or imperatives
informing us	recommending
of knowledge claims	choices of action
which can be true/false	which are advised or not
so are cognitive.	so are non-cognitive.

Think about

Do the following propositions merely state facts or make value judgements?

- That's a beautiful picture.
- You must not smoke in this café.
- The notice said, you must not smoke in this café.
- You ought to consider this university.
- She is wearing flared trousers.
- Great outfit!
- It's healthy to take regular exercise.
- That's a clever plan! She's intelligent.

Can the fact–value gap be bridged?

The above separation of factual statements from moral claims endorses the view that no factual truth entails a moral conclusion. This position undermines the naturalist claim to know moral truth. Two challenges to this position are considered below. The first relates back to Foot (1974) and her comparison of the word 'good' to the word 'dangerous'. Pinchin (1990) refers to her attack on a 'free-floating' view of moral attitudes, that good or bad can be hung 'on any peg in a cloakroom'.

We can't value anything we like

Foot (1974) argues that moral reasoning is constrained by moral facts or a moral reality external to us. In consequence of the facts about human welfare and flourishing, we can reach moral conclusions.

So while she does not deny that 'good' has a recommending function, she argues that it is tied to certain objects, since there is a limit to the objects that can meaningfully be called good. For example, collecting buckets of water from the sea could not be called morally good, unless one constructs a specific moral and religious framework to explain its benefits. It is not possible to have a moral attitude, which is independent of some content that makes sense. So she attacks the notion of the happy, unjust man to deny that an evil person could be considered good. If she is right, then 'it is quite impossible to call anything you like good'.

In this attack on extreme, moral subjectivity, she counters the claim that what counts as evidence for goodness is just a personal choice. So supposing a person claimed that being vindictive, dishonest and unjust was good. Plato similarly reviews this in his myth of 'The Ring of Gyges'. In order to survive, the unjust man will have to be a very cunning liar, and constantly on his guard that he will be betrayed and dealt with. We simply cannot get away with evil, except in isolated circumstances. Therefore the facts are that injustice is never more profitable than justice *in the long run*, because we can only function in a social context, where we can depend on others and safely trust them. The consistent, unjust person would be plagued by insecurity that he will be found out, so 'good' is inextricably linked to justice and virtuous behaviour, because only the just flourish.

Synoptic link

'The Ring of Gyges' is discussed in AQA AS Philosophy Chapter 3, Why should I be moral?

Evaluation

Not everyone will be convinced that there is an inevitable link between human welfare and behaving virtuously. The link is contingent and dependent on circumstances, rather than necessary. One might cite certain dictators, for example Chairman Mao in China, who behaved abominably and hypocritically, as he indulged in many pleasures that he denied the people, yet died apparently revered and peacefully. As a pragmatic argument, it is not entirely effective, and at worst reduces morality to expediency. As Pinchin argues, 'sooner or later Foot is going to have to offer a non-moral consideration as to why one should be moral. Once you set off on that road, you end up with a corrupt account of morality' (Pinchin, 1990).

Furthermore, the argument seems to beg the question of what we mean by human flourishing, or that it is even the highest good. A fascist might claim that the exploitation of others (Nietzsche 'the herd') is justifiable for a great man, and a religious zealot may cite God's will rather than humanistic values as their end goal. A previous quotation from Mill is relevant: that questions about ultimate ends are particularly difficult to decide. If one rejects that there are objective facts about goodness, then the fact–value gap remains unbridged. A meaningful use of the word therefore remains relative to culture and context.

Social institutions

Whereas Foot tries to derive value from facts via human needs and interests, Searle attempts to do so via institutional and social facts, – that certain human conventions entail values. He uses the practice of promising as an example (Fig. 4.1).

So if one utters a promise to someone (fact), then one enters into a social practice, which in turn entails a moral obligation to carry it out (value). To offer another example, if I accept Sheila's proposal of marriage and utter: 'I will marry you Sheila', this necessarily commits me to obligations to go through with a wedding, not to commit adultery etc. So from entering into a social convention can be derived moral values.

Evaluation

Critics will argue that implicit in the initial act are concealed values and choices. To say 'I hereby …' is not just a matter of behaviour, but an endorsement and commitment to the importance of keeping one's word, and to affirm the values of the convention. In the case of marriage, the commitment is highlighted in the rituals of exchanging rings etc. So, with reference to Figure 4.1, (1) is not just a matter of fact, since values are concealed in the act.

Secondly, (3) does not necessarily follow from (2). Moral obligations are contestable and there can be disagreements over (3) dependent on circumstances and moral interpretation. Whereas (2) is a matter of truth or falsity, (3) is a matter of right and wrong. We can envisage a situation where despite making a promise, an obligation is denied because of duress or adverse consequences etc., so that (3) is a matter of moral debate rather than incontrovertible fact. Hare also claimed that there is a concealed premise – that one ought to keep one's promises.

Nevertheless, Hare perhaps over-emphasises the extent to which we can stand outside social institution and make autonomous choices. Foot and Searle remind us that ethical choices are grounded in our way of life. If we do not base our morality on the fundamental conditions of life, how do we choose our values? We cannot simply ignore that we have to live in the world, labour and that life is finite. The implications of this surely, cannot be entirely ethically neutral. Nevertheless, it is not possible to determine a logically necessary connection between any fact and any value.

Supervenience

Some philosophers, therefore, have argued that the relationship between facts and values is one of supervenience. Values supervene on facts, rather than necessarily deriving from facts, so 'good' is not defined as 'happiness' but is supervenient on happiness.

The relationship of supervenience means first that values are dependent on facts; and secondly, that there can be no difference or change in moral values, without a difference or change in non-moral properties, so values are not entirely free floating. So, for example, if good is supervenient on happiness, then two actions that deliver identical amounts of happiness are equally good, and any alteration in the value of one, is consequent on a change in the amount of happiness produced. Hare in *The Language of Morals* offered this example.

> Suppose that we say 'St Francis was a good man'. It is logically impossible to say this and to maintain at the same time that there might have been another man placed exactly in the same

Fact: Jones says 'I hereby promise to pay you, Smith $5

↓ Implies

Fact: Jones promises to pay Smith $5

↓ Implies

Fact: Jones is under obligation to pay Smith.

↓ Implies

Value: Jones ought to pay Smith.

Fig. 4.1 *Searle argues certain human conventions entail values*

Synoptic link

AQA A2 Philosophy Chapter 1, Philosophy of mind, p45.

circumstances as St Francis, and who behaved in exactly the same way, but who differed from St Francis in this respect only, that he was not a good man.

Hare (1963)

Thick and thin concepts

■ **Think about**

Consider such thick concepts as 'kind', 'cruel', 'dishonest', 'courageous'. What is the descriptive content? Could it be possible to agree on the facts of a case, but disagree on the use of these terms? You may want to refer back to Foot on words such as 'dangerous'.

It may be helpful to distinguish between different ethical terms. Words such as 'courageous', 'cruel', 'generous' and 'dishonest' have a high descriptive content and are labelled 'thick' concepts (Williams, 1995). So to be generous, for example, one has to fulfil certain criteria, such as giving money to deserving causes. In this realm of discourse, our moral judgements cannot significantly differ because the meaning of such words is determined by facts. It would not be possible to call someone generous if they never helped their friends or gave to charity.

Now, terms such as 'good', 'right' and 'ought' that have much less content are called 'thin' concepts. They are much freer floating, but it is argued they supervene on thick concepts. So the word 'good' is dependent on 'kindness', 'honesty', 'truthfulness' etc., and so cannot be used about anything at all. Furthermore thick concepts cannot be fully grasped without grasping their evaluative implication. One does not fully understand generosity, if one does not realise its positive nature.

Thus the question of whether moral words are tied to particular facts and the case for cognitivism depends on the nature of the concept. It is hard to deny that there can be knowledge of thick concepts and that they to some extent determine our understanding of thin concepts.

Secondary properties

■ **Synoptic link**

AQA AS Philosophy Chapter 2, Knowledge of the external world, p40.

Some moral philosophers have borrowed an analogy from the Philosophy of perception and compared moral opinions to secondary properties. This implies that our moral perception is dependent on a network of beliefs and a conceptual framework, which we impose on the world. This point was originally made by Hume:

> Vice and virtue may be compared to sounds, colours, heat and cold, which … are not qualities in objects but perceptions in the mind.

Hume (1969, Bk III.i.1)

The distinction between primary and secondary qualities in perception is as follows. Primary qualities of an object, such as size and motion, belong to the object and are inseparable from it. We all acknowledge an object has a size and shape that we can measure. These qualities are independent of a person's perspective. However, secondary qualities such as colour and sound are a product of the powers of the object but are dependent on the way our senses interpret the sensations and the way in which they appear to our minds. Thus perception of colours depends on the structure of our eyes (dogs can only see in black and white); and whether a sound is high or low is an interpretation of the sound. Hume argues that moral qualities are similarly subject to our passions and sentiments so at least partly dependent on the state of our minds. A vice is a feeling of disapproval towards a behaviour – 'it lies in yourself, not the object'.

A first point to notice is that to give the same status to morality as colours would be sufficient to maintain a case for moral realism.

> Secondary-quality experience presents itself as perceptual awareness of properties genuinely possessed by the objects.
>
> *McDowell (1985)*

Although we might accept that colours and sounds vary according to the perception of the observer, we still retain a notion of normal or standard vision. A colour-blind person is mistaken and a deaf person who denies the existence of a sound is inaccurate. More recent moral realists also argue that, like colours, moral opinions can be determined true or false by the way things are in the world. Thus McNaughton in *Moral Vision* (1988) explains the realists' view that we can see the beauty in a sunset or the cruelty in a spiteful act. While there may be some difference of opinion, they reject the position implied by Hume, that moral perception is a two-stage process, whereby we see the event, such as the sunset, and we contribute the feeling of pleasure that is designated beauty. According to McNaughton, 'the beauty of the sunset is woven into my experience of it' and 'I am thrilled by the sunset because I see it to be beautiful; I do not take it to be beautiful because I and others, are thrilled by it'. Similarly we *observe* cruelty, we do not *judge* an act to be cruel. Thus the world has 'power' which determines what we see, and moral beliefs are determined by the way things are in the world. Therefore there are moral truths – an act can be identified as generous, courageous and so on, independently of any individual's perspective.

The non-cognitivist might reply that matters of fact do not entail a particular moral stance, and that we can accept an account of events yet reject the moral conclusion. The cognitivist will respond that while there may be some variety of opinion, widely differing moral positions will be unreasonable and lack coherence with other shared moral beliefs. Just like 'dangerous', the words 'fearful' or 'worrying' can only be used about situations that genuinely merit fear and concern.

This theory is developed by McDowell in 'Values and Secondary Qualities' (1985). He argues that moral rightness is a matter of perception, but that rightness cannot be a primary quality because:

1 Whatever is right is tied to human sensibility.
2 We would need a faculty by which these objective moral qualities were comprehended – a mysterious intuition, about which we can say nothing.

However, moral properties, like colour, are both:

1 Subjective: because they are not independent of human perception, they are 'phenomenal'.
2 Objective: as we experience them as properties of objects that make certain demands on us.

These properties will elicit appropriate responses, under normal circumstances to those who are suitably sensitive, just as the structure of an object stimulates a colour in normal light to those whose eyesight is properly functioning. So just as it is straightforwardly false to say that London buses are green, it is similarly false to say unwarranted suffering is okay.

As David Clark (2003, Chapter 9) explains, the 'suitable sensitivity' is Virtue, which is knowledge that can be learnt just as people learn to distinguish colours. Thus the virtue of kindness allows the agent to read a situation and know the appropriate response. These virtues can be taught by experts and we can make moral progress in understanding

Synoptic link

Whether this distinction holds in perception is discussed in AQA AS Philosophy Chapter 2, Knowledge of the external world, p40.

Think about

Compare and contrast the statements. 'Lemons are yellow' and 'Torture is wrong'. In what respects do they express something which is objective? In what respects do they express something which is subjective? Do they both express truths?

situations (see the section 'Virtue theory' later). If we do not respond correctly to the features of an object or event, that is, show proper concern for the welfare of a friend, then our sensibility is incomplete. So the features of the event should under normal circumstances give rise to appropriate feelings – things are good when they elicit sentiments of rightness and vice versa. The test for the truth of a moral belief becomes first whether it is used in judgements for which there are developed standards of rational argument, and secondly whether it makes otherwise inexplicable events meaningful. So moral properties will be no less real than colours, smells, quarks or black holes.

McDowell, however, also notes a disanalogy between rightness and colour. This is no causal relationship between acts and sentiments as there is with the structure of objects and colour. In the case of sense experience, there is an identifiable correlation between cause (wavelengths) and effects (eye structure). Now Hume suggests that there is a similar correlation between suffering and disapproval (because of our sympathy). However, McDowell describes the relationship as one of *merit* not *cause*: whereas objects have the power to cause perceptions of colour, moral properties merit a certain normative response. But surely 'merit' allows for much more disagreement and variety of opinion that 'cause'; and therefore the non-cognitivists will claim aesthetic and moral judgements are much more subjective. We can witness the same event and have very different emotions, for example fox hunting. Can we speak of correct, normal, moral vision? While differences in human perception are limited and accountable, can the same be said of morality? It can be argued that facts about the world do not have the same causal power to produce moral beliefs in the way that physical objects cause sensations.

Wright, in a recent work (1992) quoted by Tollefsen (2000) has described realism as committed to two claims about moral objectivity:

1 'The modest claim' that moral facts are as they are, independent of all perceivers.
2 'The self-assured claim' that perceivers can gain some form of access to moral facts without terribly distorting them.

To come to a conclusion on moral truth, it is necessary to decide whether either of these claims can be substantiated. Some might contend with regard to (2), that despite superficial or local variations, there is a universal core of moral agreement – for example, cheating on your friends is nowhere approved of. The utilitarian principle could similarly be offered as evidence of some objectivity.

However, with colour there are independent circumstances to check whether the London bus is really green or is in fact red, but there are no such independent and objective checks to ascertain whether the features of the event should elicit kindness of not. What makes it easy to talk about the objectivity of colours is that there are standard conditions of perception that we all share, that is, normal vision, daylight etc. But are there such standard conditions in moral situations? In the section 'Virtue theory' below, we will argue that there are conditions pertaining to human flourishing that are standard, while subjectivists will claim that every situation is unique and that even deceiving your friends can never be ruled out.

Thus Clark points out that the problem is that:

> Moral objectivity depends upon the availability of a means of validating the sensibilities of some while exposing that of others as misleading of chimerical. And for this is seems we must get outside our sensibilities.

Clark (2003)

Think about

'Independent "scientific" checks ultimately rely on human judgement just as all judgement of value and morality do.' Is that statement illuminating or misleading?

It was this detached, absolute standard of value that Plato was attempting to provide. Furthermore, it would not even be enough to argue that the virtuous sensibilities are coherent and the rightness derives from their coherence, because it is possible to ask of any moral code:

'Yes it is coherent – but is it right?'

A final point is that Hume's account appears to be a return to naturalism, except that the quality common to all good acts is not in the observed, but in the observer. The source of goodness is our capacity for selfless sympathy for others, our natural tendency to be moved by the happiness and suffering of others. So 'good' becomes identified with virtuous sentiments that are useful and agreeable to ourselves and others, such as benevolence and cheerfulness. As a naturalist theory it will be subject to the controversy of deriving value from facts. In this case, it moves from the fact 'we feel sympathy for others', to the fact 'such behaviour is useful' to the value 'we ought to adopt this behaviour as right'. Can you spot the exact moment when Hume moves from 'is' to 'ought':

> Sympathy, we shall allow, is much fainter than our concern for ourselves, and sympathy with persons remote from us much fainter than that with persons near and contagious; but for this very reason it is necessary for us, in our calm judgements and discourse concerning the characters of men, to neglect all these differences and render our sentiments more public and social... The intercourse of sentiments, therefore, in society and conversation makes us form some general unalterable standard by which we may approve or disapprove of characters and manners.

> *Hume (2006)*

Moral beliefs and actions

A significant aspect of moral situations is that when we understand a moral dilemma, we are usually required to act. A specific issue for cognitivists is to explain the connection between moral understanding and moral action. If we say that value statements can be straightforwardly factually true, the question then arises as to how moral beliefs taken in this way motivate action:

> mere awareness of the facts ... can never be sufficient to provide the agent with reason to act.

> *McNaughton (1988)*

So do we need another desire, the desire to do the right thing? This, it will be seen, is not a problem for non-cognitivists.

Moral realists respond in two ways. *Externalists* maintain that what is good for someone is a factual matter, which can be decided by a study of human societies. However, only those who are concerned for others will be motivated to be good and it is quite possible not to be moved by moral considerations. They conceive of morality as a complex system of rules for promoting human welfare (McNaughton, 1988), and rather like a scientist acting on experimental knowledge, any questions of how to live is a factual one.

One odd implication of externalism is that they must allow that one could admit of a duty to do something, yet still feel no motive to do it, and so 'someone who personally has no concern for human welfare may still recognise the moral truth that inflicting unnecessary suffering is

Think about

Are the following responses inevitable, because of the universal nature of human beings:

- Harming others is wrong.
- Promoting one's own happiness.
- Showing care and concern for others.
- Maintaining self-respect.
- Promoting trust and truthfulness.
- Treating everyone consistently and fairly.

(Some intuitionists claim these are self-evident moral principles.)

wrong' (McNaughton, 1988) and act accordingly. It would seem strange that someone would accept a moral duty yet at the same time claim he had no reason to do it. The question therefore still remains how a moral truth can exhibit a moral demand to which we must conform, regardless of any personal wants.

In contrast, the *internalist* would only admit that they have a reason to do a duty if they have come to the conclusion that *x* is the right thing to do and consequently desire it.

We can understand this by contrasting it with the standard Humean model of how action is motivated. Hume claims that an action is caused by two mental states:

1 a belief, which is passive, and

2 a desire, which is active.

He separates the cognitive state (1), from the motivated state (2), so that moral beliefs can only elicit action if there are also appropriate desires. McDowell (1985), however, denies this and claims that a perception of truth (i.e. belief) justifies both the action and the desire; for how could we understand a desire except as part of a belief? Thus he presents a position which is realist, cognitivist and also internalist.

> It is cognitvist, and internalist because the virtuous person's way of understanding a situation is sufficient to motivate her.

Tollefsen (2000)

Thus when two people see a situation and only one is motivated to act (morally), it is not the case that they see the same facts, but one has a different, independent desire. What accounts for the different response is how they conceive of the facts. One is 'virtuously sensitive' and the other is not. It is the beliefs of the former that he is required to act which is sufficient to motivate action. Thus an agent can be motivated by a cognitive state and moved to intervene by her understanding of a moral requirement. Cognitive states are not passive.

On the belief-desire theory, we can picture the desire as distinct from the beliefs and additional to the beliefs. This account is rejected by the internalist realist.

✔ *After working through this topic, you should:*

- understand and be able to evaluate the case for God-independent moral truths
- be able to assess whether moral knowledge can be based on natural facts
- understand the open question argument and the naturalistic fallacy, and be able to discuss whether the fact–value gap can be bridged
- know why moral values have been compared with secondary properties and be able to criticise the analogy
- appreciate issues in the connection between moral beliefs and actions.

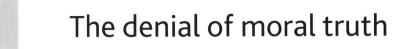

The denial of moral truth

Relativism

Discussion of ethical relativism usually begins with factual and descriptive accounts of the wide variety of conflicting values found in different cultures and at various times in history. The reader might like to research some of the more eccentric beliefs about what constitutes right and wrong. Suffice it to say that cannibalism, polygamy, slavery, paedophilia and rape have all been regarded as acceptable practices by one civilisation or another.

The first thing to note is that no factual account of people's different values leads to any normative or ethical conclusion in particular. Having surveyed different beliefs, one could adopt any of the following responses:

- these practices are wrong and we must stop them
- we should leave people alone to develop their own values
- since there is such a wide variety of moral values, there are no absolute values – cannibalism is right for some people
- although we cannot prove these values are wrong, we should be intolerant, and criticise and suppress them
- we should be tolerant, and when in their country, respect their culture
- these values are primitive and we should help these people to make moral progress.

Normative relativism

From the above position of descriptive relativism, it can be argued that accounts by themselves do not justify any particular conclusion. However, normative relativism advocates that different moral outlooks are appropriate in their own time and place. Whatever is thought to be right in a culture is right, so when in Rome, do as the Romans do. Moral values ought to be considered as cultural preferences, and behaviour must be judged relative to the culture from which it arose. So the ritual killing of the elderly is justified in a culture where survival is a key issue.

The above position is a normative one – a prescription, that is itself a value about what is permissible and acceptable. It embodies a form of tolerance.

Some philosophers argue that regarding moral values as simply a cultural preference leads to unacceptable conclusions, such as:

1 It would be difficult to criticise the standards of any culture or to make comparisons. So, slavery was right at the time, and we have not made moral progress in abolishing it.

2 Moral values should be justified according to their origin, rather than according to modern and civilised standards of decency and justice. This is a form of the **genetic fallacy**, that because a practice originated out of particular needs or beliefs, it is justified.

Synoptic link

AQA AS Philosophy Chapter 6, Tolerance, p184; AQA A2 Philosophy Chapter 10, Philosophical problems in Nietzsche. This can be found at **www.nelsonthornes.com/aqagce**

AQA Examiner's tip

Cultural relativism is often superficially used to argue that there are no absolute moral values. After reading this section, you should be able to explain why this is not so.

And furthermore:

- It assumes that cultures are homogeneous and accepted by all within it. But in any culture, some people will feel alien and uncomfortable and will argue that moral mistakes have been made.

- It perpetuates the belief that moral truths are not 'discovered' and 'out there' but rather 'invented' and 'created' by people who could change their beliefs and interpret events differently. It is possible to have more than one coherent value system to accommodate facts.

- It suggests that if consenting adults, or the most powerful sections of society, agree to something, no matter how degrading or disgusting, then it should be allowed.

Conclusion

While all of the above positions have pros and cons, relativism can logically have nothing to say about how we should behave. If it does, it contradicts itself, by advocating one unique, absolute, universal value.

Yet it does suggest that we should adopt a 'humility' (Williams, 1995) in making moral judgements about others, because others 'may not' and perhaps 'should not' recognise our standards, if they themselves are being authentic. The fact that our moral perspective is contingent could be used as a case for tolerance, but that is open to debate.

First, it is necessary to examine two theories that deny moral realism and moral truth: emotivism and prescriptivism.

Emotivism (A.J. Ayer)

Ayer is concerned with what is meaningful. To begin with, he identifies two kinds of ethical statements that are meaningful:

1 Propositions which define terms and unpack the meanings of words – for example, 'cruel means spiteful' etc.

2 Propositions about the phenomena of ethical experience – for example, accounts of what people believe.

But the most interesting utterances are the third class of statements that make moral judgements, such as cannibalism is wrong. These propositions do not seem to have factual content and would therefore appear to be meaningless. Since Ayer accepts the 'is → ought' fallacy, normative propositions cannot simply convey empirical information, and they are not telling us anything about the world. This includes whether I am experiencing a feeling of approval. Since there is no way of ascertaining whether or not someone has such a feeling, it cannot be substantiated that whenever P says 'X is good', they are describing their feeling. So nothing is being claimed by moral statements that can be true or false.

Furthermore, Ayer makes use of a similar argument to the 'open question' argument. If 'X is good' means 'I approve of X', then it could not be meaningful to say that I approve of something bad, yet, this is not contradictory.

So Ayer concludes that moral terms *express* rather than *describe* feelings and attitudes. When I say 'X is good' I am expressing a feeling of approval, with a secondary purpose of encouraging and evoking the same feeling in others. This has been likened to saying Hurrah (or Boo) to X or shouting X with a thumbs up gesture. So the significant feature of moral propositions is not their descriptive content, but their expressive quality. Whether or not I actually have a feeling is beside the point.

An implication of this theory is that if ethical terms are purely emotive, it would be possible to express approval/disapproval for anything, since the evaluative component has been separated from any factual content. I could say 'hurrah for pencils' and hope to arouse the same feeling in you. Thus Ayer agrees that moral language is not indicative, and informative, but a form of command – something like, 'approve of pencils!'

From this, it follows that ethical statements have no objective validity or claim to truth. They do *not* provide knowledge (non cognitive), refer to a natural property (non-naturalistic) or claim there is a moral reality (anti-realism). They do not even assert the existence of feelings. Thus Ayer admits his theory is 'radically subjectivist' and distinguishes this from 'orthodox subjectivist' theory. The latter claims that moral judgements *are* simply feelings, but on Ayer's theory, 'tolerance is a virtue' makes no claim about the state of anyone's feelings, but purely expresses approval:

> I can express boredom, without actually saying 'I am bored'

> *Ayer (1971)*

Ayer admits that this theory entails that one cannot argue about value. If I say 'X is good' and you say 'X is bad', we have just expressed different emotions, so we are not contradicting one another. If there is a dispute, it is about relevant matters of fact and these can be argued about. So if I bolster my disapproval of stealing by appeals to the unhappiness it brings, we can conduct surveys and dispute the facts about unhappiness. But in the end, if we agree on the facts, there is no way of resolving a difference of attitude. This seems to agree with a familiar position, that in the end, you cannot prove that someone is wrong, if they adopt a different attitude to the same events. Moral arguments fail us, once the differences over fact are dealt with. It is rather like two people looking at the same painting and expressing different tastes. All we can do is praise or blame, but matters of taste and sentiment are beyond argument. Emotivism captures this feature of moral discussion.

Furthermore, it is consistent with the dynamic aspect of moral beliefs. We know that we can change our mind or develop different moral attitudes to something. How many people, in recent times, have altered their feelings towards racism, sexism and homosexuality? So this theory accommodates a change in our sentiments and our approval of different kinds of behaviour.

Evaluation

This separation of the factual content from the expressive quality causes great uneasiness because of its radical subjectivity. The analysis implies that we can express approval about anything we like. It would in theory be possible to approve of paedophilia or genocide, or to give purely neutral accounts of facts and allow people to add on their emotive attitude. But surely this is not possible. It is not possible to sustain this separation, because our values determine how we interpret behaviour, or even what we consider to be a relevant fact. It would be impossible to use words such as 'generous' or 'suffering', because you cannot understand these words without their positive and negative associations. In any civil war, there is rarely agreement on the description of the facts because they are viewed through different spectacles. A shooting, for example, is seen as 'provoked' or 'a retaliation' or 'premeditated' or 'an over-reaction'. Remember the oft-quoted dictum that one man's terrorist is another man's freedomfighter. So it can be maintained that there are rarely

Think about

Describing, expressing and describing Factual statements indicate and describe; emotive statements express emotion and taste; but moral statements prescribe and recommend action.

Identify these propositions:

- You cannot smoke in the café.
- The notice said, 'you cannot smoke in the café'.
- You should not watch that kind of programme.
- She is such a sweet child.
- You ought to consider this university.
- Great picture!

And more difficult!

- Cornflakes are good for you.
- It is healthy to take regular exercise.
- That is a clever plan.
- You should have watched football last night.

Can you distinguish between expressing emotion and prescribing behaviour?

neutral matters of fact that are incontrovertible, because events are viewed through a web of beliefs.

A second concern is that Ayer seems to have trivialised moral debate. In the end, he agrees that it is reduced to 'mere abuse', since all we can do is swap slogans and exchange expletives. I say that I approve, you say that you disapprove – end of story. If, as Ayer claims, we are solely expressing feelings, then neither of us is wrong and there is no actual contradiction. But moral disagreements *are* contradictions about *values*, *choices* and *actions*. If we disagree about stealing, we cannot adopt both views, since we are either going to thieve or not thieve.

We can and do have reasoned debates about value systems, their consistency, their implications and their importance for life choices. Should one universalise, consider the consequences or admit social facts? This is the important difference between moral debate, and propaganda and advertising. The former is distinguishable by its appeal to rational concepts and considerations that invoking feelings and prejudices is not. For example, on Ayer's account, I could adopt one attitude today and a different attitude tomorrow, without contradicting myself and being charged with inconsistency, hypocrisy and insincerity. Emotional pleas and expletives can seek to influence moral argument, but they are not themselves moral arguments. There is much more to a moral conversion, because as we shall see with prescriptivism, it involves a change of commitments and rational implications.

The last point suggests that the focus of emotivism is wrong. Moral debates are primarily about actions and behaviour, not just about feelings. Debates about what time a teenager should return home become emotive because there is a contradiction about what to do. They cannot both be out at 10.00 pm and home at 10.00 pm.

For this reason, the theory does not sufficiently distinguish between aesthetic and ethical discussion. While we can agree to differ on how we feel about a work of art, so the discussion is largely emotive; but we cannot agree to differ on how to behave, which is more significant and urgent. Morality is not just about a matter of taste, but choices of action that have important repercussions for others. So there is a definite distinction between moral and aesthetic utterances, and 'it is right' cannot be reduced to 'I am glad' (see subjectivity).

Prescriptivism

Richard Hare argued that moral thinking takes place at two levels, a lower level where we prescribe principles without questioning and a higher level to decide principles and resolve conflicts between them. This theory evolved out of emotivism, but changed the focus from *expressing* and trying to influence *feelings*, to *prescribing* and *action*-guiding. There is also more emphasis on the rationality of moral utterances, that moral judgements should be universal, and that there are logical relations between moral statements. Aspects of this theory were referred to in the previous section, but key points will again be summarised.

Prescriptivism denies that there is a moral reality or moral truths. The common feature in all good acts is not that they exhibit a certain quality, but that they are commended. Moral language is characterised by its form (e.g. it is an imperative) rather than its content, which is contingent. We are the sources of value, it is a matter of personal decision making and so it is non-cognitivist – there are no objective moral values to be discovered and no moral experts.

Key philosophers

Richard Hare (1919–2002): Taught at Oxford University from 1947 to 1983 and published influential texts such as *The Language of Morals* and *Freedom and Reason*.

To sum up, moral statements are prescriptions and recommendations about choices of behaviour, according to our personal values.

Now, once we utter a recommendation, it would be insincere and hypocritical if we did not apply it to our own actions. Consistency demands that I act according to the moral imperatives I give to others. Furthermore, I am also committed to universalise my beliefs that in all similarly relevant situations, people ought to behave according to my guidance; and that moral prescriptions override other particular or aesthetic commands, since moral imperatives apply to *all* similar circumstances.

Once more we have an important separation between the descriptive content and the prescriptive, evaluative add on. So 'good' cannot be wholly identified with something's function or certain criteria – their natural qualities. Hare also uses a version of Moore's open question argument, which is explained by Pinchin (1990). If we identified a good picture as that which is 'admired by the Royal Academy', then to say something is good because it is admired by the RA would be a tautology like 'all bachelors are unmarried'. But it is possible to ask: 'are all pictures admired by the RA good pictures?' This is a meaningful, open question, to which a significant 'yes' or 'no' answer is possible. So 'good' cannot be identified with 'admired by the RA'. This will apply to any criteria. Because as well as a descriptive element, there is also an evaluative, commending 'add on' to any use of the word good, as we discussed with the example of shmakums. This evaluative element, unlike Ayer, is not an expression of approval, but a recommendation to choose and to act – a kind of imperative.

Non-cognitivism: moral beliefs and actions

The question is whether we actually desire value *x* because it is desirable (cognitivism) or, value *x* is desirable because we desire it (non-cognitivism). If one accepts the distinction between facts and values, then we could argue, as Hare does, that only moral statements, which are prescriptive, entail that we perform our duties. As the word 'good' does not refer to a truth independent of the views of any individual, but is an action-guiding word, the issue of motivation becomes simply a matter of coherence and authenticity: that recommendations should be internally consistent. Contradictory beliefs can seem ungenuine and hypocritical.

According to Hare, there are three implications of a sincere moral belief:

1 that I am obliged to carry it out, unless other moral considerations intervene

2 that I must believe everyone in a relevantly similar situation has a similar obligation – universalisation

3 that moral imperatives override other particular imperatives or aesthetic imperatives.

This is the rational aspect of morality.

It would be a contradiction to hold a prescriptive principle, yet not commit oneself when the opportunity arose.

However, Hare also points out that moral beliefs can be refined, so that for example, a belief that stealing is wrong might be ignored to feed a starving family. So the principle is modified to something like: 'do not steal except in cases of saving life'.

In (2), Hare argues that moral commands are different from ordinary commands by their feature of universality. Having a principle requires that the command remains in force whenever a relevantly similar situation occurs. So if I wish to imprison someone for dishonesty, then I must accept that I can be imprisoned for the same reason, unless there are morally significant differences. An interesting implication here, which Hare discusses, is the case of fanatics, for example those who impose strict religious discipline on others, and accept it themselves. Is it the case that to be authentic, one must accept the freedom of others to make their own choices?

With regard to (3), moral imperatives have superior force over other commands. So if a soldier is ordered to torture a prisoner, his moral objection overrides the requirement to obey an officer's orders. Hare gives the example of his wife giving him cushions which do not match the colour of his sofa. He acknowledges an aesthetic imperative not to allow clashing colours, but this does not take precedence over much more important moral imperatives, such as to be grateful (to his wife) for well-meaning gifts.

Evaluation of prescriptivism

We have already discussed the issue of whether a prescriptive add-on can be applied to any descriptive content, or whether 'good' can be fixed to certain facts that are meaningful. This would allow the possibility of moral truth. The discussion with Foot should be revised.

The cognitivist will object that non-cognitivism means that anyone can accept the evidence that is used to support a moral position, and yet without contradicting himself reject the moral conclusion and an imperative to act. But surely moral reasoning not only involves the requirements of internal consistency and universalities, but also a careful and sensitive appreciation of the salient facts. In our observations of selflessness, kindness and courage we are noticing goodness, and when we observe cruelty such as the Holocaust, we are witnessing evil and must act accordingly. This recognition of good and evil (belief) also motivates action.

Also, as we identified with Ayer, there is a problem with what is to count as 'similarly relevant' situations. Since what the facts are is not entirely a neutral matter, but open to interpretation, so there will be an element of choice and perspective on what is to count as 'similar' and relevant.

It might be argued that every situation is unique, and what might count as a relevant similarity is open to interpretation. In the extreme case, one might argue that the individuality of someone's character and interests precludes any application of a moral principle. Sartre in *Existentialism and Humanism* (1974), cites the example of a man who fails at school, in work and in his love life. The man interprets this as a sign that he should become a Jesuit priest. But Sartre points out that this is a subjective choice and interpretation of his predicament that cannot be prescribed to others. Each of us 'interprets the signs as he chooses'. While I can advise someone, 'that if I were in your position, I would do *X*', I also invite the retort that, 'you are not me'. The most that one can claim is, 'do unto others as you would be done by', and that you cannot make yourself a special case.

So moral language cannot be distinguished by its form alone, there must be some content. It is not only prescription and consistency that is at the heart of moral disputes, but also correctness. Otherwise someone who we would describe as a fanatic would be a model of moral behaviour, since they never waiver from their chosen course of action. But a suicide bomber is wrong because of *what* they do, and morality is not only about *how* we apply our principles.

▌ Think about

Is a belief in moral truth required to make sense of the notions of 'moral progress' and 'moral mistakes'? Does emotivism and prescriptivism rule out these notions?

In fact, lack of consistency or flexibility is not always to be condemned as insincere and ungenuine. To 'turn a blind eye', to 'tell a white lie', to be sensitive to a situation is a sign of a subtle and sophisticated or at least human approach to morality. Good can come from not treating everyone the same, and suspending the rigorous application of moral imperatives.

Furthermore, universality should not be confused with impartiality. Again, it is purely a test of consistency. Norman points out that it does imply that if X is wrong because he did Z, then Y is also wrong if he does Z. However, it does not entail that I have to consider everyone's interests impartially. He uses Hare's example of the two trumpeters to illustrate the point.

Imagine that two musicians live in rooms next door to one another, and that one wants to practise jazz, and one classical music. Now if you hold the belief that people should consider their own interests, then you are committed to the universalisation that other people may consider their own interests too, but you are not committed to the impartial consideration of other people's interests. Both musicians could be consistently egoist and each practise their style of music. One could say genuinely and consistently since I play my style of music, then he must be allowed to play his style of music. But Hare wants to argue that they must 'give weight to (each other's) interests' and limit how long and loudly they play. But this further commitment to the impartial consideration of everyone's interest, to become a sympathetic and disinterested observer, is not the same as a simple test of consistency.

Finally the thesis in (3), that moral imperatives must override others, is also questionable. Hamilton (2003) points out that I may consider an aesthetic imperative, such as preserving old buildings and natural landscapes, more important than a commitment to human welfare, such as the construction of new homes. If the reply is that this aesthetic principle is really a moral principle in disguise, about perhaps, human pleasure or freedom, then this could apply to any aesthetic judgement, and so does allow aesthetic values to trump moral ones.

☑ *After working through this topic, you should:*

- understand normative and descriptive relativism and be able to discuss their implications

- be able to explain and assess emotivism and prescriptivism

- be able to present a debate on the existence of moral truth

- know how to explain and evaluate the fact–value gap.

> ### Synoptic link
>
> For further discussion of the denial of moral truth, see AQA A2 Philosophy Chapter 10, Philosophical problems in Nietzsche. This can be found at **www.nelsonthornes.com/aqagce**

Moral decisions

Think about

Which of these arguments is teleological and which deontological?

- With limited resources available, hospitals should give treatment to those who will gain the most quality years of life from being treated.

- Some religious groups believe that blood transfusions are morally wrong. So one day, when a young boy was seriously hurt in a car accident and rushed to hospital, his parents who held this belief refused to give permission to the doctors to give him blood and save his life.

- Doctors take a Hippocratic oath to save life and therefore should never perform a mercy killing.

- If a prisoner on Death Row is miserable and wretched because of remorse and a life sentence, it is better to execute them. This will also act as a deterrent to other would-be criminals.

Introduction

Once you have developed your position on moral truth, the next step is to apply your decision to moral dilemmas. Thus if you agree that the natural quality common to all good acts is happiness, then moral decisions will be made on the criteria of maximising happiness. We have already seen how Mill bases the desirability of an action on what is actually desired. Some non-cognitivists have also advocated maximising the satisfaction of people's preferences. Hare develops the notion of consistency and universalisability to also argue for a form of utilitarianism.

One of the most important distinctions in moral judgements is the distinction between teleological and deontological theories.

Teleological theories, such as utilitarianism, claim that a decision should aim to produce the most beneficial consequences. Thus killing is usually wrong because it generally leads to negative results, but if the consequences were to be good, such as in the assassination of a homicidal maniac, then it would be morally justified.

Deontological ethics, however, argue that it is the rightness or wrongness of the act itself that matters, regardless of the consequences. So if you believe in the sanctity of human life, then killing is always wrong, despite any positive results. It is your duty to adhere to ethical principles, regardless of particular situations, such as always obeying the Ten Commandments.

First, we will consider the most influential of all teleological theories: utilitarianism.

Utilitarianism

The classical version of this theory is usually attributed to **Bentham**, who in a eureka moment, discovered the idea of 'the greatest good of the greatest number', which he named the Principle of Utility.

He applied this principle to law, which we should note is prescriptive, commanding what citizens ought to do. He claimed that human beings have two 'sovereign masters' which 'govern' how they behave (fact). These are pain and pleasure. The utility principle recognises this and defines good as happiness, which is the absence of pain and suffering, and the presence of pleasure. The moral value of the action or law will therefore depend on the amount of pleasure and pain it produces, which can only be calculated through assessing the consequences. Happiness is the overall sum of pleasure over pain. This exposition of the theory is described as:

- act utilitarianism – every action must be judged on the principle of utility.
- hedonistic – the aim is to produce pleasure.
- teleological – the action is good if the consequences produce the greatest happiness for the greatest number.

Let us deal with some immediate issues that are often raised with this theory.

Can you measure pleasure?

Utilitarianism has been criticised for proposing the idea that the feeling of pleasure can be quantified. Bentham actually proposed a 'hedonic calculus', which determined the value of a pleasure according to intensity, duration, certainty, remoteness, fecundity, purity and number of persons. Few people, however, have claimed to use it successfully! Nevertheless, we can and do roughly estimate how happy people will be when considering the presents we will buy them. The issue is whether this can be applied to moral considerations. For example, we can be fairly sure that killing a mature oak tree will cause more distress than destroying an acorn. But can the same be said for an adult human and a foetus?

Is it a pig philosophy?

The theory has been accused of not discriminating between bestial satisfaction and refined pleasure. Bentham is quoted as saying, 'pushpin is as good as poetry'. And furthermore, can we identify moral goodness with gaining pleasure? Surely the two are quite distinct. Mill's response will be considered later, but Bentham can be defended on the grounds that he is not advocating short-term, unenlightened, sensation seeking. Poetry will probably give more enduring, varied and stimulating pleasure than repeated games of a trivial nature, and if moral behaviour does not make us happy, then surely we have a serious question as to why we should perform our duty. While people may not get immediate satisfaction from keeping a promise, we all recognise the happiness derived from trust and friendship. So most people take an enlightened approach and aim for the best long-term consequences. Can the same be said for respecting other people's rights?

Can we calculate consequences?

A further common complaint against any teleological theory is that it is impossible to predict the consequences, and to foresee the consequences of those consequences. If we cannot do something, then it is fruitless to say we ought to do it (**'ought' implies 'can'**).

Yet Bentham might reply that we can and do and ought to. We all consider the consequences of our actions on a daily basis, and it is inconceivable that, for example, a woman contemplating an abortion or a government preparing for war would not imagine the likely outcomes. While it is not an exact science, we usually have sufficient experience of the past to prepare for the future. And some issues are judged almost entirely on their consequences. Would rash exploitation of the earth's resources be of concern if it did not lead to global warming and detrimental results?

Crossing from facts to values?

Bentham's argument can also be criticised for its illogical move from the fact that human beings seek pleasure and avoid pain, to the conclusion that we ought to draw up our laws on that basis. Yet Bentham might reply that this is a reasonable assumption. If we are governed by pleasure and pain, then it is justified to legislate for what we all recognise is of supreme importance. If we cannot help but seek pleasure and avoid pain, then it would be foolish to demand otherwise. Again, 'ought' implies 'can'. Mill, indeed is content to argue that it is reasonable to base what is desirable on what is desired, rather than present it as a logical inference.

Happiness is the intrinsic good

Many philosophers have therefore wished to examine the claim that the sole end of human action is happiness, a balance of pleasure over pain, and that it is the only thing desirable as an end. They point out that typically people desire many things, such as love, respect, wisdom, virtue, power and so on. However, Bentham could reply that these are not desired for their own sake, but because they lead to happiness. Only pleasure is an intrinsic good, because we value it for its own sake, it is an end in itself. If we ask 'why do you want to be loved?', it is possible to reply 'because I want to be happy'. But if we then ask 'why do you want to be happy?' no further justification is possible. It is the end of the line. Thus happiness is desired as the ultimate good.

An immediate response to this is that people actually desire many different things, that cannot easily be reduced to one sole aim. In Huxley's *Brave New World* (1977), citizens are administered drugs to keep them happy, and there are even a variety of drugs to give you adrenalin and excitement, and 'soma' to create the feeling of calm and virtue. But would one wish to live a life of false happiness? In the story, the Savage says defiantly, 'I'm claiming the right to be unhappy'. What he implies is that he wants truth and reality rather than a fake, perfectly happy world, even when that includes fear, sickness and impotence. The utilitarian reply might be that truth is part of utility (Mill, 1985, Ch 2), but then it looks as though anything is going to count as happiness! Even unhappiness and pain is part of happiness! This makes the claim look rather empty.

The problem is that utilitarianism has conflated the psychological satisfaction of achieving an end, with the end itself. The goals that people seek are typically love, respect, success etc., and if they achieve them, they will be satisfied. The utilitarian position is to say that this psychological condition of satisfaction is in fact the ultimate end. This is neither logical or necessary. It would be perfectly meaningful to retain the position that you seek love and success, even though the chances of satisfying your preferences and thus the possibility of happiness is slim.

Conflict with egoism?

There is also a further problem of reconciling the individual's desire for happiness for themselves (egoism), and the desire for the greater happiness of everyone else. Why should I act to maximise happiness for everyone else, if it conflicts with my own happiness? One reply is that benevolence and sympathy for others make life much more agreeable for all, but that does not mean that my personal pleasure is always to be identified with what will make the whole group happy. As Mill admits in *On Liberty*, 'it is the government of each by all the rest' (1985, Ch. 1). If I find myself in a minority culture, I will forever have to sacrifice my goals to the tyranny of popular pleasure, or as Ayn Rand (1957) dramatically declares, 'you surrender your soul to promiscuous love for all comers'.

We see this in a common argument against euthanasia (mercy killing). While it may be possible to justify giving someone a gentle and easy death because the individual is in such a painful and wretched state, we cannot make it a law because of the 'slippery slope' which might allow the possibilities for euthanasia to be employed in less deserving circumstances. So the individual is sacrificed for the good of all, and euthanasia remains illegal.

These implications of utilitarian theory lead some to argue that the theory is too demanding. It suggests that if I am wealthy, I should be forever giving to charity, rather than lavishing money on personal luxuries. Singer (1993) makes this case for the alleviation of poverty. He maintains that if we impartially consider the happiness of the majority, then affluent individuals could deny themselves trivial pleasures of marginal utility, in order to significantly increase the happiness of starving and oppressed people. He suggests that any family of above average income give about 10 per cent to charity, to reduce poverty around the world. Clearly, satisfying the basic needs of people and improving life chances is more important than entertainment and fashion. He underpins this with the claim that 'there is no intrinsic difference between killing and allowing to die'. The obvious intention in the former cannot disguise the fact that the consequences are the same. Yet the reader might decide that having the intention to kill is the significant difference. Otherwise we could on the basis of 'not acting' be held responsible for all sorts of evils that surround us.

Singer's chapter on poverty raises a number of consequentialist issues, some of which are listed below:

- If you are in a crowded lifeboat, do you try to save more people if you risk overturning the boat?
- If we contribute to charity, we could raise education standards and manage world resources and population.
- Do we have special responsibilities to help our own 'family' rather than care for 'strangers', that is, can we be impartial?
- We cannot expect 'moral heroism'.
- 'Not acting' can sometimes lead to more suffering than acting. Letting die could cause more pain than killing.

Actions and motives

The above discussion raises the importance of motives, which utilitarianism overlooks. Consequentialist theories are forward looking and judge an action solely on the beneficial results. But deontology stresses the need to look backwards to the agent's intention, before awarding praise and blame. This issue was illustrated some years ago, by a car thief in London, who broke into the boot of a parked car and found a cache of IRA weapons. His intention had been to steal the car, but instead he handed the information over to the police. In court, the judge made it clear that he was still to be punished, because although the results were beneficial in the confiscation of harmful weapons, his intention had been to steal. While we might feel that consequences should be taken into account, surely part of the moral worth of an action, and certainly the agent, depends on the motive. Otherwise we could let any cheat or thief carry out their action, provided they do not get caught, and there is an overall gain. Cheating in exams and stealing from large retailers could be justified, when we know the actions themselves are wrong.

The end justifies the means

One of the implications of teleological theory therefore is that providing the overall consequences of our actions are beneficial, we can employ any means to achieve them. This 'Robin Hood' approach to ethics underlines that no action is in itself wrong, if it leads to the happiness of the majority. Thus at the end of the Second World War, a nuclear bomb was dropped on Hiroshima with devastating consequences for the population, but the greater good was the swift end to a global war that otherwise would have prolonged even more suffering. Yet some will argue that despite the end result, some acts are so abhorrent that they should never be considered. This will be developed under the section on 'The problems of duties, rights and justice'.

The issue is particularly apparent in any discussion of the treatment of animals. Utilitarianism is committed to reducing suffering to improve the sum total of happiness, and Singer argues that this should not be restricted to a particular species. Animal suffering must also be taken into account:

> if a being suffers there can be no moral justification for refusing to take that suffering into consideration.

Singer (1993)

This highlights the egalitarian and thus fair aspect of utilitarianism that everyone's interest is considered to the degree that they are affected by an action, without favour or discrimination. Any person or creature that is conscious and **sentient** deserves their interest to be taken into account. Bentham himself recognised this and declared, 'the day may come when the rest of the animal creation may acquire those rights, which never could have been withholden from them but by the hand of tyranny'.

So the exploitation of animals in zoos, laboratories, factory farms must be reviewed. 'A mouse does have an interest in not being tormented' (Singer, 1993).

The difficulty for Bentham is that utilitarianism will not necessarily deliver animal rights. Since decisions have to be made on the sum total of happiness produced, it might be argued that a few animals in cages provide huge interest for human beings; that the discovery of new drugs for human beings and animals justifies experimentation; and affordable meat is necessary for human consumption. The debate will become a calculation. Set out below are factors that may help decide which way to vote.

The utility monster

While utilitarianism appears to be just in terms of its consideration of interests, and could be regarded as democratic and egalitarian, it could result in a grossly unjust decision, for several reasons that are outlined below. First, it is the sum total of happiness that matters, rather than whose happiness. This favours the 'utility monster', a term employed by Nozick (1974), for the person or group that, given the same amount of resources as everyone else, manages to convert it into more pleasure. The decision will therefore always favour the people with prodigious appetites for pleasure, or those who are more liable to suffer. Resources will therefore not be allocated in any equal manner at all, but tend to be directed to the persistently needy, the large consumer, and the inefficient. When dividing up a cake, it would be natural to give everyone an equal share, but to make everyone equally happy and satisfy their appetite, some will demand more and some less. The same could be applied to world resources.

Agent-centred ethics

Thus the problem with utilitarianism is that it is not sufficiently focused on the moral character of the agent. A moral decision involves a consideration of motives, moral history and life projects, not just a calculation of consequences.

To illustrate this, Smart and Williams (1973) construct the story of Jim, who enters a small town in South America to find 20 Indians about to be executed by soldiers. Jim is offered the chance to save 19 of the Indians, if he will shoot the other one himself. The utilitarian would balance the 19 lives saved over the one.

However, the bad consequences of not accepting the offer will be because of what *other people* will do. Utilitarianism is only interested in the overall result, and does not give sufficient weight to the responsibility that an individual has. If Jim accepts the offer, he will become a killer. If he accepts *he* will kill an Indian, if he declines *someone else* will kill 20; and surely in the latter case, his responsibility is less direct. It may be that if he kills an Indian, he will be racked with guilt, even though he saved 19. Supposing he is a pacifist, could we expect him to give up his most deeply cherished beliefs, which are integral to his identity as a person and a moral agent, to achieve beneficial consequences?

The utilitarian might reply that Jim's guilt will be part of the calculation of happiness. But individual moral responsibility goes deeper than just feelings of unhappiness. It is about moral integrity and a person's whole character. Why should someone ruin their own life project, because of other people's actions?

The importance of being the moral agent is absolutely evident in the case of abortion. The special position of the mother, since her whole self-image and life project will be determined by the decision, must override simple calculations of happiness that will be influenced by the feelings of the father, the doctor and society as a whole.

A possible response, offered by Hare (1981), is that Jim is right to feel a distaste and reluctance to kill, but the rule 'do not kill' should be broken on utilitarian grounds, and in this case it would be right to overcome his repulsion to killing to save the lives of 19 people and he ought to do the act. However, is this view simply a matter of the numbers involved? Supposing an elderly person is suffering greatly from a terminal disease, which also distresses the relatives greatly. The person requests euthanasia. Should a doctor, whose whole life is dedicated to saving life, be required to perform a mercy killing? The utilitarian calculation might demand it, but is the case so compelling?

The problem of duties, rights and justice

Many feel that utilitarianism does not adequately defend our notions of justice. While it would alleviate suffering if Jim and the doctor acted in a utilitarian fashion, we also feel that they have a right to refuse. A moral decision should recognise that we have duties to other individuals, which respects their value and autonomy, regardless of calculations of happiness.

A common example is the scenario of prison guards torturing a prisoner. Even if their happiness outweighed the suffering of the victim, this violation of human rights is simply wrong. Torture is evil in any circumstances. That is the position of deontological ethics. Similarly, if several patients are all awaiting organ donors for different organs, it cannot be morally justified to kill one person and distribute his organs in order to save many lives.

The problem for utilitarianism is well illustrated by Singer's conclusion on the killing of severely disabled infants. If a severely disabled child is born, their right to life is protected by our regard for the sanctity of human life. However, Singer discusses the possibility of ending its life in order to replace it with a healthy baby. On a calculation of happiness, this could be justifiable. To overcome our repugnance, Singer constructs the following scenario. A woman is informed that if she goes ahead to become pregnant, her child will be seriously disabled, but if she waits three months and tries again, her child will be healthy. In this case, we would not think it wrong for the woman to wait to bring about the best possible outcome. So 'possible' people are replaceable. If this is agreed, then cannot the same principle be applied to a foetus and a new-born infant? In all three cases, a possible person is terminated and replaced by a healthy child, which maximises happiness for all. He concludes, 'killing a disabled infant is not morally equivalent to killing a person. Very often it is not wrong at all.'

However, surely there is a significant difference between 'not creating' life and 'taking life'. But can such a distinction be ensured by utilitarians? While it may be argued that birth is not necessarily a morally defining event, and the human life is a continuum from conception to old age, our abhorrence at the destruction of any human life has to be enshrined in basic human rights. The genuine problem is, when in the life of a foetus, does 'human life' begin?

Mill and rule utilitarianism

Like Bentham, Mill endorses the view that 'pleasure and freedom from pain are the only things desirable as ends'. However, unlike Bentham, he emphasises the variety and complexity of pleasures and especially the *quality* as opposed to just *quantity*. He argues that 'higher' pleasures are more desirable because of their distinctive, refined quality. Thus noble pleasures and pleasures of the intellect, such as disinterested sympathy for others and enjoyment of art and music, are preferable to sensual and physical lust:

> Few human beings would consent to be changed into any of the lower animals for a promise of the fullest allowance of a beast's pleasures ... no person of feeling and conscience would be selfish and base.

Mill (1948)

The evidence for this is that people who have experienced higher and lower pleasures (and thus are experts), express preferences for higher. The fact that we do not always choose higher pleasures, is that lower ones are more immediate and easier to satisfy. We therefore sink through ignorance or laziness to sensual indulgence rather than strive for spiritual aesthetic enjoyment. With this distinction, Mill can defend utilitarianism from such problems as the sadistic guards, and the utility monster.

To avoid complicated calculations for every act, on the part of individuals who may not be experienced, and therefore may need guidance on the best qualities of pleasure, it is possible to formulate rules about how to behave. These will be based on the wealth of human knowledge about what produces real happiness, and can accommodate virtuous behaviour which is an essential element of wellbeing. Thus Mill, through rules, can acknowledge both the complexity of happiness and the unique importance of the noble life. **Rule utilitarianism**, for example, can protect human rights, if it is clear that in the long run, the benefits of having rights make everyone's lives happier. Thus, for example, while a judge may be tempted under act utilitarianism to sentence an innocent man to death, to placate public opinion, under rule utilitarianism, he knows that a rule which violates basic rights will breed increased fear and insecurity.

Evaluation

Mill's version of this theory has been criticised on a number of grounds.

First, to talk of qualities of pleasure is to conceal a value judgement. One pleasure is superior to another in respect of *X*, which cannot be pleasure but must be something else. This quality of *X* is thus another value, such as 'intellectual' or 'virtuous'. Thus the pleasure of watching Shakespeare rather than a TV soap opera lies in his emotional complexity. Then complexity is itself a value. So Mill is introducing under the guise of higher and lower pleasures, a set of values, such as mental, intellectual and spiritual which themselves need to be justified, and cannot be justified in terms of pleasure. He will have to refute someone who is ecstatic over football and pop music, that other values are integral to the quality of pleasure. Thus animal life is inferior to human life, not in terms of pleasure, but these other considerations.

There is also something suspect about the apparent empirical basis of the argument. The justification that Mill gives for happiness being the ultimate end and more especially quality happiness, is that 'happiness alone' is 'what people desire'. Now this could be taken as a logical definition, in which case it is trivial. If whenever we talk about 'what people desire', we call it happiness, then it is a tautology such as 'bachelors are unmarried'. However, if it is not a logical point, then it is a factually significant statement that is capable of being proved true or false. We can conduct empirical tests and if anyone does not desire happiness as the sole end, it is falsified. Suppose that someone says, 'I don't desire happiness, I desire God's will be done'. Now if the utilitarian response is that desiring God's will is actually happiness by another name, then whatever one desires is going to be called happiness. This is to return to defining happiness as 'whatever people desire', which is not factually significant.

There are also issues concerning the rules, which utilitarians may wish to make. First, the status of these rules is unclear. Mill claims that a rule should never be broken unless it conflicts with another rule. Then there should be an appeal to the greatest happiness principle. Thus in the Robin Hood scenario the rule 'do not steal' and 'help the poor' could both be utilitarian rules, but are nevertheless in conflict. The solution therefore is to return to act utilitarianism and resolve the issue by consideration of how to maximise utility in this particular dilemma. But this will reintroduce all the problems of possible injustice, lack of consideration for the agent and the utility monster etc., which rule utilitarianism was designed to avoid. So the very likely conflict of rules will leave utilitarianism with all its original problems.

From another perspective, Foot criticises the theory for being too impersonal. Good (happiness) is 'speaker relative', and related to one's commitments and life projects. So one would only wish that many people are happy if one accepts the virtue of 'benevolence', and if one has the virtue of wisdom or justice, then making the majority happy will not be desirable. Thus utilitarians have misunderstood the relationship between happiness and goodness. They claim that 'doing what makes people happy' is 'the good', whereas it is 'doing what is good' that makes people 'happy'. This is reflected in Mill's contention that there are rules. This alternative view of the relationship between goodness and happiness is developed in the section 'Virtue theory'.

Preference utilitarianism

With the difficulties surrounding the nature and importance of happiness, some utilitarians choose instead to talk of preferences. Hare makes a case

Synoptic link

AQA A2 Philosophy Chapter 2, Political philosophy, p76.

Key terms

Preference utilitarianism: the theory that we ought to maximise the satisfaction of people's preferences.

for maximising the satisfaction of people's interests or preferences, and Singer also employs this version of utilitarianism.

They argue that the basis of moral behaviour involves the consideration of other people as well as oneself. Once we consider something as appropriate for ourselves, then consistency entails that we also allow other people's interests to count. This universalising has the consequence that we reflect on issues and make decisions in an impersonal and impartial way. If we recall Hare's example of the trumpet players, then all ought to be treated without fear or favour and that means an equal consideration of interests. When contemplating an act which will affect someone else, then consistency demands that I not only consider my own interests, but give equal consideration to the interests of everyone else affected. This would affect the decision of the trumpet player on how much time and when to play the trumpet.

We then need a principle to judge people's interests by and surely a majority interest should outweigh the minority. We should note that this avoids the problems of identifying happiness as the sole end and makes no judgement about what people desire. We talk only of interests or preferences, so even though for example, going to school may not bring a pupil much pleasure, they choose to attend for their welfare. So instead of happiness, Hare identifies a moral decision 'to maximise satisfactions'. Singer concludes: 'the utilitarian position is a minimal one … that we reach by universalising self-interested decision making'.

Evaluation

While this may seem a very reasonable position, it cannot be reached by a consideration of consistency alone. Norman argues that the move from universalising to a claim for impartiality is a suspect one. After all, one could be consistently egoist and pursue one's self-interest while consistently agreeing that other people can seek their preferences too. The outcome would probably be a Hobbesian 'war of all against all' where the trumpet players and musicians drown each other out. Consistency alone does not demand that we consider other people's interests as our own, although it is reasonable to suggest that most people would prefer to harmonise our interests in an impartial way rather than risk conflict, with the result that no-one is satisfied.

A further implication of preference satisfaction developed by Singer is that animals also have preferences, and some human beings have limited preferences. He contends that newborn infants 'cannot see themselves as beings who might or might not have a future', and since at least some sensitive and sentient animals can have interests in their future, we are not justified in using these animals for experimentation or enjoyment where we would not use a human infant. Of course there are the interests of the parents to be considered, and of wider society, and the potential interests as the infant matures. But since we have returned to a calculation of interests, the problems of the tyranny of the majority and the absolute nature of justice reappear. Supposing it was in the interests of a majority to enslave a minority?

Thus assessing interests could be as complex as understanding happiness. Some people would be seduced by short-term interests (e.g. to drown their sorrows in alcohol), rather than the long-term interests of health. But once we try to discover a person's *real* interest as opposed to their *expressed* interest, we enter into all kinds of irresolvable disputes and while the process of consulting everyone's preferences has the merit of being democratic, some will argue that all we arrive at is a popular decision, not a moral one.

Finally, not only do I have preferences for myself, I also have preferences for others. For example, I would prefer to be rich and I would like everyone else to be poor. So there are both (a) personal preferences and (b) external preferences. Now it could be argued that we should only consider personal preferences and that our preferences for others should be discounted. However, in practice, this looks impossible, because they are so entwined and intermingled. After all, my preference to be rich necessarily entails that a significant number of people are poor. To counteract this, we could construct theories of rights, so that people's bigoted, biased preferences for others are ruled out. However, as we have seen, utilitarianism cannot secure absolute values of justice. For this we have to turn to deontology.

Deontological ethics

To those who are troubled by the claim that the moral worth of a decision depends entirely on how events turn out, it is reasonable to appeal to deontology and the moral value of the act itself, regardless of the consequences. After all, if you are a true friend, you would help out and protect a friend in trouble, even if it was unpopular or had negative effects for you and your friend, because it would be the right thing to do. True friendship, love and respect should be unqualified; it is the right thing to do and should not be affected by how you happen to feel at the time or fear of consequences. This is the approach to moral decisions that we shall now consider.

Moral motivation

Kant maintains that an action of moral worth must emanate from a good will. In other words, it is the motive or intention that matters. Our sole motivation should be to do right for its own sake, to perform our duty. If we do duty for duty's sake, if we act out of respect for the goodness of the act itself, out of reverence for the principles we uphold, then this is a truly moral decision. We stand up for what we believe in and perform actions, which we believe are intrinsically good, then even if the consequences are unfortunate, we still did the right thing. If we act solely from a good will, which means we have the right intention, and act out of respect for the moral law, then we cannot be blamed or criticised.

Kant emphasises that we must not be motivated out of self-interest, or even out of love or sympathy for others, because emotions and inclinations can be variable, love can be selfish and sympathy narrowly focused or dependent on circumstances. Whereas our duty is something we must do, whether we are inclined or not, it is consistently binding in all situations and cannot be swayed by how we feel. Moreover, since our duties must be the same for all people everywhere, and are universal and absolute, they cannot be decided by 'subjective impulses', but determined by reason alone. Reason will command that we must do the right thing, even if we do not feel like it, reason can inform us what our unconditional duties are and emancipate us from personal bias. Everyone will come to the same conclusion and realise they must accept their duty, it is a categorical imperative.

Synoptic link

This section should be read in conjunction with AQA AS Philosophy Chapter 3, Why should I be moral?, p86, where deontological ethics was introduced.

The categorical imperative

Kant proposes three versions of the categorical imperative. The first formulation is:

> **i** Act only on a maxim or rule that you can will to be a universal law.

This tells us the *form* of a moral duty that you should act as if you are making law for everyone to obey, without exception. It is the test of consistency and universalisability that you would not allow yourself or anyone else to act differently. You ask 'what if everyone did this?'

The second formulation of the categorical imperative is:

> **ii** Treat humanity, never solely as a means but always also as an end.

This follows from (i) and provides some *content*, that universalising our actions implies also that we treat other rational beings as 'ends', valuable in themselves, and therefore with respect. It would be inconsistent to favour some people and not others, so our duties apply to all and reflect the universal value of all human beings. It is similar to the religious command that we treat others as we ourselves wish to be treated. Clearly sometimes we cannot avoid using people, just to function in our daily lives, but we should never *solely* use them as a means, but always have respect for them as a person.

The third formulation derives from the second:

> **iii** Act as if by your maxims and rules, you were legislating for a universal kingdom of ends.

Some commentators see this as the political aspect of the categorical imperative that our respect for the free and autonomous decisions of all requires we grant rights to all. Raphael (1981) links it to the three aims of the French Revolution: liberty, equality and brotherhood.

Kant offers four examples of the categorical imperative:

1 We should not commit suicide but respect life.

2 We should not break promises but keep trust.

3 We should not be lazy but develop our talents.

4 We should not ignore the happiness of others but help them.

The important test of these four duties is that if we attempted to will the opposite, it would result in a contradiction and would therefore be irrational and not universalisable. For example, although I could wish to break a promise on a particular occasion, I cannot wish that everyone would do that, because the breakdown in trust would mean that promises, including my own, would cease to be believed. This would defeat my intention to use people by making false promises. It would contradict my will, and therefore cannot become a universal law. We can note, once more, that universalising not only is a test of consistency but also encourages impartiality.

The first two duties are what Kant calls 'contradictions in the law of nature'. The rule that we would make will clearly contradict itself when universalised. As Palmer (1991) explains, 'such a rule would be "Do this but don't"'. Thus in the case of suicide, Kant claims that it is a natural law that we act out of 'self-preservation' or 'self-love'. But if out of self-love, I wish to end my life, I am contradicting the fundamental law of self-preservation, which is the most basic principle of nature. From this he derives the sanctity of human life, and the wrongness of killing, which is consistent with the intrinsic worth of human beings and rights. 'There is nothing more sacred in the wide world than the rights of others.'

The second two duties are 'contradictions in the will'. It would theoretically be possible, for example, to not help others and not expect others to return help when you were in need. This is not a straightforward contradiction, but it would be utterly unacceptable and unworkable for everyone to act selfishly, that one could not will it.

Kant also called the first two duties, 'perfect duties', and the second pair, 'imperfect duties'. Perfect duties admit of no exceptions and override imperfect duties, where there might be a clash or conflict of duties. Where imperfect duties clash, some will have to be forsaken for others.

Thus, for example, not destroying life is a perfect duty, but preserving life (benevolence) is an imperfect duty. The importance of this distinction is seen in the issue of euthanasia. While one must not kill, one does not always have a duty to take all necessary steps to preserve a life. Thus some philosophers would distinguish between active and passive euthanasia. They claim that while it is wrong to take direct action to kill, it is permissible to allow a patient to die, if he is suffering unbearable pain from a terminal illness. The former is active euthanasia, where death is the result of direct action and the latter is passive euthanasia where death is the result of the illness and not acting to preserve life. Passive euthanasia appears justified on the grounds that:

1 the imperfect duty to seek another's happiness outweighs the imperfect duty to preserve life
2 the patient will die of the illness, not the action of the doctor, so the perfect duty to not kill is observed.

Rachels, in 'Active and Passive Euthanasia' (1979) argues that the distinction is not valid or morally sound. He points out that from a consequentialist perspective, passive euthanasia can cause more suffering than a quick, lethal injection to terminate the life. From a deontological perspective, he claims that the motive in both cases is the same – the doctor wants the person to die. Furthermore, 'not giving medical treatment' is equivalent to acting and that refraining is simply a different kind of behaviour from intervening. In both cases, if the patient had a *curable* illness, the doctor would be blamed and held responsible for the death. So in respect of the moral law, in these particular circumstances, 'not killing' and 'preserving life' are equivalent duties. There is no moral difference between active and passive euthanasia. The full article is reproduced in Palmer.

Rachels has been countered, however, by those who argue that the motive is not the same in both situations. The same point was made with respect to Jim and the Indians. In terms of active euthanasia, the doctor does not wish to be a killer, it is part of an ongoing project and commitment to save life. The doctor can still maintain the ultimate importance of the sanctity of life, whereas in passive euthanasia, concern for the quality of life outweighs the sacredness of life itself.

A further distinction between Kant's perfect and imperfect duties is that **1** and **2** clearly state what we should not do: not commit suicide and not break promises. However **3** and **4** are positive in this respect that we should not, not help others, i.e. help, and to use our talents. Whereas **1** and **2** can always be wrong, **3** and **4** can be performed to a degree or might admit of exceptions. Negatives are more absolute. Furthermore, Kant is not saying that we ought to do anything that is universalisable, but if there is no contradiction, then there is no reason not to do it. Clearly there are many ridiculous laws that I could universalise, that I would never wish to be a duty, and are not obligatory. Duties derive from clear contradictions such as breaking trust or destroying life.

> **Think about**
>
> Which side of the argument do you think is more coherent? Would you agree with Kant's argument, or place more importance on the quality of life? Would this contradict Kant's argument?

Evaluation

Clearly Kant's insistence on universalising is what most people regard as integral to moral behaviour. Ethical life begins when we start thinking of others and modifying our own behaviour to treat others as we wish to be treated ourselves. While it is true that we use each other all the time to pursue our own self-interest, we learn also in important respects to value others and their choices, as though they were our own. The rights to self-determination and freedom from torture among others are universally sacrosanct and inalienable. Thus deontological ethics appear strong on issues of justice and human rights.

However, while some general principles might be established on this basis, there are also many issues to be resolved. We have already noted that the test of consistency does not necessarily entail impartiality, since I could be a consistent egoist.

But the first issue is that the universalising process is not at all clear. In fact, the more detail one adds to the maxim or law the less clear it becomes. So while the concern for the sanctity of life seems a perfect duty, suppose that I add to the maxim 'never take a life', the condition 'never take a life except in self-defence'. This would not appear to result in a contradiction, but now it opens up, for example, the possibility of abortion, where the mother's life is threatened. We could add other conditions such as 'never have an abortion unless the pregnancy was unintended' or 'never take life unless to assassinate a tyrant who is suppressing the rights of others'. No contradictions appear obvious, so it seems that the more particular the conditions, the less clear the duty will be.

Secondly, the contradictions in the will appear to consider (a) the consequences of the action and (b) an appeal to self-interest. While it is true that I cannot universalise living off the hard work of other people, I could universalise not developing my talents as long as I do not harm other people. The duty to maximise my potential or help others is justified by the unacceptable consequences if I do not, and the benefit to myself.

Thirdly, the potential conflict of duties is a common criticism and Kant's own example of not lying to protect a friend from a murderer is much used. A more plausible example, which directly impinges on his two perfect duties, is the assisted suicide of a marriage partner. The marriage ceremony contains a solemn oath to care for your partner's welfare, which might mean assisting their suicide, to free them from the wretched agony of a terminal illness. Yet suicide is unequivocally wrong and assisted suicide is still legally categorised with murder. This direct clash of duties is irreconcilable, unless one duty is permitted to override the other.

The role of reason

Kant has also been criticised for his over-emphasis on concern for duty which has supplanted a love of humanity. The rational concern for consistency, impartiality and obedience to law is only half of the moral experience. The emotions, such as sympathy and compassion, the happiness of the interested parties and the genuineness of moral action are also important:

- Kant under-rates our capacity for consistent and selfless love, which is surely one of the noblest aspects of the human character.
- Furthermore, to act out of duty and not out of genuine care and concern for others implies a lack of authenticity in one's motivation. Weil's example of the father who plays with his son out of a sense of duty, rather than love and joy illustrates the point well.

Think about

What conditions could you add to the sanctity of life duty which would allow killing, without producing a contradiction?

- Morality is not like mathematics. In mathematics, propositions can be tested for consistency and are true or false. Morality is about choice and action, and the goals or ends are as varied as human creativity. For example, animals would not be rational ends, for Kant, but we are capable of including them in our moral consideration.
- Kant must explain why we should act morally and do our duty and ultimately this must be related to human happiness and fulfilment.

Kant's account of motivation seems to lack the humanity which we associate with genuine moral intention. To obey laws for their own sake can seem superficial and lacking emotional integrity. Surely we respect a person more if they have experienced a moral struggle between inclination and reason, and arrive at a choice with a deeper (emotional) understanding of the dilemma, than someone who follows rules and duties for which they may have no particular inclination. It is important not only to perform duty for duty's sake, but also to have a genuine and authentic belief in the importance of that duty. The Victorian novel is full of examples of satire on do-gooders (e.g. Mrs Pardiggles and Mrs Jellyby in Dickens, *Bleak House*) whose commitment to duty lacks real love and concern.

The general nature of rational laws also means that they will have to be applied to the particular situations in which we find ourselves. The principle of ends demands that we do not use people or disregard their free, moral choices, yet often this is not possible. It is in difficult situations that we have to be creative and choose personal commitments. Sartre's example of the 'pupil', torn between fighting for the French resistance or staying at home to support his mother makes the point. Either way, he will fail in a duty, to fight for freedom against oppression, or to protect and sustain his mother through the war. Sartre's point is that general rules cannot provide answers to particular dilemmas, and which rules we regard as relevant and choose to obey has to be a personal choice.

Who has moral status?

Kant's theory also entails that we respect other rational human beings, because in universalising, we must consider that others are permitted to make the same choice and we cannot be an exception to the rule. The kingdom of ends therefore is a community of beings, who are capable of making autonomous decisions, and who thereby acquire rights. This would seem to exclude from the moral community the foetus and young children, the unconscious and those in a permanent vegetative state and animals. The problem of when and how we grant rights and moral status therefore arises.

The rights of the unborn child

The granting of rights to an unborn foetus would resolve the problems of replaceability, which concerns the utilitarian argument. However, since the foetus is no more rational or self-aware than an animal, there is still the problem of when and on what basis we grant rights and define duties. One argument that might be offered is that a foetus has the *potential* for rational thought and self-awareness, and therefore has a claim to protection and the right to life. However, the problem has still not disappeared, since everything has potential, even the unfertilised egg has potential. So where would we stop in assessing potential for human life? Singer provides the imaginative scenario of an IVF laboratory, where a sperm and an egg are separately flushed down the sink. But there is a blockage in the sink and it is possible that by accident the egg has been fertilised. Should the embryo be regarded as potential human life? He concludes, 'potentiality seems not to be such an all or nothing concept' (Singer, 1993).

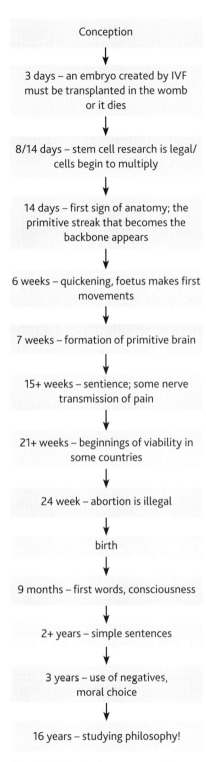

Conception

↓

3 days – an embryo created by IVF must be transplanted in the womb or it dies

↓

8/14 days – stem cell research is legal/ cells begin to multiply

↓

14 days – first sign of anatomy; the primitive streak that becomes the backbone appears

↓

6 weeks – quickening, foetus makes first movements

↓

7 weeks – formation of primitive brain

↓

15+ weeks – sentience; some nerve transmission of pain

↓

21+ weeks – beginnings of viability in some countries

↓

24 week – abortion is illegal

↓

birth

↓

9 months – first words, consciousness

↓

2+ years – simple sentences

↓

3 years – use of negatives, moral choice

↓

16 years – studying philosophy!

Fig. 4.2 *When is a foetus a person?*

Think about

Fig. 4.2 illustrates the life of a foetus with significant moments in its development.

Can you identify at what point and why we have a good reason to grant the right to life? Would this claim have consequences for animal welfare too?

When is a foetus a person? Examine the life of a foetus, infant and young person and decide when, if at all, an abortion would be acceptable.

Conflicting rights

Even if we can determine the rights of the foetus, there will be some conflict with the rights of the mother. The mother must have a right to determine what happens to her own body, which opposes the right to life of a foetus. To consider the claims of both sides, Thomson (1991) offers a series of imaginative examples, including the possibility that you enter a hospital, only to find that you are kidnapped, and a famous violinist who urgently needs treatment, is plugged into your body to help him cure his otherwise fatal disease. It will only last nine months, but if you unplug him, he will die. The article is reproduced in Palmer (1991).

Thomson then unpacks what a right to life means. Does it mean that it is right to have one's life sustained, at any cost? Does it mean that another person has a claim on your body? She concludes that a right to life does not mean that you have a right not to be killed, but a right not to be killed *unjustly*, and so you have a right to unplug the violinist. However, a variety of factors affect the justice of the situation. For example, if a woman knowingly consented to becoming pregnant and deliberately brought another being into life, this clear intention would affect her ethical position.

So, there are possible problems with Thomson's position. While the violinist knowingly violates your right to self-determination, the foetus is entirely innocent. It is the events surrounding the mother that have brought it into being. Surely a right not to be killed is paramount if the being is entirely innocent of any wrongdoing.

Palmer also offers a second criticism, that while we are not obliged to save lives, we are obliged not to kill. We may not have a duty to offer our bodies to the violinist, but once the situation has arisen, we do have a duty not to kill. Yet Thomson, I feel, could respond by distinguishing between 'not killing' and 'not sustaining life'. How long do we feel obliged to stay plugged to the violinist: 9 hours? 9 days? 9 years? At some stage, the obligation to not kill has transformed into an obligation to sustain life.

The inconclusive nature of this debate suggests that a clear set of duties does not exist. Indeed it could be argued that the universalisation process itself presupposes values that need to be explicit and justified. For example, it presumes the equal value of all human beings, regardless of race and gender.

The problem with duty ethics is that it regards each act in isolation, whereas morality must be embedded in a wider understanding of what we consider to be the good life and how best to achieve it. We need to have an answer to the question – why should I do my duty? – and we need to assess the moral worth of an action in the context of a person's situation, and their moral development. An abortion for a young girl who has barely started life cannot be considered in the same way as for a mature and self-aware woman. To accommodate the complexity of moral decisions, to provide a framework in which they can be understood, and to acknowledge the importance of practical wisdom, we need therefore to examine virtue ethics.

■ Practical wisdom

In a world of apparent conflict, dysfunctional relationships and moral crises, it is instructive to enquire who has the greatest sense of wellbeing, and what kind of person do you have to be to achieve the fulfilled life.

In fiction, from Jane Austen to the Simpsons, this question hangs over every story. Who achieves the happy ending and why? Which kind of

AQA Examiner's tip

You may be asked to compare rule utilitarianism with deontological ethics. Make a list of similarities and differences.

character thrives and how do they approach moral decisions? This is the subject of virtue ethics.

Virtue theory

Rather than examining moral actions, the focus of this theory is on the moral agent, their character and the cultivation in ourselves and others of traits that we admire. We ask, 'what sort of person do I want to be?', rather than 'what should I do?'; and 'what kind of society do I want to live in?', rather than determining rights and duties.

The virtues are:

- dispositions of character
- acquired by ethical training and practice
- displayed by emotional response as well as action
- that promote excellence
- and enable the virtuous person and society to flourish.

According to Aristotle (1953), the virtuous person has the practical wisdom, 'to have these feelings at the right times on the right occasions towards the right people for the right motive and in the right way'; and to have these feelings 'in the right measure' is 'somewhere between the extremes'. The reader might be tempted to see this as encouraging a subjective assessment of a dilemma, but Aristotle assures us, '(there) is only one way of being right … it is easy to miss the bull's eye'.

So although there is built-in flexibility according to the situation, the virtuous character guided by reason will achieve the optimum response. Aristotle uses comparisons with playing musical instruments – that an accomplished flautist will practise and develop skills and excellence that enable them to produce the ideal performance. With the necessary education, eventually wise and virtuous behaviour will flow naturally as good music emanates from a disciplined and talented musician. So good role models and teachers are essential to acquire the virtues.

The strong version of this theory holds that virtues are more basic than rights and duties, and that an understanding of the good (virtuous) life is fundamental and prior to any theory of moral behaviour. So the issue arises of whether a theory about what makes a good character can provide clear rules for concrete situations or whether we still need an independent theory of rights.

Application

Traditionally, virtue ethics has stressed the importance of the community in the life of the virtuous individual. Because the individual is insufficient and has need of society to provide education, friendship etc., then our wellbeing is dependent on being part of a flourishing community, in the same way that a student makes more progress when the whole class is well motivated and studious. An important aspect of virtue theory, which is understood by the possessor of practical wisdom, is the importance of positive and fulfilling relationships, because 'each of us being a main character in his own drama, plays subordinate parts in the drama of others' (MacIntyre, 1981).

The good life

A crucial aspect of the theory is the link between the virtues and wellbeing. This link is presented as both a conceptual and an empirical relation. There are issues with both approaches.

AQA Examiner's tip

Useful reading is *The "Simpsons" and Philosophy?* (Irwin, 2001, chs 4, 5, 10–15). This will help you develop imaginative examples for your essays.

Synoptic link

Much of the classical theory was introduced in AQA AS Philosophy Chapter 3, Why should I be moral?, and this is recommended additional reading. We have also covered some aspects of the theory in the discussion of moral truth.

Think about

Plato identified and early Christians adopted four cardinal virtues (essential virtues). Do you agree that these virtues are fundamental to our wellbeing?

- *temperance*: self-discipline and moderation of the appetites, rather than over-indulgence in physical pleasure
- *courage*: showing spirit in the face of adversity and overcoming fear
- *justice*: being well balanced and rational in our dealings with others to achieve a harmony of interests
- *prudence*: practical wisdom and good judgement.

Would a lack of any of these virtues lead to a less flourishing life?

In mediaeval theology, faith, hope and charity were added. Would you support this?

Are there any other virtues, you might argue are missing?

1 **The conceptual account** of virtue ethics unpacks the meaning of terms in order to establish the relationship between virtues and the good life. Thus virtues are defined as skills or excellences of character, and when one acquires these and can function as an effective human being, this enables the individual to live well and flourish. Thus virtues entail the moral health which entails the good life. However, this conceptual link is regarded by many as rather empty and circular.

It can be presented in the way shown in Fig. 4.3.

It therefore seems that we have done little more than define words, but have little meaningful content. To provide substance, we need empirical demonstration.

2 **The empirical account** takes one of two forms. It either explains human flourishing by appeal to a hypothesis about the purpose or function of human beings and a demonstration of how the virtuous life delivers genuine happiness and eudaimonia; or describes how living a life that meets the historical and cultural standards of a tradition enables that community to thrive. So the virtues are grounded either by appeal to universal truths about the human condition; or by claiming that they give a narrative order to life and are part of a meaningful tradition. Thus the Homeric virtues were appropriate for societies that were regularly threatened by external enemies and needed loyalty and valour in order to survive, while Aristotelian virtues of self-esteem, magnificence and good taste were appropriate for the development of a sophisticated civilisation. Neither approach is entirely convincing.

The human condition

The theory of teleology proposed by Aristotle based on the supposed, unique faculty of human reason is discussed in the relevant AS chapter, and is generally regarded as outmoded and untenable.

Foot provides a more modern approach based on the conditions of human existence. One example is the concept of injury, where clearly damage to the body prevents the human being from fully functioning. This is something that all people wish to avoid and we all have a desire and interest in the effective use of our limbs and organs, otherwise we cannot satisfy our wants. These universal needs must be taken into account and so entail a list of relevant virtues. So the virtues can be derived from what any human being would reasonably want, such as health, prosperity and so on.

However, as Norman identifies, there is a problem with the virtue of justice. On Foot's account, the virtues would appear to be a form of enlightened egoism, and self-interest, so that I show courage or prudence because it benefits me. But it does not seem adequate to base a sense of justice on enlightened personal gain. As Kant would argue, we perform a just act because it is the right thing to do rather than because is suits our interests. As Foot later admits, the virtue of justice only provides a reason for acting, if one already has a moral point of view. The AS chapter also raises the issue of whether the virtue of justice is necessary for mental health and whether it successfully explains altruism.

Also in this chapter, we have already discussed the crossing of the fact–value gap, and the problem of arguing from what *is* human nature, to what we *ought* to do.

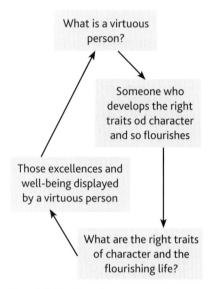

Fig. 4.3 *What is a virtuous person?*

Synoptic link

AQA AS Philosophy Chapter 3, Why should I be moral?

Synoptic link

AQA AS Philosophy Chapter 3, Why should I be moral? p80.

Tradition and context

There are also problems if one argues that the virtues depend on
a meaningful historical context. MacIntyre argues 'we cannot …
characterise behaviour independently of intentions, and we cannot
characterise intentions independently of their settings' (1981). The
significance of a person's action depends on their motive, which in
turn must be interpreted through the history of that person and their
relationships and the social and cultural context. For example, the moral
significance of abortion has changed through history. There was a time
when self-induced abortion was commonplace, among the poorest class
of women, in a society where the poor could barely keep themselves alive,
and the infant mortality rate was high anyway. Such an occurrence, while
still a personal tragedy, was arguably less important than virtues, such as
obedience to superiors or attending church. Similarly the importance of
female chastity and pregnancy within wedlock seems to have coincided
with the importance of establishing property rights and inheritance.

These examples highlight the difficulty that the virtues are relative to
their context and very often conflict. Aristotle, for example, leaves out
kindness and overrates pride. Christians in contrast emphasise humility
and patience, while Franklin praised frugality. Yet the Homeric virtues
advocate honour, cunning and patriotism. While this position may have
its advantages, it has two clear problems:

1 One culture cannot judge another.
2 For those who seek absolute and universal moral values, virtue theory
   cannot provide an answer.

Before we pursue the difficulties with developing practical wisdom,
however, it is clear that there are a number of advantages.

The advantages

1 Realistic

It is argued that the theory does justice to the complexity and subtlety of
moral issues. Where rules and duties or formulars for producing happiness
are clearly too generalised, rigid and simplistic, the emphasis on developing
a virtuous character capable of making wise judgements is more realistic. So
with Aristotle's doctrine of the mean, the difference between right and wrong
is not an either/or but a matter of degree. The doctrine of the mean, Norman
suggests, is not just a moderated response but more an appropriate response.
An emotion such as anger is wrong if excessive or deficient, but properly
moderated, will be appropriate to the seriousness of the vice: 'Aristotle's ideal
is that of the rational, emotional life'. This enables a more sophisticated
approach, to say, the Robin Hood attitude to stealing, which could be
justified to feed the starving, and so is not always wrong. Practical wisdom
can accommodate the richness of human experience.

2 Holistic

Virtue theory is also generally applauded for recognising the importance
of the emotions and the complete person. The genuinely virtuous agent is
encouraged to feel the appropriate sentiments and the love and sympathy
which was lacking in duty ethics is a significant aspect of virtuous
response. Virtue ethics also recognises that moral judgement cannot be
divorced from a person's life perspective and ongoing commitments. We
cannot treat each moral decision as a separate issue, which leaves our
moral life fragmented. Instead the unity of moral experience and the
effect decisions have on the moral agent are acknowledged, as illustrated
by the case of Jim and the Indians. The virtues cannot be switched on

▦ Think about

Consider the following. What
judgement would you come to?

- The motive for the experiment
  e.g. to test cosmetics or to find a
  cure for cancer.
- The number of animals used.
- The kind of animals used, e.g.
  social, self-aware etc.
- The attitude to any suffering and
  the degree of suffering.
- The range of alternative
  procedures and whether tests on
  animals give accurate results.
- The use of the results to obtain
  maximum benefit, e.g. widely
  available or highly priced
  exclusive medicines.

and off like a tap, but a moral decision will be dictated by the person we are, and will influence the person we will become. If we are committed to non-violence, we cannot be required to kill even one Indian:

> someone who genuinely possesses a virtue can be expected to manifest it in very different types of situations.

Norman (1998)

3 Flexible

As already acknowledged, the theory allows for the importance of cultural factors and historical differences.

> What the good life [is] for a fifth century Athenian general will not be the same as it was for a medieval nun.

MacIntyre (1981)

There are conditions of human life which determine what we conceive of as virtues, but these can be re-interpreted and adapted by each generation. The 'catalogue of virtues' may vary, but will embrace the same purpose:

> to sustain ... the kind of political communities in which men and women can seek for the good together.

MacIntyre (1981)

4 Acknowledges education and progress

Finally, a theory of practical wisdom is able to understand the importance of social conditioning and education and explains how as individuals and cultures we can make moral progress. Williams identifies the significance of 'pattern books of virtues', and the fact that much ethical education is 'top down', whereby we learn and practise virtuous dispositions and can debate the examples offered by different role models. This seems much more akin to the actual discussions about people's lifestyles that we have, than the rather artificial procedures of the categorical imperative or the hedonic calculus. The latter oversimplify the moral process.

Disadvantages

1 Conflicting virtues

Virtue ethics is often criticised for its vagueness and lack of clarity in decision making. Just as there is the problem of conflicting duties in duty ethics, so there will be conflicting virtues. In a case of euthanasia, a doctor will be torn between the virtue of benevolence, to end the unbearable suffering of a patient, and the virtue of justice to balance the interests of the community, and possibly the Christian virtue of hope, that suffering is educative and ennobling. Thus no clear guideline emerges, and if we rely on the virtue of practical wisdom to find a solution in each individual case, then that might result in euthanasia for some and not others. Critics point out the danger of a lack of consistency and the need for a clear law or rule, which virtue ethics does not supply.

2 What is human flourishing?

The virtues are conceptually and empirically linked to a vision of the good life, but a historical analysis, such as MacIntyre's, shows that such a vision has varied enormously throughout history. There is a very wide disparity between the Christian virtues of love, compassion, faith, hope and charity and the Machiavellian virtues of vitality, pride, genius and success. Machiavelli's noble and flourishing individual is one who has the ability to achieve 'effective truth' and impose his will on society. Contrast this with a Christian tombstone, cited by MacIntyre:

> Be good, sweet maid and let who will be clever.

MacIntyre (1981)

3 No agreement on human nature

Following on from this, the theory is in trouble grounding the virtues in an account of human nature and a concept of essence. This issue is identified by MacIntyre: 'a moral philosophy … characteristically presupposes a sociology' and his succeeding chapters review a number of sociologies.

In the end, the discussion may boil down to an assessment of the relative merits of different accounts of human nature, and in Chapter 18 it is proposed that the modern debate should be between the Aristotelian tradition and the liberal individual tradition. This in itself is, of course, a matter of opinion, so the essential difficulty of finding a consensus on human nature remains.

4 No necessary link between virtue and flourishing

We can ask meaningfully: 'are all virtuous people flourishing?' and 'are all flourishing people virtuous?' and answer no on both accounts. History is littered with examples of virtuous people (such as Joan of Arc?) who are martyred and deprived of a fulfilled life, and rock and roll stars who have lived life to a full and satisfactory conclusion, but who could hardly be called virtuous.

5 Deontological ethics

Those who advocate duty will point out, therefore, that in real life we do not condemn people for having bad character traits, but for committing evil actions. Some acts are so intolerable that we must devise a special list of offences which are prohibited, and virtue theory cannot supply such a list. It is not sufficiently clear how virtues such as courage, temperance, prudence, and kindness, for example, lead to corresponding duties. Thus the theory does not give sufficiently clear guidance on practical issues such as euthanasia, where we need to know, not only the manner of behaviour, but what our duties and rights are.

6 Utilitarianism

Those who contend that the consequences of our action must be considered will also not be satisfied with the emphasis on character and style. Sometimes we have to choose a less than virtuous means in order to achieve the greatest good for the greatest number. So virtue theory is regarded as too preoccupied with the manner of acting, rather than the results. Great music, art, feats of engineering and political decisiveness – in other words the genius that produces great happiness for mankind is not necessarily linked to virtuous character.

✔ *After working through this topic, you should:*

- be able to explain utilitarianism, duty ethics and virtue theory
- understand their approach to practical moral dilemmas
- be able to discuss the merits and demerits of each method for making moral decisions
- appreciate issues surrounding the importance of consequences, motive and moral character.

Synoptic link

AQA AS Philosophy Chapter 3, Why should I be moral?, p80.

AQA Examiner's tip

In the exam, you will be expected to compare different theories and their application to practical problems such as euthanasia, abortion and the treatment of animals.

Summary questions

1. Explain two possible sources of moral truth.

2. Discuss the issue of whether moral values are relative or subjective.

3. What is the fact–value gap? Can it be bridged?

4. With reference to one practical issue, compare utilitarianism, deontological theory and virtue ethics.

5. Can moral actions be judged solely by their consequences?

■ Further reading

■ Atherton, M., Cluett, C., McAdoo, O., Rawlinson, D. and Sidoli, J., *AQA AS Philosophy*, Nelson Thornes, 2008. This provides simple, clear background reading.

■ Cardinal, D., J. Hayward and G. Jones, *Moral Philosophy*, Hodder Murray, 2006. This provides entertaining accounts and exercises on all the relevant issues.

■ Irwin, W. (ed.), *The "Simpsons" and Philosophy: The D'oh of Homer*, Open Court Publishing Co, 2001. Provides contemporary and entertaining illustrations of many moral issues.

■ Warburton, N., *Philosophy: The Basics*, Routledge, 2004. This offeres a concise and clear summary of the theories mentioned on the chapter.

■ **www.philosophersnet.com** offers various interative games on ethics.

■ References

Aristotle, *Ethics*, Penguin, 1953.

Ayer, A., *Language, Truth and Logic*, Penguin, 1971.

Bentham, J., *An Introduction to the Principles of Morals and Legislation*, ed. J.H. Burns and H. Hart, Methuen, 1982.

Clark, D., *Empirical Realism*, Rowman and Littlefield, 2003.

Foot, P., *Theories of Ethics*, Oxford University Press, 1974.

Hamilton, C., *Understanding Philosophy for AS*, Nelson Thornes, 2003.

Hare, R.M., *The Language of Morals*, Oxford Paperbacks, 1963.

Hare, R. *Moral Thinking: Its Levels, Method and Point*, Oxford University Press, 1981.

Hume, D., *A Treatise on Human Nature*, Penguin, 1969.

Hume, D., 'An Enquiry Concerning the Principles of Morals', Cosimo Inc., New York Public Library Digitized, 2006.

Huxley, A. *Brave New World*, Penguin, 1977.

Kant, I., 'Groundwork of the Metaphysics of Morals', translated in H. Paton, *The Moral Law*, Hutchinson, 1972.

Locke, J., *Essay Concerning Human Understanding*, Oxford University Press, 1984.

MacIntyre, A., *After Virtue*, Gerald Duckworth & Co. Ltd, 1981.

McDowell, J, 'Values and Secondary Qualities' in *Morality and Objectivity*, ed. T. Honderick, Routledge and Kegan Paul, 1985.

McNaughton, D., *Moral Vision: An Introduction to Ethics*, Wiley-Blackwell, 1988.

Mill, J.S., *Utilitarianism, Liberty and Representative Government*, Dent and Sons, 1948.

Mill, J.S., *On Liberty*, Penguin Classics, 1985.

Moore, G.E., *Principia Ethica*, Cambridge University Press, 1968.

Nietzsche, F., *Beyond Good and Evil*, Oxford University Press, 1998.

Norman, R., *The Moral Philosophers: An Introduction to Ethics*, Oxford University Press, 1998.

Nozick, R., *Anarchy, State and Utopia*, Basic Books, 1974.

Palmer, M., *Moral Problems*, Lutterworth Press, 1991.

Pinchin, C., *Issues in Philosophy*, Palgrave Macmillan, 1990.

Plato, *The Republic*, Penguin, 1955.

Rachels, J., 'Active and Passive Euthanasia', 1979 (reproduced in Palmer, 1991).

Rand, A., *Atlas Shrugged*, Random House, 1957 (reproduced in Palmer, 1991).

Raphael, D.D., *Moral Philosophy*, Oxford University Press, 1981.

Rorty, R., *Contingency, Irony and Solidarity*, Cambridge University Press, 1989.

Sartre, J., *Existentialism and Humanism*, Methuen Publishing Ltd, 1974.

Singer, P., *Practical Ethics*, Cambridge University Press, 1993.

Smart, J. and Williams, B., *Utilitarianism – For and Against*, Cambridge University Press, 1973.

Thomson, J.J., 'A Defence of Abortion' (reproduced in Palmer, 1991).

Tollefsen, C., *Disputatio*, The Philosophy Centre of the University of Lisbon, May 2000.

Weil, S., reprinted in Winch, P., *Ethics and Action*, Routledge, 1972.

Williams, B., 'Ethics' in *Philosophy I*, ed. A. Grayling, Oxford University Press, 1995.

Wright, C., *Truth and Objectivity*, Harvard University Press, 1992.

Philosophy of religion

Arguments for the existence of God

The cosmological argument

- to be able to explain the cosmological argument, and how the idea of a 'cosmological relation' exemplifies difficulties in talking about God

- to understand the centrality of religious experience for religious belief, and be aware of the variety of religious experience and the associated problems

- to consider the possibility of naturalistic explanations

- to think about what counts as responsible and rational belief and why.

AQA Examiner's tip

It is important to bear in mind that this module is about the *philosophy* of religion. While you can certainly make use of your own religious (or atheistic) views in the exam, you must not let them overshadow philosophical argument.

Think about

Is Clifford right about those already prone to believe? Always?

Suppose nobody had ever experienced God and no events had ever occurred that we might call miraculous. Justifying the belief that 'God exists' could not depend on drawing attention to extraordinary supernatural events. If people believed there was a God, the justification for their belief would have to be grounded in premises provided by the ordinary course of nature. Also, suppose nobody claimed to have any special sensitivity to religious realities or to be guided in their thinking by any unusual presence or spirit. When people reasoned about the existence of God, how they reasoned would not be different in kind from the sort of reasoning they employed whenever they thought about other familiar topics. You might think that unaided reason, contemplating facts about the natural world, would still be compelled or persuaded to accept the hypothesis that 'God exists'. Why? Just because the existence of God is the only or best explanation for what we all observe. This way of reckoning that God exists has been the strategy employed by what has traditionally been labelled 'natural theology'. Theology means, literally, the study of God.

One advantage of this approach to thinking about whether or not God exists is that it grants authority to what appears to be the ideal truth-seeking investigator. Clifford brings this out by contrasting the virtues of a truth-seeking investigator with the vices of the thinker who has already prejudiced their judgement:

> No man holding a strong belief on one side of a question, or even wishing to hold a belief on one side, can investigate it with such fairness and completeness as if he were really in doubt and unbiased.

Clifford (1970)

If we agree with Clifford about what makes believing 'responsible believing', then those who think God exists ought to provide a justification for the truth of the proposition 'God exists'. The burden of proof lies with those who want to assert that something is the case. Only when judgement is swayed one way or another by the evidence and argument, will the ideal truth-seeking investigator assent to belief. Now we shall consider whether the cosmological argument provides sufficient reason to assent to the belief that God exists.

Let us begin by acknowledging what we all accept; there is what there is. Why is there what there is? 'Why is there a stain on the kitchen ceiling?' The pipe in the bathroom above leaks, so water has escaped, seeping down through the floor, causing the stain. 'Why is John ill?' He ate spinach kept beyond its sell by date, and now the bacteria in his stomach are producing a reaction. Tracing causes back to their origin is a familiar way of making sense of things. In each case I identify a cause that produces what it is I am trying to explain. Read 'Why is there what there is?' as a question seeking a causal origin.

■ The argument

> Beginning with sensible things, our intellect is led to the point of knowing about God that He exists, and other such characteristics that must be attributed to the First Principle.

Aquinas (1976)

So we think the events and things we experience occur and exist because something has made them so – a prior cause. Now suppose everything has a prior cause. If everything has a prior cause then the series of prior causes will stretch back infinitely. But an infinite regress of prior causes is impossible. Yet we know that there is a series of prior causes which has produced what we experience now. So, because an infinite regress of prior causes is impossible, there must be something that is not itself caused, but is the causal origin of all subsequent causes producing what there is now. What could be the uncaused cause? Only God.

■ Issues

The cosmological argument does not appeal to any controversial evidence. We all agree that something *is*. Next, the argument proceeds to draw inferences, guided by our intellect, towards the existence of God. We shall work backwards through the argument. Following the procedure already outlined, each claim ought to be assessed impartially: and unless there is some decisive reason one way or another, an ideal truth-seeking investigator will withhold their assent to believe.

'What could be the uncaused cause? Only God'

Are the uncaused cause and God really one and the same thing? We need to establish what makes one thing identical to another. According to Leibniz's Law one thing is identical to another if and only if anything that can be said truly of the one can be said truly of the other. For instance, 'John is the murderer' is true if and only if the profile of the murderer is also the profile of John. If there is something true of the murderer that is not true of John, then John cannot be the murderer. And if there are facts true of the murderer that might not be true of John then a responsible jury ought not to conclude 'John is the murderer'. Now apply this kind of thinking to the uncaused cause and God: are they one and the same thing?

The Bible says that God created everything and if both the uncaused cause and God are said to be the origin of everything, then it looks like we are referring to one and the same thing. But the biblical understanding of the genesis of the World regards it as quintessentially the act of a loving Creator, whereas there is nothing about being simply the uncaused cause of everything else that requires an act of love. Likewise, God is said to be eternal, whereas nothing about being the uncaused cause of everything else necessitates existence beyond what is required to subsequently cause the World. And must an uncaused cause have supreme authority over everything, as anything being God must? So whether God's activity and the activity of an uncaused cause should be understood as being one and the same activity, of the same thing, is undecided.

'Something not itself caused, but the causal origin of all subsequent causes'

Must we accept at least, there is an uncaused cause of everything else? This asks two things: must we accept there is a single uncaused cause, and must we accept that an infinite regress of prior cause is impossible?

■ Think about

Which part of the argument refers to 'sensible things' and which part is under the guidance of the 'intellect'?

AQA Examiner's tip

■ It is crucial in the exam that you do not confuse the cosmological argument with other arguments for God, such as the ontological one.

■ Following on from this, it will be helpful if you know specific versions of the cosmological argument, such as Aquinas's first three ways and Leibniz's Principle of Sufficient Reason.

■ Synoptic link

For more on Leibniz's Law, see AQA A2 Philosophy Chapter 1, Philosophy of mind, p3.

It turns out that in neither case are we forced to accept, simply by thinking about it, any particular conclusion.

How many uncaused causes?

Even if everything must derive from an uncaused cause, it does not follow that everything derives from the same uncaused cause. As Paul Edwards puts it:

> even if otherwise valid, the argument would not prove a **single** first cause. For there does not seem to be any good ground for supposing that all the various causal series in the universe ultimately merge.

Edwards (1959)

So merely admitting every causal series must originate in an uncaused cause is neutral between there being a single origin or many origins. Reason authorises both possibilities and so we are not swayed either way and ought to withhold our judgement.

What would it be like supposing there is no single point of origin? It would be like conceiving the possibility that once each independent causal story has been told, there is nothing else left to account for. Hume's character Cleanthes puts it like this:

> In each chain ... or succession of objects, each part is caused by that which preceded it, and causes that which succeeds it. Where then is the difficulty? But the **whole** you say, wants a cause. I answer that uniting of these parts into a whole, like the uniting of several distinct countries into one kingdom, or several distinct members into one body, is performed merely by an arbitrary act of the mind, and has no influence on the nature of things.

Hume (1998)

If we assume that 'the whole' is a single entity, then we might expect a single cause of 'the whole'. But according to Cleanthes, only an arbitrary act of the mind could insist that 'the whole' is something that demands a single origin. Think about this: expecting that there is a causal explanation for the existence of life on Earth appears reasonable because biological organisms really are a kind of thing, sharing common distinctive properties and behaviour; and we have at least some idea how life on Earth might be explicable in terms of some common basic laws of nature. Even admitting all this, there might not be a single point of origin for all life because there might be a number of separate starting points. Contrast this expectation with someone who demands an explanation for all the 'stuff presently in my room'. What is presently in my room is a totality, but it is not obvious how cups, chairs, books, a computer, a dog, carpets, bricks, glass and so on could be a kind of thing or a real 'whole'. Thinking about the room as a totality appears to be a mere arbitrary act of the mind and it would be confused to insist that there must be a single, unifying explanation. Obviously, in the case of all those things presently in my room, we would anticipate diverse and independent accounts for all the particular objects that happen to fall under the non-natural classification 'stuff in my room'. Returning to 'what there is', we can imagine that 'the whole' is a single kind of thing, and with that presumption, it appears plausible that 'the whole' derives from a single cause. But we can just as easily imagine that 'the whole' might not be a single thing and according to this way of thinking, a multiplicity of causes seems reasonable. Nothing about things themselves appear to sway our judgement either way.

Think about

How could you decide whether 'everything' refers to a single thing, or many things?

Is an infinite regress of prior causes impossible?

Because most of our thinking concerns what is finite, having to think about 'infinity' is bound to be unusual: the notion of 'infinity' has struck some philosophers as difficult to the point of obscurity. According to **Hobbes**, when we think of 'infinity' we are aware of 'no conception of the thing, but of our own inability'. **Locke** (1996) provides a careful diagnosis of the difficulty we have trying to think of a past stretching back through eternity:

> what do we but, beginning from ourselves and the present time we are in, repeat in our minds the ideas of years, or ages, or any other assignable portion of duration past, with a prospect of proceeding in such addition with all the infinity of number.

Locke (1996)

Yet reflecting on finite things and multiplying 'in our thoughts as far as we can' can never capture accurately the reality, because when our understanding has:

> added together as many millions, &c., as it pleases, of known lengths of ... duration, the clearest idea it can get of infinity, is the confused incomprehensible remainder of endless addible numbers, which affords no prospect of stop or boundary.

Locke (1996)

And so trying to imagine a past stretching back forever overreaches our limited powers:

> whilst men talk and dispute of infinite ... duration ... it is no wonder if the incomprehensible nature of the thing they discourse of, or reason about, leads them into perplexities and contradictions, and their minds be overlaid by an object too large and mighty to be surveyed and managed by them.

Locke (1996)

Exactly what sorts of 'perplexities and contradictions' come up when we contemplate the possibility of an infinite past? Suppose you are asked to count all the prior causes in the series that produced what there is up until now, but this series has no beginning and instead regresses infinitely. You will have an infinite quantity of prior causes. Also suppose what there is now causes something next and you count everything again. Even though the previous collection is only a part of your updated collection, your previous collection is the same size as your updated collection (both contain an infinite quantity). Not only is this odd, but also it looks as if what happens next cannot add to what has already been counted because both collections are of equal infinite size, always. And so, according to Locke, if someone claims to have a clear idea about a boundless infinite past we should be suspicious. The idea of an infinite past lacks clarity because an infinite past is incomprehensible and incoherent: a person who asserts that there is an infinite past is in the same position as a person who claims to have:

> a clear idea of the number of the sands on the sea-shore, who knows not how many there be, but only that they are more than twenty.

Locke (1996)

Key philosophers

Thomas Hobbes (1588–1679): English philosopher best known for his political writings; notably *Leviathan*, in which he proposes his own version of the social contract.

John Locke (1632–1704): Early English empiricist and proto-psychologist. Highly influential in a wide range of fields, notably political philosophy; a field in which he held republican views. Locke was also a doctor of medicine.

But is an infinite regress of prior causes really so difficult to grasp? Certainly I cannot mentally survey all the items making up an infinite collection, but nevertheless the idea that 'things and events always have been' appears comprehensible; things exist, events occur, and causes operate as now, always. Because understanding the sense of 'an infinite regress of prior causes' is not the same as trying to hold in my understanding each and all those things and events the idea refers to, I can have a 'conception' of 'an infinite regress of prior causes'. Using my reason I can manage counting infinite collections by distinguishing between the way to deal with finite collections, and the way to deal with infinite collections. Understood on their own terms, infinite collections are logically well behaved: Cantor developed sound mathematical concepts for distinguishing between infinite subsets and the infinite wholes of which they are part, as well as an appropriate arithmetic for adding to and subtracting from these collections. Treated properly the apparent paradox generated by infinite collections disappears and counting an infinite regress of prior causes is no longer contradictory: and so no longer incoherent. For this mathematics can be applied to things and events, so an infinite causal series of things and events is possible; it might be like this.

Hume insists that reason alone cannot draw any decisive conclusions about what is. Hume insists this is true for all cases; only truths about 'what can be thought' and never truths about the existence and nature of events or things can be determined just by reason. A priori, any imaginable event or thing or arrangement of event and thing is, as a matter of fact, just as possible as any other. Because a past with a beginning and a past without a beginning are equally imaginable, reason authorises both possibilities. Kant tried to show that there were equally compelling reasons for thinking there was and that there was not a beginning. He wanted to show that pure reason, if allowed to speculate free from the counterweight of sense experience, will authorise all kinds of contradictory truths: Kant calls these paradoxes **antinomies**, and the metaphysical decrees which produced them 'the euthanasia of reason'.

Response: the Big Bang

Pope Pius XII wrote how the scientific evidence supporting the Big Bang account of creation:

> has succeeded in bearing witness to the august instant of the primordial Fiat Lux [Let there be Light], when along with matter, there burst forth from nothing a sea of light and radiation, and the elements split and churned and formed into millions of galaxies .... Thus, with that concreteness which is characteristic of physical proofs, [science] has confirmed the contingency of the universe and also the well-founded deduction as to the epoch when the world came forth from the hands of the Creator. Hence, creation took place. We say: therefore, there is a Creator. Therefore, God exists!

Pope Pius XII, Pontifical Address to the Academy of Science (1951)

Cosmological observations appear to confirm that the material universe did, as a matter of fact, begin to exist at a single point in the finite past before which it in no way existed. So it looks as if the past is finite. This point of origin is called the singularity. So it looks as if all causal series do merge on a single point in the finite past. The material universe is, as a matter of fact, a unit ('the whole') whose singular causal history begins with the Big Bang. And so, a cosmological argument appears to come back into sharp focus:

> Since everything that begins to exist has a cause of its existence, and since the universe began to exist, we conclude, therefore, the universe has a cause of its existence … Transcending the entire universe there exists a cause which brought the universe into being …
>
> *Craig (1979)*

For the moment, concentrate on the claim that the Big Bang appears to establish that there is a beginning and single point of origin. The Big Bang hypothesis is compatible with the singularity being an event occurring in a pre-existing reality. The 'universe', or our universe, can just refer to a huge homogeneous domain, emerging from a sea of more or less distinct multiple universes. On this model, the Big Bang is just a specific phase or local fluctuation within eternally existing space-time 'foam'. And the series of 'causes', that transcend the beginning of this material universe, could stretch back through infinite space-time. As such, the Big Bang event might only be 'the beginning of everything' in a qualified sense and the 'whole' might only be part of a greater totality which is more or less integrated. Whether this more extensive reality has itself a single origin, multiple origins or is without beginning is still an open question.

Everything has a prior cause

Hume stresses how thinking about the cause of the beginning of the material universe is like thinking about nothing we have ever experienced:

> Here indeed lies the justest and most plausible objection against a considerable part of metaphysics, that they are not properly a science; but arise … from the fruitless efforts of human vanity, which would penetrate into subjects utterly inaccessible to the understanding.
>
> *Hume (1967)*

Consider two competing causal hypotheses:

1 The dog chased the sheep over the cliff.
2 The cat chased the sheep over the cliff.

If no one saw it happen, how should we choose between **1** and **2**? Well, we have no experience of cats chasing sheep, but lots of experience of dogs chasing sheep. Therefore, the evidence implies that **1** is more likely. Now consider competing factual hypotheses regarding the unobserved cause of the material universe. In this case there are no other instances of like events we can refer to for guidance; there isn't any relevant evidence making any particular causal hypothesis more probable, one way or another.

Perhaps we could draw an analogy between the material universe coming into being and the coming to be of events and things we are familiar with. Even if we had never seen another dog, if this dog is like a wolf and we have seen wolves chase sheep, then 'this wolf-like dog chased the sheep' seems more likely than supposing it was the cat. But what on Earth is 'causing the material universe' like? What about the suggestion that the cause of the universe is like a mental act – a choice – that brings about an action? The singularity is understood as the beginning of matter. Whatever caused matter to begin existing cannot itself be matter, but must be something other, **transcending** *the entire universe*. What kind of being could exist other than materially, and be capable of acting independently of prior causes? It could only be a mind that has chosen freely to create the World.

> ## Think about
>
> Is speculating about the origins of 'the Big Bang' science?

> ## Synoptic link
>
> AQA A2 Philosophy Chapter 6, Philosophical problems in Hume, Ideas. This can be found at **www.nelsonthornes.com/aqagce**

> ## Key terms
>
> **Transcending:** something is said to be transcendent if it is absolutely beyond the limits of our own existence.

> In the beginning was the Word, and the Word was with God, and the Word was God. He was in the beginning with God; all things were made through him, and without him was not anything made that was made.

John 1:1

But such a Divine Mind, bringing the material universe into being by an act of will, is nothing like anything we have ever experienced. At best, the minds we know modify and arrange material, but never create matter from nothing. Led by familiar experience, we are unable to decide between competing causal hypotheses regarding the origin of the material universe.

If a person asks 'what is the cause of the World?' what exactly are we being invited to think about? They might tell us to think of things being 'brought about', 'made', 'created', 'produced', and so on. But all these examples are of familiar causal relations: what we have been asked to consider is the truth about a radically unfamiliar causal relation. Hume argues that the idea of 'cause' is inseparable from our experience of the successive repetition of like events and things: Kant develops this idea. We have already seen that applying ideas, or concepts, familiar and authoritative in one area (e.g. our familiar understanding of 'parts and wholes' in relation to finite collections), can lead to paradox and incoherence when applied beyond their appropriate range (e.g. when applied to unfamiliar infinite collections). For Kant the rules laid out by his **Copernican revolution** prescribe for any and all rational beings what rightful thinking about causal relations demands. 'Space', 'time' and 'causality' are rules that jointly designate the requirements that must be satisfied in order for any experience to qualify as an experience of an object. These rules dictate that if I think about an object, for instance my house, then I must be thinking about something with spatial dimensions, causally interacting with other spatial objects, over a period of time. Because the role of 'causality' is to regulate the objects we experience in space and time, the notion of 'cause':

> has no meaning and no criterion for its application save only in the sensible world. But in the cosmological proof it is precisely in order to enable us to advance beyond the sensible world that it is employed.

Kant (2004)

Causal concepts allow us to make inferences from one actual or possible event or thing to another actual or possible event or thing, relating each to each, as either a cause or an effect. Legitimate causal inferences have their form and authority delegated from and within experience: any causal inference regarding a reality beyond experience will overreach its jurisdiction; thus being an exception to the rules that regulate and legitimate causal inferences in general. Hence metaphysical causal inferences are impossible because they are prohibited by the restrictions our understanding lays down regarding the limits of what makes sense. Our metaphysical causal inferences are merely empty gestures.

Can we at least know a priori that there must be a cause – even if we admit we cannot know what it is or how it operates – a kind of abstract 'because of …'? For instance, can we not insist, simply on the basis of reflection that 'nothing can come from nothing'? As Pope Pius XII thinks, because there might not have been a Big Bang, the material universe need not exist: 'science has confirmed the contingency of the universe'. So, the existence of the material universe must be, in some abstract sense 'because of …' something. According to Hume, as you are guided a priori,

Key terms

Copernican revolution: just as Copernicus' astronomy displaced the Earth from the centre of the universe in favour of the Sun, Kant claimed that his philosophy displaced the fixed nature of objects in favour of our perception of them. In other words, objects conform to our knowledge of them, as our perceptions shape our world.

anything that is not impossible is equally possible and that also includes the possibility of a causeless beginning:

> as all distinct ideas are separable from each other, and as the ideas of cause and effect are evidently distinct, 'twill be easy for us to conceive any object to be non-existent this moment, and existent the next, without conjoining to it the distinct idea of a cause or productive principle. The separation, therefore, of the idea of a cause from that of a beginning of existence is plainly possible for the imagination, and consequently the actual separation of these objects is so far possible, that it implies no contradiction or absurdity.

Hume (1967)

And so the coming to be of the material universe might merely be a brute fact, and that is all there is to it. Hume has uncovered a structural catastrophe that no argument of this form can avoid. Nothing about our understanding of 'sensible things' can guide our judgement regarding a super-sensible or transcendent reality: our intellect alone is unable to establish truths about what is; our intellect can only determine both what could be, and what must be impossible. It is conceivable that the material universe just exists and nothing we can draw from experience can sway our judgement one way or the other.

So should we just admit that there is no effective method for deciding the argument? There does not appear to be anything we would experience differently about the World, whether it is or is not a brute fact. What should we conclude as responsible truth-seeking investigators? Hume insists that all arguments must be decidable – in principle – if they are to count as arguments proper. The cosmological argument cannot be decided on the basis of observation: and reason alone cannot determine what is probable or actual; and so the cosmological argument is 'nothing but sophistry and illusion'.

> ### Think about
> - Is the hypothesis that the material universe just is, any more or less probable than the hypothesis that God created it from nothing?
> - Are there any circumstances in which 'God is the uncaused cause of everything else' reads as a respectable factual hypothesis?

Cosmological awareness: faith seeking understanding

Hume and Kant appear to have undermined any hope that a cosmological argument can demonstrate the existence of God as envisaged by traditional natural theology. Perhaps the cosmological 'argument' can serve another function. According to Hepburn, the cosmological argument is not merely an exercise in traditional natural theology. Rather, the cosmological leap attempted by the argument is a particular expression of something more general and pivotal to a religious point of view: as the believer shifts their attention from a focus on the sorts of dependence-relations that hold between the temporary and particular to an awareness of the possibility of something 'other' which transcends the World, and against which the existence of everything else stands out. Hepburn recognises and acknowledges the 'utter uniqueness of the relation between God and the world' exposed and exploited by Hume and Kant in criticising the cosmological argument, but he reasons as follows:

> No examples of this relation can be reasonably demanded, for they would have to be drawn from the relations of finite, created thing with finite, created thing. At best we could see the whole cluster of dependence-relations, such as cause-effect, parent-child, etc. ... as

preparing one to make a final, and still sharp, transition in thought to the unconditional dependence of the cosmological relation itself.

Hepburn (1971)

So, however God is supposed to be in relation to the World, the relation cannot be like a causal dependency that holds between any kinds of familiar events and things. McCabe is sure that whatever God could be, God cannot be:

> a member of everything, not an inhabitant of the universe, not a thing or a kind of thing … an existent among others. It is not possible that God and the universe should add up to make two.

McCabe (2000)

Grappling with the cosmological argument makes the believer aware of what God is not and thereby discloses God's transcendence. But, if the relation between World and God is so unique and utterly transcendent, how is a thinker supposed to make a final, sharp transition in thought to an understanding of the 'cosmological relation itself'? Unless we can specify positively what that relation might be like we might wonder what talk about the 'cosmological relation' means; if it means anything at all. What is the difference between a person who says they do not understand what this sort of talk is getting at and a person who says that they do? McCabe thinks the difference comes out in the following contrast:

> a genuine atheist is one who simply does not see that there is any problem or mystery here, one who is content to ask questions within the world, but cannot see that the world itself raises a question.

McCabe (2000)

This atheistic attitude is then compared with the awareness of the believer who experiences 'the World as a problem': and McCabe contrasts the atheist's unresponsiveness to the World with his own commitment to seek understanding; likening his devotion to the commitment a researcher ought to have towards pushing at the boundaries of conventional science.

> In my view to assert that God exists is to claim the right and need to carry on an activity, to be engaged in research, and I think this throws light on what we are doing if we try to prove the existence of God. To prove the existence of God is to prove that some questions still need asking, that the world poses these questions for us.

McCabe (2000)

If we can be struck by the thought of the World as a limited whole, then we might have an insight into the possibility of something immeasurable and entire: like the horizon encapsulating my visual field. McCabe refers to Wittgenstein's thought:

> It is not *how* things are in the world that is mystical, but *that* it exists.
>
> To view the world sub *specie aeterni* is to view it as a whole – a limited whole.
>
> Feeling the world as a limited whole – it is this that is mystical.

Wittgenstein (2001)

The cosmological argument is then transformed into something like a spiritual exercise:

> All of us … are led beyond the region of ordinary facts. Some in one way and some in others, we seem to touch and have communion with what is beyond the visible world. In various manners we find something higher, which both supports and humbles, both chastens and transports us. And, with certain persons, the intellectual effort to understand the universe is a principal way of thus experiencing the Deity. No one, probably, who has not felt this, however differently he might describe it, has ever cared much for metaphysics.

Bradley (1963)

Think about

Is McCabe getting at something 'deep' or just waffling? How would you decide?

The argument from religious experience

We began by considering whether we could justify believing in God by reflecting on familiar facts accessible to anybody: events occur, things exist and causes operate. Such facts were to be considered 'impartially'; whereby the responsible truth-seeker should only ever believe if evidence and reason points their judgement towards one conclusion instead of another. In this next section we will consider reasons for believing in God that draw attention to peculiar facts accessed by those who claim to have encountered the divine through religious experience. Also, we shall complicate the issue 'what counts as rational belief?' by considering how **William James** thinks the phenomena of religious experience ought to be understood and estimated in situ.

The centrality of religious experience

In his groundbreaking study, *The Varieties of Religious Experience*, James asserts:

> I doubt if dispassionate intellectual contemplation of the universe, apart from inner unhappiness and need for deliverance on the one hand and mystical emotion on the other, would ever have resulted in the religious philosophies we now possess.

James (1983)

Key philosophers

William James (1842–1910): American philosopher and psychologist. Best known for his pragmatism and support of functionalism. James's interests were very wide. In philosophy of religion, he was particularly interested in mysticism. He was the brother of the novelist Henry James.

What does he mean? Well suppose there was a world just like our own, except there were no religious believers, and religious practices and institutions had never existed. If, in such a world, a 'dispassionate' cosmological argument had occurred to and persuaded philosophers that a supreme uncaused cause must exist then James would say that what we call 'religious belief' on our world would not, as a consequence of this philosophical reflection or natural theologising, emerge on their world. According to James, natural theology is irrelevant for religious belief.

For many believers, a personal encounter with God is at the heart of their faith. Not only because the religious think the experience confirms that God exists, just as observations can confirm a hypothesis: but also because people who have had such experiences feel that through this overwhelming personal encounter with the Divine, a loving God has directly intervened in the course of their lives. Because of their religious experience, believers are engaged in a special relationship with God. As we will discuss further, James thinks that religious belief is only a *forced momentous and live option* because it is animated by a chance for personal transformation and salvation.

Think about

What could religious belief be apart from believing the proposition that 'God exists'?

James was particularly interested in the impact religious experience had on individual lives. There are other ways in which encounters with the divine sustain religion. Anthropologists and sociologists have highlighted how shared religious experience, often mediated through ritual and preserved through tradition and scripture, provide groups with their distinctive religious identity and modes of thought. As a matter of fact, all the major world faiths are committed to scriptures that record, in one way or another, the experiences of human beings who believe they are encountering what we might describe broadly as ultimate reality. These experiences are the bedrock on which any subsequent authoritative religious teachings are sustained. What these experiences reveal and how these revelations were acquired and preserved is fundamental in forming the normative character of a religion. As we shall see, the extent to which religious experience can be understood independently of the particular religious traditions in which they are expressed is a problematic issue.

The argument

Testimony

You claim you are acquainted with God – I should trust you

That a report of an experience ought to be accepted as **prima facie** true, is a general requirement of rational life is brought out by Reid:

> The wise and beneficent Author of Nature, who intended that we should be social creatures, and that we should receive the greatest and most important part of our knowledge by the information of others, hath, for these purposes, implanted in our natures two principles that tally with each other. The first of these principles is, a propensity to speak truth, and to use the signs of language, so as to convey our real sentiments … Another original principle … is a disposition to confide in the veracity of others, and to believe what they tell us.
>
> It is evident that, in the matter of testimony, the balance of human judgement is by nature inclined to the side of belief; and turns to that side of itself, when there is nothing put into the opposite scale. If it was not so, no proposition that is uttered in discourse would be believed, until it was examined by reason; and most men would be unable to find reason for believing the thousandth part of what is told them.
>
> *Reid (2000)*

Reid's insight into the economy of rational life suggests that unless there is something 'put into the opposite scale', I ought to believe your reports.

Competing truth claims

Here is a consideration to put into the opposite scale. Whatever aspect of religious experience you focus on, that kind of experience will be testified throughout the religions of the world, and each religion will understand and infer something different by it. Paul, a Christian, claims to know God through his experience on the road to Damascus. The Almighty Creator and final Judge of all things has sent His Son into Paul's heart who, moved by the Holy Spirit, is now a changed man. Mohammed says that his epoch-transforming experience is the result of hearing the command of Allah: and on the basis of his revelation Muhammad, the prophet of Islam, now claims to be the last authoritative messenger of the one true

God. Through his experiences, Mohammed has come to understand that Paul's references to 'God', the 'Son' and 'Holy Spirit' is befuddled:

> Say: He is God, the One and Only; God, the Eternal, Absolute; He begetteth not, nor is He begotten; and there is none like unto Him.

The Qur'an (112:1-4)

But Siddhartha Gautama, the Buddha, has learned through his revelation, or enlightenment, that this World of impermanent contingency unfolds against a backdrop of continuous necessity captured by the ceaseless wheel of Dukkha: and in explaining what he has come to understand through his experience, Siddhartha Gautama has no place for a supreme creator 'God' or a final Day of Judgement:

> this cycle of continuity (samsara) is without a visible end, and the first beginnings of beings wandering and running round, enveloped in ignorance (avijja) and bound down by the fetters of thirst (tanha) is not to be perceived.

Rahula (1978)

Paul, Mohammed and Siddhartha Gautama disagree fundamentally about the character of 'ultimate reality': they cannot all be right. And so, the testimony of the witnesses – the balance of the scale – is in question. Amid this lack of consensus, what epistemic authority could any particular religious experience have? Where testimonies conflict and contradict, the reliability of all the witnesses is undermined unless we can establish why one report should be preferred over any other. How can this be done? Whether or not any particular witness is ordinarily reliable is no decisive indicator; as the question posed by the conflicting claims involves weighing up the reliability of testimony regarding something radically other than the ordinary. Without independent access to the reality Paul, Mohammed and Siddhartha Gautama have supposedly experienced, on what basis could a neutral judge credit any particular witness with unique expertise? The conflicting and contradictory testimonies render all their claims null and void.

Could subsequent conduct be used as a mark of authentic and authoritative experience? If so, we would have rational grounds for discriminating between the weights of different conflicting and contradictory testimonies. Although 'how you subsequently act' is used to decide whether your experience is either genuine or sham within a particular religion, when trying to decide between religions 'how you subsequently act' cannot help. Each religion has its own expectations of conduct derived from the original and authoritative conduct of its founder. Simply asserting the authenticity and authority of one tradition of religious experience and practice, begs the question. Even if one testimony might be right, considering the various testimonies there is no way of telling which. Unable to justify any particular inference from religious experience to the nature of supernatural reality, the situation resembles Kant's complaint against metaphysics:

> a battle-ground quite peculiarly suited for those who desire to exercise themselves in mock combats, and in which no participant has ever yet succeeded in gaining even so much as an inch of territory, not at least in such a manner as to secure him in its permanent possession.

Kant (2004)

Think about

There is a broad agreement among scientists regarding the nature of reality and how that reality is to be explored. Do you find the same broad agreement among religions?

Credulity

It seemed I became acquainted with God – I'll trust myself

From the 'outside' – based on what Reid calls 'the information of others' – it might be difficult to justify taking any particular religious experience as an authoritative disclosure of reality: but from the 'inside' could an individual argue that the beliefs they uphold because of their religious experience are warranted just as legitimately as other beliefs sustained by experience? Just as I am not an impartial judge when it comes to trusting my own sense experience so likewise, I cannot be reasonably expected to be an impartial judge when I assess whether to trust my own religious experience. My experience has served me well in the past and that warrants my trust in it. Experience, or how things seem to me, has a certain prima facie first person authority. The Principle of Credulity makes explicit that it is:

> a principle of rationality that (in the absence of special considerations) if it seems (epistemically) to a subject that x is present, then probably x is present; what one seems to perceive is probably so. How things seem to be is good grounds for a belief about how things are.

Swinburne (1979)

Certainly, we take sense experience as good grounds for a belief about how things are. But certain kinds of religious experience are commonly not like typical sense experience in content or form. Mystical experiences are typically described using paradoxical and obscure phrases. Consider Blake's description of the disclosure of a mystical 'truth':

> To see a World in a Grain of Sand
>
> And a Heaven in a Wild Flower,
>
> Hold Infinity in the palm of your hand
>
> And Eternity in an hour.

Blake (1977)

> ### Think about
>
> How would you distinguish between a person who does and a person who does not understand Blake's meaning?

Mystics will insist the nature of the reality they encountered cannot be put into words: their experience has an ineffable quality. That such an encounter is ineffable might merely reflect the limitations of our understanding in the presence of ultimate reality:

> Our intellect occupies in the order of intelligible things the same rank as our body in the expanse of nature.

Pascal (2003)

Ayer is less sympathetic. He argues that unless the mystic can specify 'in intelligible terms' what they have experienced then their attempts to express their experience are literally meaningless:

> If a mystic admits that the object of his vision is something which cannot be described, then he must also admit that he is bound to talk nonsense when he describes it.

Ayer (2001)

Now consider the form of religious experience: the way in which it is supposedly presented to us. Some 'visions' of God, describe His appearance, or hearing His voice or literally feeling God's presence. For instance, Isaiah reports 'I saw the Lord sitting upon a throne, high and lifted up' (Isaiah 6:10) and Ezekiel provides a wonderfully vivid account of his encounter with God (Ezekiel 1: 1–28). However, 'God' is often understood to be beyond time and space, incorporeally. If so, how can we experience God? Consider this explanation offered by one mystic:

> I perceive, not with my fleshy eyes ... but with the eyes of my mind and understanding, the invisible truth of Thy face ... Thy true face is freed from any limitation, it hath neither quantity nor quality, nor is it of time or place, for it is the Absolute form, the Face of faces.

Nicholas of Cusa (2007)

Another example – Simone Weil describes a moment where she became aware of:

> a presence more personal, more certain, more real than that of a human being, though inaccessible to the senses and the imagination.

Weil (1992)

How much credulity should we grant such extraordinary and obscure 'perceptions'? It is far from obvious that mystical religious experience ought to be deferred to in the same way as other kinds of experience. But not all religious experience is as unusual as mystical experience and is much more like familiar sense-experience. If so, should such religious experience be granted the same prima facie authority as sense experience? One objection is that with sense experience, even if you and I disagree about a particular observation, we both agree that sense experience is for all, as a rule, a prima facie reliable way of discovering truth: the reliability of sense experience is inclusive. In the case of religious experience, if I assert the authority of my experience over the conflicting and contradictory testimony of others, then I am asserting that, as a rule, religious experience is delusory: except in my own case, or in cases revealing the same truths revealed to me. As such, unlike sense experience, religious experience is not taken as generally reliable. Rather, religious experience is regarded as peculiarly reliable: only experiences like mine qualify as authoritative. So, because religious experience is exclusive, it is not like sense experience; it has none of its prima facie inclusive authority. Because there is no analogy, the authority of sense experience does not carry over to religious experience.

Mere psychology?

> To say he hath spoken to him in a Dream, is to say no more than to say he dreamed that God spake to him.

Hobbes (2008)

Descartes experienced sitting by the fire in his dressing gown, reading. However, it turned out that he was, in fact, all the time in bed dreaming. The cause of Descartes' experience was not what he took it to be: what his experience was about (sitting by the fire in his dressing gown, reading) and what caused that experience (the process of dreaming) were not the same. Likewise, consider the suggestion that when it comes to religious experience, the cause of the experience is not the same as the supposed mind-independent object the experience is about: rather, the experience is caused by processes occurring within the subject of the experience. No wonder there appears to be such disagreement: if religious experience is the product of various individual psychologies, conditioned differently by their contrasting social environments, then we would expect to see a great diversity among reports of supposed encounters with God or

Synoptic link

AQA A2 Philosophy Chapter 9, Philosophical problems in Descartes. This can be found at **www. nelsonthornes.com/aqagce**

Ultimate Reality. According to Hobbes, if we treat religious experience as natural phenomena, like dreaming, then the testimony of religious experience:

> is not of force to win belief of any man that knows that dreams are for the most part natural, and may proceed from former thoughts.

Hobbes (2008)

Consider the following experiment. On Good Friday 1962 a group of theology students attended a service at Marsh Chapel, just outside Boston. Half the group were given psilocybin, a hallucinogen that produces vivid sensory images and distorted perception. The other half got a placebo. After the service, unlike the students given a placebo, the drugged students described having vivid religious experiences. What could this show? If we know that religious experience has been produced by natural causes on this occasion then it is plausible that natural causes have produced religious experience on other occasions. Because the experiences are the outcome of internal natural processes, there is no need to appeal to any external supernatural causal agency – God is redundant. As Ayer puts it:

> In describing his vision the mystic does not give us any information about the external world; he merely gives us indirect information about the conditions of his own mind.

Ayer (2001)

However, we might still value religious experience as a psychological mechanism because it performs an important function maintaining our internal psychological harmony and regulating our social interactions. For instance, the psychoanalyst Jung saw religious experience as a means by which the personality seeks to integrate itself at crucial periods in our psychological maturation. Equally, we might understand the natural production of religious experience as the outpouring of a distorted psychology, as a symptom of a dysfunction in the way we live our lives. Marxian sociologists often interpret religion as an ideological soporific dulling our awareness of the contradictions disfiguring the economic and social system we inhabit, and they understand 'God' as an alien projection of ourselves.

However, there is never sufficient evidence to rule out the possibility of supernatural intervention altogether. James, who conducted his own comparative research into the varieties of religious experience, admits that naturalism is a plausible option when it comes to explaining the immediate origin of religious experience; and it might be an exhaustive explanation. But merely correlating religious experience with natural processes does not rule out the possibility 'that the divine is actually present ... and between it and ourselves relations of give and take are actual'. James points out that psychology assumes that 'the dependence of mental states upon bodily conditions must be thorough-going and complete'. If so, just because religious experience has a physiological basis, cannot in itself undermine its potential for disclosing truth:

> otherwise none of our thoughts and feelings, not even our scientific doctrines, not even our dis-beliefs, could retain any value as revelations of the truth, for every one of them flows from the state of their possessor's body at the time.

James (1983)

And the method of deliverance, however much it resembles a natural occurrence, is always compatible with it being the deliverance of a 'higher power':

> If there were such a thing as inspiration from a higher realm, it might well be that the neurotic temperament would furnish the chief condition of the requisite receptivity.

James (1983)

That the experiences in Marsh Chapel were induced by psilocybin need not, in itself, rule out the possibility that the experience is truth disclosing:

> Today, Mike Young is the Rev. Mike Young, pastor of the Unitarian Universalist Church in Tampa. He was one of the 10 who took psilocybin that Good Friday three decades ago. 'Of course I remember it. All of it,' he says. 'Experiencing death is something you don't forget.' Those wild and colourful seven hours showed him a new mode of perception that was nothing short of ecstatic. The drug trip helped solidify his career path in the ministry. And it conquered his fear of death.

Malmgren (1994)

> **Think about**
>
> To what extent, if at all, can naturalistic explanations rule out the possibility of supernatural interventions?

Experiencing as

Is there a way of overcoming the problem of the conflicting experiences among religions and accommodating the insight that religious experience appears to be saturated by the religious culture in which it is embedded? Consider Hick's example:

> An elephant was brought to a group of blind men who had never encountered such an animal before. One felt a leg and reported that an elephant is a great living pillar. Another felt the trunk and reported that an elephant is a great snake. Another felt a tusk and reported that an elephant is like a sharp plough share. And so on ... Of course they were all true, but each referring only to an aspect of the total reality and all expressed in very imperfect analogies.

Hick (1977)

> **AQA Examiner's tip**
>
> The use of illustrative examples such as this one are very helpful in the exam when trying to get complicated points across.

The blind men are each describing an aspect of the same thing, interpreted from a different perspective. Understood like this, the various descriptions each man gives complement, rather than conflict and contradict, one another. Likewise, perhaps the various testimonies given by those who have had a religious experience are really partial, culturally conditioned, experiences of one and the same thing. If this is the right way to think about it then, at least, it would appear that in principle the problem of competing truth claims can be resolved. Also, if at some level of abstraction we can discover a common denominator among all religious experience, then we have the following argument:

> When there is a nucleus of agreement between the experiences of men in different places, times and traditions, and when they all tend to put much the same kind of interpretation on the cognitive content of these experiences, it is reasonable to ascribe this agreement to their all being in contact with a certain objective aspect of reality, unless there be some positive reason to think otherwise.

Broad (2000)

> **Think about**
>
> Could all religions be talking about the same reality?

A nucleus of agreement?

Because we already know what an elephant is, we can see how we could reconcile the different experiences. Without knowing what sort of thing an elephant is, the suggestion that the blind men's conflicting testimony might be reconciled appears less persuasive:

> One felt … and reported … a great living pillar. Another felt … and reported … a great snake. Another felt … and reported …a sharp plough share. And so on …
>
> *Hick (1977)*

Subtracting the elephant, why would you believe they were referring to one and the same thing at all? Even if we made that assumption, on what reliable basis could we construct the 'object' which they all speak of? Is it more like a pillar or a plough? In what way is it snake like? Without already knowing it is an elephant, it is not obvious that there is a nucleus of agreement. As far as religious experience goes, it looks as if I am equally unable to establish that the experiences are each of the same object; what could this 'common' object be? This question has great practical significance:

> People may succeed in relating their thoughts to the true God even though they have a partly erroneous view of his attributes … However, there are limits to the possibility … A sufficiently erroneous thought of a God will simply fail to relate to the true and living God at all.
>
> *Geach (2001)*

> **Think about**
>
> Is the Supreme Being a bit like Thor, or more like Zeus, or Baal? How alike? How can you tell?

■ The will to believe

Earlier we said we would think about 'what counts as rational belief?' by considering how religious experience ought to be understood and estimated in situ. James argues that it is rational and responsible for me to believe in the reality of a higher power based on your religious experience. In order to show this, James argues that it makes sense to interpret religious experience as experience of a single supernatural reality. In order to establish this commonality, James needs to distinguish between religious institutions or traditions such as Christianity, Islam, Judaism, and so on, and what he calls 'personal religion pure and simple'. He then tries to show that, given the circumstances in which religious belief is presented as an option, it is responsible and rational to choose belief instead of unbelief.

Experience of a higher power

James thinks the object of religious experience might be made sense of in terms of the role it is supposed to play in effecting change in an individual. He conceives of this 'higher power' as that which brings about life-enhancing experience and subsequent transformation:

> the various religions do indeed cancel each other, but there is a certain uniform deliverance in which all religions all appear to meet. It consists of two parts:
>
> An uneasiness; and
>
> Its solution

The uneasiness to its simplest terms, is a sense that there is something wrong about us as we naturally stand.

The solution is a sense that we are saved from the wrongness by making proper connection with higher powers …

James (1983

Apart from the similarity of function, James also notices a shared **phenomenology** among religious experience:

When we survey the whole field of religion, we find a great variety in the thoughts that have prevailed there; but the feelings … are almost always the same.

James (1983)

And the common feeling is that the individual, divided by inner turmoil:

becomes conscious that this higher part is coterminous and continuous with a more of the same quality, which is operative in the universe outside of him, and which he can keep in working touch with, and in a fashion get on board of and save himself when all his lower being has gone to pieces in the wreck.

James (1983)

The religious option

James is a pragmatist: whether a belief is warranted or not, is determined by the success possessing that belief achieves in securing our interests. Even abstract theory, if it is of any real value, must be put to work. Unless our beliefs have practical consequences they are literally useless: 'what could it matter, if all propositions were practically indifferent, which of them we should call true or false'. A reflective philosopher cannot have a single set of criteria against which the legitimacy of all beliefs, as one, should be measured. Instead, the philosopher must pay attention to the way the belief functions in the context in which it is put to work. Different pursuits in different contexts require different rules of assessment, and as our practical interests change, so the rules of engagement change. Failure to recognise that 'what counts as rational' is sensitive to context just reflects prejudice:

This very law which the logicians would impose upon us … is based on nothing but their own natural wish to exclude all elements for which they, in their professional quality of logicians, can find no use.

James (2003)

James applies his pragmatism to the question of adopting religious belief. His scientific research has confirmed that, in general, the common feelings produced by religious experience are, ultimately, life enhancing:

Religious feeling … like any tonic, freshens our vital powers … overcomes temperamental melancholy and imparts endurance to the subject, or a zest, or a meaning, or an enchantment and glory to the common objects of life.

James (1983)

As we have seen, James acknowledges that these life-enhancing effects could be the result of natural processes, rather than being the product of an actual 'higher power'. From the perspective of the theoretician, the evidence is inconclusive. Nevertheless, concluding his scientific study *The Varieties of Religious Experience*, James expresses what he describes as his 'over belief' that the 'higher power' is not merely imagined, but is real:

> the unseen region in question is not merely ideal, for it produces effects in this world. When we commune with it, work is actually done upon our finite personality, for we are turned into new men, and consequences in the way of conduct follow in the natural world upon our regenerative change.

James (1983)

James's pragmatism informs him that what counts as warranted or unwarranted belief in the pursuit of science, need not count as warranted or unwarranted belief in different circumstances. Believing that there is a higher power at work in effecting religious experience could be the rational thing for me to do, here and now.

> If religion be true and the evidence for it be still insufficient, I do not wish, by putting your extinguisher upon my nature (which it feels to me as if it had after all some business in this matter) to forfeit my sole chance in life of getting upon the winning side ... This command that we put a stopper to our heart, instincts, and courage and wait – acting of course meanwhile as if religion were not true – till doomsday, or till such a time as our intellect and senses working together may have raked in evidence enough – this command, I say, seems to me the queerest idol ever manufactured in the philosophic cave.

James (2003)

When evaluating a scientific hypothesis I can afford to withhold my judgement in order to avoid error, whereas the possible reality of a higher power demands a different kind of response. Among the variety of religious experience there is a core, but inconclusive, testimony that I can be saved and my life transformed for the better, as long as I embrace the reality of a higher power. The religious option is forced. Unlike deciding whether a scientific hypothesis is more or less true, the possible reality of a 'higher power' requires a decisive response: either you put your faith in there being a higher power, or you do not put your faith in there being a higher power; you cannot hedge your bets. Also, the religious option is momentous for my personal wellbeing and fulfilment. The respectable scientist must detach him or herself from the hypothesis being considered. As an ideal observer the outcome cannot matter to him/her personally. In contrast, my embracing the reality of a higher power is essentially a decision of unique individual significance. Now, the practical alternative of taking up a religious life makes embracing the reality of a higher power a real possibility. The religious option is live. As such, embracing the reality of a higher power is, in these circumstances, what James regards as a genuine option.

> The religious hypothesis gives to the world an expression which specifically determines our reactions, and makes them in a large part unlike what they might be on a purely naturalistic scheme of belief.

James (2003)

In these circumstances, admitting that the evidence is indecisive, would embracing the reality of a higher power be the rational thing to do?

> We see, first that religion offers itself as a momentous option. We are supposed to gain, even now, by our belief, and to lose by our non-belief, a certain vital good. Secondly, religion is a forced option, so far as that good goes. We cannot escape the issue by remaining sceptical and waiting for more light, because, although we do avoid error in that way if religion be untrue, we lose the good, if it be true, just as certainly as if we positively chose to disbelieve … Now, to most of us religion comes in a still further way that makes a veto on our active faith even more illogical. The more perfect and more eternal aspect of the universe is represented in our religions as having personal form. The universe is no longer a mere It to us, but a Thou, if we are religious; and any relation that may be possible from person to person might be possible here … If the hypothesis were true in all its parts, including this one, then pure intellectualism, with its veto on our making willing advances, would be an absurdity; and some participation of our sympathetic nature would be logically required. I, therefore, for one, cannot see my way to accepting the agnostic rules for truth-seeking, or wilfully agree to keep my willing nature out of the game. I cannot do so for this plain reason, that **a rule of thinking which would absolutely prevent me from acknowledging certain kinds of truth if those kinds of truth were really there would be an irrational rule**. That for me is the long and short of the formal logic of the situation, no matter what the kinds of truth might materially be.

James (2003)

For James, choosing faith or religious belief is warranted by the circumstances.

> I simply refuse obedience to the scientist's command to imitate his kind of option, in a case where my own stake is important enough to give me the right to choose my own form of risk.

James (2003)

But which version of the 'higher power' should you worship, which practice and ritual should you adopt, whose beliefs should you accept? Because James thinks that 'the religious life is spiritual and no affair of outer works and ritual sacrament' he thinks that what matters is the possibility of an inner relationship; the mere outward expression of belief is not that important. We should adopt the religion that, in our particular circumstances, is practically viable. Roughly: in Thailand choose Buddhism; in Saudi Arabia choose Islam; in Italy choose Christianity.

Assessment

James has defended the right to embrace the reality of a higher power when the evidence is indecisive but 'the reality of a higher power' presents the individual with a genuine option. James's analysis of the situation stresses that what Hume called 'the religious hypothesis' is not much like a scientific hypothesis at all: the circumstances in which we assent to believe are very different in the cases of religion and science. Should we follow James's advice? Briefly consider the following issues:

- Is James right to treat 'outer works and ritual sacrament' as extrinsic and accidental? Can a religious experience be understood or can religious feeling be understood except from within the language and practice which express that experience and feeling? We could criticise James because he has failed to recognise that the 'cash-value' of religious experience is inseparable from the currency of a particular religious form of life.

■ Does James confuse estimating the probability of a proposition with weighing up the possible consequences embracing a proposition might have for the individual? James might respond by insisting that all he wants to show is that what appears 'a good bet' depends on weighing up possible gains and losses. My chances of surviving a thirty-foot jump remain constant, but I ought to be more willing to take the risk if I am leaping from a burning building, and less willing to take the risk if I merely wish to avoid walking down the stairs in normal circumstances.

■ Can I adopt, with appropriate conviction, a religious belief in the reality of a higher power by an act of will? I appear to be able to use my will when evaluating all kinds of propositions: I might insist on further evidence, offer an alternative interpretation, or stress different aspects as more or less important and so on. Even if we grant that these strategies are subject to my will, and that they are common whenever evidence is assessed, it is not clear that I can will myself to full-blown religious belief.

■ Even if I could do this, the kind of strategy James recommends has been criticised for being dishonest and self-seeking: a kind of wilful self-deception. Kant puts it like this:

> The hypocrite regards as a mere nothing the danger arising from the dishonesty of his profession, the violation of conscience, involved in proclaiming even before God that something is certain, when he is aware that, its nature being what it is, it cannot be asserted with unconditional assurance.

Kant (1998)

Think about

Do any of these issues undermine James's argument? Which and why?

☑ *After studying this topic you should:*

- understand the motivation and structure of cosmological arguments

- know the reasons why Hume and Kant object to a cosmological proof

- know how the cosmological argument illustrates problems with religious language

- know how the cosmological relation is pivotal to religious thinking

- understand the nature and significance of religious experience

- be able to discuss the problems posed by conflicting truth claims and possible solutions

- understand the difficulty of establishing an objective, independent cause of a religious experience.

Reason and faith

Learning objectives

- to understand how the relation between faith and reason can be conceived
- to understand the role volition has been described as playing in faith.

Synoptic link

AQA AS2 Philosophy Chapter 8, God and the world, pp263–5. This can be found at **www.nelsonthornes.com/aqagce**

Think about

- Do we have an obligation to believe 'as reason directs'?
- What kind of obligation could it be?

James has argued that, given the circumstances, it is rational to choose belief. How have others understood the relation between faith and reason and the legitimacy of choosing to believe? Locke does not see an opposition between reason and faith. In fact, our capacity to reason and arrive at truth is a gift from God, and God will judge our faithfulness to that gift:

> Faith is nothing but a firm assent of the mind: which if it be regulated, as is our duty, cannot be afforded to anything, but upon good reason; and so cannot be opposite to it. He that believes, without having any reason for believing, may be in love with his own fancies; but neither seeks truth as he ought, nor pays the obedience due to his maker, who would have him use those discerning faculties he has given him, to keep him out of mistake and error. He that does not this to the best of his power, however he sometimes lights on truth, is in the right but by chance … This at least is certain, that he must be accountable for whatever mistakes he runs into: whereas he that makes use of the light and faculties God has given him, and seeks sincerely to discover truth … may have this satisfaction in doing his duty as a rational creature … for he governs his assent right, and places it as he should, who in any case or matter whatsoever, believes or disbelieves, according as reason directs him. He that does otherwise, transgresses against his own light, and misuses those faculties, which were given him.

Locke (1996)

Because Locke thinks both that faith is a matter of being properly guided by reason and that reason shows that the existence of God is highly probable, he thinks there is no need to think of faith in the proper sense as having to extend beyond the evidence. For Locke, faith is just rational belief in God. Presumably, if Locke were to conclude that reason cannot establish the high probability that God exists, he would conclude that religious faith is illegitimate.

Aquinas also sees faith and reason as complementary, but he argues that some religious truths are not demonstrable by reason; he also stresses the role of volition in faith. Having faith, for Aquinas, is a virtue. As a virtue, faith must involve a volitional aspect: it is something I can be responsible for, and God will judge whether my conduct has merit. Unlike the kind of forced belief that comes with logical compulsion (such as: if *A* is *B* and *B* is *C*, then *A* is *C*), faith involves my free will. I ought to choose to believe in God. The possibility of exercising my free will depends on the articles of faith being less certain than the truths delivered by logical compulsion. Nevertheless, faith is stronger than belief because it is animated by the grace of God, which guides our judgement to the Truth. Aquinas believed that the cosmological argument was a proof of God. But he did not think that the essential truths of Christianity, for instance the trinity or incarnation, could be demonstrated philosophically. These essential truths can only be held through faith: but they are acceptable to reason; which is faith's ally in coming to an understanding of God.

Key philosophers

Søren Kierkegaard (1813–55):
Danish philosopher and theologian. Often wrote under pseudonyms and in a very literary style which left his work highly open to interpretation. His fame increased enormously after his death and he is now held to be a founding father of existentialism.

Compare the medieval Aquinas with **Kierkegaard**, who is thinking about faith in the wake of Hume and Kant:

> *To stand on one leg and prove God's existence is a very different thing from going on one's knees and thanking him.*

Kierkegaard (1973)

Faith and reason are opposed. Reason cannot know God or acknowledge God for what God is. Reason is no longer an ally, but a pompous impostor:

> The existence of a king or his presence is commonly acknowledged by an appropriate expression of subjection and submission; what if, in his presence, one were to prove that he existed.

Kierkegaard (1973)

But Kierkegaard is aware that from the perspective of reason, faith in the reality of God must always appear absurd, because reason is the currency of thought:

> As soon as I talk I express the universal, and if I do not do so, no one can understand me.

Kierkegaard (1973)

Kierkegaard thinks about three examples of 'the tragic hero':

1 King Agamemnon who must sacrifice his own daughter Iphigenia to the goddess Artemis. Agamemnon is preparing his fleet for war, but after offending the goddess by killing a sacred stag and bragging about his own god-like prowess at hunting, Artemis becalms the sea unless Agamemnon appeases her.

2 Jephtha, the Hebrew leader whose victory against his enemies is secured by a promise made to God to sacrifice as a burnt offering the next person entering his house and unbeknown to him that person will be his only daughter.

3 The Roman Consul Brutus, who orders his own son's execution, because he plotted to overthrow the republic that Brutus represents.

In each case the sacrifice of the father can be made intelligible as a tragedy: an individual who personifies 'the rule of law' is bound by that law to sacrifice what is most dear to him. The protagonists have no choice given their commitments and duty; we all know this and recognise their nobility in choosing duty over passion. In Lockean terms, each protagonist can have the satisfaction of doing his duty as a rational creature, acting according as reason directs.

Next Kierkegaard considers Abraham's imperative to sacrifice his only son Isaac. Unlike the other cases, Abraham's situation is not obviously tragic. As Kierkegaard says, we can both admire and be appalled by Abraham's choosing to sacrifice his son. Abraham's dilemma does not even make sense, it is a paradox: how can the God of Abraham demand that 'the father shall love his son' and at the same time require his sacrifice? The imperative to sacrifice Isaac cannot be 'a temptation' or a test of dutifulness. Unlike the cases of Agamemnon, Jephtha and Brutus we have no idea what standard Abraham will be judged by, and he cannot tell how he will be judged. Abraham's decision to suspend 'The Universal' and sacrifice Isaac must be made in complete existential anguish and despair:

Is it possible that this can be anything else but a temptation? And if it be possible, but the individual was mistaken – what can save him? He suffers all the pain of the tragic hero, he brings to naught his joy in the world, he renounces everything – and perhaps at the same instant debars himself from the sublime joy which to him was so precious that he would purchase it at any price. Him the beholder cannot understand nor let his eyes rest confidently upon him …

Kierkegaard (1973)

Like Aquinas, Kierkegaard stresses the volitional aspect of faith but characterises it as a passionate personal commitment, in opposition to the duties imposed by the universal regulations of reason. And, in direct conflict with universal reason, Kierkegaard stresses the need for the individual to choose to believe in the paradox of God – to make a passionate leap of faith. In place of grace, our will is guided by the appropriate attitudes of fear and dread; as exemplified by 'the knight of faith', Abraham. For Kierkegaard, understanding the limits of reason clarifies our duty to God: a life of faith.

☑ *After working through this topic, you should:*

- understand the nature of faith and its relation to responsibility
- know how 'faith' has been used differently by different thinkers.

Miracles

Learning objectives

- to think about the role miracle stories have in authorising and sustaining religious belief
- to consider how the occurrence of miracles might be accommodated within our general understanding of how the world operates
- to consider the extent to which we ought to believe testimony reporting miracles.

What kind of document is the Bible? Although it records and interprets past events, for many believers it is not simply a historical record or even a 'history' in the conventional sense at all. Troeltsch explains that for traditionalists, even though the Bible:

seeks to bind men to individual facts of history … its facts are different from ordinary history … they are substantiated by a miraculous tradition and are confirmed by an inner seal of substantiation in the heart.

Bowden (1988)

For now, think about the miraculous tradition Troeltsch identifies. That miracles are to be taken as marking the supernatural authority of the biblical message is made clear in the Gospel of John:

Jesus did many other miraculous signs in the presence of his disciples, which are not recorded in this book. But these are written that you may believe that Jesus is the Christ, the Son of God, and that by believing you may have life in his name.

(John 20:30)

The miracles of Jesus illustrate his power over the spiritual and natural realm, as he heals the sick, exorcises demons, and calms the stormy sea. The miraculous resurrection of Jesus, a unique event in history, confirms that Christianity is the only true religion and validates the teachings of Christianity.

> If there is no resurrection of the dead, then Christ has not been raised either. And if Christ has not been raised, then all our preaching is useless, and your faith is useless … and you are still guilty of your sins … But in fact, Christ has been raised from the dead.

1 Corinthians 15:12-21

And the miraculous is not only limited to the acts of Jesus. Throughout the Bible miracle stories testify to a personal God intervening in human affairs, disclosing his will in the details of salvation history. The widow who willingly uses up her last supplies to feed the prophet Elijah is rewarded; as God ensures that from then on she always has a supply of flour and oil; investing Elijah with the power to raise her son back from the dead. When the Hebrews Shadrach, Meshach and Abednego refuse to worship an idolatrous image, the enraged gentile King Nebuchadnezzar has them thrown into a fiery furnace 'seven times hotter than usual'. The soldiers escorting them are all killed by the intense heat, but Shadrach, Meshach and Abednego are unharmed, and their clothes are not damaged in any way. There are many extraordinary episodes like this witnessed in the Old and New Testaments: miracles have a crucial role to play in sanctioning the peculiar authority the Bible has. These miraculous events, by their very nature, would not have happened, all things being equal.

Are miracles, in principle, permissible?

Can we make sense of the idea that miracles happen, if we also believe that the occurrence and existence of events and things is explicable scientifically? This was not a dilemma the biblical writers had to face, because they lived in a pre-scientific age. The uniformity of nature, articulated through constant and universal causal laws, appears to keep out God's personal and momentary interventions. **Diderot**, *writing in the 18th century, describes seeing the universe as a self-contained causal system*:

Key philosophers

Denis Diderot (1713–84): French rationalist philosopher of the Enlightenment. Best known for the key role he played in the development of the *Encyclopédie*, an early and very influential 27 volume encyclopaedia, which Diderot both edited and contributed many important articles to.

> It is not from the metaphysician that atheism has received its most vital attack … If this dangerous hypothesis is tottering at the present day, it is to experimental physics that the result is due … the world is no longer a God; it is a machine with its wheels, its cords, its pulleys, its springs, and its weights.

Diderot (2000)

Perhaps describing an event as a miracle is compatible with a scientific explanation of that event. Holland thinks that even if we accept the exclusive authority of science to rightful causal explanations, it still makes sense to talk about miracles:

> the significance of some coincidences as opposed to others arises from their relation to human needs and hopes and fears, their effect for good or ill upon our lives … And the kind of thing that outside religion we call luck is in religious parlance the Grace of God or a miracle of God … But although a coincidence can be taken religiously as a sign and be called a miracle … it cannot without confusion be taken as a sign of divine interference with the natural order.

Holland (1965)

Holland imagines a child playing on the railway track: neither the child nor the train driver know of the other's location.

> The child's poor mother is up the hill from this developing tragedy, and can see both her son and the train, but because of distance, is unable to do anything. Suddenly, the train slows, and comes to a halt, only a few feet from her child. The mother thanks God for the miracle, which she never ceases to think of as such although, as she in due course learns, there was nothing supernatural about the manner in which the brakes of the train came to be applied. The driver had fainted, for a reason that had nothing to do with the presence of the child on the line, and the brakes were applied automatically as his hand ceased to exert pressure on the control lever.
>
> *Holland (1965)*

Holland's example confirms a legitimate religious use of the word 'miracle' which does not imply any scientific laws have been breached or that supernatural causes have operated. Holland draws attention to the fact that 'miracles' are not merely extraordinary events: miracles have personal significance (the Hebrew for miracle *nes* or *oth* means 'sign'). Hick stresses that experiencing an event as a miracle involves interpreting the event. Even if the atheist and the mother agree about the causal trajectories leading up to the incident, the mother, unlike the atheist, draws inferences from the event and sees it as disclosing a meaning in a way that contrasts with the response typical of atheism. The difference between the mother and the atheist is not a disagreement about the facts, but what the facts mean:

> In order to be miraculous, an event must be experienced as religiously significant.
>
> *Hick (1977)*

In fact, according to some thinkers, any occurrence can be described as a miracle as long as it reveals some religious significance:

> Every event in so far as it is embraced within the divine providence, can be understood as potentially an event manifesting God's action, yet some particular concrete events stand out in a special way in the experience of individuals or communities as vehicles of divine action.
>
> *Macquarrie (1977)*

Just as my action is interpreted as meaningful by you, irrespective of any particular causal processes that contribute to it so a miracle can be regarded as a meaningful act, irrespective of any causal processes that contribute to it. Wittgenstein imagines one way of seeing the World:

> A miracle is, as it were, a gesture that God makes. As a man sits quietly and then makes an impressive gesture, God lets the world run on smoothly and then accompanies the words of a saint by a symbolic occurrence, a gesture of nature. It would be an instance if, when a saint has spoken, the trees around him bowed, as if in reverence.
>
> *Wittgenstein (1984)*

> **Think about**
>
> Between the mother and the atheist, which account do you think 'gets it right'? Why?

Winch makes the point that understanding the World as exhibiting such gestures is not something derived solely from the event or thing as a mere bare particular. Rather, just as,

> A certain disposition, or movement, of a human body can be called a 'gesture' only within a context where it is possible for it to be recognised and/or reacted to as a gesture.

Winch (1995)

So Winch concludes that reading an event as a miracle 'depends, at least in large part, on the reigning culture within which the action occurs'. Just as talk about mere physical behaviour cannot disclose the significance a person's action has, so only referring to the causal dimension of an event will fail to capture the significance a miracle has as an act of God. So a miracle can be an event that believers regard as especially expressive of God's relation to his creatures. J.A.T. Robinson develops this line and suggests:

> The miracles are seen by Jesus, not as things he alone could do because he was divine but as what any man could do who was really open to the love of God.

Robinson (1963)

Bultmann takes this radical option. The resurrection story is an attempt to understand the religious significance of the historical crucifixion of Jesus. The writers of the gospel drew upon their pre-scientific understanding of the world as they tried to articulate and express this significance. Yet, from our scientific perspective, their mythological reading is now incomprehensible and obscures the real religious significance of the act from us:

> What a primitive mythology it is, that a divine being should become incarnate, and atone for the sins of men through his own blood.

Bultmann (1990)

Key philosophers

Martin Heidegger (1889–1976):
German phenomenologist who reinvigorated the study of ontology. Despite a period during which he allied himself with National Socialism, Heidegger remains one of the most important and influential 20th-century thinkers.

Bultmann recommends that we demythologise the story and instead try and reread it through a contemporary conceptual scheme; and he adopts **Heidegger's** existentialism as a framework for making sense of the life and death of Jesus. Is Bultmann's demythologised rereading of the Bible the only legitimate option in an age of science? Consider this miracle. In the Old Testament, God intervenes to allow the battling Joshua time to defeat the Amorites:

> And the sun stood still, and the moon stayed, until the nation took vengeance on their enemies.

Bultmann (1990)

Read literally, the normal processes at work in nature have been suspended for the final duration of combat, by the will of God. Why not accept the story at face value? Consider the claim that the Joshua miracle would undermine our fundamental understanding of the operations of nature. The principle of the conservation of energy requires that the total amount of energy in the universe remains constant, even if it is continually transferred and transformed within the causal nexus that obtains among physical states of affairs. Whichever way God is supposed to bring about the Joshua miracle, it is difficult to see how He could have achieved such a cosmic suspension without the closure principle being violated by the external input of 'supernatural' causal forces. Although the 'closure' claim is metaphysical, the authority science now has in establishing its metaphysics is derived from its practical technological success. And so the claim goes that the pragmatic preference must be for science. The normal processes at work in nature cannot be suspended and so the Joshua story is literally false. According to Bultmann, thinking about the miracles recorded in the New Testament:

> It is impossible to use electric light and the wireless and to avail ourselves of modern medical and surgical discoveries and at the same time to believe in the New Testament world of demons and spirits.

Bultmann (1990)

Must God's intervention disrupt the causal nexus in such a way that science is no longer able to keep track of the various physical processes causally active within the physical universe? Purtill develops the following analogy. The US legal system proceeds according to rules and regulations. However, the President can intervene exceptionally, in order to pardon someone. These presidential interventions are not part of the legal system. The system cannot require the President to pardon anybody or debar the President's actions, as the authority of the President here is beyond the scope of the legal system. Once the pardon has been granted the legal system carries on exactly as it always has. A miracle, like a presidential pardon, is 'outside' the system and has no ramifications for the system in general, which works as it has always worked. As the system is not disrupted, on what basis can we rule out exceptions to the rule? Consider the objection that if a suspension of the normal processes at work in nature is not the outcome of the application of laws of nature, then the event is physically impossible? Levine speculates:

> Suppose the laws of nature are regarded as non-universal or incomplete in the sense that while they cover natural events, they do not cover, and are not intended to cover, non-natural events such as supernaturally caused events if there are or could be any. A physically impossible occurrence would not violate a law of nature because it would not be covered by (i.e. would not fall within the scope of) such a law.

Levine (1989)

So a suspension of the normal processes at work in nature is compatible with the laws of nature because no law of nature could be violated by the occurrence of a non-naturally caused event: a miraculous suspension of the normal processes at work in nature is a physically impossible occurrence brought about by God. On this account, miracles cannot be taken as evidence for supernatural interventions: the possibility of such supernatural causal intervention must be presupposed by describing the event as 'miraculous'. Unless we have decisive reasons for ruling out the possibility of supernatural causation, the uniformity of nature, articulated through constant and universal causal laws, appears to permit God's personal and momentary interventions.

Presume that suspensions of the laws of nature are conceivable and so the sun really stopped. Either God's intervention explains the suspension of the normal processes at work in nature or nothing explains the suspension of the normal processes at work in nature – it was a brute fact that the sun stopped and that event happened to coincide with a battle. The situation recalls the options we faced after considering the cosmological argument: reason does not compel us to adopt either interpretation of events. But in this case it might be a religious believer who advances reasons for rejecting the intervention of God as a possible explanation for the occurrence of the event. From the victor's point of view, the brute suspension of the normal processes at work in nature will appear to be divine providence, but we ought to reject that appearance as deceptive. How can God be supremely good if he intervenes sporadically in the course of human history, in the interests of the few? Hospers asks:

> Why not stop or prevent a major catastrophe instead of a minor one, instead of an event like turning water into wine, which made little difference one way or the other compared with the vast misery of human beings at the same time and place, none of which was alleviated?

Hospers (1992)

According to Hick, acknowledging evil and suffering while believing that there is a supremely loving and omnipotent God depends on God's keeping his distance and not interfering. McCabe's objection is more metaphysical. The idea that God might be the particular cause of particular events in the World, however spectacular, degrades the idea of God:

> God cannot interfere in the universe, not because he has not the power but because, so to speak, he has too much; to interfere you have to be an alternative to, or alongside, what you are interfering with.

McCabe (2000)

The balance of probabilities

Suppose that the sorts of events recorded in the Bible and referred to earlier are, at least, possible occurrences. Hume doubts whether it could ever be wise for us, on the basis of biblical testimony, to believe these events really happened. He identifies a principle that we are usually happy to employ:

> The maxim, by which we commonly conduct ourselves in our reasoning, is, that the objects, of which we have no experience, resemble those, of which we have; that what we have found to be most usual is always most probable; and that where there is an opposition of arguments, we ought to give the preference to such as are founded on the greatest number of past observations.

Hume (1975)

So the probability of an event should be weighed up against what usually happens. If a student once again fails to hand in an essay, the teacher will believe it is more likely that the student has once again forgotten the deadline rather than believe the student's testimony that the completed essay has been eaten by the cat. The teacher, drawing on experience, qualifies as a wise judge because he/she proportions their beliefs to reflect the balance of probabilities. This strategy of weighing up the evidence is indicative of being 'wise': 'a wise man … proportions his belief to the evidence'. Failure to adjust your beliefs to the evidence indicates that you are not wise. If the teacher believes that the cat has eaten the student's essay, even though the student has never handed in an essay on time before for all sorts of 'reasons' and no cat has ever been reported eating an essay, then the teacher is not being wise, but being naive unless there is some overriding evidence that balances the probabilities in favour of the student's testimony. For instance, the teacher sees the cat regurgitate what appears to be an essay.

Think about

Is an all-powerful God who intervenes sometimes, supremely loving or unjust?

Synoptic link

AQA A2 Philosophy Chapter 6, Philosophical problems in Hume, Miracles. This can be found at **www.nelsonthornes.com/aqagce**

Hume then points out that *'nothing is esteemed a miracle, if it ever happens in the common course of nature'*. Read this as saying that, all things being equal, the miraculous events reported in the Bible do not occur in the ordinary way of events. These miraculous happenings stand out from the familiar: they are extraordinary. Given the maxim that the probability of an event should be weighed up against what usually happens, there is a prima facie argument against believing testimony reporting miracles.

> There must, therefore, be a uniform experience against every miraculous event, otherwise the event would not merit that appellation … the proof against a miracle, from the very nature of the fact, is as entire as any argument from experience can possibly be imagined.

Hume (1975)

Notice that what matters is the contrast in frequency. Because miracles are extraordinary, the probability of their occurring always approximates towards zero relative to the normal course of nature. That people find it easy to believe in miracles indicates that they are not following common sense or being wise judges. Hume suggests that this could be because they are attached emotionally to the story in some way, just as a teacher's judgement might be obscured by wanting to see a student that everyone else has written off succeed 'against the odds'. As far as miracles go, it could be that the sheer marvel of a miracle story excites a believer's imagination, or the moral of the miracle story ignites their reformist or revolutionary zeal. That the response is disproportional to the evidence indicates that common sense might have been suspended in this case. Hume allows a probability that miraculous events could occur, just as there is a probability that a cat can eat an essay – both events are conceivable – but it is always more likely that the witness is unreliable in one way or another:

> no testimony is sufficient to establish a miracle, unless the testimony be of such a kind, that its falsehood would be more miraculous, than the fact, which it endeavours to establish.

Hume (1975)

One criticism of Hume is that he has failed to take into account the numbers of people who are said to have witnessed miracles in the Bible. The more witnesses then the more credible the report. Whether or not Mary really was a virgin is a difficult claim to substantiate from testimony, given the inevitable lack of available witnesses; but when Moses parted the Red Sea, thousands witnessed the event. However, we do not know that thousands witnessed the event, all we know is that thousands are *said* to have witnessed the event. Deciding whether or not the event was likely has to make reference to our present experience, as the reliability of the biblical witness is not historically certain. Unless we assume that the past is like the present then we have no way of making sense of the fragments of evidence we have from that time and, as a matter of fact, none of our contemporaries report similar kinds of events occurring now. This is strange, considering the wealth of information we now have about what occurs globally and the frequency with which miracles occur in biblical history. A more powerful criticism that responds to the lack of analogy between our familiar experience and the miraculous events recorded in the Bible is to argue that if a miracle is the occurrence of a physical impossibility then it is not obvious how reference to the normal course of nature, or laws of nature, could be relevant. How can the ordinary be a guide to the extraordinary? Yet, even if ordinary experience cannot be a standard against which we can judge the likelihood of miracles – and Hume would insist we have no other option – the probability of any particular religious testimony being true is undermined by the competing testimonies of different religions. As we have seen, these conflicting and contradictory testimonies appear to cancel each other out: 'whatever is different is contrary'. Hume thinks the unconvincing return made by venturing into the extraordinary ought to deter the prudent inquirer from further speculation:

> When you go one step beyond the mundane system, you only excite an
> inquisitive humour, which it is impossible ever to satisfy.

Hume (1975)

☑ *After working through this topic, you should:*

- understand the significance of miracles for believers

- understand the challenges and responses to the claim that miracles occur

- know how the term 'miracle' can be used differently.

Making sense of religion

Learning objectives

- to understand the verificationist challenge to religious belief and different responses to it

- to appreciate the various ways religious language has been interpreted

- to understand the relation between religious language and religious life

- to appreciate the question whether religion ought to be understood from the 'outside' or the 'inside'.

Isaiah provocatively asks:

> To whom then will you liken God, or what likeness compare with him? The idol! A workman casts it, and a goldsmith overlays it with gold and casts for it silver chains. He who is impoverished chooses for an offering wood that will not rot; he seeks out a skilful craftsman to set up an image that will not move. Have you not heard? Has it not been told you from the beginning? Have you not understood from the foundation of the earth? It is he who sits above the circle of the earth, and its inhabitants are like grasshoppers; who stretches out the heavens like a curtain, and spreads them like a tent to dwell in; who brings princes to nought, and makes the rulers of the earth as nothing ... To whom then will you compare me, that I should be like him? says the Holy One. Lift up your eyes on high and see: who created these?

Isaiah 40:18

Does it make sense to make a transition in thought from Hume's mundane system to the 'Holy One'? Whatever the source of all being and intelligibility is, Isaiah's 'Holy One' escapes the attempts of ordinary expression to capture its concrete nature. What does 'Holy One' mean? Certainly we can use metaphors, draw analogies or tell stories, but as Hepburn says:

> The question which should be of the greatest concern to the theologian is not whether this or that myth may be re-expressed in language less flagrantly pictorial, more abstract in appearance, but whether or not

the circle of myth, metaphor and symbol is a closed one: and if closed then in what way propositions about God manage to refer.

Hepburn (1971)

The verification principle

Hume drew a limit beyond which factual inferences lost any claim to authority: experience. Kant confirmed that freed from 'the sensible world' our concepts were no longer properly regulated, leading to absurdity. Philosophy was given the task of exposing the conditions and parameters of our thinking and using this clarification to illuminate how the various aspects of experience must be understood by us. Knowledge could not transcend how the world appears. But Ayer acknowledges that even if someone asserts something is the case without any justification, what they say could still be true. And so the epistemological restriction inherited from Hume and Kant is still too accommodating: Ayer wants something comprehensively destructive. Ayer sets out to show that assertions about the non-empirical world could not be true, but not because they were false:

the labours of those who have striven to describe such a reality have all been devoted to the production of **nonsense**.

Ayer (2001)

Ayer concentrates on language: the line of attack on metaphysics in general is established 'in a criticism of the nature of the actual statements which comprise it'. He introduces the verification principle, which he employs to decide whether a given statement is meaningful. If the statement fails the test, then it is literally nonsense. The verification principle states:

a sentence has literal meaning if and only if the proposition it expresses is either analytic or empirically verifiable.

Ayer (2001)

Ayer understands the distinction between analytic and empirical statements as follows. We verify analytic statements from definitions by means of only logical laws. Ayer believes (erroneously, it turns out) that the truths of mathematics are all analytic. Analytic truth does not depend on how anything happens to be, because it makes no reference to anything: it is not contingent, but necessary. As analytical truth consists in logical derivation alone, it can be known a priori. The truth or falsity of an empirical statement, in contrast, is determined by reference to experience. Whether the assertion 'I am six feet tall' is true depends on the facts, what happens to be my height, and this can only be known a posteriori. If an assertion is neither analytic nor empirical, then it is literally nonsense. Consider the assertion:

For from him and through him and to him are all things. To him be glory for ever. Amen

Romans 11:36

It does not express a logical truth; neither is it obvious how we could confirm it or disconfirm it by observation. The assertion is literally nonsense. Perhaps we might find out if it is true in the future? Descriptions of the presently unobservable are legitimate: what matters

Synoptic link

AQA AS Philosophy Chapter 8, God and the world, pp254–7; AQA A2 Philosophy Chapter 10, Philosophical problems in Nietzsche. Chapter 10 can be found at **www.nelsonthornes.com/aqagce**

is that the assertion proposes a particular confirming experience. For instance, we can speculate whether there is water in other solar systems even though, right now, we are unable to settle the issue: in principle we know what it would be like to determine the truth of the hypothesis that 'there is water in other solar systems'. Current limitations on our capacity to make relevant observations do not count against meaningfulness; as long as we can suppose how a relevant observation might be made. What kind of observation could settle whether the assertion ' from him and through him and to him are all things' is true? Unlike empirically verifiable assertions, religious assertions make claims about a 'Holy One' whose existence transcends any possible sense-experience. Even if religious assertions appear meaningful because of their grammatical form; they are exposed as literally nonsense, on analysis. Ayer is not saying that religious claims are false: simply nonsense.

> It is important not to confuse this view of religious assertions with the view that is adopted by atheists ... For, if the assertion that there is a god is nonsensical, then the atheists' assertion that there is no god is equally nonsensical.

Ayer (2001)

Think about

How could you establish whether or not a supernatural intervention had been the cause of a physically impossible outcome?

Responses to the verification principle

> For a more adequate treatment of theological discourse we must abandon the closely circumscribed techniques of verificational analysis and search for a style of linguistic analysis which can better appreciate the extraordinary variety of the functions of language.

Ferre (1969)

Religious language as expressing feeling

One person says the glass is half full, the other says the glass is half empty. What is the difference between the two? Nothing about the glass. Rather the two descriptions express a different mood; the two speakers feel differently, but they do not disagree. Wisdom proposed that religious language could be meaningful as long as it was interpreted as expressing feelings, not stating facts. As such, religious 'assertions' do not conflict with the assertions of the scientist. Talk about the Big Bang and talk about God creating the World are compatible because the latter talk makes no real truth-claims, but rather expresses a feeling. Wisdom followed the guiding imperative of the verification principle: if you assert a fact, for instance 'God exists', then there should be a possible observation that could either confirm or disconfirm the assertion. Otherwise, if everything is the same whether God exists or not, asserting 'God exists' says nothing different from asserting 'God does not exist'. Whereas Ayer concluded that neither proposition makes sense, Wisdom thought they expressed different emotional responses. He imagines two people looking at a long-neglected garden. They both describe the garden similarly, but one person says 'there is an invisible gardener' and the other says 'there is no gardener':

> and with this difference in what they say about the gardener goes a difference in how they feel towards the garden.

Wisdom (1953)

Perhaps the response of the mother in Holland's example where she 'thanks God for the miracle' can be interpreted as stressing the emotive aspect of religious language. She understands that the event could be described as 'just a coincidence' but is overwhelmed by a feeling of gratitude which she expresses in a prayer. Understood in this way, what would it mean to assert that 'miracles happen'?

Religious language as action-guiding

Braithwaite accepts Ayer's analysis of empirical assertions and subsequent conclusion that religious language is not literally meaningful. However, like Wisdom, Braithwaite thinks that religious language can be meaningful in a non-literal way. Whereas Wisdom focused on feeling, Braithwaite focused on conduct. According to Braithwaite, religious language should not be thought of as primarily concerned with describing a transcendent reality. Rather, the primary function of religious language is to prescribe courses of acting and inspire and encourage virtuous conduct. He writes:

> A religious assertion, for me, is the assertion of an intention to carry out a certain behaviour policy, subsumable under and sufficiently general to be a moral principle, together with the implicit or explicit statement, but not the assertion, of certain stories.

Braithwaite (1964)

For Braithwaite, what is being expressed is the 'intention to follow the **agapeistic** way of life', and the stories we find in the Bible are ways in which that commitment is expressed and inculcated:

> A man is not, I think, a professing Christian unless he both proposes to live according to Christian moral principles and associates his intention with thinking of Christian stories: but he need not believe that the empirical propositions presented by the stories correspond to empirical fact. But if the religious stories need not be believed, what function do they fulfil? ... It is an empirical psychological fact that many people find it easier to resolve upon and carry through a course of action which is contrary to their natural inclinations if this policy is associated in their minds with certain stories. And in many people the psychological link is not appreciably weakened by the fact that the story associated with the behaviour policy is not believed.

Braithwaite (1964)

Braithwaite's analysis stresses that religious language and the beliefs expressed by that language have an action-guiding role to play in human lives. Because Braithwaite believes that such language cannot refer to a transcendent reality, this prescriptive function becomes the hub of religious meaning. But, why would a believer feel the need to 'act contrary to their natural inclinations' unless they thought that another way of acting was required by God? Social scientific explanations of religious belief can share both Braithwaite's stress on the action-guiding function of religious language and his scepticism regarding its literal significance; but the social sciences can also offer some explanation of the factors that generate the stories and keep the believer 'on track'. For instance, a psychoanalyst might argue that 'God's Will' is really the voice of a sublimated father figure, or a Marxian sociologist could interpret the guiding stories as an ideological construct emerging out of the dynamics of material production. If the understanding a believer has of the reasons

 Think about

Could you be genuinely religious if you thought your faith was merely an expression of your feelings or attitude?

 Key terms

Agape: in Christian theology, agape refers to the form of unconditional love for others promoted by Jesus.

for their own conduct is literally nonsense, then these social sciences can offer empirically meaningful explanations of religious behaviour: whereas the religion itself cannot. Although he might not describe religious assertions as nonsense in Ayer's sense, Durkheim is sure that the only satisfactory way to make sense of religion is to 'see through' the appearances and consider the underlying mechanisms animating religious belief. Consider Durkheim's description of the real interactions that are occurring during a religious service and his subsequent understanding of what religious 'faith' amounts to. Whatever is really occurring cannot be what is apparent to the sociologically sophisticated observer:

> The true justification of religious practices does not lie in the apparent ends which they pursue, but rather in the invisible action which they exercise over the mind and in the way in which they affect our mental status ... when preachers undertake to convince, they devote much less attention to establishing directly and by methodical proofs the truth of any particular proposition or the utility of such and such an observance, than to awakening the sentiment of the moral comfort attained by the regular celebration of the cult. Thus they create a predisposition to believe, which leads the mind to overlook the insufficiency of the logical reasons, and which thus prepares it for the proposition whose acceptance is desired. This favourable prejudice, this impulse towards believing, is just what constitutes faith.

Durkheim (1976)

■ Think about

Is Durkheim right about the 'real nature' of faith?

Whether or not we can make sense of religious belief and faith, or interpret the real meaning of religious language 'from the outside', as a scientist observing a causal process, is something we shall return to.

At least, the action-guiding nature of religious language distinguishes religious assertions from the language of scientific theory, which does not require we act one way or another. Evans develops an account of the relation between religious language and action that tries to make explicit what he calls its self-involving character. In doing this, Evans shares Braithwaite's view that religious assertions engage the speaker in ways that Ayer's mere pseudo-empirical statements do not. Evans asks:

> In saying, 'the Creator made the world', does a man commit himself to any further conduct, or imply that he has a particular attitude or intention, or express a feeling or attitude? Or is the utterance a neutral, impersonal statement of fact, like saying, 'Jones built the house'?

Evans (1963)

■ Key terms

Performative: a word or phrase, the uttering of which carries out, or 'performs' its meaning. Another example is 'I now pronounce you man and wife'.

Is 'the Creator made the world' just like the hypothesis 'Jones built the house'; except the former hypothesis about a Creator is unverifiable and therefore meaningless? Admitting that an assertion might not be all that it appears, Evans thinks the assertion 'the Creator made the world' should be interpreted differently. Consider 'I promise you £5'. It looks like a description of something done, an act of promising. However, as I utter it, I am not simply reporting an event: the sentence 'I promise you £5' is a **performative**. Unless I understand the performative meaning of the sentence I cannot understand the way in which uttering it involves me. By uttering the sentence I involve myself in a series of commitments and acknowledge a background (the kind of world where promising is possible) that makes my action intelligible. Evans rejects the suggestion that the only role world-engaging language can have is to propose actual or possible observations; and with it he rejects the suggestion that a philosophical analysis of language is primarily concerned with trying to devise a 'principle' that can determine whether or not empirical statements and 'the way the world is' match up. The relationship between my words, the social and communicative institutions I participate in and my experience is more complex:

> In the biblical context, the utterance 'god is my Creator' is profoundly self involving … if I say 'God is my Creator', I acknowledge my status as God's obedient servant and possession, I acknowledge my role as God's steward and worshipper, I acknowledge God's gift of existence, and I acknowledge God's self-commitment to me.
>
> *Evans (1963)*

So if Evans is right, in order to understand the meaning of creation language we need to pay attention to the context in which it is uttered, the social and communicative institutions that make it intelligible, and the conduct that understanding it entails. Macintyre maintains:

> If the Cosmological argument is what I have taken it to be, it becomes clear that it is not a proof in the rationalist metaphysician's sense … Where the difference lies between the adherent of the argument and a sceptic is in a willingness to adopt the whole vocabulary and set of concepts in terms of which the argument is phrased.
>
> *Macintyre (1959)*

Still, do assertions containing the term 'God' attempt to refer to some reality that transcends the context in which the assertion is uttered, the social and communicative institutions that make the assertion intelligible and the conduct that understanding the assertion entails? If so, unless there is some way of knowing whether they 'hit the target', such assertions look like empty gestures.

Eschatological verificationism

Hick thinks there is, in principle, a way of knowing whether talk about God hits the target. As such, the verification principle can be complied with: the assertion that 'God exists' is, in principle, verifiable. He provides a story to illustrate:

> Two people are travelling together along a road. One of them believes that it leads to the Celestial City, the other that it leads nowhere, but since this is the only road there is, both must travel it. Neither has been this way before; therefore, neither is able to say what they will find around each corner. During their journey they meet with moments of refreshment and delight, and with moments of hardship and danger. All the time one of them thinks of the journey as a pilgrimage to the Celestial City. She interprets the pleasant parts as encouragements and the obstacles as trials of her purpose and lessons of endurance, prepared by the sovereign of that city and designed to make her a worthy citizen of the place when at last she arrives. The other, however, believes none of this, and sees their journey as an unavoidable and aimless ramble. Since he has no choice in the matter he enjoys the good and endures the bad. For him there is no Celestial City to be reached, no all-encompassing purpose ordaining their journey; there is only the road itself and the luck of the road in good weather and in bad. During the course of the journey, the issue between them is not an experimental one. That is to say, they do not entertain different

expectations about the coming details of the road, but only about its ultimate destination. Yet, when they turn the last corner, it will be apparent that one of them has been right all the time and the other wrong. Thus, although the issue between them hasn't been experimental, it has nevertheless been a real issue. They have not merely felt differently about the road, for one was feeling appropriately and the other inappropriately in relation to the actual state of affairs. Their opposed interpretations of the situation have constituted genuinely rival assertions, whose assertion-status has the peculiar characteristic of being guaranteed retrospectively by a future crux.

Hick (1957)

If God exists then there will be an afterlife; and if there is an afterlife then 'God exists' can be confirmed: **eschatological** verification. Because 'God exists' can be verified then the language which expresses God's nature, God's will and relationship to His creatures can also be verified. Therefore, the assertion 'God exists' and the proposed implications of that assertion, are each as meaningful as any other body of assertions that still await confirmation. A theory might fail to be true: but that does not make it meaningless; merely untrue. The differences between the two travellers' descriptions are differences over the way the World is, but they cannot make the crucial confirming observation now. But is the idea of an after-life coherent or plausible? Ayer doubts whether the idea of an 'immaterial soul' makes sense and so 'an 'immaterial soul' might verify 'God exists' is nonsense and therefore, impossible. Whether an after-life is impossible is not a question we can think about here.

Seeing as

Hick's story also draws attention to the role of interpretation. Both travellers are confronted with the same reality as they journey through life, but they interpret reality differently. According to Hick, attempts to prove or disprove on the basis of the evidence we possess here and now, is inevitably inconclusive. Both 'God exists' and 'God does not exist' are compatible with the available evidence. Nevertheless, this open-endedness of interpretation does not count against the rationality of religious belief, but rather animates faith. Faith is the 'interpretative element in human experience' which is a necessary condition for our being free and responsible agents capable of choosing to enter into a mature and loving relation with God. Nothing about the journey forces the traveller to choose or reject God.

Faith now becomes a mode of understanding and interpretation in which believers consciously engage with events in their personal experience and events in history and experience them as manifestations of God's work. The story of the travellers reminds us of Hick's remarks about miracles as events interpreted as religiously significant and his example of the blind men and the elephant. Hick draws on Kant's model of experience regulated through concepts and categories and Wittgenstein's remarks where he points out that when experiencing some 'thing' we experience it as being a something: for instance, 'a snake', 'a pillar' or a 'plough share'; depending on the understanding we bring to the object. Faith becomes the activity of discerning God, where life is 'experienced as' or even 'experienced for' God. For example, the writers of the Old Testament saw the history of their people as revealing the will of God; their history became the medium through which the Divine was manifest. Unlike John Wisdom's example, the difference between the travellers is a real disagreement over the facts which can be settled post mortem, and so faith is an attitude towards the truth not merely an expression of feeling.

Must God keep an 'epistemic distance' in order to allow us our freedom? Hick explains:

> God does not become known to us as a reality of the same order as ourselves. If God were to do that the finite being would be swallowed by the infinite Being. Instead, god has created space-time as a sphere in which we may exist in relative independence, as spatiotemporal creatures. Within this sphere God is self-discovered in ways that allow us the fateful freedom to recognize or fail to recognize God's presence. The divine actions always leave room for that uncompelled response that theology calls faith. It is this element in the awareness of god that preserves man's cognitive freedom in relation to an infinitely greater and superior reality.

> *Hick (1957)*

Death by a thousand qualifications

Flew is suspicious about this 'elusiveness' of God. Religious believers make assertions about God, His nature and will, here and now. Do those assertions mean anything? Flew challenges the believer:

> What would have to occur or to have occurred to constitute for you a disproof of the love of, or the existence of, God?

> *Flew (1963)*

If the believer cannot point out anything which would disprove God's existence, then the believer is admitting that 'God exists' is compatible with any state of affairs. If I assert something is the case ('the door is open') and it is true, then as a matter of logic there will be at least one other statement which is false ('the door is not open') and as a matter of fact, we can expect that other statements follow from it ('if the door is closed then the light will not shine through from next door'). Hence to assert a fact is at the same time to assert that something else is not a fact, as well as implying that other things will be different. As such, the hypothesis that God exists, if it is a fact, implies that certain other asserted facts are not true. If no facts are ruled out by my assertion then it appears that my assertion is not asserting anything of significance. Flew recalls Wisdom's example of the invisible gardener:

> They set up a barbed wire fence. They electrify it. They patrol with bloodhounds … But no shrieks ever suggest that some intruder has received a shock. No movements of the wire ever betray an invisible climber. The bloodhounds never give cry … At last the sceptic despairs, 'but what remains of your original assertion? Just how does what you call an invisible, intangible, eternally elusive gardener differ from an imaginary gardener or even from no gardener at all?'

> *Flew (1963)*

Although Hick might appeal to eschatological verification as a test for distinguishing between there being a real gardener rather than not, what do we actually mean when we refer to 'an invisible gardener' – what sort of being do we have in mind?

> Someone tells us that God loves us as a father loves his children. We are reassured. But then we see a child dying of inoperable cancer of the

throat. His earthly father is driven frantic in his efforts to help, but his Heavenly Father reveals no obvious sign of concern. Some qualification is made – God's love is 'not a merely human love' or it is 'an inscrutable love, perhaps – and we realize that such sufferings are quite compatible with the truth of the assertion that 'God loves us as a father (but, of course…). We are reassured again. But then perhaps we ask: what is the assurance of God's (appropriately qualified) love worth, what is this apparent guarantee really a guarantee against …

Flew (1963)

And so Flew draws his memorable conclusion:

Someone may dissipate his assertion completely without noticing he has done so. A fine brash hypothesis may thus be killed by inches, the death by a thousand qualifications.

Flew (1963)

Crombie responds to Flew's challenge by acknowledging that religious assertions straddle between the familiar and the transcendent, and that this can appear a cheat:

The atheist alleges that the religious man supposes himself to know what he means by his statements only because, until challenged, he interprets them anthropomorphically; when challenged, he retreats rapidly backwards towards complete agnosticism.

Crombie (1963)

The believer confidently explains God's nature and His will, until challenged; at which point the 'mystery' of God is affirmed. The atheist's complaint is that you cannot have it both ways. Either 'God' can be understood using familiar concepts, by drawing analogies or through metaphors, similes and parables and so on; or else 'God' is understood as totally other, and so, says nothing to us. Nevertheless, Crombie thinks that God talk can be legitimate – in context. How a believer uses expressions is inseparable from 'the concrete process of living the Christian life'. Crombie points out that the meaning of a word in one context might not carry over in another context. Contrast the logicians' use of the expression 'contingent' with the meaning that 'contingent' has for the religious believer. For the logician contingency is a property of propositions: contingent propositions can either be true or false. In contrast, for the believer, 'contingency' is in the nature of things. However, 'the contingency of things' is grasped, what the religious believer understands by contingency and what the logician means by contingency can only be elucidated by paying attention to the experiential context in which the expression is used. So, what is the experiential context for the religious use of the word 'contingent'? According to Schleiermacher what is distinctive about religious experience is its characteristic 'feeling of absolute dependence':

the immediate consciousness of the universal existence of all finite things, in and through the Infinite, and of all temporal things in and through the Eternal.

Schleiermacher (1996)

Hepburn refers to Otto's account of 'the numinous':

> numinous experience is characterised by a sense of out-and-out dependence, derivativeness, and creatureliness, and by a peculiar haunting strangeness – an awesomeness or weirdness. But all descriptions are held in the end to fail. The strangeness and awesomeness prevent the sense of dependence from being construed as simply cause-effect dependence or as dependence of any other familiar intelligible type.
>
> *Hepburn (1971)*

This understanding of 'contingency' is typical of cosmological arguments, where everything else depends upon God for its being or intelligibility:

> Creator of all things, visible and invisible … who, by His almighty power, from the beginning of time has created both orders in the same way out of nothing.
>
> *The Fourth Lateran Council, Section 1 'A New Profession of Faith' (1215 AD)*

So, what 'contingency' means can only be drawn out by paying attention to the experiential context and conceptual associations that regulate its use for religious believers. As Goodall puts it:

> Religious language is discourse sponsored by a special sort of experiencing; it commends this experience, by showing how from the distinctive viewpoint which it affords a pattern is disclosed which furnishes explanation of human experience.
>
> *Goodall (1966)*

Crombie maintains that religious assertions can be tested against experience, but there is no particular crucial observation or experiment. Rather, the truth of religious assertions becomes apparent within the framework of religious life, discourse and belief. The resurrection promises The Truth can be known, understanding God's nature through His earthly incarnation in Jesus Christ and his teaching provides an exemplar and check on what can and cannot be said or inferred, and what God's love means is shown through the religious life of His followers. Can this body of assertions be confirmed or falsified by experience as a whole? Crombie responds:

> Does anything count against the assertion that God is merciful? Yes, suffering. Does anything count decisively against it? No, we reply, because it is true. Could anything count decisively against it? Yes, suffering which was utterly, eternally and irredeemably pointless. Can we then design a crucial experiment? No, because we can never see all of the picture.
>
> *Crombie (1963)*

When a religion can no longer provide a narrative against which a believer can cast the significance and course of their journey through the World, it stops being told.

Think about

Has Crombie met Flew's challenge?

Synoptic link

AQA A2 Philosophy Chapter 1, Philosophy of mind, The private language argument, p12.

Synoptic link

AQA A2 Philosophy Chapter 9, Philosophical problems in Descartes. This can be found at www.nelsonthornes.com/aqagce

Religious language games

Wittgenstein pioneered the method of logical analysis that Ayer uses to expose religious assertions as meaningless. But Wittgenstein became convinced that the kind of once for all standards that Ayer, and Hume and Kant before him, applied to philosophical problems was itself part of the source of philosophical confusion. Ideas or concepts examined apart from their role, or use, in language inevitably appear peculiar: 'philosophical problems arise when language *goes on holiday*'. He recommended that philosophy should pay attention to the situations and purposes of language. His later work is an extended exploration of these details, and he is struck by:

> the multiplicity of the tools in language and of the ways they are used, the multiplicity of kinds of word and sentence.

Wittgenstein (1998)

Wittgenstein did not deny that our thinking was governed by rules, legitimated by reason or authorised by experience. However, he doubted whether rationality could be explored independently of the various activities we engage in. What is and what is not rational is a question we cannot answer apart from examining the multifarious practices in which judgements are made and endorsed. In order to draw out the notion that being rational is being engaged in a rule-governed activity, Wittgenstein suggested that we could think of language as a game. Games have explicit and implicit rules, rules determining purposes and rules of application, rules that must be followed and rules that can be followed. Just as games develop or deteriorate, so does language. The language-game analogy was just that; an analogy that might be more or less illuminating. Wittgenstein also wanted to undermine the idea that unless we had 'proof' our beliefs were somehow unwarranted. This was the central claim that had animated philosophy since Descartes set about doubting all his opinions. For Wittgenstein, once we admit the possibility of philosophical global doubt we are inevitably led astray. Therefore, he emphasised how doubt presupposes a certainty that does not rest on philosophical foundations, but is a given; a form of life:

> If you are not certain of any fact, you cannot be certain of the meaning of your words either ... the questions that we raise and our doubts depend on the fact that some propositions are exempt from doubt ... If I want the door to turn, the hinges must stay put ... my life consists in me being content to accept many things.

Wittgenstein (1998)

These two ideas merged into what became known as Wittgensteinian philosophy of religion. In this view, religious assertions can only be understood by paying attention to their use. However, the language-game analogy transforms into an account of language that sees it as a highly structured network of inferences and meaning associations; a particular game, with its own rules. This religious language-game is autonomous: it does not need to be justified or legitimated; it is a self-governing form of life. Winch advocated this kind of reading of Wittgenstein:

> intelligibility takes many and varied forms ... criteria of logic are not a direct gift from God, but arise out of, and are only intelligible in the context of, ways of living or modes of social life as such. For instance, science is one such mode and religion is another; and each has

criteria of intelligibility peculiar to itself. So within science or religion actions can be logical or illogical; in science, for example, it would be illogical to refuse to be bound by the results of a properly carried out experiment; in religion it would be illogical to suppose that one could pit one's own strength against God's; and so on. But we cannot sensibly say that either the practice of science itself or that of religion is either logical or illogical; both are non-logical.

Winch (1977)

And Phillips insisted that Wittgenstein's approach to religious language and belief was incompatible with philosophical doubt:

philosophy can claim justifiably to show what is meaningful in religion only if it is prepared to examine religious concepts in the contexts from which they derive their meaning ... And when the philosopher understands that, his understanding of religion is incompatible with scepticism.

Phillips (1977)

This approach to religion insists that it can only be understood from the inside:

Consider the parable of the Pharisee and the Publican. Was the Pharisee who said 'God, I thank Thee that I am not as other men are' doing the same kind of thing as the Publican who prayed 'God be merciful unto me a sinner'? To answer this one would have to start by considering what is involved in the idea of prayer; and that is a religious question. In other words, the appropriate criteria for deciding whether the actions of these two men were of the same kind or not belong to religion itself ... if the judgements of identity – and hence the generalisations – of the sociologist of religion rest on criteria taken from religion, then his relation to the performers of religious activity cannot be just that of observer to observed

Phillips (1977)

According to Phillips religious belief can only be criticised within the religious language game. Just as the rules of cricket are irrelevant when judging football, so the rules of science are irrelevant when judging religion. According to Winch, religion cannot be explained away from some more 'knowing' perspective. Understanding religion rules out the possibility that religion is anything else apart from what it understands itself to be.

One very important criticism of this position is that it isolates religious belief from other forms of rational enquiry and makes relative the meaning of religious concepts so that they become quite alien, unless you also share the religious form of life. Hence this position is often dubbed Wittgensteinian Fideism. But this goes both ways. Religion can have nothing relevant to say to secular forms of life and the non-believer cannot feel obliged to enter into a practice that they cannot, as a non-believer, understand. And the kind of autonomy the language-game model insists upon is an implausible description of the facts. Our practices and the language we use to make sense of what we think and do is not a monolithic structure, but a more or less open-textured and fluid economy of ideas, aims and activity. This is precisely the point Wittgenstein makes when he introduces the notion of a language-game:

how many kinds of sentence are there? ... There are countless kinds ... And this multiplicity is not something fixed, given once for all; but

> **Think about**
>
> How does this link to what we said about conduct authenticating religious experience from the inside?

new types of language, new language-games, as we may say, come into existence, and others become obsolete and get forgotten…

Wittgenstein (1998)

Whether or not religious language is significant or otherwise becomes obsolete and is forgotten, will depend on how the multiplicity of religious expression finds its place in our evolving understanding of the World and us. As the religious poet T.S. Eliot reflects on his task:

For us there is only the trying. The rest is not our business.

Eliot (1954)

☑ *After working through this topic, you should:*

- know the challenge of the verification principle to the meaningfulness of religious language

- understand the attempts to make sense of religious language that stress its role in the attitudes and activity of religious believers

- recognise that the notion that religious language has its own rules of rationality and problems with that claim.

Summary questions

1 Has the cosmological argument been thoroughly refuted?

2 Could you have your own private religion?

3 Is faith intrinsically good, or would we be better off with knowledge?

4 Are there any convincing arguments for miracles, in the light of modern science?

5 Can a belief which is compatible with any state of affairs ever be a meaningful belief?

■ Further reading

■ Davies, B. (ed.), *Philosophy of Religion: A Guide and Anthology*, Oxford University Press, 2000. This book collects together some very important historical and contemporary extracts.

■ Hick, J., *The Existence of God (Problems of Philosophy)*, Macmillan, 1964. This book collects together some very important historical and contemporary extracts.

■ Hick, J., *Philosophy of Religion*, Prentice-Hall, 1989. A very good introductory book.

■ Hume, D., *Dialogues Concerning Natural Religion* (World's Classics), Oxford Paperbacks, 1994. This is a classic.

■ James, W., *The Varieties of Religious Experience*, Penguin, 1993. This is a classic.

■ Quinn, P.L. and Taliaferro, C., *A Companion to Philosophy of Religion* (Blackwell Companions to Philosophy), Wiley-Blackwell, 1999. Offers a thorough overview of the subject as it is presently undertaken.

■ Rowe, W., *Philosophy of Religion*, Wadsworth Publishing, 2000. A very good introductory book.

References

Aquinas, T, *Summa Contra Gentiles*, University of Notre Dame Press, 1976.

Ayer, A.J., *Language Truth and Logic*, Penguin, 2001.

Blake, W., *The Poems of William Blake,* Penguin, 1977.

Bowden, J., *Jesus: The Unanswered Questions*, SCM Press, 1988.

Bradley, F.H., *Appearance and Reality*, Oxford University Press, 1963.

Braithwaite, R.B., 'An Empiricist's view of the nature of Religious Belief', reprinted in *The Existence of God*, ed. by J. Hick, Macmillan, 1964.

Broad, C.D., *Religion, Philosophy and Psychical Research: Selected Essays*, Routledge, 2000.

Bultmann, R., *New Testament and Mythology and Other Basic Writings*, Augsburg Fortress, 1990.

Clifford, W.K., 'The Ethics of Belief', in *Belief, Knowledge and Truth* ed. by R. Ammerman and G. Singer, Scribners, 1970.

Craig, W., *The Kalam Cosmological Argument,* Barnes and Noble, 1979.

Crombie, I., in *New Essays in Philosophical Theology*, ed. by A. Flew and A. MacIntyre, SCM Press, 1963.

Diderot, D., *Thoughts on the Interpretation of Nature*, trans. by Lorna Sandler, Clinamen, 2000.

Durkheim, E., *The Elementary Forms of the Religious Life*, Routledge, 1976.

Edwards, P., 'The Cosmological Argument', *Rationalist Annual*, 1959.

Eliot, T.S., *Selected Poems*, Faber and Faber, 1954.

Evans, D., *The Logic of Self-involvement*, SCM Press, 1963.

Ferre, F., *Making Religion Real*, Collins, 1969.

Flew, A. 'Theology and Falsification: The University Discussion' in A. Flew and A. MacIntyre (eds.), *New Essays in Philosophical Theology*, SCM, 1963.

Geach, P., *God and the Soul*, St Augustine's Press, 2001.

Goodall, J.L. *An Introduction to the Philosophy of Religion*, Longmans, 1966.

Hepburn, R., 'God and World', in B. Mitchell, *The Philosophy of Religion,* Oxford University Press, 1971.

Hick, J., *Faith and Knowledge: A Modern Introduction to the Problem of Religious Knowledge*, Cornell University Press, 1957.

Hick, J., *God and the Universe of Faiths*, Macmillan, 1977.

Hobbes, T., *Leviathan*, Longman, 2008.

Holland, R.F., 'The Miraculous', *American Philosophical Quarterly*, vol. 2, 1965.

Hospers, J., *Introduction to Philosophical Analysis*, Routledge, 1992.

Hume, D., *A Treatise of Human Nature*, Oxford University Press, 1967.

Hume, D., *Enquiries Concerning Human Understanding*, Oxford University Press, 1975.

Hume, D., *Dialogues Concerning Natural Religion*, Oxford University Press, 1998.

James, W., *Varieties of Religious Experience*, Penguin, 1983.

James, W., *The Will to Believe and Other Essays in Popular Philosophy*, Dover, 2003.

Kant, I., *Religion within the Boundaries of Mere Reason and Other Writings*, trans. and ed. by Allen Wood and George di Giovanni, Cambridge University Press, 1998.

Kant, I., *Critique of Pure Reason*, Dover, 2004.

Kierkegaard, S., *A Kierkegaard Anthology*, ed. by R. Bretall, Princeton University Press, 1973.

Levine, M., *Hume and the Problem of Miracles: A Solution*, Kluwer, 1989.

Locke, J., *An Essay Concerning Human Understanding*, Hackett, 1996.

MacIntyre, A., *Difficulties in Christian Belief*, SCM Press, 1959.

Macquarrie, J., *Principles of Christian Theology*, SCM Press, 1977.

Malmgren, J., 'The Good Friday Marsh Chapel Experiment, Then – Rev. Mike Young – Now. "Tune In, Turn On, Get Well?"', *St. Petersburg Times*, 27 November, available online at: **http://leda.lycaeum.org/?ID=16491**

McCabe, H., in *Philosophy of Religion: A Guide and Anthology*, ed. by B. Davies, Oxford University Press 2000.

Nicolas of Cusa, *The Vision of God*, Cosimo, 2007.

Pascal, B., *Pensées*, revised edition, Penguin Classics, 2003.

Phillips, D.Z., in P. Sherry, *Religion, Truth, and Language-Games*, Barnes & Noble, 1977.

Rahula, *What the Buddha Taught*, Gordon Fraser, 1978.

Reid, T., *The Works of Thomas Reid*, BookSurge, 2000.

Robinson, J.T., *Honest to God*, John Knox Press, 1963.

Schleiermacher, F. von, *On Religion: Speeches to its Cultured Despisers*, Cambridge University Press, 1996.

Swinburne, R., *The Existence of God*, Oxford University Press, 1979.

Weil, S., *Waiting for God*, Harper Perennial, 1992.

Winch, P., in P. Sherry, *Religion, Truth, and Language-Games*, Barnes & Noble, 1977.

Winch, P., 'Asking Too Many Questions', in *Philosophy and the Grammar of Religious Belief*, ed. by T. Tessin, and M. von der Ruhr, St Martin's Press, 1995.

Wisdom, J., 'Gods' *Philosophy and Psychoanalysis*, Blackwell, 1953.

Wittgenstein, L., *Culture and Value*, trans. by P. Winch, ed. by G.H. von Wright, Blackwell, 1984.

Wittgenstein, L., *Philosophical Investigations*, Blackwell, 1998.

Wittgenstein, L., *Tractatus Logico-Philosophicus*, Routledge, 2001.

Glossary

A

A priori: a judgement which is justified without appeal to the tribunal of our experience. (Truths which have to be justified by such an appeal are called a *posteriori*.)

Ad hominem: an attack upon the person making an argument rather than the argument itself. This method of attack is generally ruled out of court in philosophy because it leaves the argument itself intact, by failing to distinguish the motives behind a belief from the truth conditions and consistency of the belief itself.

Agape: in Christian theology, agape refers to the form of unconditional love for others promoted by Jesus.

Altruism: an altruistic doctrine holds that individuals have a moral obligation to help others even if it is to their own detriment.

Analytic philosophy: a branch of philosophy developed during the early part of the 20th century which has come to dominate the English speaking world. Among other things, analytic philosophers attempt to examine concepts and language by means of formal logic in order to determine their relationships and limits.

Anomalous: irregular, inconsistent, does not fall under a law-like (nomological) description.

Antimony: a way of presenting opposed arguments side by side with each other. Kant's antimonies are demonstrations of how opposed inferences may be equally justifiable if reason is pushed beyond its proper limits.

Aphorism: a form of compressed writing expressing a point in very few words. Nietzsche is generally recognised as master of the form, even by his opponents.

B

Basic belief: one that might be seen either as self-evident, or an ultimate justification not to be justified in terms of something more basic.

Begging the question
Begging the question: a logical fallacy in which the argument in favour of a proposition depends upon the assumption that the proposition itself is correct.

Binary oppositions: paired words such as right and wrong or male and female in which if one applies one term to an object, it automatically excludes the other term.

C

Categorical imperative: a moral command that you must obey. It is universal and impartial.

Coerce: forcing a person or group of people to do something they would not choose to do.

Coherentism: the theory that beliefs are justified to the extent that they cohere with one's other beliefs in a mutually supporting framework or force-field which need not rest on any foundational certainties.

Communitarians: hold that individuals can only flourish as part of a wider community of which they form a part and with which they identify.

Compatibilist: compatibilism is the doctrine that free will, or liberty, is not inconsistent with determinism.

Conservatism: a political philosophy which generally opposes change and especially large scale change. One reason for this is that conservatists believe human beings are flawed by nature.

Contiguity: being next to each other.

Copy principle: the way in which impressions become imprinted upon the mind as ideas.

Critique: A detailed critical analysis. Generally a philosophical analysis in this context, although this may be open to dispute.

D

Deduction: a form of reasoning that begins from general propositions. The opposite of induction, which begins from particular cases.

Democratic government: one in which the people choose those who are to govern them.

Deontological
Deontological: from the Greek 'deon' meaning 'duty'. Actions should obey our duties, it is the nature of the act itself which matters.

Desert: assesses effort and quality of work and therefore is backward looking.

Despotic state: a state which denies political rights to its citizens and may pass laws which oppress all or part of the population.

Dialectics/Socratic method: a form of philosophical argument in which one interlocutor draws out the implications of another's position in order to highlight contradictions and thereby strengthen his or her own argument. This should not be confused with Hegelian or Marxist dialectics, which are altogether different.

Difference in kind/degree: this is a distinction between two types of difference. Differences in kind are absolute differences, such as that between being at rest or in motion. Differences in degree are relative differences, such as that between fast and slow.

Dualism: the theory that mind and matter (body) are two distinct and fundamentally different kinds of thing, or have irreducibly different kinds of property (such as, respectively, *thought*, which cannot *be at* any point in space, and *extension*, which cannot *look from* any perspective).

E

'Ecce Homo': latin for 'Behold the Man': supposedly the words uttered by Pilate when he displayed Christ to the crowd prior to crucifixion. Some commentators have argued that Nietzsche's application of this term to himself was a sign of his crumbling sanity; others have suggested that he was being ironic.

Eliminativism: the view that our everyday, folk, psychology of 'experiencing' this and 'believing' that is imprecise and deficient. It can and should be replaced with a better, more scientific, vocabulary.

Epistemological: to do with the nature and processes of knowing (from Greek *episteme*, knowledge)

Epistemological: epistemology is the study of knowledge: what we know and how we come to know it, so an epistemology is a particular account of knowledge.

Epistemology: the branch of philosophy concerned with what knowledge is: how we acquire knowledge and what we can have knowledge of (from Greek *episteme*, knowledge).

Eschatology: the study of the end of the World.

Etymology: the study of the historical development and meaning of words.

Eugenics: the practice of selectively breeding humans for desired traits, coupled with the restriction or prohibition of breeding outside of chosen bloodlines.

Extrinsic good: something that is valued because it makes another thing possible. For example, for most people money is an extrinsic good because it is possible to use it to buy things that one needs or wants. Money is a good because it can obtain other goods, hence its extrinsic character.

Faculty: in philosophy in general, a faculty is a power that has the ability to effect change in some way; usually towards a goal of some kind. In this chapter, the

faculties in question are all mental ones.

Flourishing life: a life in which they exercise and improve those faculties distinctive to a human being.

Folk psychology: our commonsense understanding of psychological events; the psychological concepts (such as belief and desire) we employ on a daily basis.

Formal reality: the reality of anything's existence as itself;

Foundationalism: the philosophical theory that knowledge of the world rests on a foundation of beliefs which are certain, and from which further beliefs are

inferred to produce a structure of known truths.

Genetic fallacy: this is the claim that it is a mistake to accept or reject an idea, because of where or whom it came from, rather than on its own merits.

Hegemony: control of ideas.

Homunculus: the Latin term for little man. It is employed here to illustrate the functioning of a system in terms of the causal roles played by its component parts.

I

Ideologies: in this sense simply means a set of ideas and values associated with different political standpoints

Individual: a single, conscious, reasoning and responsible human being.

Individual autonomy: the freedom from constraint to make one's own decision based on the exercise of reason.

Individual political rights: opportunities to engage in certain political activities which are enforceable by law; for example, the right to vote.

Individualist: a person primarily concerned with individual people and their interests, rights and responsibilities.

Induction: a form of reasoning in which the reasons given support but do not entail the conclusion. The conclusion is a generalization from a consideration of individual instances.

Inference: drawing a conclusion from supporting reasons or evidence.

Inference to the best explanation: in the philosophy of science, is linked to hypotheses that typically provide simple, coherent, and causally adequate explanations of the evidence or phenomena in question.

Innate ideas: knowledge that we are born with.

Intension: in logic, the intensional meaning of a symbol, or proposition, is an exhaustive

list of the things it could possibly describe. The opposite of intension is extension: an exhaustive list of things in the world that a symbol or proposition actually describes.

Inter-theoretic reduction: the reduction of one theory to another Implies a change of ontological attitude towards reduced entities (so that, for example, mental states come to be seen as physical states), while simultaneously assuming the existence of both: both mental states and physical states really do exist just as heat and motion really do exist.

Intrinsic good: something that is valued in itself rather than for the purposes of obtaining another thing. For most people happiness is an intrinsic good. They want to be happy because happiness is good in itself, not because it results in some other good.

Irony: a form of writing in which the author's choice of words is deliberately ambivalent leading to uncertainty as to his or her intentions.

L

Law of contradiction: one of the fundamental principles of logic which states that something cannot simultaneously belong and not belong to the same category. For example, no-one can be alive and dead (i.e. 'not alive') at the same time.

Leibniz's Law: this law states the identity of indiscernibles. Simply put, if two substances, X and Y, have exactly the same properties so that there is no possibility of distinguishing between them, if all the attributes of X are also attributes of Y, and vice versa, then X is Y. To put it another way, if X has a property that is not possessed by Y then X is not Y.

Liberalism: a political philosophy which emphasises the importance of individual freedom and opportunity based upon assumptions about the rationality and goodness of human beings.

Love of wisdom: the word 'philosophy' is derived from the ancient Greek 'philosophia' which literally means love (philo) of wisdom (sophia).

Merit: entails meeting criteria and therefore is forward looking.

Meritocracy: a state where the division of social classes is based upon intellect, or talent of some kind.

Monism: single; there is only one kind of 'stuff' (in this case, matter). Monistic theories are opposed to theories such as mind/matter dualism.

Moral realism: this means that there is an ethical reality. Just as there is an atomic structure to the world, so there is one moral structure to events in the world, that local variations reflect.

Motivational analysis: a method whereby one examines the grounds from which something is presented in the way it is, as opposed to simply asking questions about the thing itself. So if one aspect of Socratic method is to ask 'what is the Good?', a motivational analysis would enquire why it is that Socrates desires to hold the Good up as the highest Form.

Natural language: the philosophical term for everyday spoken and written languages, as opposed to formal languages such as those of logic or mathematics. Note that while 'H_2O' can substitute for 'water' in natural language, 'water' cannot substitute for 'H_2O' in the formal language of chemical equations.

Naturalism: a philosophical position claiming that the world can be fully understood in scientific terms without recourse to metaphysics or theology.

Necessary/contingent: logically, a property of an object is necessary if and only if the object must always possess that property. Contingency is the opposite of necessity: a property is contingent if the object may or may not possess it.

Negative concept of freedom: Briefly, negative freedom is concerned with a lack of constraint. I am free to the extent that I can do as I wish without interference by other individuals or the state.

Negative freedoms: those which give you freedom from something. Freedom of speech is a negative freedom because you can say what you wish without interference from the state or others.

Nihilism: nothing is true or worthwhile, therefore there is nothing to seriously care about.

Nomological dangler: something which lies outside of a scientific law of nature.

Normative: relating to or deriving from a standard or norm.

Objective reality: the representational reality which makes a mental content what it is.

Occam's razor: the view that the simplest explanation of any given phenomena is the best explanation. Entities should not be multiplied beyond necessity, so an explanation that refers to one entity and which does the same work as an alternative explanation that refers to two entities is to be preferred.

Ontological: to do with the nature of being or existence (Greek root *ont-*, being)]

Ontology: the branch of metaphysics concerned with questions about what there is, with what sort of entities exist. In the philosophy of mind ontological questions concern whether there are minds and brains, just brains, or just minds.

Other-regarding actions: actions that have an effect on other people.

'Ought' implies 'can': if we claim that a person ought to do something, then a necessary precondition is that it is possible for them to do it.

Performative: a word or phrase, the uttering of which carries out, or 'performs' its meaning. Another example is 'I now pronounce you man and wife'.

Phenomenology: the study of what an experience feels like to a conscious individual.

Philology: the study of languages, especially in relation to their development over time, and relationships between languages. Particular emphasis is laid upon the study of literature as a means of doing this.

Polemic: a form of aggressive argument; often against the grain of accepted opinion.

Positive freedoms: the freedoms to do certain things or have certain things, for example the right to health care.

Postmodernism: in philosophy, postmodernism is most often taken as the doctrine that there are no overarching theories, or 'metanarratives', that provide an ultimate justification for the solutions to theoretical problems.

Predicate: part of a sentence that adds something to the subject of the sentence.

Preference utilitarianism: the theory that we ought to maximise the satisfaction of people's preferences.

Presupposition: an assumption about a subject that is taken for granted rather than argued for. Something one believes without requiring any proof.

Prima facie: on first examination.

R

Reductio ad absurdum (reduction to absurdity): a form of logical argument where one grants the initial premises, and then draws a conclusion from them that is so counter-intuitive that it throws those premises into doubt.

Representative democracy: exists where voters choose people to govern who exercise their judgement on the people's behalf and are held responsible for their judgements at periodic elections.

Ressentiment: Nietzsche uses the French form of 'resentment' as a technical term indicating a particular feeling of hostility felt by one group towards another as a result of the former's feeling of powerlessness and inferiority. While the term does not appear in *Beyond Good and Evil*, you will undoubtedly come across it in secondary texts.

Rule utilitarianism: an action is right if it conforms to a particular rule, which has been determined on past experience, to create the greatest overall happiness in the long run.

S

Scepticism: traditionally questioned how reliable our beliefs are, how much we can actually know and whether we can really know *anything*. Famous sceptics on whom Descartes drew included Sextus Empiricus and Pyrrho; an important sceptical thinker who came after him was David Hume.

Self-regarding actions: actions that only have an effect on the person who chooses to carry them out.

Sentient: capable of feeling pain, suffering and experiencing pleasure.

Solipsism: sometimes expressed as the view that 'I' am the only minded being, but is more properly expressed as the view that, in principle, 'I' can attach no meaning to the supposition that there could be thoughts, experiences, and emotions other than my own.

Sophistry: empty argument. Named after the Sophists of Ancient Greece who, according to Plato, taught techniques for winning debates rather than genuine philosophy.

Substance: the notion 'substance' has various uses: it may refer to that which persists while attributes change (as in Descartes' example of the wax) and/or to that which is logically capable of existing independently (as, for example, in Descartes' view that mind could exist independently of body).

Substantive justice: this refers to the content or substance of the decision and involves normative principles, such as equality of need, desert and rights.

Supervene: a supervenient property is one that is dependent upon its subvenient base without being reducible to that base, so that mental properties supervene upon physical properties without being reducible to them.

Synthetic a priori: a judgement may be said to be a priori if it can be known independently of experience. Generally, such judgements are held to be analytic in that they tell us nothing new. Kant denies this, claiming that there are a priori judgements that deliver new information, which are therefore synthetic.

T

Tautology: generally, two things with identical meanings, but different wordings. In philosophy, a tautology is a proposition in which the meanings of both sides are identical.

Teleological: from the Greek, 'telos' meaning 'end'. Actions should be taken to achieve an end. Any doctrine which stresses necessary movement towards an ultimate goal may be said to be teleological. For example, if you believe that humans have become more civilised as the ages have progressed and will continue to do so, you take a teleological view of history.

The Enlightenment: a movement in 18th-century Europe characterised by increasing confidence in, and reliance upon, reason and the natural sciences and progressive politics; mostly at the expense of traditional Ecclesiastical authority. One of the major historical outcomes of this period was the French Revolution of 1789.

The state: the body, or set of institutions, which governs a territorial area, and secures obedience from those who live within its boundaries. It is the entity that has sovereignty and jurisdiction over all matters within its boundaries.

Totalitarianism: a form of centralised, one party, government in which the needs and desires of individual citizens are subordinated to the will of the state.

Transcendence: something is said to be transcendent if it exists separately from the world of experience. For example, the Christian concept of God is a transcendent one. The opposite of transcendence is immanence.

Transcending: something is said to be transcendent if it is absolutely beyond the limits of our own existence.

Two world view: the theory that the world of experience is not the only one, but that there is another realm separate from it, yet somehow accessible.

U

Übermensch: early English translations of Nietzsche rendered this important term as 'superman'. However, 'overman' is now preferred because, while the Übermensch is certainly what comes after man, he is not necessarily superior to all those who have gone before him.

V

Validity: as used here is a technical term of logic. An argument is valid when, if its *premises* (the reasons which it gives) are true, its *conclusion* (what it is giving reasons for) must be true. Arguments are valid in virtue of their logical form, and the *form* of an argument is the structure it has apart from its specific propositional content: argument (2) has the valid form: p is true only if q is true; and p is true; so q is true.

Veridical: a veridical experience is a non-illusory experience which accurately captures reality.

Vicious infinite regress: a logical failure which occurs when any attempt at the solution of a problem requires the reintroduction of the same problem in its solution, meaning that it can only be explained in terms of itself. This causes the infinite reoccurrence of the problem.

W

Will to power: Nietzsche's later philosophy is centred on the idea that everything is struggle; the will to power is a universal force which drives that struggle. On an individual level, it could be described as manifesting itself as the series of drives or instincts which make us strive to overcome or dominate others.

Index